Opening the Black Box

The Turkish Military Before and After 15 July 2016

Metin Gürcan

Helion & Company

To Senem…

Helion & Company Limited
Unit 8 Amherst Business Centre
Budbrooke Road
Warwick
CV34 5WE
England
Tel. 01926 499 619
Fax 0121 711 4075
Email: info@helion.co.uk
Website: www.helion.co.uk
Twitter: @helionbooks
Visit our blog http://blog.helion.co.uk/

Published by Helion & Company 2018
Designed and typeset by Mach 3 Solutions Ltd (www.mach3solutions.co.uk)
Cover designed by Paul Hewitt, Battlefield Design (www.battlefield-design.co.uk)
Printed by Hobbs the Printers, Totton, Hampshire

Text and figures © Metin Gürcan 2018

Every reasonable effort has been made to trace copyright holders and to obtain their permission for the use of copyright material. The author and publisher apologize for any errors or omissions in this work, and would be grateful if notified of any corrections that should be incorporated in future reprints or editions of this book.

ISBN 978-1-912390-15-1

British Library Cataloguing-in-Publication Data.
A catalogue record for this book is available from the British Library.

All rights reserved. No part of this publication may be reproduced, stored in a retrieval system, or transmitted, in any form, or by any means, electronic, mechanical, photocopying, recording or otherwise, without the express written consent of Helion & Company Limited.

For details of other military history titles published by Helion & Company Limited contact the above address, or visit our website: http://www.helion.co.uk.

We always welcome receiving book proposals from prospective authors.

Contents

List of Figures

Introduction

> *I swear by my honour that, in peace and at war, on land, in sea, and in air, always and everywhere, I will serve my Nation and my Republic with truth and honesty, that I will obey the Law and my superiors, and that I will not hesitate to willingly and lovingly sacrifice my life for the honour of soldiership and the greatness of the Turkish flag.*

The Turkish Military Oath[1]

Modern militaries are complex organisations relying on human force provided by society, budget, weaponry and other resources delivered by state, being strictly founded on three pillars: traditional institutional setting, a framework of values, norms and rituals, or professional ethos; discipline, a sense of unity, devotion, responsibility and common interest, or cohesion; and e*spirit de corps*, shared among their soldiers. This inherent complexity reflecting the structure-culture-action nexus often means that scholars study modern militaries with separated disciplines: Political Science, International Relations, Sociology, Anthropology, History, Administrative Sciences, Economics and Security Studies. The scholarship of these studies examining modern militaries is rich in diversity, despite the fact that they often seem disconnected as they look like "separate tables".[2] The existing knowledge and scholarship about the Turkish military, or Turkish Armed Forces (TAF), is no exception.

This book, however, in contrast to the conventional scholarship on modern militaries, conceptualises the TAF as a "messy center [*sic*] of convergence" so as to go beyond the "separate tables" approach.[3] Not only by describing the TAF as a security actor in organisational terms but also defining it as a socio-political institution interacting with wider society and the civilian government, and elucidating officership as

1 Turkish military's Internal Service Act, Article 37.

2 Mark Irving Lichbach and Alan S. Zuckerman, *Comparative Politics: Rationality, Culture and Structure* (New York: Cambridge University Press, 2009).

3 Mark Irving Lichbach and Alan S. Zuckerman, *Comparative Politics: Rationality, Culture and Structure* (New York: Cambridge University Press, 2009).

a profession, this book attempts to delve into the black box of the TAF to explore it more and explain the whats, whys and hows of its change over the last decade.

The Rationale and Arguments of the Book

With this book, the author's hope is to make connections reflecting the structure-culture-action nexus explicit to better understand change both within the Turkish military and the Turkish Civil-Military Relations (CMR) before and after the failed military uprising on 15 July 2016.[4] To better understand change, the book, which has benefited greatly from the author's PhD research, seeks to follow a pragmatic multi-method approach at different levels of analysis (i.e. data and method triangulation). To overcome the problem of complexity, the book's theoretical setting is an eclectic construction which borrows theoretical elements from both institutionalist literature and literature on military sociology. This eclectic theoretical construction seeks to select what appear to be the best elements in various theoretical approaches in the literature to explain the change within the institutional identity of the TAF as a security organisation, as a socio-political institution and officership as a profession, and elucidate transformation of the Turkish CMR before and after 15 July 2016. In this sense, the author does not aim to propose an institutionalist versus military sociology dichotomy; instead he endeavours to benefit from both in a complementary fashion by cherry-picking relevant elements of both approaches. That is why he seeks to explain the Turkish military's change with a theoretical framework in which one may see some elements from James Mahoney and Kathleen Thelen's theory of gradual institutional change at the organisational level,[5] and some elements from Theo Farrell and Terry Terriff's military sociological approach at the individual level.[6] It is this eclectic

4 Contrary to conventional thinking, the author is inclined not to define the act on the night of 15 July 2016 as a classical coup attempt, but rather as an "attempted military uprising" by a small clique comprising Gulenist officers, officers with strong sentiments against Erdogan and his Justice and Development Party, elements being blackmailed or deceived by the Gulenist network, careerists and others merely obeying orders. Indeed, the putschists were not guided by a profound ideology or coherent *esprit de corps*, a strong and all-encompassing motivation to break the will of pro-government forces or a clear political road map for the transfer of political power. For many senior officers who had been on the government's monitoring or detention lists owing to their links to Gulenists, participation in the attempted overthrow was instead a kamikaze-like gesture. Had they not acted on that night, they would have been dismissed at the Supreme Military Council meeting in early August 2016 and then subjected to legal investigations. Their involvement appeared to be their only pre-emptive bet.

5 James Mahoney and Dietrich Rueschemeyer, 'Action in Comparative Historical Social Science', in *Comparative Historical Analysis in the Social Sciences* (Cambridge: Cambridge University Press, 2003), 270–301.

6 Theo Farrell and Terry Terriff, *The Sources of Military Change: Culture, Politics,* Technology (London: Lynne Reinner Publishing).

construction that enables him to achieve a big-picture pragmatism and to get through the challenge of studying the military, or messy centre of convergence.

What is the scholarly concern that drives the author writing this book?

First, relying on his both 20 years-long insider experience within the Turkish military (both on the field and in the strategic corridors of the Turkish General Staff) and academic career, the author provides two 'inside-out' snapshots, one about the TAF before 15 July 2016 and the other about it after that date. It is worth noting that these snapshots have been enriched by empirical insights (both quantitative and qualitative).

Regarding the TAF's pre-July 15 snapshot, this book aims at opening the black box of the Turkish military by presenting the findings of a survey conducted among 1,240 officers in May-August 2015 as a part of the author's PhD research. The findings show that there are some main drivers of change influencing the officer corps, and still shaping change within the military after the 15 July Uprising. Heterogenisation and diversification of officers' opinions, a shift from a collectivist to individualist understanding of life, from an elitist to an egalitarian view of society, a change from value-centric service to a focus on financial goals and career opportunities, and a shift from the centre-left spectrum into centre-right in the political portfolio are some examples of those drivers of change. The findings also indicate that the Turkish Army (Land Force Command), the Air Force and the Navy's organisational cultures are dissimilar regarding their stance towards military transformation, organisational restructuring and some socio-political issues such as the extent of secularist sentiment, religiosity and political orientations. The author argues that drivers like the increased submission of the military to the civilian government over the last decade, officers' increasing awareness of the significance of democracy and of rule of law, heterogenisation and diversification among the officer corps and officers' more egalitarian view of society, the combination of which created a power-distributional effect within the TAF, played a decisive role in the failure of the 15 July Uprising as endogenous institutional resistance within the military prevented this heinous attempt from becoming a full-fledged uprising with the participation of the majority of the officers. Simply, the differentiation among the TAF in terms of change drivers, change types, change agents, change pathways and change modes created a power-distributional effect of change in the TAF, the factor functioning as a braking mechanism on the night of 15 July 2016. The author also suggests that these drivers shaping the mindset and thus determining the behaviours/preferences of the officer corps do still actively influence the institutional setting of the post-5 July military and officers' opinions.

To better elucidate the snapshot of the TAF after 15 July, on the other hand, one should focus on the impact of the uprising and the following mass purges on the Turkish military's institutional identity, emphasising a transition from a monolithic identity symbolised and embodied by the agency of Chief of General Staff, to a polylithic one composed of many but separated micro-identities in terms of the military elites' stance towards change and reforms, their political affiliations, the service commands' (the Army, Navy and Air Force) stance towards organisational transformation and the attitudes and worldviews of the senior (generals, colonels, lieutenant colonels) and junior (majors, captains, first lieutenants and lieutenants) officers.

This is also a book about the changing nature of Turkish CMR. Regarding the post-15 July setting, the book first emphasises Turkey's overarching dilemma after 15 July 2016: whether to monopolise or democratise CMR for more effective control of the TAF. The monopolisation of CMR implies *transfer of power* from the military elites to the elected executive presidency.[7] For pro-executive presidency circles, the most effective remedy for Turkey to diminish these risks is to first formalise and then institutionalise the executive presidency, a 'practical reality' that has seemed to turn into an 'urgent need' after 15 July.[8] Burhanettin Duran and Nebi Mis, for instance, suggest that the lack of strong government was closely related to the fragmentation of political parties and resulting parliamentarianism and growing friction between various identity groups, which led to periods of instability in Turkey.[9] Following this line of thought, first quickly civilianising and then slowly monopolising CMR under the strict civilian control of the elected executive presidency is not only the solution to preventing the occurrence of another 15 July but also the means to developing more effective security forces. On the other hand, democratisation of CMR enables *diffusion of power* among the elected president, elected government and parliamentary and civil society actors such as academia, think tanks and media so as to create a more effective oversight and monitoring system over the military and establishing check and balances within the CMR. As seen, these definitions – civilianisation of the CMR after 15 July 2016 or the transfer of power from the military elites to the executive presidency – does not necessarily mean, or automatically lead to, the democratisation of CMR, or the diffusion of power among different political actors including the ones within civil society to establish more effective oversight/monitoring mechanisms and checks and balances within the system. It is thus of the utmost importance to ask the following questions: how can the state prevent the occurrence of another 15 July which attempted to hijack the state power? Will monopolising/accumulating power under an executive presidency enable stricter control of the state apparatus, or does democratising power represent the better option in that it will create checks and balances, institutional oversight and monitoring mechanisms within the state apparatus? The book aims to provide insights regarding these questions.

Regarding the impact of 15 July on the nature of CMR, the author argues that the post-15 July setting, shaped by concurrent military reforms and mass purges, led

7 Burhanettin Duran, 'The Executive Presidency and Turkey's Future', *Daily Sabah*, 31 January 2017.
8 *Ibid.*
9 Burhanettin Duran and Nebi Mis, 'The Transformation of the Turkey's Political System and Executive Presidency', *Insight Turkey*, 18:4 (2016), pp.11-27.

to a paradigm shift. The shift took place in the nature of Turkish CMR, implying a transition from the Huntingtonian paradigm focusing on the *management of the gap* between the military and civilian worlds to the Janowitzian paradigm aiming to *diminish the gap* between the military and society so as to anchor the military to society as a whole.

To elucidate the impact of this paradigm shift, this book analyses the possible implications of such a hasty and large-scale civilianisation process after the 15 July Uprising on the nature of Turkish CMR. It then explores the extent to which the military's institutional identity has evolved from a monolithic whole embodied and represented by the Chief of General Staff into a polylithic formation involving many but separated micro-identities in terms of the military elites' stance towards change, their worldviews, the service commands' stance regarding transformation and split between junior and senior officers. It is also worth mentioning that this transition from monolithic to polylithic institutional identity is driven by the weakening of the agency/institutional power of the General Staff both against executive presidency (power transfer to the civilian executive presidency) and within the military (power diffusion to the service commands) and seems to be the prime risk factor in Turkish CMR in years to come, and is thus in need of delicate management.

The Need for 'Inside-out' Insights to Open the Black Box

Despite the fact that the literature on the TAF and Turkish CMR is rich in size, the literature includes only 'outside-in' insights by 'civilian' researchers who have sought to explore the military. This book emphasises the need for more social research from within to better dissolve the fog around the black box of the Turkish military. Indeed, the absence of 'inside-out' insights from within the Turkish military would be listed as the first shortfall in the literature. Another handicap of the literature may be the dominance of dichotomous approaches, which stereotypically conceptualise Turkish CMR as a power relation between the 'secular, patriotic and modern soldier' and 'the elected, but inefficient and anti-secular politicians'. The third handicap visible in the literature is the conceptualisation of the TAF as a monolithic and time-proof institution with unchanged norms, values, ways of thinking and doing things. Exaggerated secrecy restrictions that are common in defence matters in Turkey may have exacerbated the impact of these obstacles. Thus, scholars have had limited access to the military, which in return, has limited the number of studies conducted by civilian researchers on the military. Another objective of this book is to tackle these three handicaps. The author fully acknowledges that the book is surely not immune to substance-related and methodological weaknesses. One should, however, give credit that, despite all these weaknesses, with this contribution, the literature has an empirical piece on the Turkish military relying on primary data sources that may have a potential to elevate the scholarly debates about the Turkish military and the Turkish CMR to a more quantitative level. Lastly, these two snapshots provided in this book could enable scholars to generate comparative scholarly insights after conducting a similar survey in the post-15 July environment with a similar research design, survey questions and methodology.

As emphasised, this is a book aiming to examine change within the Turkish (CMR) over 15 years. General CMR literature revolves around the nature of relationship between what is civilian (governments, civil society, academia, media, thinks tanks) and what is military. As Peter Feaver states, CMR "is a very broad subject, encompassing the entire range of relationships between the military and civilian society at every level".[10] It is mainly because of the problem of explaining the complex relationship between what is civilian and what is military, that historians, political scientists, sociologists, anthropologists and military strategists have all made important contributions to expand the scholarly grasp of the field. The three categories proposed by Feaver on CMR research in political science are: normative studies, which mostly follow sociological approaches that endeavour to explain how civilians (elites and civil society) and militaries should interact to achieve and maintain democratic and civilian control; empirical or descriptive studies, which mostly follow institutional approaches and examine the characteristics, nature and evolution of CMR in a particular polity; and theoretical works, which attempt to explain factors or conditions that are most likely to produce outcomes such as military interventions or effective civilian control of the military.[11] When following Feaver's categorisation, it likely to suggest that this book sits at the intersection of the theoretical and empirical analysis categories. It is, on the one hand, theoretical work because it seeks to follow an eclectic theoretical design seeking to provide novel aspects on endogenous factors and processes from a multi-method perspective. It is also an empirical analysis emphasising those endogenous factors within the Turkish military as the prime drivers of the Turkish military's change by providing quantitative and qualitative 'inside-out' insights from within the Turkish military. The book aims therefore to achieve this goal by studying the problematic on two levels: CMRs on one level, and the TAF itself on the other.

Indeed, because we fear others, we create an institution of violence to protect us, but then we fear the very institution we have created. Peter Feaver calls this paradox the "civil-military *problematique*",[12] implying the need to receive protection both by and from the military. On the night of 15 July 2016,[13] Turkey bitterly experienced the

10 Peter D. Feaver, 'The Civil-Military Problematique: Huntington, Janowitz and the Question of Civilian Control', *Armed Forces and Society*, 23:2 (1996).
11 Peter D. Feaver, 'The Civil-Military Problematique: Huntington, Janowitz and the Question of Civilian Control', *Armed Forces and Society*, 23:2 (1996).
12 *Ibid.*
13 Please see these pieces for the earlier version of this article: Metin Gurcan and Megan Gisclon, 'From Autonomy to Full-fledged Civilian Control: Changing Nature of Turkish Civil-Military Relations After 15 July', IPC-Mercator Policy Brief (Istanbul: Istanbul Policy Center, August 2016); Metin Gurcan and Megan Gisclon, 'What is the Turkish Military's Strategic Identity after July 15?', IPC-Mercator Policy Brief (Istanbul: Istanbul Policy Center, September 2016).

need for the latter, the need to be granted protection from the military. On this night, Turkey passed a major democracy test that included a military uprising seeking to hijack state power, a coup attempt, the worst form of terror in Turkey ever against its citizens, the disproportionate use of military power against government institutions and extrajudicial execution attempts to the elected civilian elites.[14]

Since 20 July 2016, just five days after this shocking attempt that claimed 249 lives, Turkey has been under a perpetual state of emergency – by means of which the government can issue executive decrees in a rapid fashion for the de-Gulenification of the state bureaucracy. While initially this state was declared for a single 90-day period, the Justice and Development Party (AKP) government faced few complications in extending this period past its intended expiration. It is likely that the constitutional referendum of 16 April 2017, involving a set of 18 proposed constitutional amendments ending the parliamentary system in Turkey and establishing an executive presidency, will be put to vote under the state of emergency, which will last, in President Tayyip Erdogan's words, "until everything is settled down".[15] Turkey has indeed been going through challenging times after 15 July 2016, seeking to diminish those risk factors that would put the country's future at peril.

It is indeed possible to define the military uprising of 15 July as the act of putschists attempting to hijack state power both to redesign the state apparatus and, in the case of strict Gulenists, to rule people until society adapts to Fethullah Gulen's totalitarian political vision militarised by the Gulenist putschits. These two factors distance the events of 15 July from past coups in the history of the Republic of Turkey, which had sought to topple the elected government and eventually hand over political power to elected civilians.

In a nutshell, the attempted military uprising of 15 July imposes upon us the call to carry the argument on the CMR and the military into the most existential (ontological) ground. The work entitled *Qualitative Methods in Military Studies* by Helena Carreiras and Celso Castro emphasises the need for more "social research of familiar" and "social research from within", in addition to the "social research of the other" to better understand strategic preferences and behaviours of modern militaries. This suggests that some amount of 'insider-ness' is needed to get a more accurate understanding of civil-military interactions.[16]

Why has the military side of the CMR always been in heavy fog, or why does then the TAF still remain as a 'black box' waiting to be explored by academics with 'inside-out' insights?

Surely this is not Turkish academia's fault. Difficulty with opening this black box may likely be associated with the TAF's self-imposed distance from the academic

14 Metin Gürcan, 'Why Turkey's Coup Didn't Stand a Chance', *Al-Monitor*, 17 July 2016.

15 See <http://www.diken.com.tr/erdogan-khk-ve-ohale-devam-dedi-referandum-icin-uzerime-duseni-yapacagim/> (Turkish) (accessed 3 March 2017)

16 Helena Carreiras and Celso Castro, *Qualitative Methods in Military Studies* (London: Routledge Press, 2014), pp.18-24.

world, the lack of civilian expertise on security issues in academia and a general absence of a cooperative environment and mutual trust between the TAF and academia. Exaggerated secrecy restrictions that are common in defence matters in Turkey may have exacerbated the impact of these obstacles. An attempt to take a holistic picture of the TAF on socio-cultural, security-related and political issues may, therefore, shed light on (and either confirm or falsify) the common portrayal of the TAF as a monolithic and homogenous organisation with unchanged norms, values and ways of thinking and doing things (i.e. organisational culture).

Research Questions

The following research questions directed this body of research:

- Is the TAF a monolithic and homogenous organisation as commonly assumed in the pre-15 July literature?
- Do all officers in the TAF think and behave alike concerning the military as a profession, a security organisation and a social institution?
- What is the extent and nature of change in the Turkish military? If change exists, then in which domains has it changed and what can be said about the characteristics of this change?
- In the 'military as a profession' domain, what are the variables defining the professional ethos in the TAF? Are there any differences among the Turkish officer corps in terms of ranks and service?
- In the 'military as a social institution' domain, how does the TAF define society? What does the TAF think about concepts such as politics, democracy, secularism and civilian control of the military? Has there been a generational difference in the attitudes and opinions of the junior (lieutenants, first lieutenants, captains and majors) and senior (lieutenant colonels, colonels and generals) officers in the TAF? If that is the case, then in what sense and in which realms? Is there a cross-sectional attitudinal difference between the Army, Air Force and Navy? What are the political views of the officers in the TAF? How does the Turkish military change as a social institution?
- In the domain of the 'military as a security organisation', what are roots of the TAF's threat perception? How does the TAF define its roles and missions? Has there been a change in the traditional conceptualisation of the TAF as 'the guardian of the state' against internal threats such as religious fundamentalism and Kurdish separatism? Do variables such as NATO, knowing a foreign language and serving in an international mission or fighting against terrorism have an impact on the thinking patterns of the officers in terms of the TAF's tasks and role in society?

- How, in which domains and through which kind of mechanisms does the 15 July military uprising affect the institutional identity of the TAF and nature of Turkish CMR?

Methodological Terrain

In order to answer the questions listed above, it is necessary to conduct a comprehensive analysis that spans time, employ both qualitative and quantitative data and provide both casual and descriptive inferences (multi-method analysis) at the organizstional and individual levels (multi-level analysis). Such a comprehensive approach would help us open the black box of the Turkish military. Therefore, a single case research method using multiple data sources at the different levels of analysis can both get a better grasp of the current patterns of the military's organisational culture in a holistic fashion, and conduct a causal analysis of change in the Turkish military. Simply put, our dependent variable is the Turkish military's culture, and the research phenomenon is institutional change in the Turkish military over the last 15 years. Thus, for this research, to get a more valid and holistic picture of the Turkish military, the Turkish CMR literature needs such single-case studies using multiple data sources generated with both qualitative and quantitative techniques in a complementary fashion. This is why this research was designed as a single case study utilising multiple data-gathering techniques both at the individual and organisational levels.

This research is multi-level because it both attempts to examine, at the organisational level, the change in the Turkish military as an institution over the last decade, and, at the individual level, the opinion and attitudes of the officer corps. It utilises multiple data sources (both qualitative and quantitative). In the qualitative strand, on the one hand, it applies both textual/discourse analysis (statements and speeches of top brass of the TAF and TAF press releases since 2004, for instance) and in-depth interviews with serving and retired officers conducted both before and after 15 July. In the quantitative strand, on the other hand, the research has a representative survey applied to the serving officers to examine the possible factors contributing to military change in the last decade.

Why does this research follow this methodological approach? Complex institutions such as militaries are inherently hard to grasp in their entirety with one research method and difficult to be captured by a single data-collection technique. Thus, no single method or means of social research can achieve the objective of this research, which is to get a 'valid' and 'holistic' picture of the Turkish military and factors that have shaped this picture. Therefore, this research embraces 'triangulation' as its methodological strategy, believing that it is useful to triangulate in order to compensate the weaknesses of other data-collecting techniques to have a current holistic view of the Turkish military's organisational culture and possible factors affecting it. Indeed, the use of qualitative and quantitative methods in studying the same phenomenon (i.e. institutional change) to get a more valid picture has received significant attention among scholars and researchers. As a result, it has become an accepted practice to use some form of triangulation in social research.

Jacob Alexander notes the following:

> By combining multiple observers, theories, methods, and empirical materials, researchers can hope to overcome the weakness or intrinsic biases and the problems that come from single-method, single-observer, single-theory studies. Often the purpose of triangulation in specific contexts is to obtain confirmation of findings through convergence of different perspectives. The point at which the perspectives converge is seen to represent reality.[17]

Triangulation, actually a military technique seeking to use multiple reference points to locate an object's exact position, is a process of verification that increases validity of casual and descriptive inferences, which this research equally takes into consideration when studying military change. By incorporating several viewpoints and data sources in the social research, triangulation is used to combine the advantages of both the qualitative and quantitative approach during the same time frame and give equal weight to compare data results or to validate, conform or corroborate qualitative findings with quantitative ones. The researcher seeks to merge the findings of the qualitative and quantitative approaches, which should interact with each other to interpret and transform data during analysis, to supplement measures of social and political behaviour drawn from interviews and questionnaires with measures drawn from physical trace evidence, test any given hypothesis repeatedly using the different measures of key concepts, and lastly to treat the hypothesis as more credible if all the tests converge in support.[18] Triangulation is thus not aimed merely at validation, but at deepening and widening one's understanding, and tends to support interdisciplinary research.

Why does this research embrace triangulation as the method to study change in the Turkish military? To better capture the nature, extent and characteristics of change the TAF has been experiencing over the last 15 years, and factors leading to this change, one needs a more complete, holistic and contextual portrayal of the TAF. In this portrayal, only the usage and interpretation of both descriptive and casual inferences in a complementary fashion may increase the validity of the research findings. That is, beyond the analysis of overlapping variance, the use of multiple measures may uncover some unique variance within the TAF, which otherwise may have been neglected by a single research technique.

17 Jakob Alexander, 'On the Triangulation of Quantitative and Qualitative Data in Typological Social Research: Reflections on a Typology of Conceptualizing "Uncertainty" in the Context of Employment Biographies', Forum: Qualitative Social Research, 2:1 (2001).

18 For more, see the International Encyclopedia of Political Science: <http://knowledge.sagepub.com/view/intlpoliticalscience/n619.xml> (accessed 23 December 2014).

The research's qualitative analysis includes three strands. The first strand is qualitative content analysis of official texts released by the Turkish military, such as press releases, and a discourse analysis of statements made by military elites through media outlets.[19] The second is the institutional analysis of the TAF's strategic preferences and behaviours over the last decade. Then, to achieve the objective of yielding the analytically rich qualitative insights to triangulate the quantitative findings, semi-structured in-depth interviews with the focus group of 80 serving officers in the TAF were conducted.

Methodological Self-Awareness to Overcome the Question of Reflexivity

At the end of the methodological introduction, it is also significant to note that the author is fully aware of the challenge of reflexivity coming with his 'insider' status when doing this research. The challenge of reflexivity is that it is not possible for a social researcher to be detached from what he or she is observing. That is, the reflexive process challenges the researcher to explicitly examine how his or her research agenda, assumptions, methods, personal beliefs and, more importantly, emotions enter into the research. Mainly because of this reflexive process in research, the researcher may unconsciously become an active part of knowledge production rather than remaining a neutral bystander throughout the research. How can a researcher prevent the effect of their position on their research? He/she should first recognise the challenge of reflexivity, and then stay firm by both becoming methodologically self-aware and by following a constant process of assessment of their own contribution and influence both in cognitive and emotive domains in shaping the research findings. The extent of the researcher's provision of their findings and how they present them are two factors that directly reveal this notion of becoming self-aware. Lastly, the critical capability to make explicit that their position and the possible impacts of this position on the research findings constitutes the third factor shaping methodological self-awareness. The author, having resigned from the military at the rank of major in January 2015, in the second year of this project and becoming a civilian since, assures the reader that he can critically engage in his findings so as not to be so submissive to his career in the Turkish military. One should also note that the author's both being an active service member of the Turkish military and a resigned officer provides him a unique position to enjoy different degrees of 'insiderness'. During the first two years of his research, the author conducted social research from within the Turkish military, then after his resignation in January 2015 and becoming civilian, the author started conducting the 'social research of the familiar' of the Turkish military. This was a stimulating point for the author, enabling him to look from different angles at his academic subject of

19 Klaus Krippendorff, *Content Analysis: An Introduction to its Methodology* (Newbury Park: Sage Publications, 2004).

the Turkish military. One should note that the research design and author's academic focus on his academic subject of the Turkish military has not changed after his resignation. One may assert that, throughout the thesis, the author has an attitude of "I know what I am doing, and thus, you should trust me", and this attitude could be a validity-related problem, as it would automatically raise the question of "Why should I trust you?" The author knows that trustworthiness cannot be self-declared, meaning that trust has to be earned and maintained. Reliability, the degree to which a measurement tool produces stable and consistent results, is not a problem for this piece of work, as any researcher may replicate this research by operationalising exactly the same protocols, and then compare/contrast the findings of this research and the findings of his/her research. The question is, however, whether the findings of this research portrays accurate or credible snapshots of the TAF. This is in fact a question about validity, the concept implying the necessity that the results obtained meet all of the requirements of the scientific research design. The author's assertive attempt to maintain his objectivity when studying his old institution as his scholarly subject, his attempt to conduct the research with a representative sample to generalise findings back to the officer corps, and his methodological self-awareness emphasising his strict adherence to his multi-method and multi-level research design for more triangulation of findings, would be stated as three factors consciously utilised by the author to maximise the both the internal and external validity of the research. Lastly, one should also note that, as can be seen in the literature review chapter, there is not a single scholarly work in the literature so far claiming to take 'accurate' snapshots of the TAF enabling one to compare the approximate truth of propositions, inferences and conclusions. The author is fully aware that this inherent deficiency constitutes a setback for this research. Last but least, this high degree of insiderness and 'you should trust what I say' attitude felt in some parts of the dissertation would be the weakest side of the research when recognising the fact that this research is the first of its kind in the literature, but also its strongest side.

Road Map

This book proceeds as follows:

The Literature Review (Chapter 1), which is designed to set the stage, is a background chapter for readers to get familiar with the scholarly debate about the TAF and Turkish CMR. This chapter first presents literature seeking to explain the civilianisation process and shift from 'confrontation' to 'delicate harmony' between civilian governments and the military that had started in the early 2000s, long before the 15 July Uprising. Particularly, it attempts to provide a thorough overview of the five arguments (The European Union effect, the argument of empowered civilian elites, the argument of strong governments, the argument of changing public perceptions towards the military and the argument of changing threat perceptions), emphasising the exogenous factors, the combination of which has likely contributed to the civilianisation of the Turkish CMR in 2002-16. This chapter, then twisting its grasp to the military culture and dynamics leading to change in the military, provides insights from Samuel Finer's classic book entitled *The Man on Horseback* in which the Turkish military was classified as one of those 'self-aware' militaries with an interventionist mentality.[20] Then, in the light of Finer's conceptualisation, this chapter turns to the few available works in the literature focusing on the military and providing endogenous scholarly insights within the military. Particularly, the themes from Mehmet Ali Birand's *Shirts of Steel*, the only available source which presents a "holistic picture of the Turkish military" in the early 1990s, are presented in detailed fashion to better compare and contrast the findings of the research with Birand's findings.[21]

Coming to the Theoretical Discussion (Chapter 2), the first thing that should be mentioned is that the TAF is a complex institution relying on men, women and other resources provided by society, being founded on values, norms and rituals as well as producing security (and kinetic power, if required) for polities with means and ways available to achieve the strategic objectives. While the first track in this chapter seeks to explain the Turkish military's change with institutional analysis, the second track, with a sociological twist, aims to understand this change through the examination of the evolution of the Turkish military's strategic culture. It is this theoretical diversity that enables this research to get through the challenge of studying the complex phenomenon of the military. That is why this chapter on theoretical discussion starts with the classic debate between Samuel Huntington (the institutionalist track) and Morris Janowitz (the sociological track), which dates back 60 years but is still relevant for contemporary debates regarding CMR. Huntington's 1957 *The Soldier and the State* and Janowitz's 1971 *The Professional Soldier* not only methodically combined empirical research on CMR with systematic theorizing for the first time, but also initiated the split of civil-military research into a sociological tradition and a strand of political science.[22] That is, political science studies of CMR, on the one hand, have followed Huntington's institutionalist tradition, and are mostly concerned with the question of how civilian political leaders can maintain civilian control, or the subordination of the military under legitimate elected civilian leaders. Military sociology, on the other hand, concentrates more on the cultural norms, values and societal factors affecting the relationship between soldiers and civilians. Because this research sits at the intersection between institutional analysis and military sociology, Huntingtonian and Janowitzian approaches are equally important. This chapter concentrates on the general literature and theoretical discussions on both the institutional and sociological

20 Samuel E. Finer, *The Man on Horseback: The Role of Military in Politics* (New York: Praeger, 1962), p.62.

21 Mehmet Ali Birand, *Shirts of Steel* (London: IB Tauiris, 1991).

22 P.D. Feaver and E. Seeler, 'Before and After Huntington: The Methodological Maturing of Civil-Military Studies', in S.C. Nielsen and D.M. Snider (eds), *American Civil-Military Relations: The Soldier and the State in a New Era* (Baltimore: Johns Hopkins University Press, 2009).

tracks to better highlight those dynamics leading to change within the Turkish military. Particularly, this chapter emphasises the model of gradual change and institutional change proposed by James Mahoney and Kathleen Thelen,[23] and the sociological framework for military change proposed by Theo Farrell and Terry Teriff.[24]

The Qualitative Analysis (Chapter 3), being the first empirical chapter, seeks to point out the 'whats, whys and hows' of the reaction of the TAF to the changing socio-economic and political context from 2002 onwards at both organisational and individual levels. The first aim of this qualitative analysis is to determine the patterned preferences and behaviours of the TAF when addressing the institutional challenges it has faced as an organisation in the last decade. These institutional challenges could be political, such as the 'de-securitisation' of the Kurdish question and the transfer of decision-making responsibility from the military to the civilian elites on the PKK-related issues; economic, such as the relative decline of monthly wages of military personnel when compared to their civilian counterparts; or social, such as the changing public perceptions regarding the military. These institutional challenges could also be rooted within the military, such as the struggle of non-commissioned officers (NCOs) for their status and rights against the Turkish General Staff, or outside the military, like the allegations of abuses of soldiers' rights and debate over the allegedly high suicide rates within the military. How and through what kind of institutional mechanisms has the Turkish military first responded and then addressed those challenges to change and adapt to the new environment? Simply, these are the sorts of questions this chapter seeks to elucidate to emphasise the fact that the gradual institutional change within the TAF had already started long before the 15 July Uprising. In this chapter, the qualitative content analyses of the statements of the top brass in the Turkish military and the Turkish General Staff's press releases in 2004-15 are provided to better understand the nature of change, particularly in the strategic narratives of the Turkish military in the last decade. Turning to the individual level, this chapter then provides the findings of the semi-structured, in-depth interviews of 82 military elites, among whom are still serving and retired officers, to provide their perspectives on drivers, actors and pathways of change within the TAF. At the end of this chapter, charts showing the change domains, change actors, change drivers and change pathways transforming the TAF as a security organization, as a social institution and officership as a profession are worth mentioning as, for the author, these charts are still relevant to explain the change within the TAF after 15 July.

Chapter 4, entitled Quantitative Analysis, twisting its grasp to the quantitative approach, provides statistical analyses based on the data derived from the survey research[25] applied to 1,240 officers in the Turkish military, a representative sample of

23 James Mahoney and Kathleen Thelen, *Explaining Institutional Change: Ambiguity, Agency and Power* (Cambridge: Cambridge University Press, 2010).

24 Theo Farrell and Terry Terriff, *The Sources of Military Change: Culture, Politics, Technology* (London: Lynne Reinner Publishing, 2002).

25 See Appendix A for the survey questions in Turkish.

the officer corps of 39,845 officers in the Turkish military (including the Gendarmerie Command and the Coast Guard) as of May-August 2015.

Chapter 5 provides an analysis of the paradigm change in Turkish civil-military relations as a result of the military reforms triggered by the attempted 15 July Uprising and also delves into how the continuing mass purges have impacted the TAF's institutional identity. The following discussion section in this chapter elucidates and then assesses the risks and challenges faced in the post-15 July setting in the domains of state institutions, Turkish CMR and the military's institutional identity. This section also presents the findings of the pre-15 July snapshot of the TAF, such as heterogenisation and diversification, transition from idealist-type officership to a pragmatist one, collectivist to individualist understanding of life, from an elitist to an egalitarian view of society and change from value-centric service to a focus on financial goals and career opportunities among the officer corps, as the prime endogenous drivers that played a major role in the failure of the attempted 15 July military uprising, as those factors prevented this act from turning into a full-fledged military uprising. The author suggests that those drivers visible in the pre-15 July snapshot have already degraded Turkish military self-awareness about its interventionalist mentality and thus severely dissolved its capacity to intervene in politics in a coherent and collective fashion. Simply, if those putschists had been aware of the findings of the pre-15 July military snapshot, they would not have dared to implement their plan of making the TAF wholly involved in this heinous act on that night. The second section delves into how the continuing mass purges have impacted the strategic identity of the TAF. The third section of the chapter provides an analysis of the paradigm change in Turkish CMR as a result of the military reforms triggered by 15 July. The discussion section first elucidates and then assesses the risks and challenges faced in the post-15 July setting in the domains of state institutions, the military's strategic identity and Turkish CMR. This section also presents some risk domains that should be managed delicately after 15 July.

The concluding chapter provides a summary of the key findings, theoretical and practical implications of the research, future prospects and possible avenues offered by this research for following researches.

1

Literature Review

To better emphasise the fact that civilianisation of the Turkish CMR had already started long before the 15 July Uprising, the first part of this review provides a brief overview of change in the basic characteristics of Turkish CMR over 15 years. One should note that the literature available explains the civilianisation as a process solely driven by non-military, or exogenous, dynamics. This chapter critically engages in the debate and discusses why these non-military factors may have been necessary, but not sufficient in themselves, to fully explain the civilianisation of Turkish CMR that has been the case over 15 years.

After elucidating these perspectives, the review then seeks to provide a picture of the Turkish military as portrayed in the existing literature to better compare/contrast it with the findings of the research. To provide conceptual insights at the beginning of this section, this chapter first reviews Samuel Finer's classic *The Man on Horseback*,[1] particularly Finer's conceptualisation of mentality and motivation of militaries as the endogenous drivers for military intervention and his classification of the Turkish military as an example of those "self-aware militaries inclined to intervention". After this conceptual prelude, the review turns to Mehmet Ali Birand's *Shirts of Steel*,[2] the first ever source-providing insights from within the Turkish military. Birand's work is highly relevant for this research, as its insights would be defined as a snapshot of Turkish military in the early 1990s. At the end of this section, some other scholars' observations/findings about the characteristics of the Turkish military are also provided to enrich the literature's picture of the Turkish military.

1 Samuel E. Finer, *The Man on Horseback: The Role of Military in Politics*, p.62.
2 Mehmet Ali Birand, *Shirts of Steel* (London: IB Tauiris, 1991).

Historical Terrain: Civilianisation before 15 July 2016

Turkish CMR before 2000

The Turkish military has always been an important actor since the foundation of the Turkish Republic in 1923.[3] Gareth Jenkins writes:

> The role of the military in Turkey is rooted in Turkish society, history and culture. The military has always lain at the heart of how Turks define themselves; and most still regard the institution of the military as the embodiment of the highest virtues of the nation.[4]

In addition to its empowered status and pre-eminent role in Turkish socio-cultural life,[5]the Turkish military has been entrusted by laws recognising its 'special status'.[6] The Turkish military, as Zeki Sarıgil puts it, "has had a special position of *de facto veto player* in the Turkish political system".[7] During all interventions, the Turkish military has adopted a profile for itself of being above politics, that is of being distant to fractional demands but certainly in defence of the state's interests and for the sake of the whole nation. This may be defined as an illustration of a hegemony construction in Gramscian terms, in which the military disperses its values to the society and state's bureaucratic machine by making the soldiers hegemonic and dominant in the political system, but in a tacit way.

Ersel Aydınlı suggests that the nature of Turkish CMR reflects the centuries-long historical experience of the Ottoman Empire (and its gradual decline), a distressing War of Independence (1919-23), a Cold War that was essentially quite hot in Turkey

3 William Hale, *Turkish Politics and the Military* (London: Routledge, 1994).
4 Gareth Jenkins, *Context and Circumstances: Turkish Military and Politics* (Oxford: Oxford University Press, 2001), p.15.
5 Gareth Jenkins, *Context and Circumstance: The Turkish Military and Politics*, pp.21-35.
6 The three main laws relating to the status and legal responsibilities of the TAF are:
The Turkish Constitution (1982). For the full text of the constitution see: <http://global.tbmm.gov.tr/docs/constitution_en.pdf> (accessed 14 January 2015). Particularly Chapter 3 of the Constitution, privileging military judicial system as an independent judicial branch in the state, Article 145 regulating the military judicial system, Articles 156 and 157 regulating the Higher Military Courts, Article 117 regulating the national defence, and Article 118 recognising the National Security Council as a constitutional institution and assigning tasks to it.
The TAF Internal Service Law (1961). For the full text (in Turkish) see: <http://www.mevzuat.gov.tr/MevzuatMetin/1.4.211.pdf> (accessed 12 January 2015).
The National Security Council Law (1983). For the full text (in Turkish) see: <http://www.mgk.gov.tr/index.php/kurumsal/mevzuat/mgk-ve-mgk-gensek-kanunu> (accessed 12 January 2015).
7 Zeki Sarıgil, 'Europeanization as Institutional Change: The Case of the Turkish Military', *Mediterranean Politics*, 12:1 (2007), pp.39-57.

and an enormous modernisation project which was eventually adopted to the Turkish military itself.[8] He then concludes that, after the initiation of the multi-party system in 1946, the Turkish military was never the army of a single party, and never the tool of radical politicians. Yet being a guardian army, it was also never truly a predatory military that wanted permanent power possession with a long-term vision, always having returned power promptly to civilians after the various military interventions. Along the same lines of Aydınlı, Ali L. Karaosmanoğlu highlights that, after grasping control of administrations, the military immediately assigned power to the civil governments and passed into the multiple-party regime.[9] This is one of the important characteristics that make the situation in Turkey different from the military dictatorships of Latin America[10] and the Middle East.[11] David Lion-Perlin, for instance, finds that while the Turkish military ruled only for brief periods, relying instead on extracting legal constitutional guarantees to maintain influence, Latin American militaries ruled for lengthier periods with less constitutional rewriting.[12] However, for Karaosmanoğlu, after each coup, the Turkish military has expanded its "autonomous" or "above-politics" sphere of influence by making changes to the constitution as well as other laws and legal regulations.[13] The military, for instance, achieved important privileges through constitutional and legal regulations to intervene in the political Service Law, the State Security Courts (DGMs), the right of the military to select one of the members of the Higher Education Council (YÖK) and the right of the Secretariat General of the National Security Council (MGK) to nominate one member of the Supreme Board for Radio and Television (RTÜK). The military also directly intervened in politics through informal mechanisms, such as public statements, press releases and declarations given by top-ranking officers. The reason for this, according to Aydınlı, is that the military was never convinced that the level of democracy in Turkey and the quality of civilian politics were good enough to become fully subordinate to them.[14]

One could then assert that the military, during much of the Republican Period, shared political power with civilian governments, with Steven Cook's words, "to rule"

8 Ersel Aydınlı, 'A Paradigmatic Shift for the Turkish Generals and an End to the Coup Era in Turkey', *Middle East Journal*, 63:4 (2009), pp.581-96.
9 Ali L. Karaosmanoğlu, *Armed Forces And Democracy* (Bilgesam Publications, 2011).
10 David Pion-Berlin, 'Turkish Civil-Military Relations: A Latin American Comparison', *Turkish Studies*, 12:2 (2011).
11 Nil S. Satana, 'Civil-Military Relations in Europe, the Middle East and Turkey', *Turkish Studies*, 12:2 (2011), pp.279-92.
12 David Pion-Berlin, 'Turkish Civil-Military Relations: A Latin American Comparison', *Turkish Studies*, 12:2 (2011).
13 Ali L. Karaosmanoğlu, 'Armed Forces And Democracy', p.8.
14 Ersel Aydınlı, 'Ergenekon, New Pacts and the Decline of the Turkish Inner State', *Turkish Studies*, 12:2 (2011).

by leaving the daily routines of governance to the civilian governments.[15] Through its role as the protector of the whole nation and the guardian of the state both against internal and external threats, the military has had a powerful position in the affairs of the state, which eventually led to the ability to decide the fate of governments and politicians as well as a privileged position in the eyes of the people. On four occasions (1960, 1971, 1980 and 1997), the military directly intervened to change the course of the political system and replace the government. All were effective for the military in the sense that the military was able to change the course of events in their own favour. Directly placed under the office of the Prime Minister instead of the Ministry of Defense, and the Chief of General Staff remaining in fourth place on the state protocol list after the President, the head of Parliament and the Prime Minister, the military enjoyed sufficient autonomy to influence decisions made by the political leadership. These decisions were not only on security-related issues but also in other domains such as judicial and legislative processes, as well as budgetary, education and broadcasting matters.[16] The officer corps has been a privileged group in Turkish society, respected and trusted by the population and enjoying special privileges in the form of high-quality education, secure employment, housing and various other welfare benefits.[17] Generally, the military and society have had a good and strong relationship.[18] Known for its adherence to law and order and incorrupt ways, the military has been the most trusted institution in the country, recording much better in opinion polls than any other civil-political organisation.[19] For instance, a Gallup poll in May 2007 found that Turks are more likely to express confidence in the country's military than any other national institution, with 81% of respondents saying they had confidence in the military.[20] Similarly, a Eurobarometer opinion poll of 2008 indicated that the vast majority of Turkey respected the military as an institution, 84% of Turks naming the military as the most trusted institution in the country.[21] One should note that military interventions in politics were also, by and large, accepted by society as a necessity during times of political unrest.[22]

15 Steven Cook, *Ruling But not Governing: The Military and Political Development in Egypt, Algeria and Turkey*, p.17.
16 Eser Karakaş, 'State Protocol and Politics', *Today's Zaman*, 8 November 2012.
17 Gareth Jenkins, *Context and Circumstances: Turkish Military and Politics* (Oxford: Oxford University Press, 2001), p.15.
18 Zeki Sarıgil, 'The Turkish military: Principal or Agent?', *Armed Forces & Society*, 40:1 (2014), pp.168-90.
19 Yaprak Gürsoy, 'The Impact of EU-Driven Reforms on the Political Autonomy of the Turkish Military', *South European Society and Politics*, 16:2 (2011), pp.293-308.
20 For the poll results see: <http://www.gallup. com/poll/28351/military-turkey-elicits-highest-levels-public-confidence.aspx> (accessed 12 June 2015).
21 Gareth Jenkins, 'Court postpones Semdinli Hearing once again', *Eurasia Daily Monitor*, 5 (2008), p.109.
22 Metin Heper and Aylin Güney, 'The Military and the Consolidation of Democracy: The Recent Turkish Experience', *Armed Forces& Society*, 26 (2000), pp.635-57.

In sum, one may suggest that, until the turn of the millennium, CMR in Turkey were characterised by relatively weak civil-political institutions and political elites on the one hand, and a strong military institution and powerful generals on the other, or in Zeki Sarıgil's words, "the period of military supremacy rather than a civilian supremacy".[23] However, during the last decade, the power dynamics have changed in favour of the civilian institutions. But how has this shift started, or which factor caused the beginning of this shift? Turkey's EU candidacy process, which led to the wide-ranging EU harmonisation packages, the first of which was taken by the three-party coalition comprised of the Democratic Left Party, the Nationalist Movement Party and the Motherland Party in 2000, was the answer that was proposed in the literature.[24]

The Coalition Government: Civil-Military Relations (2000–02)

Turkey was declared a EU candidate country at the European Council's Helsinki Summit in December 1999, upon which several democratisation reforms were introduced to meet the requirements for full membership. One dimension of these reforms was concerned with the democratisation of Turkish CMR, aiming to eliminate the military's privileges and autonomous status within the political system. In contrast to some who associate the civilianisation of Turkish CMR with the first AKP government's ruling period that started in 2002, Sarıgil suggests that, in fact, the decline of the Turkish military's political influence was triggered by the EU's decision of granting candidacy status to Turkey after the Helsinki Summit.[25] Simply, when the EU recognised Turkey as an official candidate country for membership, Turkey was forced to initiate major legal and institutional changes to curb the military's political powers. The result of the summit decisions triggered a rapid reform process. This first wave of civilianisation can be grouped under three broad reform categories: reforms strengthening civilian power over defence-related issues; reforms curbing the military's presence in the judiciary; and reforms amending the structure of the MGK. In addition, the reforms aimed at increasing democratic liberties, such as freedom of speech and minority rights. Several packages that were enacted in the early 2000s changed the anti-terror law and granted the right to broadcast and obtain education

23 Zeki Sarıgil, 'The Turkish military: Principal or Agent?', *Armed Forces & Society*, 40:1 (2014), pp.168-90.

24 Şule Toktaş and Ümit Kurt, 'The Turkish Military's Autonomy, AKP Rule and the EU Reform Process in the 2000s: An Assessment of the Turkish Version of Democratic Control of Armed Forces (DECAF)', *Turkish Studies*, 11:3 (2010), pp.387-403.

25 Sarıgil, Zeki, 'Europeanization as Institutional Change: The Case of the Turkish Military', *Mediterranean Politics*, 12:1 (2007), pp.39-57.

in languages other than Turkish, including Kurdish.[26] Accordingly, in 1999, the seats of the military judges were removed from the DGM. In 2001, an amendment was made to Article 118 of the Constitution, increasing the number of civilians participating in MGK meetings by adding the Minister of Justice to the MGK, the latter of which was comprised of five military members (Chief of General Staff and four Force Commanders) and four civilian members (the Prime Minister, the Minister of Interior, the Minister of Foreign Affairs and the Minister of Defence). In addition, in Article 118 of the Constitution, the statement "Any MGK decision would primarily be taken into consideration by the Cabinet" was changed to "would primarily be evaluated by the Cabinet", not to degrade the credibility of the cabinet.

The First AKP Government: Civil-Military Relations (2002–07)

After the AKP entered office as a single party in the 2002 general election by receiving 34.28 % of total votes, the seventh harmonisation package was implemented in 2003.[27] Through this package, the method of electing the MGK Secretary General from among civilian members was ensured; the authority of the Chief of General Staff on selecting and assigning a three-star general as the MGK Secretary General was transferred to the Prime Minister as a civilian bureaucrat; the monthly meetings of the MGK were determined to be held bi-monthly; and the authority of the MGK Secretary General was drastically narrowed. Most importantly, while the authority of the MGK was reduced to an advisory role on issues such as determining, assigning and applying the national security policy of the state, an explicit initiative was presented to the Prime Minister and his cabinet about whether or not to apply these decisions. Therefore, the MGK was legally turned into an advisory body. Within the scope of regulations made after the military's 1971 memorandum, which increased the political autonomy of the military, the DGM were established and entrusted with "the task of trying the crimes related directly to national security and crimes against the Republic, with its qualities such as the unity and integrity of the state with the country and the nation, and having a free democratic order determined in the Constitution". The military judges in these courts were removed.

In May 2004, the eighth harmonisation package was approved in parliament, bringing increased civilian supervision of defence expenditures by expanding the Court of Auditors' purview to oversee the budget, including what was previously considered confidential property. In this reform process, the DGMs, which had included both military and civilian members, were completely abolished; the

26 Yaprak Gürsoy, 'The changing role of the military in Turkish politics: democratization through coup plots?', *Democratization*, 19:4 (2012), pp.735-60.

27 For the full texts of all harmonization packages (in Turkish) see: <http://www.abgs.gov.tr/files/pub/abuyp. pdf> (accessed 16 January 2015).

provision allowing for the selection of one member of the YÖK by the General Staff was removed from the Law on Higher Education; and the provision allowing for the nomination of one member of the RTÜK by the MGK's Secretariat General was repealed from the Law on the Establishment of and Broadcasting by Radio and Television Corporations. Among these reforms, one should note that the reform of the MGK was a remarkable step toward curbing the military's capacity to intervene in politics in a direct and formal fashion.[28] The military was no longer represented in institutions that oversee higher education and the media,[29] and military judges no longer served on the benches of the DGM.[30] Several amendments made in conjunction to the harmonisation packages increasingly restricted the military courts' jurisdiction regarding hearing court cases against civilians, and in 2006 finally ended the trial of civilians by these courts during peacetime.[31] One should note that the first AKP government (2002–07) intensely supported Turkey's EU bid, kept a distance from political Islam and refrained from any direct confrontation with the military on critical political issues such as the wearing of the headscarf and secularism.[32] In a way, the pledge to the ideal of EU membership provided the AKP with legitimacy, which had been under inquiry by the military due to the party's Islamist background. This legitimacy indirectly served to lessen the military's political power. It is likely that both the AKP and the military tried to accomplish a *modus vivendi* with each other by equally respecting the EU process.[33] It is, however, important to note that the self-proclaimed role of the Turkish military – that is, dominating the national security agenda by way of securitisation, especially on issues such as political Islam and Kurdish nationalism – continued.

It is also worth mentioning the changing strategic preferences among military elites. Some suggest that, despite the deep-rooted involvement of the Turkish military in civilian affairs due to institutional background and historical experience, another important factor that shapes this relationship is the personality of the individuals in the position of the chief of staff. For example, during General Hilmi Özkök's term of office as Chief of General Staff between 2002 and 2006, the Turkish military had a relatively low political profile. The military respected the AKP's election victory

28 Linda Michaud-Emin, 'The Restructuring of the Military High Command in the 7th Harmonization Package and its Ramifications for the Civil-Military Relations in Turkey', *Turkish Studies*, 8:1 (2007), p.36.

29 Joost Lagendijk, 'The Times are Really Changing in Turkey: Security Matters', *Newsletter from the Centre of European Security Studies* (2010), p.12.

30 Gareth Jenkins, 'Continuity and Change. Prospects for civil-military relations in Turkey', *International Affairs*, 83:2 (2007), pp.339–55.

31 Yaprak Gürsoy, 'The Impact of EU-Driven Reforms on the Political Autonomy of the Turkish Military', *South European Society and Politics*, 16:2 (2011), pp.293-308.

32 Fuat Keyman and Ziya Öniş, *Turkish Politics in a Changing World: Global Dynamics and Domestic Transformation* (Istanbul: Bilgi University Press, 2007), pp.9-34.

33 Metin Heper, 'Civil-Military Relations in Turkey: Toward a Liberal Model?', *Turkish Studies*, 12:2 (2011), pp.241-52.

in 2002. Özkök did not force the AKP leaders and the political elite to come to terms with the military's opinions on security issues but instead opted for methods of negotiation and persuasion. Özkök was in favour of a more democratic solution as he questioned the understanding and rationale of direct or indirect involvement of the military in the political scene. In line with the conventional TGS's ideal of westernisation, General Özkök also supported Turkey's EU membership. Metin Heper summarises Özkök's relatively liberal attitude as follows:

> Özkök was also of the opinion that pious people might pursue secular politics. He wished to develop a *modus vivendi* with the AKP. At times, he changed his mind when the AKP government came up with a persuasive argument. Most significantly he kept restlessness under control among some commanders at the top particularly about 'the hidden agenda' of the AKP government. When he spoke up, often he seemed to appease the detractors of the AKP government within the military: "The February 28 was the consequence of certain developments in Turkey. The effect would not be different if the cause continues to exist."[34]

After the relatively smooth period of Hilmi Özkök, Turkish CMR severed in the following period when Chief of General Staff Yaşar Büyükanıt was appointed in 2006 and remained in office until 2008. The friction between the AKP government and the military increased during the period of the 2007 presidential elections. The military sought to change the AKP's decision to nominate Abdullah Gül, the then-Minister of Foreign Affairs, as its presidential candidate. The military's strategic preferences and behaviours before and during the presidential elections process were reminiscent of previous military involvements in political processes. In a conference on 12 April 2007, the Chief of General Staff, General Yaşar Büyükanıt, announced that the military must concern itself with the presidential elections as the President of the Republic was also the Commander in Chief of the Turkish military. He also stated that, "as a citizen and as a member of the armed forces, I hope someone who is loyal to the main principles of the Republic and committed to the secular, unitary structure of the state – not just in words, but in essence – will be the President."[35] Yet, despite this warning and the military's other formal and informal mechanisms to influence the government's decision, the AKP did not rescind Abdullah Gül's candidacy to be president. In reaction, on 27 April 2007, the military introduced a new way of expressing its opinions about developments in the Turkish political system. The Turkish General Staff published a memorandum on its official website warning of the danger to secularism.[36] It was the harshest statement by the military since the intervention on 28

34 *Ibid.*

35 William Hale and Ergun Özbudun, *Islamism, Democracy and Liberalism in Turkey: The Case of the AKP* (New York: Routledge, 2010), p.91.

36 *Ibid*, pp.91-93.

February, which was a confrontation with the Welfare Party coalition in 1997. The e-memorandum stated the following:

> It is observed that some circles who have been carrying out endless efforts to disturb the fundamental values of the Republic of Turkey, especially secularism, have escalated their efforts recently ... An important portion of these activities was carried out with the permission and the knowledge of administrative authorities, who were supposed to intervene and prevent such incidents, a fact which intensifies the gravity of the matter.[37]

The direct method employed by the military to block Gül's nomination for the presidency also led to some criticism in civil society. One should note that some civil society organisations, the media and business circles alike gave significant support to the AKP in its standoff with the military. Even participants in demonstrations against the AKP expressed their ambivalence towards the military with the slogan 'No *Sharia*, but no coup either'.[38] Thus, the military did not achieve its main objective to organise public, press and non-governmental organisations against the AKP government in overturning its decision to hold Abdullah Gül as its presidential candidate. With this civilian response, citizens, including both opponents and proponents of the AKP, sent a clear message that the military needed to keep out of this debate. This is a very critical juncture in Turkish CMR, in the sense that the legitimacy of the military as a veto player in the political realm was questioned by the public, giving authority to civilian rule rather than to the military's guardianship role. That is why, in 2009, General Yaşar Büyükanıt confessed that he was the one who had penned the e-memorandum but was against the idea of shutting down the AKP (2009, 'Retired General confesses…'). It is also worth remembering that, in September 2011, the very first month after his appointment as the Chief of General Staff, General Necdet Özel removed the controversial 27 April statement from the official website of the Turkish military (www.tsk.tr).

In sum, the CMR in the AKP's first governmental term (2002–07) would be marked by two entirely contradictory stages. The first stage is the period up until 2006 when there was a robust motivation for EU membership by the government; a positive pro-Turkish climate amongst the political and bureaucratic elite of the EU and its member states; an enormous legislative reform process that emphasised the civilian supremacy in Turkish politics; General Hilmi Özkök, who as Chief of the General Staff, stuck to democratic processes and respected civilian supremacy; and

37 In a well-known TV news programme called '32. Gun' broadcast on Channel D on 5 May 2009, then-Chief Yaşar Büyükanıt declared that he wrote the text of the e-memorandum himself.

38 Şule Toktaş and Ümit Kurt, 'The Turkish Military's Autonomy, AKP Rule and the EU Reform Process in the 2000s: An Assessment of the Turkish Version of Democratic Control of Armed Forces (DECAF)', *Turkish Studies*, 11:3 (2010), pp.387-403.

smooth relations between the AKP and the military, which seemed to tacitly endorse the EU candidacy process. The second stage, however, would be marked by a change of office in the Turkish General Staff; a more enthusiastic Chief of Staff, General Yaşar Büyükanıt, who often reminded people of the military's guardianship role of the Turkish state; chaos during the presidential nomination and election processes, as well as the military's involvement in these processes with Büyükanıt's public speeches and e-memorandums published on the TAF's official website; the AKP government's counterattack by making public speeches against the memorandums in favour of democracy instead of using executive power in appointing or resigning military cadres or retreating; and reactions by some civil society institutions to the military for this attempt of direct intervention in politics, political instability and civilian incapacity in the outbreak and, later on, in the management of the crisis in Turkish CMR. The general elections in 2007 were timely for the civilian elites to stress the importance of parliamentary democratic politics. As a last note, Gül's presidency can be considered both a success of elected civilians over the military in a delicate political matter and an indicator of the military's declining ability to shape the politics.

The Second AKP Government: CMR (2007–11)

The AKP won the 2007 general elections by increasing its share of the national vote from 34.3% in the 2002 general elections to 46.7%. A self-confidence empowered by the election results endowed the AKP with new life to rekindle the reformist spirit of Turkish CMR. In June 2007, however, the publication of the diaries of retired general Özden Örnek in the weekly news magazine *Nokta* was followed by an alleged coup conspiracy against the AKP government and eventually triggered the ignition of a legal investigation, later to be known as the *Ergenekon* case.[39] More than 300 people, including journalists, academicians and retired and active duty military officers from various ranks, were implicated in the coup plans and were put on trial in October 2008. In early 2010, another alleged plot entitled *Balyoz* (Sledgehammer) was discovered, resulting in the start of a separate trial in December 2010 against almost 200 suspected retired and serving officers. The number of armed forces personnel being prosecuted was unprecedented in Turkish history, especially once it is considered that *Balyoz* and *Ergenekon* led to the arrest of one-in-ten generals and admirals in the TAF, a group including both retired and serving four-star generals.[40] Yaprak Gürsoy suggests that the exposure of alleged coup plots in 2008 and the following trials of the retired and serving officers have shaken the guardian role of the Turkish military

39 Ersen Aydınlı, 'Ergenekon, New Pacts, and the Decline of the Turkish Inner State', *Turkish Studies* 12:2 (2011).

40 Ersen Aydınlı, 'A Paradigmatic Shift for the Turkish Generals and an End to the Coup Era in Turkey', *Middle East Journal*, 63:4 (2009), pp.581-96.

in politics.[41] This is an accurate observation, as investigations into the coup plans have also discouraged officers from political expression.

In January 2010, the AKP government abolished the Police-Public Security Cooperation (EMASYA) protocol, which had formed one of the legal bases for the military to carry out internal security operations in urban areas. In August 2010, for the first time in more than two decades, the AKP government got involved in the decisions of the High Military Council regarding promotions. Later in the year, the government prepared a constitutional package, which was approved by the majority of the electorate in a referendum on 12 September 2010. The package included changes such as that soldiers would be adjudicated in civilian courts for non-military offences, it would be possible to try the generals who had staged the military intervention of 1980, and the decisions of the High Military Council on purges from the military would be subjected to judicial review. Accompanying these legal changes, the inclination of civilians to challenge military autonomy in practice has also increased. A 2010 constitutional amendment permitted military officers to face trial in civilian courts for criminal offences against state security. The execution of this constitutional order made a significant contribution to decreasing the military's ability to informally yet directly intervene in politics through statements, declarations and press releases given by high-ranking officers. This amendment almost completely ended the military's usage of such informal mechanisms to influence politics.

In the second governmental term of the AKP, to bypass these newly appeared restrictions in the political context, the Turkish military started to change its communication strategy. After General İlker Başbuğ replaced Yaşar Büyükanıt as the Chief of General Staff in 2008, the Turkish military initiated a new media and public relations strategy to directly inform the public about security matters as an actor independent of the government. This shift in the communication strategy would be defined as being respectful of civilian authority, meaning not being in open dispute with the elected civilians, but instead being open to discussing security matters with the public. To achieve this, the military extended the accreditation list to include new media outlets, which had not been invited to their events before. In this new approach, high-ranking generals briefed these media outlets about military operations against targets of the Kurdistan Workers' Party (PKK) and accepted questions in press conferences. As the Chief of General Staff, General İlker Başbuğ was interviewed by many leading journalists in the media during this time (2010: 'Başbuğ: A demoralized…'). In his speech at the War Academies Command in Istanbul on 14 April 2009, for instance, General Başbuğ articulated the military's position *vis-à-vis* the main internal political issues, such as the Kurdish question, the *Ergenekon* case and political Islam. Despite the form and style of his speech seeming softer compared with previous speeches by former chiefs of general staff, the content of his speech indicated that Turkish CMR were still

41 Yaprak Gürsoy, 'The Final Curtain for the Turkish Armed Forces? Civil-Military Relations in View of the 2011 General Elections', *Turkish Studies*, 13:2 (2012), pp.191-211.

not in line with a democratic one. What this speech indicated was that, like between 2008 and 2010, the military still attempted to exert its influence on politics and that the military's involvement in political and public affairs still continued. As seen in the first empirical chapter providing an institutional analysis of the Turkish military's change, this method of communicating directly to the public against the elected civilians was to create a backlash effect that eroded the public image of the Turkish military.

While the Turkish military followed the method of directly communicating with the public to complain about the preferences and behaviours of the elected civilians and behaviours the military deemed improper or anti-secular, the AKP government continued with more civilianization. The newly founded Secretariat for combating terrorism called the Secretariat for Public Order and Security under the realm of the Ministry of Internal Affairs in 2009 is another sign of the shift in the state's security structure. The new Secretariat's aims include the recruitment of civilian security specialists to develop strategies to fight terrorism and to coordinate intelligence services of the state. One of the problems in the democratic control of the military has been the Turkish National Intelligence Organisation. It is currently a semi-independent organisation under military dominance, whereas constitutionally, it is an office under the Prime Minister. The Ministry of Internal Affairs has an intelligence organisation under the General Directorate of Security. The military also has its own intelligence organisation. The new Secretariat aims to civilianise these different units of surveillance by creating a coordination centre at the Ministry of Internal Affairs.

In sum, through various institutional reforms, the Turkish military's power in politics has been significantly narrowed by reforms carried out by the AKP governments and the fact that the public embraced these reforms despite the military pleading with them not to do. For instance, the military could not react to the government's lifting of the ban on headscarves in universities in 2010, the amendment allowing officers to be tried in civilian courts the same year, and the government's negotiations with the leader of the PKK, known by the public as the Oslo Process.[42]

It is possible to suggest that, as of 2009, the only rigid domain in which elected civilians confronted the military was the Kurdish question and the armed conflict between the PKK and the security forces. On 19 October 2009, 34 members of the PKK surrendered through the Habur border gate, and there were peaceful demonstrations organizsd by the pro-Kurdish Democratic Society Party (*Demokratik Toplum Partisi*, DTP). All returnees were freed as part of the rapprochement and reconciliation initiative of the AKP without legal proceedings. Then-Prime Minister Erdoğan said that he was "considering far-reaching steps to resolve the conflict" (2009, 'In a symbolic move…'). Indeed, the same year, state television channel TRT launched a groundbreaking channel, TRT Şeş, broadcasting in Kurdish.[43] The Turkish military

42 Mustafa Akyol, 'Turkey considers new peace process with PKK', *Al-Monitor*, 3 January 2015.
43 The first public broadcasting in Kurdish took place in June 2004, following 2001 amendments by the coalition government. At that time, it was for only two hours a day.

reacted strongly against the warm reception and the release of the PKK members without penalty (2009, 'Turkey denies Öcalan...'). Families, veterans and friends of martyrs protested against celebratory events welcoming members of the PKK (2009, 'Martyrs' families continue...'). The then-Secretary General of the General Staff, General Ferit Güler, said in a weekly press conference that "the developments which took place on 19 October and the following days are unacceptable" (2009, 'Military and HSYK...'). Government officials shared a similar criticism by saying "excessive celebration will have negative repercussions for the Kurdish resolution" (2009, 'Reception for returnees...'). Historically, in military discourse, practice and mindset, the Kurdish question was provoked by PKK terrorism. Accordingly, there was no need for a political solution but a fight against terror. The AKP's recent Kurdish resolution project, which is likely to result in the purge of the PKK in the long run, has been purely a civilian initiative. It was met with relative silence by the military, reflecting the military's confirmation of the ongoing process. One may then suggest that the resolution process, despite all its shortcomings and drawbacks, contributed to the process of desecuritisation, demilitarisation and civilianisation in the Turkish polity, particularly as the hottest issue of the Kurdish question and ongoing PKK-initiated conflict in south-eastern Turkey.[44]

The Third AKP Government: CMR (2011–15)

The AKP won a third term in parliamentary elections by increasing its vote to 49.8% during the 2011 general election. With this result, the AKP became the only political party in Turkish history to win three consecutive general elections, each time receiving more votes than in the previous election. This is indicative of the empowerment of the single-party majority in Turkish politics.

After General İlker Başbuğ's retirement, General Işık Koşaner became Chief of General Staff on 27 August 2010. Koşaner did not follow Başbuğ's approach of direct communication with the public during his term in office. However, he continued to defend the military against investigations carried out during the alleged *Ergenekon* case and coup plans by using both formal and informal mechanisms, especially via strategic talks with the Prime Minister and the President, and released press statements on the General Staff's website. He made these statements in a milder manner compared with Başbuğ. However, an unanticipated development occurred in July 2011. On 29 July 29, Prime Minister Erdoğan stated that the government would not approve the promotion of detained officers in the Supreme Military Council, which would start on 1 August. After this, Koşaner pointed out that a total of 250 officers – 173 active and 77 retired – were detained and these detentions were against universal

44 Yaprak Gürsoy, 'The Final Curtain for the Turkish Armed Forces? Civil-Military Relations in View of the 2011 General Elections', *Turkish Studies*, 13:2 (2012), pp.191-211.

legal principles, fairness, justice and conscientious values. On the same day, Koşaner, along with the Land, Air and Naval Force Commanders, resigned by requesting their retirement. While Turkey confronted mass resignations of its commanders for the first time in the country's history, public opinion turned fearful over the possibility that Turkey was heading toward a serious crisis. However, the government weathered the storm in a very short time by assigning a new command echelon, including the General Staff. The EU viewed the event as Turkey "becoming a more democratic country in which democratic institutions have control over military decisions".[45]

Another critical juncture towards civilianisation was the revision of Article 35 of the military's Internal Service Law. The previous version of this article stated: "The duty of the TAF is to protect and preserve the Turkish homeland and the Turkish Republic as defined in the Constitution." This article was an important legal justification for the military leaders to legitimise the coup of 1980. In July 2013, Article 35 was revised to the following: "The duty of the armed forces is to protect the Turkish homeland against threats and dangers coming from abroad, to ensure the preservation and strengthening of military power in a manner that will provide deterrence, to fulfill the duties abroad according to the decisions of the Parliament and help maintain international peace." With this revision, which placed emphasis to external threats, the military's ability to use the pretext of internal threats to stage coups and intervene in politics was abolished.

In August 2011, General Necdet Özel, an officer with moderate views and strong democratic commitments (2011, 'Profile of Necdet…'), was appointed as the new Chief of the General Staff. When taking his soft engagement approach with elected civilians into account in the domain of CMR,[46] one may assert that Özel has disinclined from direct confrontation with the political elites as a "reformist dove",[47] particularly with regard to the *Ergenekon* and *Sledgehammer* cases.[48]

The 2013 EU Turkey Progress Report summarizss the civilianisation of Turkish CMR over the last decade as follows:

> Civilian oversight of the security forces was further consolidated. The General Staff abstained from exerting pressure on political issues beyond its remit. A law overhauling the Turkish Armed Forces' disciplinary system, adopted in January 2013, provides for the conversion of disciplinary tribunals into administrative disciplinary committees, the abolition of solitary confinement and the strengthening of appeal mechanisms for disciplinary punishments. The report of an inter-party Parliamentary Commission tasked with investigating coups and alleged

45 Constanze Letsch, 'Turkey military chiefs resign over Sledgehammer "coup plot" arrests', *The Guardian*, 30 July 2011.

46 Metin Gürcan, 'Turkish military wages war on Social Media', *Al-Monitor*, 9 March 2015.

47 Metin Gürcan, 'Turkish hawks want to settle past injustices', *Al-Monitor*, 20 March 2015.

48 See Cansu Çamlıbel's interview with Bilgin Balanlı, a four-star Air Force general who was arrested and jailed for four years during the *Sledgehammer* trial: <http://www.hurriyet.com.tr/gundem/28656351.asp> (accessed 15 April 2015).

'deep state' networks was published in December. Judicial investigations into the 1980 coup and the 'Postmodern Coup' of 28 February 1997 continued. In November, a Court heard the two surviving perpetrators of the 1980 coup via videoconference. 103 suspects have been charged with involvement in the 28 February 'Postmodern Coup' of 1997.

Amendments made to the Law on Provincial Administrations, which is used as the legal basis for the use of military force upon request of governors in domestic security incidents, gave civilian authorities a broader oversight of military operations. In July, the Internal Service Law of the Turkish armed forces, which broadly defined the duties of the military and contained one article to justify military intervention in politics, was amended. Military service has been re-defined and the amendment also clarified that members of the Turkish Armed Forces cannot engage in political activities. Civilian oversight of the Gendarmerie's law enforcement activities, in particular, remained insufficient. There was only limited access to the Turkish Court of Accounts audit reports on security, defence and intelligence agencies. Military and civilian judicial investigations into the December 2011 Uludere incident in which 34 civilians lost their lives as a result of a military airstrike remained subject to a secrecy decision and were not finalised. No administrative measure was taken to punish any individual for the incident. A parliamentary investigation report was published – with dissenting opinions – but did not clarify political or operational responsibility.[49]

The report also emphasises the following points in Turkish CMR:

> The civilian and military court systems continued to run in parallel. Increasing civilian control of the military requires the amendment of legal provisions on the composition and powers of the Supreme Military Council. Pending the finalization of a new constitution, the Chief of the General Staff continued to report to the Prime Minister rather than the Minister of Defense. Overall, progress was made in consolidating civilian oversight, in particular with the parliamentary investigation into past military coups and legislative amendments, confirming the profound shift in the balance of civil-military relations in favor of the civilian authorities. However, further reforms are needed, particularly as regards the military justice system and civilian oversight of the Gendarmerie.

When reviewing the literature seeking to explain the civilianisation and the military's diminishing political influence over the last 15 years, one can find five major arguments, all exogenous in the literature.

49 European Union, 'Turkey 2013 Progress Report', 16 October 2013. For the full report see: <http://ec.europa.eu/enlargement/pdf/key_documents/2013/package/tr_rapport_2013_en.pdf> (accessed 12 December 2014).

Exogenous Arguments Attempting to Explain Civilianisation of CMR over last 15 years

The 'EU Effect' Argument

The main point of the 'EU effect' argument is that the EU harmonisation process in Turkey has required reforms in Turkish CMR to secure civilian supremacy over the TAF and greater transparency in its affairs, meaning that the EU emerges as an important external factor which initiated this change.[50]

After Turkey's accession to candidacy status at the European Council's Helsinki Summit in 1999,[51] one particular EU requirement for Turkey to fulfill the Copenhagen political criteria was the elimination of the involvement of the military in civilian affairs and politics. Meeting this requirement would mean that Turkey would have the same CMR standards as those of other EU member states. To achieve this objective of civilian supremacy and oversight, Turkey abolished or reduced military representation in civilian governmental bodies, introduced greater transparency in defence policy-making and budget, and improved parliamentary oversight of the military.[52] The EU membership process required Turkey to enact certain political reforms, particularly in Turkish CMR as, among these reforms, the establishment and consolidation of civilian supremacy and oversight over TAF was a prime one. This argument also suggests that these reforms were accepted by the TAF, even if they meant that the military lost autonomy in the state structure and political influence. Why, then, did the TAF obediently endorse these EU-mandated reforms? The answer is that the TAF, which has always supported Westernisation and the modernisation of Turkey, perceived the EU candidacy process and possible membership as an important step forward for the country to become a fully democratic European state with a strong economic and

50 Aylin Güney and Petek Karatekelioğlu, 'Turkey's EU Candidacy and Civil-Military Relations: Challenges and Prospects', *Armed Forces and Society*, 31(3) (2005), pp.439-62.

51 In the Copenhagen Criteria, the articles concerning the CMR are presented below:
The representative of the National Security Council on the High Audio-Visual Board (RTÜK), responsible for preparing the regulations for the implementation of laws such as broadcasting in languages other than Kurdish, would be withdrawn.
The representative of the National Security Council on the High-Education Board (YÖK) who oversees the administration of universities would be withdrawn.
The decisions of the Supreme Military Council would be no longer immune from judicial oversight or review, assuming that the judiciary would also become independent.
Extra-budgetary funds available to the military, for example the defence industry support fund, would be brought under full budgetary control of the Parliament.
For more about the Copenhagen Criteria see: Michael Emerson, 'Has Turkey fulfilled Copenhagen political criteria?', Center for European Political Studies Brief (2004), p.48.

52 Nilüfer Narlı, 'Changes in the Turkish Security Culture and in the Civil-Military Relations', *Western Balkans Security Observer*, 14 (2009), pp.56–83.

political structure, and surely with a more modern military. Embracing an institutionalist approach, Sarıgil explains why the Turkish military, a veto player in the Turkish political system, has accepted its loss of power in the last decade by proposing the concept of "rhetorical entrapment".[53] He suggests that the Turkish military's commitment to further integrate with the EU on several occasions has led it to become rhetorically entrapped. Thus, the military refrained from blocking the civilianisation process due to the likely damage such an action would cause to its ideational interests (legitimacy and credibility).[54]For Sarıgil, when this institutional model is applied to the civilianisation of Turkish CMR, one can draw the following conclusions. First, for him, the EU played an important role in changes in Turkish CMR because the EU was the primary factor that led to shifts in power relations among the civilian and military sides in post-Helsinki Turkey. Second, even though the military was highly concerned about the consequences of reforms for its own political powers, it could not block them due to the likely damage such an action would cause to its validity and integrity.

The military also believed that the EU membership process offered the best options in confronting domestic threats such as political Islamism and Kurdish separatism.[55] Thus, particularly from 2002-07, the TAF's commitment to the ideal of EU membership provided legitimacy to the AKP, which had been under scrutiny by the TAF due to its Islamist background, and indirectly served to reduce the TAF's political power. For Toktaş and Kurt, this EU-imposed legal and institutional framework, which functioned as an "exogenous" control mechanism, has necessitated democratisation in Turkish CMR and served as an external stimulus in empowering the civilian voices for the civilianisation of the military-dominated legal and institutional setting in Turkey. For them, the EU effect has strengthened the stance of political elites *vis-a-vis* military elites.[56] In the same vein, for Ümit Cizre, the adoption of EU harmonisation reforms played a significant, but not in itself sufficient role in the AKP's strategy to reduce the military's influence in politics. For her, in spite of the recent developments that curb the TAF's role in politics, the TAF did not abstain from undermining the AKP government. She concludes that the reform packages, which represent a major move towards weakening the military's role in politics, has not really led to a significant disengagement of military officers from politics, nor to a rethinking of their role in areas that should be under civilian control.[57] Similarly, Hale

53 Zeki Sarıgil, 'Europeanization as Institutional Change: The Case of the Turkish Military', *Mediterranean Politics*, 12:1 (2007), pp.39-57.

54 *Ibid.*

55 Ahmet T. Kuru, 'The Rise and Fall of Military Tutelage in Turkey: Fears of Islamism, Kurdism, and Communism', *Insight Turkey*, 14:2 (2012), pp.37-57.

56 Şule Toktaş and Ümit Kurt, 'The Turkish Military's Autonomy, AKP Rule and the EU Reform Process in the 2000s: An Assessment of the Turkish Version of Democratic Control of Armed Forces (DECAF)', *Turkish Studies*, 11:3 (2010), pp.387-403.

57 Ümit Cizre, 'The Justice and Development Party and the Military: Recreating the Past after Reforming it?', in Ümit Cizre (ed.), *Secular and Islamic Politics in Turkey: The making of the Justice and Development Party* (London: Routledge, 2008), pp.132-71.

Akay emphasises that the constitutional changes and legal amendments in accordance with the EU's Copenhagen criteria were perceived as a mistake by some of the generals.[58] Yet the option of staging a coup was closed, since public opinion at the time was pro-EU and supported the reforms. Accordingly, she asserts that, "indirectly, the EU-induced reforms of 1999 and 2005 contributed to the split in the military and the weakening of the armed forces."[59]

From 2005, however, despite the fact that Turkey has slowed down the EU reform process and Turkey's EU bid has lost its positive impact on Turkish CMR, the trend of civilianisation of Turkish CMR has continued. In this vein, Ali Karaosmanoğlu (2011) highlights that many works in the literature assert that changes between 2002 and 2006 took place due to the EU effect, but then he asks: "What about post-2007 changes and how to explain the close and effective collaboration of the TAF with the civilian decision makers?" If it is assumed that the explanatory power of the EU membership process has been diminishing when it comes to the TAF's commitment to Turkey's democratisation, one may then assert that some other dynamics, either exogenous or endogenous, could in fact be the drivers of the TAF's continued commitment to the democratisation process.

The 'Governmental Power' Argument

The followers of this argument suggest that, since 2002, Turkey has enjoyed a decade of almost unprecedented and continuous civilian political empowerment, with three succeeding majority, single-party governments formed by the AKP, which have had both the willingness and capability to restrict the military's influence over political matters.

Table 1: AKP's Election Successes over the Last Decade

2002 General Election	2004 Local Elections	2007 General Election	2009 Local Elections	2010 Const. Referend	2011 General Election	2014 Local Elections	2015 7 June General Election	2015 1 Nov General Election
34.28% 363 seats	41.67%	46.58% 341 seats	38.39%	Votes for yes: 57.88%	49.83% 327 Seats	43.39%	40.87% 258 seats	49.5% 317 seats

For this approach, which poses a negative correlation between the extent of civilian political power accumulation in a polity and the military's power to influence politics,

58 Hale Akay, Security Sector Policy Report 1: The Security Sector in Turkey: Questions, Problems and Solutions (December 2009).

59 *Ibid.*

if there is a strong government, which provides political empowerment of elected civilians, a healthy civil-military balance can be attained. But if there were a weak and inefficient government, it would be relatively easier for the military to become involved in the civilian sphere.[60] When taking the electoral popularity as a proxy for governmental power, for instance, only five years after Turkey's first ruling "Islamic government was forced to step down through military pressure, the AKP won 34.28% of the vote in November 2002".[61] The party has held an unprecedented single-party rule by popular vote in three general elections since 2002 and remains a very strong political power. Furthermore, as seen in Table 1 above, the portion of the vote that the AKP achieved has only increased over the years. In 2007, the AKP held 46.58% of the vote, rising to 49.83% in 2011. Until the Gezi Park protests in June 2013, it seemed that nothing would stand in the way of the AKP's re-election. However, an increase of fractionalisation within the Islamic sector of Turkish politics in recent years has caused many scholars to speculate about the ability of the party to retain power. Nevertheless, despite these concerns, the party was able to again gain majority support in municipal elections that took place on 30 March 2014. The results of the election allowed the AKP to maintain control in Istanbul and Ankara, with the AKP grabbing almost 44% of the total vote. This representation marks an increase from under 39% support in the 2009 municipal elections.[62] When faced with a choice between the AKP and other parties, the population voted with outstanding approval of the AKP, giving the ruling party 46.58% of the vote in July 2007.[63] The party's ability to increase its share of votes from about 47% to nearly 50% in the 2007 and 2011 general elections respectively left no question about the public's preference and forced the military "back into their barracks".[64] Moreover, during the rule of the AKP governments, Turkey experienced sustained economic growth, adding to the popularity of and support for the AKP – including from constituencies that do not identify with the ideological aspects of the party. This has greatly empowered the civilian government, enabling it to change existing institutions and practices. Civilianisation of Turkish CMR has been an important objective of the AKP, and due to its parliamentary majority and large voter constituency, it has been possible for AKP governments to push for reform regarding CMR. The strong performance and political tenacity of the AKP has also

60 Linda Michaud-Emin, 'The Restructuring of the Military High Command in the 7th Harmonization Package and its Ramifications for the Civil-Military Relations in Turkey', *Turkish Studies*, 8:1 (2007), p.36.

61 Hugh Pope and Nicole Pope, *Turkey Unveiled: A History of Modern Turkey* (Woodstock: The Overlook Press, 2000), p.322.

62 Bayram Balcı, 'Turkey: Local Elections Gave Huge Victory to Erdogan', *Foreign Policy Journal*, 3 April 2014.

63 Hugh Pope and Nicole Pope, *Turkey Unveiled: A History of Modern Turkey* (Woodstock: The Overlook Press, 2000), p.322.

64 Müge Aknur, 'The Impact of Civil-Military Relations on Democratic Consolidation in Turkey', in Müge Aknur (ed.), *Democratic Consolidation in Turkey* (Boca Raton: Universal-Publishers, 2012) p.234.

made it difficult for the Turkish military to influence policymaking during the AKP governments or to resist the governments' attempt to curb its autonomy. For this approach, under the favourable and stable political and economic conditions Turkey has enjoyed in recent years, the Turkish military would have been hard-pressed to find the necessary legitimacy to become involved in politics yet again.

What would be the limitations of this argument? The latent assumption of this argument is that, after many confrontations with a single-party majority rule empowered by victories in three elections and its popular base, the military has tacitly and unwillingly accepted and endorsed the supremacy of the civilian political power. This argument proposes a sort of zero-sum game between the military and elected civilians in which all losses of the civilians are exploited by the military to expand its influence. It is likely to suggest that, in the summer of 2013, due to the Gezi protests,[65] and on 17 and 25 December 2013, with the alleged corruption investigations made public,[66] the AKP's unrestricted political authority has been severely challenged. The military, however, has not seemed to take advantage of this imbalance, which would provide a window of opportunity to intervene in politics. Similarly, the military did not exploit the foreign policy-related crises that caused fierce friction between the AKP elites and Turkey's traditional allies in NATO, such as the parliamentary motion for cross-border operations in Syria;[67] instead it kept its position of sitting on the fence. Why, then, is the Turkish military so unwilling to fill these power vacuums caused by AKP confrontations with the domestic and international actors?

It also worth remembering that, on 27 May 1960, the Turkish military intervened in politics by carrying out a *coup d'etat* against the Democrat Party (DP) government under Adnan Menderes.[68] One should note that, despite the fact that Menderes' DP won three consecutive elections with a great majority and governed Turkey as a single party for a decade, the military did not refrain from taking action. Thus, one may suggest that, in the Turkish case, having a high degree of governmental power would not really be enough to prevent the military's intervention in politics. The intervention against a strong government is not only limited to the Turkish case. In September 2006, for instance, the Thai Rak Thai Party led by Thaksin Shinawatra, which formed a single-party government after getting the overwhelming majority of votes (60.7%) in Thailand's 2005 general election, was overthrown in a military coup organised by the Royal Thai Army.[69] Both the Turkish military's coup against the DP government

65 Nilüfer Göle, 'Secularism and Islamism in Turkey: The Making of Elites and Counter-Elites', *Middle East Journal*, 51:1 (1997), pp.56-88.
66 Berivan Oruçoğlu. 'Why Turkey's Mother of All Corruption Scandals Refuses to Go Away', *Foreign Policy*, 6 January 2015.
67 Metin Gürcan, 'Turkish NCOs fight for their rights', *Al-Monitor*, 12 December 2014.
68 Mogens Pelt, *Military Intervention and a Crisis Democracy in Turkey: The Menderes Era and its Demise* (I.B. Tauris, 2014).
69 Mark Beeson, 'Civil-Military Relations in Indonesia and the Philippines: Will the Thai Coup Prove Contagious?', *Armed Forces & Society*, 34 (2008), pp.474-90.

and the Thai Army's coup against the Thai Rak Thai Party's government indicate that the explanatory power of this argument may fall short.[70]

The 'Changing Threat Perceptions' Argument

According to this third approach, the prime source of the TAF's unchallenged control is its role in defining what constitutes security issues or threats to the nation, a privilege which serves to promote its own legitimacy and perpetuate its veto power in both domestic politics and foreign policy-making.[71] For this approach, through its weighty influence in the political system, the TAF has the capacity to militarise and thus 'securitise' some political issues as being directly related to the survival of the state. For Ümit Cizre, for instance, the TAF has branded political Islam and the Kurdish issue as internal threats to the secular character and integrity of the state.[72] She further contends that the main instrument affecting the superiority of the TAF in Turkish CMR has been this change of traditional national security discourse.[73] This change of discourse, in which the TAF decided on what counts as a security threat and what the response should be, from 2002 onwards resulted in a reduced role for the TAF in politics.

During the last decade, Turkey has also actively sought to engage its neighbouring countries in political dialogue and economic cooperation, using so-called soft power to achieve foreign and security policy goals. These developments have contributed to a more general shift in responsibility for and expertise in security policy issues from the Turkish General Staff (TGS) to government ministries, reducing further the role of the TGS in security policy formation. For Ersel Aydınlı and Nihat Ali Özcan, this new trend of civilianisation of foreign policy issues was also supported by the military, which, by the turn of the millennium, had grown weary of its ability to eradicate the threat posed by political extremism, and therefore more willing to consider a political response to security questions.[74]

This argument fits well for Michael Desch's model, which is built on the pillar that the strength of civilian control of the military is fundamentally shaped by structural factors – especially international and domestic threat environments – within which

70 Duncan McCargo and Ayse Zarakol, 'Turkey and Thailand: Unlikely Twins', *Journal of Democracy*, 23:3 (2012).
71 Ümit Cizre, 'Disentangling the Threads of Civil-Military Relations in Turkey: Promises and Perils', *Mediterranean Quarterly*, 22:2 (2011).
72 *Ibid.*
73 Ümit Cizre, 'Demythologyzing the National Security Concept: the Case of Turkey', *Middle East Journal*, 57:2 (2003), pp.216-17.
74 Ersel Aydınlı, Nihat Ali Özcan and Doğan Akyaz, 'The Turkish Military's March Towards Europe', *Foreign Affairs*, 85:1 (2006), pp.77–90.

the state operates.[75] In this line, a state that is operating in a low external and high internal threat environment, like Turkey in the 1990s, has the weakest civilian control of the military, and thus the worst CMR. Conversely, a state that operates within a high external and low internal threat environment is likely to have the strongest civilian control of the military, and thus the best CMR because the military cannot find any opportunity to engage in civilian politics. While states within both high external and internal threat environments are likely to have generally poor CMR, states with both low external and internal threats are mostly indeterminate and will have mixed results.

If one seeks to explain the current status of Turkish CMR with Desch's model, one may suggest that, since the foundation of the Republic, Turkey has seemed to operate within a 'constant' security environment characterised as one of relatively low external threat, as it has never directly engaged in inter-state war. Turkey, for instance, chose to remain neutral in the Second World War, and soon after only modestly participated in the Korean War, strictly as a member of the United Nations (UN). Although having gained NATO membership following its involvement in the Korean War in 1951, and since then remained a significant ally of the US, the Cold War never exposed a direct external threat to the national security of Turkey. Turkey maintained relatively stable and thus immune to the heightened international pressure during the Cold War years. Since then, Turkey's Cyprus Peace Operation in 1974, on the grounds that the Cypriot National Guard had organised a coup to annex the island to Greece, and the Turkish military's provision of 2,000 troops to Afghanistan/Kabul have been the only other instances of involvement in inter-state combat. Therefore, Turkey has consistently operated in a relatively stable security environment with low levels of international threat throughout the 20th century and into the 21st century, receiving no direct security threat from an adversary state, and having been involved in inter-state combat only in minimal fashion, mostly as part of international coalitions through the UN or NATO.

Conversely, Turkey has had a constant relatively high internal threat environment since the transition to multi-party politics in 1946, which has shadowed most external military operations. The two main internal threats from which the military has always derived its power and legitimacy in politics and popularity among the public continue to be the threat to territorial integrity, or to be more precise, separatist Kurdish ethno-nationalism, and the threat to the secular character of the Republic by forces of political Islam. The military's continuing efforts to maintain and intensify the spectres of these two national security threats, coupled with the Republic's "obsessive anxiety" in preserving national unity in the face of such perceived divisive forces, then further legitimized these threats and the military's hard-line stance.[76] In this line, every military coup

75 Michael C. Desch, *Civilian Control of the Military* (Baltimore: Johns Hopkins University Press, 1999).

76 Pınar Bilgin, 'The Securityness of Secularism? The Case of Turkey', *Security Dialogue*, 39:6 (2008), pp.593-614.

to date has been justified in referring to internal unrest and turmoil caused by domestic political divisions through the lines of these threats. Thus, the structural environment that the Turkish military has constantly operated in is one of a low external and high internal threat environment. In the light of Desch's model, Turkish civilian control over the military would then be extremely weak, and Turkish CMR poor, as domestic threats in the absence of external threats "divide the state and focus everybody's attention inward". This, coupled with the Turkish military's unique historical role in the state and its perception by the people, has given the military astonishing power over political affairs, as is obvious from the unrestrained history of frequent coups and military interventions in civilian governments from the 1960s onwards. Thus, Desch's model may be successful at explaining the outcome of Turkish CMR prior to 2002. However, for this model, one should then note that a shift in the degree of civilian control of the military could be explained as a consequence of the reconfiguration in the structural threat environment of the state. However, as one may easily notice, Turkey's structural threat environment (low-external and high-internal) has fundamentally remained unchanged for the period from 1945 to 2002 as well as the post-2002 period of AKP rule. Thus, it is likely to suggest that Desch's structural threat-based model ultimately fails in fully explaining the shift in CMR in the latter period.

All of these studies, which paid close attention to the role of internal threats, were valuable. However, it is no longer possible to explain CMR in Turkey through internal threats because, although these threats continue, the military's intervention in politics has been significantly narrowed through several institutional reforms.

The 'Emergence of New Political Elites' Argument

For this approach, a new stratum of elites with more conservative religious values and less sympathy towards the military has become influential within political institutions, the state bureaucracy, education and business, marginalising the stratum of traditional Kemalist elites, an important segment of which has great sympathy towards the military, and thus are submissive to the TAF's influence over politics.

The change in CMR in Turkey would also be linked to the emergence of a new class of political elites in Turkey in the last decade, starting in earnest with the liberalising reforms introduced under the AKP's first and second governments' rule from 2002-07. The emergence of this new class of political elites and state bureaucrats deprived the military of many of its former allies in the state apparatus, business circles, institutions of higher education and the media. This made it more difficult to influence and intervene in the political decision-making process in Turkey. Following Serif Mardin's centre-periphery model,[77] elites in Turkey may be broadly classified into two ideo-

77 Şerif Mardin, 'Center-Periphery Relations: A Key to Turkish Politics', *Daedalus*, 102:1 (1972).

logical categories: a secularist or Kemalist elite dominating and controlling state, politics and business for most of the period after 1923, and an Islamist counter-elite that become prominent from the 1990s onwards.[78] Due to their role as guardians of the Republic, senior military cadres have constituted a central group within the Kemalist elite and a bastion for the defence of Kemalist values in state structures and civil society. While not rigorously Islamist, the background of many leaders in the AKP is similar to that of the Islamist counter-elite described by Nilüfer Göle. In particular, after the coming to power of the AKP in 2002, this new class of political elites, espousing more conservative and religious values than the traditional secular state establishment, rose to positions of power in state institutions, business circles, the media and academia – including former Kemalist strongholds such as senior cadres of he judiciary and significant ministries such as the Ministry of Foreign Affairs, the Ministry of Interior Affairs and the Ministry of National Education. In light of this argument, one may then suggest that the senior cadres of the TAF, being staunch defenders of Kemalism and secularism, have become more isolated and contained as new political elites within the government, new elites in the state bureaucracy, business, judiciary and academia have had the upper hand.

To answer the question of what explains the rise and fall of military tutelage over Turkish democracy, Ahmet T. Kuru argues that the military's civilian allies, particularly in the judiciary, political parties and the media, had provided it with political power. For him, the reason why these civilians supported military tutelage over democracy was due to their ideological fears of Islamic reactionism, Kurdish separatism and communism. Since 2007, the military's political influence has declined due to the weakening of its ideological allies and the rise of a counter-elite, mainly the alliance of the pro-Islamic conservatives and the liberals. Kuru then suggests that these pro-Islamic conservative politicians and elites have legitimised their rule and restricted the military's way of justifying its interventions in politics by replacing the old Islamist rhetoric with a new "conservative democratic" discourse, successfully adapting to international conditions such as Turkey's candidacy to the EU and its integration in the world economy, as well as forming an alliance with liberal intellectuals.[79]

This may then beg the question as to whether or not these so-called counter-elites are homogenous. When taking into consideration the split between liberal elites favouring the EU and AKP elites, which has become visible after the 2010 Constitutional Referendum (Kalaycıoğlu, 2011: 1-22), as well as the recent division among Islamic elites such as the Gülenists versus the Erdoğanists,[80] the explanatory power of this argument, which tends to see the group of counter-elites as a monolithic

78 Nilüfer Göle, 'Secularism and Islamism in Turkey: The Making of Elites and Counter-Elites', *Middle East Journal*, 51:1 (1997), pp.56-88.

79 Ahmet T. Kuru, 'The Rise and Fall of Military Tutelage in Turkey: Fears of Islamism, Kurdism, and Communism', *Insight Turkey*, 14:2 (2012), pp.37-57.

80 Fehim Taştekin, 'War on Gulenists undermines Turkish diplomacy', *Al-Monitor*, 26 January 2015.

entity and homogenise all Islamic counter-elites into a mono-block, has seemed to wane. One may also suggest that if the rise of counter-elites weakened the influence of bureaucratic-military elites, then the current divisions among counter-elites should empower the military, which is not the case. The recent divisions among conservative elites did not yield to a re-empowered military, a phenomenon weakening the explanatory power of the counter-elite argument.

The 'Changing Public Opinion towards the Military' Argument

This approach, emphasising the public's altered opinion of the military, simply suggests that the Turkish public, while still supportive of a strong military, has grown less positive to the idea of military influence in politics in recent years.

According to this approach, which focuses on societal and cultural factors, the TAF is still the most popular and trusted institution in the country, notwithstanding the large number of senior officers accused of conspiracy and coup plans, but popular support for military intervention in politics seems to be on the wane.[81] This change, for Aydınlı, can be seen as a reflection of the consolidation of Turkish democracy, and signalling the beginning of a new era when the military's political interventions would no longer be seen by the Turkish public as feasible or desired.[82] As the TAF always cares and emphasises the significance of the 'unity of military and nation' at every occasion, it is possible to suggest that public opinion matters greatly to the TAF. This inclination to cite the strong bond between military and nation by the TAF may be seen as a historical legacy of almost mythical proportions in Turkey,[83] and the TAF owe much of their privileged status to the support they enjoy in the nation. Sarıgil notes that, among military officers, there is a sense of superiority and a strong disregard and distrust of politicians and politics, but not of the citizens of the country.[84] That is why, whenever the military elites decided to intervene, the justification for these interventions were always the same: in the name of the nation. Thus, given the special bond between the military and society in Turkey, it would be appropriate to contend that the shift in public opinion against military interventions in politics has most likely mattered to the TAF and has been an important factor when considering how to respond to the policies of the civilian governments.

81 Zeki Sarıgil, 'Civil-Military Relations Beyond Dichotomy', *Turkish Studies*, 12:2 (2011), pp.265–78.
82 Ersel Aydınlı, 'Ergenekon, New Pacts, and the Decline of the Turkish Inner State', *Turkish Studies*, 12:2 (2011).
83 Nilüfer Narlı, 'Changes in the Turkish Security Culture and in the Civil-Military Relations', *Western Balkans Security Observer* Nu:14 (2009), p.61.
84 Zeki Sarıgil, 'Civil-Military Relations Beyond Dichotomy', *Turkish Studies*, 12:2 (2011), p.265–78.

Similarly, Nilüfer Narlı emphasises that the change is not only in the context of Turkey's institutions, but there is also a change in the mindset of the citizens, a trend that eventually changes the political culture in Turkey.[85] For Ümit Cizre, for instance, the reason why the TAF was not aggressive in trials such as *Ergenekon* and *Sledgehammer* was the critical impact of the victory of the 'yes' votes in the historic referendum of 12 September 2010.[86] For her, these 'yes' votes meant a red light shown by society to the TAF. For Ersel Aydınlı, these trials functioned as a catalyst for change and reform in Turkish CMR by changing public opinion towards the military.[87]

The first thing that should be mentioned as a shortfall for the argument is that it tends to ignore structural and institutional factors such as a changing threat environment and legal reforms, which have paved the way for this civilianisation. That is why this argument, emphasising only the pressure on the military rooted from societal factors but neglecting other factors, seems to fall short when sufficiently explaining the recent civilianisation.

One common aspect of all these five approaches is that as they explain the civilianisation process in Turkish CMR in the last decade, they solely rely on exogenous factors and dynamics. In other words, they focus on non-military variables and factors shaping the CMR since the early 2000s. In addition, all these above-listed arguments assume that the decline of the military's political power occurred despite, not because of the will of the Turkish military. It is likely to suggest that these approaches, all of which have a substantial degree of explanatory power, are analytically distinct but not mutually exclusive. That is, one can defend some or all of them as they explain the declining political role of the military.

The existing literature may also be classified into two main groups in terms of the impact of the CMR on the Turkish military and its capacity for change. That is, the first explanation seems pessimistic about the TAF's internal capacity and willingness for change. Thus, it seems to rely on exogenous factors when explaining the recent civilianisation. Gürsoy, for instance, not trusting to the highest echelon of the TAF as noticed in the works of Heper, Karaosmanoğlu and Aydınlı, draws attention to the extent of the institutionalisation of the legal setting, and the impact of the exogenous legal institutions on the relationship between the military and civilians. For her, the presidential crisis in 2007 showed that legal reforms and amendments alone could not lead to behavioural changes among officers who were "inherently" inclined

85 Nilüfer Narlı, 'Aligning Civil-Military Relations In Turkey: Transparency Building in Defense Sector and the EU Reforms', *Transforming National Armed Forces in South East Europe – from the Social to the Military Challenge*, 9th Workshop of the PfP Consortium Study Group, Regional Stability in South East Europe, Lieutenant .Colonel Mag. Ernst M. Felberbauer, Mag. Predrag Jureković, Prof. Plamen Pantev (eds) (2005).

86 Ümit Cizre, 'Disentangling the Threads of Civil-Military Relations in Turkey: Promises and Perils', *Mediterranean Quarterly*, 22:2 (2011).

87 Ersel Aydınlı, 'Ergenekon, New Pacts, and the Decline of the Turkish Inner State', *Turkish Studies*, 12:2 (2011).

toward interventions. The coup allegations called into question the earlier belief that the entire military cadre tacitly endorsed the rule of the AKP and the reforms during the party's first five years in power. Consequently, for her, from the perspective of the AKP, future amendments and civilianisation should depend on cracking down on interventionist elements in the TAF with more legal institutionalisation.[88] Similarly, Ümit Cizre suggests that the adoption of harmonisation reforms for the EU membership played a significant, but not in itself sufficient, role in AKP strategy to reduce the influence of the military in politics. For her, in spite of the recent developments that curb the TAF's role in politics, the TAF did not abstain from undermining the AKP government. She concludes that although the reform packages represent a major move towards a weakening in the military's role in politics, this has not really led to a significant disengagement of military officers from politics nor led to a rethinking of their role in areas that should be under civilian control.[89] Carrying the argument one step further with the inclusion of the 'mentality' problem, Hale Akay asserts that although the EU-induced reform process has changed the power, function and composition of the MGK, these new set of institutionalisations did not result in effective civilianisation of the MSK mainly because of the absence of the mentality shift in the NSC cadres.[90] She stresses that when the AKP came to power in 2002, some groups among the public and factions within the military regarded a cabinet with Islamist roots as a threat. The electoral success of the AKP and the difference of opinion on whether this was a threat to the secular Republic contributed to the disunity of the armed forces. One may then conclude that the prevailing assumption in this camp is that, particularly in the post-2002 setting, the inconvenience of the external opportunity structures first caused a split in the higher echelons of the TAF, and then deterred the TAF from intervening in the politics, yet it still holds the 'self-important' mood and interventionist mentality.

The second type seems to be an optimistic explanation as it emphasises that the TAF is a 'learning organization' which derives its lessons from its encounters with civilians, and seeks to adapt to the changing socioeconomic, political and cultural context in Turkey. The followers of this type trusts to the TAF's endogenous capacity for change. The last sentence of Metin Heper's conclusion in his recent article entitled 'Civil-Military Relations in Turkey: Towards a Liberal Model' is as follows: "It seems from 2002 onwards, the High Command has arrived at the conclusion that the military should no longer play a guardian role even if in its view civilians made a 'mess of

88 Yaprak Gürsoy, 'The Final Curtain for the Turkish Armed Forces? Civil-Military Relations in View of the 2011 General Elections', *Turkish Studies*, 13:2 (2012), pp.191-211.

89 Ümit Cizre, 'The Justice and Development Party and the Military: Recreating the Past after Reforming it?', in Ümit Cizre (ed.), *Secular and Islamic Politics in Turkey: The making of the Justice and Development Party* (London: Routledge), pp.132-71.

90 Hale Akay, 'Turkiye'de Güvenlik Sektörü: Sorular, Sorunlar, Çözümler (Turkish)', TESEV Report, 22 (2009).

things'."[91] In the same vein, pointing out the divide within the TAF in the post-2002 setting by proposing that there are the "gradualist" and "absolutist" camps within the TAF, Ersel Aydınlı asserts that the rise of the gradualists in the Turkish military would eventually lead to a restructuring of the military's place in Turkish politics. He defines gradualists as those in the military who remain respectful of judicial processes such as the *Ergenekon* and *Sledgehammer* cases, and absolutists as those in the military who aim to block the political system in Turkey. For him, the gradualists – "who seem to be the rising force in the military" – have clearly been playing a crucial role in rather significant transformations taking place in Turkish CMR.[92] Examining the previously overlooked changes in the TAF with respect to its structure and its relations to society, Nil Şatana argues that "the lengthy but persistent transformation of the Turkish military toward a 'postmodern military' paradigm in incremental ways that [the] naked eye cannot detect, makes the consolidation of democracy more likely in Turkey and other democratizing countries".[93] She continues:

> The military's force structure is slowly modernizing with more professionals and fewer conscripts. The professional officers are trained for managerial soldier-statesman skills as well as traditional combat leadership. Instead, it occasionally explains itself to the media through dinners and social events. The public attitude toward the military is still positive but civilians no longer see military intervention as a viable option. As the Turkish society becomes more tolerant of different lifestyles, women train and serve in the military in the same conditions as their male peers. Finally, spouses of military officers are more educated and independent than they were a couple of decades ago.[94]

Şatana then contends that the paradigmatic changes within the military contribute to the consolidation of democracy in Turkey. However, she warns that, as with any other institutional change, this process is slow and risky.[95]

As seen in the debate between the optimistic and pessimistic perspectives about the Turkish military, the overall question sits at the heart of the Turkish military's mentality.

91 Metin Heper, 'Civil-Military Relations in Turkey: Toward a Liberal Model?' *Turkish Studies*, 12:2 (2011), pp.241-52.

92 Ersel Aydınlı, 'Ergenekon, New Pacts, and the Decline of the Turkish Inner State', *Turkish Studies*, 12:2 (2011).

93 Nil Şatana, 'Transformation of the Turkish military and the path to democracy', *Armed Forces & Society*, 34:3 (2008), pp. 357-88.

94 *Ibid.*

95 *Ibid.*

The Mentality of a Military

The natural question that follows is how one can conceptualise the mentality of the military. Samuel Finer, in his classic 1962 book *The Man on Horseback*, concentrates on this question. Finer takes CMR literature to another level by addressing military identity and possible means of military influence aside from direct intervention. Finer's theory attempts to elucidate the following question: why doesn't the military more often intervene in politics? For him, taking their hierarchical and disciplined organisational structures endowed with arms and public respect into account, it is surprising that they do not attempt to exert their influence on the "weaker" civilian government more often.[96] He suggests that, to intervene in politics, a military must both have the "occasion" and "disposition". He defines occasion as an external opportunity structure that paves the way for intervening in the politics, such as a major breakdown in the political order, a major crisis in the political system, a power vacuum in a state and a state of emergency due to internal conflicts. Finer distinguishes disposition for intervention from an occasion. He further divides his concept of disposition into the categories of motive and mood. The disposition to intervene related to motive includes the manifest destiny of soldiers, nationalist interests, sectional interests of the officer corps and mixed motives of the military.[97] Dispositions to intervene that are related to mood include self-awareness and elevated self-esteem of the military as a security organisation.[98] Finer's distinction between the concept of motive – a bridge concept from the cognitive domain that connects occasion to the mood – and the concept of mood, a deeper one that is related to the emotive domain, articulate the difference between preconditions and inaction versus preconditions and action. For Finer, a motive must be backed with mentality to transform into actual intervention. Finer suggests that there are three main motives for intervention. The manifest destiny of the soldiers is the first;[99] the belief that the military's role is that of the saviours of the nation. The second is the belief that the military has a unique unbiased view and can better define what is in the country's best national interest. The last and most common motives of intervention are class interest, regional interest, corporate self-interest and the motive of individual self-interest.[100] All or some of these motives may come into play at any certain time, depending on the circumstances.

Finer notes that "mentality is more difficult to describe than motives", as this concept belongs to the emotive domain.[101] The mentality of a military, or "will to intervene", he says, takes root from the centralised command structure, hierarchy with a depersonalised authority, the significance of rank but not individual, discipline – which

96 Samuel Finer, *The Man on Horseback: The Role of Military in Politics*, p.62.
97 *Ibid*, pp.20-52.
98 *Ibid*, pp.20-61.
99 *Ibid*, p.32.
100 *Ibid*, p.40.
101 *Ibid*, p.61.

requires unquestioning and prompt obedience because of the nature of the mission of this organisation – the indoctrination of new members, living arrangements, lack of communication with the outside world and finally "Esprit de Corps" that emphasises isolation and self-sufficiency.[102] The self-awareness rooted from these phenomena reflects the objective peculiarities of the military life. Specifically, Finer emphasises this self-awareness "that permits the military to conceive that they have a unique duty, a duty of supererogation, to watch over the national interest".[103] The military cultural knowledge that they are separate and different from the civilian population drives the mood. There are two elements that induce this mentality. They are a sense of power, where the military believe nothing can stop them from getting their way, and a grievance. Frustration, an emotion that comes from grievances, also plays a role in mood. When frustrated, the military acts predictably, "by responding with anger and humiliation", "projecting blame onto the civilians", "rationalizing this reaction" and "compensating for the frustration" by "taking it out on the objects of their censure".[104]

This sense of first grievance and then frustration would be defined as a difference of opinion on a political issue (foreign policy, for instance) between military officers and politicians. In this sense, Finer, in his book that was published four years after the 1960 coup in Turkey, categorises the TAF as a "self-aware" military that have a heightened opinion of themselves relative to the government or to civilians in general. He then notes that this sentiment of supremacy over civilians, in this type of military, goes beyond a professional pride in efficiency. It is this self-awareness that constitutes the source of mood. What then can be said about the TAF's mood? Is Finer's suggestion of the "self-aware" military when defining the TAF's mood still relevant? To answer this question, unfortunately, Turkish CMR literature offers very limited insights with works reflecting the Turkish military's mentality.

Setting the Stage: The 'Black Box' Waiting To Be Explored

In Turkish CMR literature, however, the military side of the story has mostly been neglected, except for a few works such as Mehmet Ali Birand's 1991 classic *Shirts of Steel*. The fundamental consequences of this negligence are two assumptions implicitly taken for granted by a great majority of work in the literature. The first assumption is the conceptualisation of the Turkish military, or Turkish Armed Forces (TAF), as a homogenous entity.[105] That is, the military has always been conceived as a monolithic agent with durable values, norms and preferences. For decades, scholarly works simply assumed that the military has always had a strict hierarchical organi-

102 *Ibid*, p.14.
103 *Ibid*, p.63.
104 *Ibid*, p.62.
105 Gareth Jenkins, *Context and Circumstances: Turkish Military and Politics*, p.15.

sation and its official view implies a blend of Kemalist principles, a strictly secular and elitist-modernist world view on which the TAF has traditionally based its value system, staunchly secular references, a nationalist stance and a modernist perspective.[106] The second assumption is that the Turkish military is an organisation immune to time and change. That is, mostly in the literature, the Turkish military's internal structures, the processes, formal and informal institutions, its organisational culture, the norms and values it embraced, and more importantly, the opinions and attitudes of the officer corps, are perceived as unchanged phenomena. Thus, the military side of the CMR has been treated as given, taken-for-granted and fixed (resisting change). For instance, it has always been emphasised in the literature that the Turkish military is a homogenous Kemalist, staunchly secular and nationalist organisation with a modernist stance,[107] which has assumed a self-appointed role of guarding the state and national interests against all internal and external threats.[108] However, scholarly analyses do not provide room for the possibility that these characteristics may change over time, and that different – even sometimes conflicting – points of view may emerge within the Turkish military.

Maybe, mainly due to these facts stated above, almost all academic researches on CMR by military personnel have not been able to promise scholarly insights within the black box of the Turkish military. This absence of 'inside-out' observations would be stated a fundamental disadvantage preventing us from getting a more accurate picture of Turkish CMR. Among those works written by military personnel on the CMR, Staff Major Hakan Şahin's unpublished PhD dissertation 'The Society and the Politics in Turkey: Reading the Military Members' Memoirs',[109] First Lieutenant Ömer Eryılmaz's master's thesis 'Turkey in the Triangle of the 1950–1960 era, the 1960 Military Coup, and the 1961 Constitution',[110] First Lieutenant Mustafa Uygun's master's thesis 'Civil Military Relations in Turkey: Motives Behind the Shift of Power From Military to Civilians after the Interventions'[111] and First Lieutenant Nihat Dumlupınar's master's thesis 'Regulation of Private Military Companies In Iraq'[112] may be defined as promising works despite the fact that they do not provide enough insider's insights to open the black box.

106 *Ibid.*

107 George S. Harris, 'The Role of the Military in Turkey in the 1980s: Guardians or Decision Makers?', in Metin Heper and Ahmet Evin (ed.), *Democracy and the Military in Turkey in the 1980s* (Berlin: Walter de Gruyter, 1988), pp.177–200.

108 Gareth Jenkins, *Context and Circumstances: Turkish Military and Politics*, p.15.

109 This work was presented as a PhD dissertation to the Political Science Department of Istanbul University in 2010.

110 For the full text of the thesis see: <http://calhoun.nps.edu/bitstream/handle/10945/41373/14Mar_Eryilmaz_Omer.pdf?sequence=1> (accessed 2 December 2014).

111 For the full text of the thesis see: <http://calhoun.nps.edu/bitstream/handle/10945/32913/13Mar_Uygun_Mustafa.pdf?sequence=1> (accessed 2 December 2014).

112 For the full text of the thesis see: <http://edocs.nps.edu/npspubs/scholarly/theses/2010/Mar/10Mar_Dumlupinar.pdf> (accessed 2 December 2014).

Coming to the domain of the Turkish military as a subject of cultural and organisational studies, the literature produced by still-serving or retired military personnel seems more promising. Retired Colonel Abdulkadir Varoğlu's article 'Volunteering for Risk: The Culture of the Turkish Armed Forces',[113] retired Colonel Abdulkadir Varoğlu and retired Colonel Ünsal Sığrı's piece 'Turkish-Dutch Encounters during Peacekeeping',[114] retired Colonel Uğur Güngör's unpublished PhD dissertation 'The Analysis of Turkey's Approach to Peace Operations',[115] retired Colonel Haldun Yalçinkaya's article 'The Nongovernmental Organizations-Military Security Collaboration Mechanism: Afghanistan NGO Safety Office'[116] and retired Colonel Salih Akyürek and retired Major Adnan Bıçaksız's Turkish book *Sivil-Asker İlişkileri ve Ordu-Toplum Mesafesi* (Civil-Military Relations and Military-Society Gap)[117] may be sorted as prominent examples in the literature, yet all mostly fall short in the provision of insights within the Turkish military.

The fact that the endogenous dynamics shaping the TAF have not been analysed in detail so far does not necessarily mean that this dimension of Turkish CMR has completely been ignored in the literature. In *Shirts of Steel*,[118] for instance, Mehmet Ali Birand provides one of the most important resources on military sociology. *Shirts of Steel*, as an observation of the TAF from the inside, delves into the underlying causes of the attitudes and opinions of Land Forces War Academy cadets on phenomena such as politics, politicians, society and the founding principles of the Republic.[119]

The first insight noticed in this work is the author's excessive emphasis of Kemalism as an ideology shaping the minds of officers. Birand writes: "Kemalism is instilled as a religion among officers."[120] In his lecture to the cadets, the commander of the War Academy notes that "your flag will be the great Atatürk. Your ideology will be his principles, your aim will be the direction he showed us. You will follow unswervingly in Atatürk's footsteps."[121] He continues: "We are opposed to anybody, no matter whether they are there by the grace of the ballot box, or the votes of the National Assembly, who attempts to violate Ataturk's principles. We have [a] right to act to this

113 Abdulkadir Varoğlu, 'Volunteering for Risk: The Culture of the Turkish Armed Forces', *Armed Forces& Society*, 31:4 (2005).

114 Abdulkadir Varoğlu, Joseph Soeters, Erhan Tanercan and Ünsal Sığrı, 'Turkish-Dutch Encounters during Peacekeeping', *International Peacekeeping*, 11:2 (2004), pp.354-68.

115 Uğur Güngör, 'The Analysis of Turkey's Approach to Peace Operations', PhD dissertation, Bilkent University, Department of International Relations (2007).

116 Haldun Yalçınkaya, 'The Nongovernmental Organizations-Military Security Collaboration Mechanism: Afghanistan NGO Safety Office', *Armed Forces & Society*, 39:3 (2012), pp.489-510.

117 For the full text of the book see: <http://www.bilgesam.org/incele/139/sivil-asker-iliskileri-ve-ordu-toplum-mesafesi/#.VH2jVTGsXCI> (accessed 2 December 2014).

118 Mehmet Ali Birand, *Shirts of Steel* (London: I.B. Tauris, 1991).

119 *Ibid.*

120 *Ibid*, p.ix.

121 *Ibid*, p.3.

end in the interests of our people, and for their protection."[122] This attitude of 'Ataturk has entrusted the country to me' has, says Birand, led to a mutually existing distrust of civilian politicians. In his book, Birand provides a telling quote from a high-ranking officer: "They [politicians] may lie and deceive people to suit themselves. I have yet to hear anything favorable about politicians. My people are poorly educated. They may be misled by politicians and the self-interested."[123] In this way, Birand places emphasis on the Turkish officer corps' proclamation of the superiority of the national interest and putting the interests of the country and the nation above all.

Birand also provided his observations on the demographic backgrounds of the officer corps. For Birand, for instance, the desire to make the family happy is a prime motivation for a great majority of the officers' decision to join the military.[124] He nonetheless notes that some join the military for material benefit,[125] and few for the love of soldiering, the love of country and the special feeling of belonging to a military nation (ideational motivations). According to Birand, the inadequacy of civilian schools and the superiority of the education available with the military is another factor that motivates the cadets to join the military. Birand presents the following direct quote from the War Academy commander: "Young men do not come to soldiering because they are in love with the career but on the whole to find employment and security."[126] This suggests that the desire to gain prestige, social status and economic motivations far exceeded the love of soldiering and the love of country. He also underlines that all the characteristics of the Turkish officer derive from middle-class influences, from his manner of speech to his world outlook, from his attitude in performing his duties to the way he regards civilians and politicians.

Birand's other emphasis on the characteristics of the officer corps can be listed as follows: autonomous, homogenous, modernist, a pro-Western mentality prevalent among the officers, dissatisfaction and annoyance to anything civilian, mutual distrust of politics and attempt to be outside and above politics, dislike of anything uncertain, high sense of moral responsibility, the aristocratic way of officership, soldiering as a way of life, feeling of superiority over and isolation from the rest of society, strong sense of superiority over civilians, staunchly secular modernist perspective blended with nationalist themes, a difference between the generals and other officers, high levels of sensitivity in hierarchy and a robust 'elitisation' process in military schools. According to Birand, self-sacrifice is the key factor shaping the attitudes and behaviours of officers, who are very hierarchical, centralised and disciplined, with high levels of duty and a high awareness of threat perceptions.

It has been two-and-a-half decades since Birand wrote these sentences. It is unfortunate to note that, since Birand's *Shirts of Steel*, not even a scholarly work providing an insider's insights on the opinions and attitudes of the officer corps in the Turkish

122 *Ibid*, p.22.
123 *Ibid*, p.23.
124 *Ibid*, p.4.
125 *Ibid*, p.23.
126 *Ibid*, p.10.

military has been published. Whilst honouring the merit of Birand's work, two points should be mentioned as pitfalls in *Shirts of Steel*. The first point is the fact that the book is a relatively outmoded work, and the second is its limited scope, which is solely concentrated on the cadets in the Military Academy, not officers in various ranks and services. As the book is a case study based on interviews with a limited number of cadets, it does not really provide a general picture of the TAF. The main reason for so far not having research that provides a real picture of the TAF has been the lack of comprehensive quantitative data. Given the changes in Turkish CMR over the last decade, the question must then be asked to what extent Birand's above-presented observations and arguments have held their relevancy since the late 1990s? Or can we suggest that the traditional guardianship role of the TAF, the attitudinal background of which was craftily laid out by Birand, is over?

According to Gareth Jenkins, who provides a more up-to date picture of the Turkish military of the early 2000s – though not as comprehensive as Birand – the traditional guardianship role of the military has continued.[127] Jenkins argues that the Turkish officer corps is still elitist, paid slightly higher than other government employees, staunchly Kemalist, nationalist and living in an excessively disciplined, strictly hierarchical setting.[128] With a "reluctantly interventionist" mentality which implies the taking of action only when they believe that the government is unable to cope with critical threats, the officers are also still contemptuous of politics and politicians, and thus very sensitive to internal threats (political Islam and Kurdish separatism).[129] He also notes that, even though there is little difference in terms of salary, there is still a huge gap in prestige between the rank of colonel and general, and states that "promotion from colonel to general also represents the tightest bottleneck in an officer's career, with an average of 24 new generals, equivalent to around 5 percent of annual graduates of military academies".[130]

In the same vein as Jenkins, Ersel Aydınlı suggests that the Turkish military still holds absolute control over the internal indoctrination of its personnel, drawing its members from the heart of society, but then doing its best to keep them independent from popular national and international ideas and trends. For Aydınlı, the Turkish military is not the army of the elite, but is rather an elite-making institution. It recruits cadets largely from rural Anatolian towns, but with its carefully crafted and closed institutions, turns these Anatolian kids into a unique new societal elite – a group neither completely inside nor outside of society. In many cases, while the immediate relatives of this new elite carry socially common ethnic and religious identities, the officers themselves become stripped of these identities through the military's own

127 Gareth Jenkins, 'Context and Circumstance: The Turkish Military and Politics', *The Adelphi Papers*, 41:337 (2001), pp.21-35.
128 *Ibid*, p.34.
129 *Ibid*, p.35.
130 Gareth Jenkins, 'Context and Circumstance: The Turkish Military and Politics', *The Adelphi Papers*, 41:337 (2001), p.25.

'eliticising' process and absorb an institutional identity. Interestingly, they still feel a part of society and believe that they are the true representatives of society.[131] Aydınlı, emphasising the division within the military, also notes that the Turkish military is not as homogenous as it seems; that is, in the last decade, there appeared to be two groups within the military leadership. The first is a traditional conservative majority group that views the Turkish military as the ultimate guard of the *status quo* – the Republican regime, its territorial integrity and its political parameters as established at the beginning of the Republic (e.g., secularism, assimilation into a unified national body and the primacy of security over politics). The second is a smaller, more progressive group that views the Army's mission as one of guarding the ongoing transformation and modernisation of the nation, without stalling this forward movement in the name of protecting the *status quo* – even if this means change within the military itself and its relationship with politics. It is difficult to trace any specific origins of such progressive thinking, but it is clear that Turkey's rapid process of integration with transnational organisations, global markets and the EU would be the main drivers.[132] Aydınlı, however, emphasises that there is no major distinction between the two groups with respect to the military's ultimate institutional goal: seeing Turkey become a modern, Westernised, Europeanised country. The division has more to do with the two camps' degrees of cautiousness. To make an analogy with the world of mutual funds, the conservatives in the military represent a more risk-averse, long-term investment, while the progressives can be seen as a riskier, speedier, growth fund. The growth fund types feel that the Turkish nation is ready for the completion of the modernisation and democratisation process, which requires putting its ultimate trust in the political realm, with the military's job being, at most, one of protecting this transformation in support of the civilian leaders. They see a better chance for the preservation of the essence of Atatürk's revolutions via forward movement rather than an emphasis on the *status quo*. The conservatives, on the other hand, emphasise Turkish society's ideological and social fragmentation, and argue that revolutionary and risky moves – foregoing the watchful eye of the guardian Army – would be disastrous. Their conservativism is embedded in the strong conviction that defending the country means much more than simply defending the country's borders. Rather, their inherited mission is more statically defined as guarding the achievements of the early Republican revolution, and can be better understood as coping with broader regime security concerns rather than territorial security.[133]The risk-averse conservatives remain cautious about the political realm's capacity to deal on its own with the country's many problems, and see the need for a continued military presence in politics to guide the nation through a difficult transformation to modernity.

131 Ersel Aydınlı, 'A Paradigmatic Shift for the Turkish Generals and an End to the Coup Era in Turkey', *Middle East Journal*, 63:4 (2009), pp.581-96.

132 *Ibid.*

133 George S. Harris, 'The Role of the Military in Turkish Politics Part I', *The Middle East Journal*, 19:1 (1965), p.59.

2

Theoretical Discussion

This chapter starts with a brief presentation of research conducted by Samuel Huntington and Morris Janowitz to fully grasp theoretical elements found in the CMR literature.

Benefitting from both Huntingtonian and Janowitzian Approaches

Work done by both Huntington and Janowitz dating back 60 years is still relevant for the contemporary debates regarding CMR. Firstly, Huntington's *The Soldier and the State* and Janowitz's *The Professional Soldier* not only methodically combined empirical research on CMR with systematic theorising for the first time, but also led to the emergence of different paths within research on CMR.[1] Political science studies of CMR, on the one hand, have mostly followed Huntington's tradition, and are mostly concerned with the question of how civilian political leaders can maintain civilian control, or the subordination of the military under the legitimate elected civilian leadership. Janowitz, on the other hand, concentrates more on the cultural norms, values and societal factors affecting the militaries, and the relationship between soldiers and civilians.

During the heady years of the Cold War, Huntington proposed a solution to reconcile two apparently incompatible social imperatives: the need to construct an institution powerful enough to defend American society against the Soviet threat, while at the same time ensuring civilian control so that this armed institution could not become a threat to society itself. Simply put, Huntington's solution to this *problematique* was the maximisation of the separation between what is military and what is

1 Peter D. Feaver and Erika Seeler, 'Before and After Huntington: The Methodological Maturing of Civil-Military Studies', in S.C. Nielsen and D.M. Snider (ed.), *American Civil-Military Relations: The Soldier and the State in a New Era* (Baltimore: Johns Hopkins University Press, 2009).

civilian. According to Huntington, the way to achieve this is to foster "military professionalism", the development of a genuine conservative military mindset focussed on corporateness, social responsibility and expertise in the management of violence.

The field of military sociology following Janowitz's work, on the other hand, has been concerned with the reciprocal influence of military and society. In *The Professional Soldier*, Janowitz's main message was that, just like other social subsystems, the military is subject to technological, socio-economic and political changes. Therefore, the role and missions, norms and values, and, more importantly, self-perceptions of the military's officer corps, as well as the function of the modern military institution itself, should not be considered as a "given fact" or constant, but change in line with the prevailing value system and dominant norms of the greater society. In this tradition, military sociologists focussed on issues such as the bureaucratic organisation of the military, the sociology of military personnel and their families, as well as the racial and gender integration in the military. Particularly, Janowitz's understanding of military professionalism may be useful in the Turkish case as it sees the institution of the military both as a product of tradition and hierarchy, but maybe more importantly as an agent shaped by its environment. This understanding provides for a more dynamic grasp of the military as a profession, a security organization and a social institution because it gives the officer corps agency and supposes that they are fully aware of their "influence" on politics and society in addition to being an actual product of them.[2]

For almost the next six decades, both the Huntingtonian and Janowitzian approaches have remained primary points of references for much of scholarly research in the field of CMR. While military sociology that followed the Janowitzian tradition has become a well-established sub-discipline of mainstream sociology, the Huntingtonian strand has remained as the sub-discipline of the larger discipline of political science.

While Janowitz agrees with Huntington on separate characteristics of the military and civilian world, he differs from his predecessor on how the military would be denied from posing a threat to democracy and society from which, in fact, it was created. For Janowitz, the military world is conservative and always prone to resist societal changes, and it is highly unlikely that the military will adapt to changes as fast as society could. Janowitz challenges Huntington's objective control and proposes outside intervention, or "subjective control" in Huntington's words, as the most viable instrument that may facilitate change of the military in a timely and effective manner. Janowitz, who then opposes Huntington's primary assumption that sees the inherent gap between the military and civilians as it is, seeks to shrink the gap either by civilianisation of the military or militarisation of society. For Janowitz, the civilianisation of the military, which means equipping the military with the norms and expectations of society, is the wiser strategy in diminishing the gap. That is why he encourages the use of conscription and reserve officer training programmes, the collaboration of the military in universities in the realms of education and technological researches so that

2 Morris Janowitz, *The Professional Soldier* (New York: Free Press, 1971), p.420.

the broadest level of influence of society on the military may be settled. Simply put, for him, the more societal norms and attitudes are digested by the military, the smaller the attitudinal and behavioural differences between these two worlds, and consequently the greater the likelihood of establishing and maintaining civilian control over the military. Thus, the key difference between the two is that Huntington separates civilian and military domains, but Janowitz defends the integration or entanglement of the two. In sum, together, Huntington and Janowitz defined the civil-military playing field. Huntington implored civilians not to attack the conservative military culture, while Janowitz lamented the consequences of a conservative military drifting too far from civilian society.

It is also worth mentioning that Charles Moskos, who followed in the footsteps of Janowitz, introduced a 'post-modern military' framework, which maintains that modern militaries of the Western world have significantly changed in terms of their culture (leadership, organisation, professionalism and so forth) since the end of the Cold War.[3] Even though criticism exists on the explanatory power of the concept of post-modern military, this study believes in the value of Moskos's post-modern framework as it suggests that not only civil society and the political institutions vary over the years, but so does the military. In the book *The Postmodern Military: Armed Forces after the Cold War*, Moskos and his co-authors define the post modern military as a more compact and mostly voluntary armed force, whose priorities are both national security and humanitarian-disaster relief missions abroad (external and internal), characterised by the increasing convergence of civilian and military domains, socially and functionally.[4] To put it differently, in the global security environment the nation-state is no longer considered the 'referent actor' in international relations and requires militaries to review their traditional roles and missions. Modern societies of the Western world have also changed and become more liberalised since the end of the Cold War as ideology becomes less divisive; the military, in turn, becomes more permeable by civilian society.

In the general CMR literature, one of the major theoretical debates has been around Charles Moskos's dichotomic categorisation of militaries as ideological or idealist versus professional or career-oriented. This debate is engaged in the question of whether modern militaries of the world are becoming less ideological or idealist in nature and more professional or career-oriented. Moskos suggests that, due to new societal and economic dynamics in modern societies, such as the replacement of conscription by a volunteer force recruited by labour force market dynamics, the military service is being transformed form a value-based vocation to an economically based job. The phrase 'idealist military' refers to a military primarily oriented by its

3 Charles Moskos, John Allen Williams and David R. Segal (eds), 'The Postmodern Military: Armed Forces after the Cold War'. Also, Charles Moskos, 'Military Systems in Twenty-First Century and New Trends', presented at Turkish Military Academy, 2 June 2003.

4 *Ibid.*

traditions, patriotic values, and a sense of community; the phrase 'career-oriented military' refers to a military primarily oriented by *homo economicus* and generally business principles. For Moskos, a career-oriented military more closely resembles a marketplace economy, where people are competitively recruited and paid salaries and bonuses based on skills and manpower needs.[5] Moskos maintains that the potential outcome of the move away from the idealist model of military organisation towards a career-oriented model is that soldiers, instead of being motivated by a desire to serve the "common good" are more concerned with pay, benefits and the quality of working life. A career-oriented military contains a greater division of labour with an increasing specialisation of skills. Members may work much like civilians by logging in a particular number of hours at the job, but then leave the work environment and their colleagues to live and socialise offsite. Members identify less with the organisation as a whole, and more with others in their occupation, including people outside of the organisation.

In sum, this research, emphasising the need for an eclectic theoretical approach including both institutional and sociological tracks to better elucidate the endogenous factors contributing to the military change, first presents the theory of gradual institutional change promulgated by James Mahoney and Kathleen Thelen in the hope that this is the best institutional approach addressing the Turkish military's change.[6] It then, turning to the military's sociology, examines the theoretical framework proposed by Theo Farrell and Terry Terriff proposing culture, politics and technology as three pathways whereby military change occurs.[7]

Military Change

For Carl von Clausewitz, the intellectual father of modern military thinking, military learning and military change were a simple matter: "If in warfare, a certain means turns out to be highly effective, it will be used again; it will be copied by others and become fashionable; and so, backed by experience, it passes into general use and is included in theory."[8] Simply put, on the battlefield, where every mistake is paid with the lives of soldiers, if something works, militaries will change their doctrines and practice accordingly; if something does not work, they pay the price with their blood.

At first glance, one may think that, as large *status quo*-oriented bureaucratic organisations, militaries are designed to produce routine, repetitive and orderly actions and

5 Charles Moskos, 'From Institution to Occupation: Trends in Military Organization', *Armed Forces & Society*, 4 (1977), pp.41-50.
6 James Mahoney and Kathleen Thelen, *Explaining Institutional Change: Ambiguity, Agency and Power* (Cambridge: Cambridge University Press, 2010).
7 Theo Farrell and Terry Terriff, *The Sources of Military Change: Culture, Politics, Technology* (London: Lynne Reinner Publishing, 2002).
8 Carl von Clausewitz, *On War* (Princeton: Princeton University Press, 1984), p.9.

seek to follow a traditional way of thinking and doing things. This would imply that they prefer continuity, not change.[9] Military rigidity covering all structures, processes, institutions and relations, from dress codes, rituals and parade practices to operational procedures, is suggestive of rigidity and conservatism in military thought. This view holds that militaries, as institutions inherently emphasising resiliency and continuity, prefer to preserve tried and tested strategies, structures, processes and relations rather than adopting new ones.

Militaries, however, may have both willingness and capacity for change. That is why, over the past decade, which has been marked by structural changes in the contemporary global security environment and changes in state-society and state-individual relations, there has been increased scholarly interest in the nature and behaviour of military organisations, with a particular emphasis on why and how they change. In the first decade of the 21st century, many scholars studying military culture and philosophy suggest that the militaries of the modern world have been changing as fast as the societies they defend. The central reason for these militaries to undertake change is quite straightforward. The end of the Cold War has resulted in a changed global strategic environment in which many traditional strategic templates and enactments no longer apply. The goals, strategies and structures of modern militaries change accordingly in this new global strategic setting that has mainly been shaped by technological and scientific change in information technologies, such as budgetary pressures, societal changes and the changing nature of conflict. In his well-known book *The Warrior Ethos*, Christopher Cooker suggests that there are three factors determining the nature, extent and characteristics of military change: changes in military technology, changing threats and changing societal norms and values.[10] Emphasising that "modern soldiers have been becoming what they defend [society] and against what they defend [threats] and how they defend [technology]", Cooker argues that even the very concept of "warrior soul", which constitutes the core of soldierhood and is associated with heroism, courage, sacrifice, mental toughness and physical fitness, has been transforming since the early 2000s with the influence of societal factors, hi-tech weapon systems and newly emerging threats.[11] What theoretical terms can be employed to explain this transformation that has forced modern militaries to change and adapt?

The theoretical literature addressing military change divides the primary contenders for understanding military change into two categories: those that look at change as a response to the external environment, as is generally embraced by the literature on Turkish CMR, and those that look at change as something internally generated.

9 Theo Farrell and Terry Terriff, *The Sources of Military Change: Culture, Politics*, Technology, p.4.

10 Christopher Cooker, *The Warrior Ethos: Military Culture and the War on Terror* (New York: Routledge Press, 2007), p.12.

11 *Ibid.*

A prominent external source of change suggested in the literature, for instance, is a change in the nature of the threat. Scholars of realist thinking argue that military change is likely only when the threat environment (or the perception of it) changes. This approach is reminiscent of the argument of changing threat perceptions in the Turkish security culture and Desch's threat-based model introduced in the previous chapter on literature review. Another source of external change would be the political direction an organisation receives. If one looks at the relationship between elected civilian elites and military organisations as a hierarchy, one might expect the military to change when civilian leaders ask (or force) it to do so. Following this line of thought, Peter Feaver's principal-agent analysis argues that military organisations are agents of the government.[12] Therefore, they suggest, one must look to the preferences of the principals (civilian leaders and ultimately the electorate) and the structure of monitoring as the key variables that affect the military's preferences for change. This approach is united in its focus on civilian leaders as initiating or mediating the process of military change, meaning that the military should change to accommodate civilian demand.

Those approaches seeking to explain change solely through examination of the nature, characteristics and evolution of the political or strategic context or environment external to the military may, however, fall short when taking the direct connection between military factors and change agents, structures and processes into account. Similar to non-military ones, the gradually unfolding military factors can be equally consequential for patterning human behaviour and shaping substantial outcomes affecting and being affected by the CMR. That is why one may need a model concentrating on change from within rather than change caused by exogenous factors, and an incremental change rather than an abrupt one.

Institutional Track: The Approach of Gradual Institutional Change

In their book *Explaining Institutional Change: Ambiguity, Agency and Power*, James Mahoney and Kathleen Thelen first suggest that, once created, institutions often change in subtle and gradual ways over time.[13] They argue that, although less dramatic than abrupt and wholesale transformations, these slow and piecemeal changes can be equally consequential for patterning human behaviour and thus for shaping substantive political outcomes. They then propose a new framework for analysing incremental change, grounded in a power-distributional view of institutions.

12 Peter Feaver, *Armed Servants: Agency, Oversight and Civil-Military Relations* (Cambridge: Harvard University Press, 2003).

13 James Mahoney and Kathleen Thelen, *Explaining Institutional Change: Ambiguity, Agency and Power* (Cambridge University Press, 2010), p.1.

Mahoney and Thelen underline the exact point this research seeks to highlight during their chapter on literature review, noting:

> In the literature on institutional change, most scholars point to exogenous shocks that bring about radical institutional reconfigurations, overlooking shifts based on endogenous developments that often unfold incrementally. Indeed, these sorts of gradual or piecemeal changes often only 'show up' or 'register' as change if we consider a somewhat longer time frame than is characteristic in much of the literature.[14]

This provides an accurate observation, as the traditional approach in the institutionalist literature often concentrates on stability over variability, continuity over change and persistence of institutions over their transformation. That is why nearly all definitions of institutions, whether explicitly or implicitly, imply the enduring and persisting nature of institutions that structure human preferences and behaviours and that cannot be changed easily. This inherently existing connection between institutions and persistence makes traditional approaches in the sociological, rational-choice and historical institutionalist branches easier to explain continuity and stability rather than change and transformation. To overcome the challenge of explaining change in traditional approaches in these three major branches of institutionalism, exogenous shocks shaking institutions in an abrupt fashion are mostly considered as the sole factors in causing institutions to change.[15] Zeki Sarıgil agrees with this by pointing out that institutionalist approaches, which provide structure-based arguments, give ontological primacy to structures, or in other words, structural factors are being 'exogenised' as the institutional explanations pay more attention to the impact of institutions on political outcomes and behaviours while neglecting institutional change. When it comes to explaining change, historical institutionalists, for instance, frequently call attention to 'critical junctures', often understood as periods of contingency during which usual constraints on action are lifted or eased.[16] Ira Katznelson, for example, sees institutions as mostly constraining in periods of stable politics, but argues that critical junctures open up opportunities for historic agents to alter the trajectory of development.[17]

14 *Ibid*, p.2.

15 Zeki Sarıgil, 'Europeanization as Institutional Change: The Case of the Turkish Military', *Mediterranean Politics*, 12:1 (2007), pp.39-57.

16 Giovanni Capoccia and R. Daniel Kelemen, 'The Study of Critical Junctures: Theory, Narrative, and Counterfactuals in Historical Institutionalism', *World Politics*, 59 (2007), pp.341–69.

17 Ira Katznelson, 'Periodization and Preferences: Reflections on Purposive Action in Comparative Historical Social Science', in James Mahoney and Dietrich Rueschemeyer (eds), *Comparative Historical Analysis in the Social Sciences* (Cambridge: Cambridge University Press, 2003), pp.270–301.

In the same fashion, to explain change, sociological institutionalists often point to an exogenous entity or force – for example, new interpretative frames, whether endogenous or imposed from outside. Rational choice institutionalists also face problems when confronted with institutional change. For Mahoney and Thelen, the basic difficulty faced by the rationalists is related to a view of institutions as coordinating mechanisms that sustain a particular equilibrium, which makes it difficult to conceptualise the gradual processes of endogenous change.[18] In short, all three variants of institutionalism provide answers to what sustains institutions over time, as well as compelling accounts of cases in which exogenous shocks or shifts prompt institutional change. What they do not provide is a general model of change, particularly one that can comprehend both exogenous and endogenous sources of change.

This insight then lends itself to the question of when does endogenous institutional change take place. For Mahoney and Thelen, institutional change often occurs precisely when problems of rule interpretation and enforcement open up space for actors of change to displace existing rules completely or to implement them in new ways and means.[19] How then can one get through the challenge of explaining institutional change? For Mahoney and Thelen, approaches that can comprehend both exogenous and endogenous sources of change in a dynamic political environment and that concentrate on the power-distributional implications of institutions as the "animator of change" are needed.[20] They then suggest that the following questions must be addressed if any institutional analysis aims to go beyond traditional trends in the literature, which mostly attempts to locate the sources of institutional change through the exogenous shocks and environmental shifts:

- Exactly what properties/domains of institutions do permit change?
- How and why do the change-permitting properties of institutions allow (or drive) actors to carry out behaviours that foster the changes (and what are these behaviours)? How should we conceptualise these actors?
- What types of strategies flourish in which kinds of institutional environments?
- What features of the institutions themselves make them more or less vulnerable to particular kinds of strategies for change?

This research embraces the idea that answering these basic questions is a critical step if scholars want to explain change within the Turkish military over the last 15 years. The theory of gradual institutional change put forth by Mahoney and Thelen emphasises the fact that institutions are vulnerable to change not just by exogenous shocks in moments of crisis but by endogenous processes on a more ongoing basis.

18 James Mahoney and Kathleen Thelen, *Explaining Institutional Change: Ambiguity, Agency and Power*, p.6.

19 *Ibid*, p.4.

20 *Ibid*, p.14.

In reaching the exact theoretical "neurological point" this research seeks to touch upon, their theory would hold the key to understanding the endogenous processes through which such change can be accomplished. Particularly, their orientations to develop casual propositions about the connections among particular types of institutions, strategies for change and modes of gradual institutional transformation would be handy to elucidate the effect of these endogenous processes in the transformation of the Turkish military.

Mahoney and Thelen's Explanation of the Modes and Types of Actor of Gradual Institutional Change

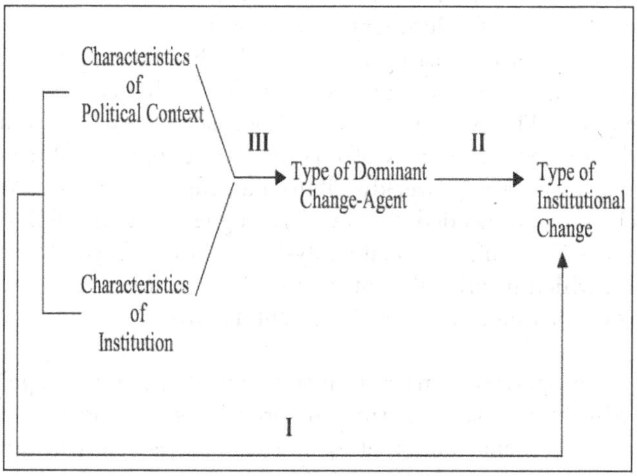

Figure 1 Mahoney and Thelen's explanation of gradual change.[21]

Mahoney and Thelen explain this figure with the following:

> Here the characteristics of both the political context and the institution in question together drive the type of institutional change we can expect. Political context and institutional form have these effects because they shape the type of dominant change agent that is likely to emerge and flourish in any specific institutional context, and the kinds of strategies this agent is likely to pursue to effect change.[22]

21 James Mahoney and Kathleen Thelen, *Explaining Institutional Change: Ambiguity, Agency and Power*, p.15.
22 *Ibid*, p.15.

They then propose four modes of institutional change. These are:

> **Displacement:** the removal of existing rules and the introduction of new ones. This kind of change may well be abrupt, and it may entail the radical shift that is often featured in leading institutional theories. The rapid, sudden breakdown of institutions and their replacement with new ones that accompanies revolutions obviously involves displacement. Yet displacement can also be a slow-moving process. This may occur when new institutions are introduced and directly compete with (rather than supplement) an older set of institutions.
>
> **Layering:** the introduction of new rules on top of or alongside existing ones, thereby changing the ways in which the original rules structure behaviour. Different from displacement, layering does not introduce wholly new institutions or rules, but rather involves amendments, revisions or additions to existing ones. Such layering can, however, bring substantial change if amendments alter the logic of the institution or compromise the stable reproduction of the original 'core'.
>
> **Drift:** the changed impact of existing rules due to shifts in the environment. When actors choose not to respond to such external environmental changes, their very inaction can cause change in the impact of the institution.
>
> **Conversion:** the changed enactment of existing rules due to their strategic redeployment as they are interpreted and enacted in new ways. This gap between the rules and their instantiation is not driven by neglect in the face of a changed setting (as is true with drift); instead, the gap is produced by actors who actively exploit the inherent ambiguities of the institutions. Through redeployment, they convert the institution to new goals, functions or purposes.

Understanding these different modes of institutional change – including the roles that institutional supporters and challengers typically play within each – sets the stage for explaining why and how one type of institutional change rather than another typically occurs.

Political Context, Institutional Characteristics and Modes of Change

In their book, Mahoney and Thelen suggest that differences in the character of existing institutional rules as well as in the prevailing political context affect the likelihood of specific modes of change.[23] The key issue is how to conceptualise the dimensions of

23 *Ibid*, pp.18-20.

institutions and political context that matter the most for explaining variations in modes of institutional change. To overcome this, they ask two broad questions:

1. Does the political context afford defenders of the *status quo* strong or weak veto possibilities?
2. Does the targeted institution afford actors opportunities for exercising discretion in interpretation or enforcement?

The analytic space presented below answers these two questions.

		Characteristics of the Targeted Institution	
		Low Level of Discretion in Interpretation/ Enforcement	**High Level of Discretion in Interpretation/ Enforcement**
Characteristics of the Political Context	**Strong Veto Possibilities**	Layering	Drift
	Weak Veto Possibilities	Displacement	Conversion

Figure 2 Mahoney and Thelen's analytical space for modes of change.

As the figure suggests,[24] differences in veto possibilities and the extent of discretion in institutional enforcement and interpretation are associated with different modes of institutional change.

They then note the following:

> Where would-be agents of change face political contexts with myriad veto possibilities, it will be difficult for them to mobilize the resources and assemble a coalition that can displace the existing institutional rules. Hence, displacement is unlikely in the context of strong veto possibilities. Likewise, efforts at active conversion will be difficult in such a context, since veto powers also apply to the realm of rule enactment. Instead of displacement or conversion, drift and layering are more promising as strategies of change in political environments

24 *Ibid*, p.15.

with strong veto players. This is true because drift and layering do not require making any direct changes to the old institutions and do not rely on altering the rules themselves or actively shifting their enactment. With drift, institutional change grows out of the neglect of an institution, or more precisely, the failure to adapt and update an institution so as to maintain its traditional impact in a changed environment. Powerful veto players may be able to defend existing institutions against outright displacement, but their veto powers are often insufficient to prevent drift since doing so typically requires supporters to take active steps to shore up support for an institution as the social, economic, or political context shifts. Monarchical political institutions, for instance, were gradually rendered into mere institutional vestiges as royal powers time and time again proved unable to successfully defend the old ways in a changing environment marked by rising parliamentary forms and their supporters. With layering, institutional change grows out of the attachment of new institutions or rules onto or alongside existing ones. While powerful veto players can protect the old institutions, they cannot necessarily prevent the addition of new elements.[25]

Types of Actors and Institutional Change

After addressing the questions of institutional change and elucidating the modes of change that are most likely to drive such change in diverse institutional settings, one may ask the following question: exactly who are the agents behind such change? Why do they bother themselves generating such change? From a distributional perspective, the first answer would be that there are two types of agents: the losers and the winners of institutional change. When taking into account the fact that the ambiguities inherent in situations and uncertainties existing in institutional enactments forces us to go beyond this dichotomic conception, one needs a new framework which can exceed this dualist and reductionist conception.

Mahoney and Thelen suggest four basic change agents after asking the questions whether the actor involved seeks to preserve the existing institutional rules and whether the actor abides by the institutional rules.[26]

Insurrectionary: these type of change agents constantly seek to eliminate existing institutions and rules, and they do so by actively and visibly mobilising against them. They reject the *status quo* and do not always abide by any rules. The insurrectionary may be, therefore, associated with the patterns of displacement, as more rapid displacement of institutions is precisely their goal.

25 *Ibid*, p.20.
26 *Ibid*, pp.23-25.

Symbiont: these type of change agents come in two forms – parasitic and mutualistic. In the parasitic type, this actor exploits an institution for private gain even as they depend on the existence and broad efficacy of the institution to achieve this gain. Parasites can flourish in settings where expectations about institutional conformity are high, but the actual capacity to enforce those expectations is limited. In the mutualistic type, symbionts also thrive on and derive benefit from the rules but use them in novel ways to advance their interests. In this case, however, in contrast to the parasites, mutualists do not compromise the efficiency of the rules or the survival of the institution.

Subversive: these type of change agents seek to displace an institution, but in pursuing this goal they do not themselves break the rules of the institution. Instead, they effectively disguise the extent of their preference for institutional change by following institutional expectations working within the system. From the outside, they may even be seen as the supporters of the institution. Depending on the political-institutional context, they may encourage conversion and the kinds of neglect that promote drift. Either way, subversion brings change as developments on the periphery make their way to the centre.

Opportunist: these type of change agents have ambiguous preferences about institutional change. They do not either actively seek to preserve the *status quo* or visibly try to change the rules. Opportunists instead exploit whatever possibilities exist within the prevailing system to maintain his/her interests. Indeed, the weight of opportunists within an institution can be a major source of institutional inertia. One should also note that opportunists' preference for making use of existing possibilities over the riskier strategy of active mobilisation makes them natural allies of institutional supporters. That is why, when they do emerge as the agent of change, opportunists often engage in strategies of conversion: ambiguities in the interpretation or implementation of existing rules provide the space for them to redeploy these rules in ways unanticipated by the initial designers.

To sum, one can generalise about the affinity between particular types of agents and modes of change as follows. Insurrectionaries seek rapid displacement but will settle for gradual displacement. Symbionts seek to preserve the formal institutional *status quo*, but their parasitic variety carries out actions that can cause institutional drift. Subversives seek displacement but often work in the short run on behalf of layering. Opportunists adopt a wait-and see approach while pursuing conversion when it suits their interests.

How can we adapt the approach of Mahoney and Thelen to the case of the TAF? According to them, institutional change can be an unintended by-product that grows out of distributional struggle in which no party explicitly sought the change that eventually occurred. This is exactly the case of the TAF for the purposes of this piece of research. Which exact properties of institutions, for instance, permit change within the TAF? How and why do the change-permitting properties of the TAF allow (or drive) actors to carry out behaviours that foster the changes (and what are these behaviours)? For the TAF, the answer to that question is every type of process, actor, structure and relation in the domains of the TAF as a security organisation, social institution and officership as a profession. Simply put, Mahoney and Thelen's power-distributional perspective of the gradual institutional change model provides a framework to explain the above-presented changes of the TAF.

Then one may conclude that, in an organization such as the TAF, change occurs through distributional effects of institutions, which trigger distrust of the pre-existing norms and divisions among those who hold the power at the elite level in the institution. Or, through elite-mass friction, change can occur if institutions disadvantage subordinate groups to the point that they organise and come to identify with one another, thereby increasing their power and capacity to break prevailing institutional arrangements. These two possibilities correspond to the themes of 'divided elites' in the TAF as a security organization domain and 'united subordinate groups vs. military elites' at the TAF as a social institution level that are emphasised in explanations of change. It is thus likely to suggest that, through distributional effects of institutions, the mega trends which will be emphasised in the following chapters, such as the prevalence of non-compliant thinking and behaviour, have forced each officer to choose one institutional identity in terms of his/her attitude towards institutional change. Unsurprisingly, the portfolio of the identity includes four types of change actor (insurrectionary, symbiont, subversive and opportunist) proposed in the Mahoney and Thelen's approach.

Sociological Track: Explaining Change through Culture

Soldiers live and operate separately from general society to be both functional and effective. To be successful on the battlefield, soldiers must learn to give their loyalty to their comrades in arms and to put personal considerations aside for the good of the service and the unit in which they serve. In doing so, they may nurture *esprit de corps*, a higher sense of responsibility to uphold the morale of the military as whole. In modern militaries, this ethical consideration, which nurtures the 'common spirit' in the fraternity, may vary, but it exists to some degree in the militaries of all long-standing democracies.[27] The sense of isolation from the rest of the society, the comrades in arms mentality, common spirit, professional ethos, discipline, ceremonies and symbolic rituals are, in fact, indicators of a distinct culture unique to militaries

27 See the 'Immersion' period of the US Marine Corps at the beginning of the training of newly admitted soldiers at <http://www.marinecorpstimes.com/class186/part1-mainbar-a.php> (accessed 12 August 2011).

within a particular society. Simply put, military culture sets soldiers apart from the civilian world. Thus, efforts to compare the military to a business organisation or a social group tend to fail as the military's mission and tasks are different, in that the soldiers stand a higher chance of losing their life than in other professions.

The term culture does not lend itself to the kind of short, sharp and clear definition usually sought by soldiers. It is a concept that transcends traditional academic boundaries in the sense that it is often used differently by historians, psychologists, sociologists and anthropologists. One should also note that most academic works defining military culture reflect American perspectives. Despite this deficiency, the definition provided by Donna Winslow is a good basis for further discussions. She states that culture represents the behaviour patterns or style of an organisation that members are automatically encouraged to follow. Culture shapes action by supplying some of the ultimate aims or values of an organisation, and actors modify their behaviour to achieve those ends. It establishes a set of ideal standards and expectations that members are supposed to follow and organise their daily worlds by locating the self and others in them and making sense of actions and motives of others.[28]

It is important to remember that culture is not only a set of values or ethos; it is also a customary style used in organising action.[29] According to Washington-based think tank the Center for Strategic and International Studies (CSIS):

> Military culture is an amalgam of values, customs, traditions, and their philosophical underpinnings that, over time, has created a shared institutional ethos. From military culture springs a common framework for those in uniform and common expectations regarding the standards of behavior, discipline, teamwork, loyalty, selfless duty, and the customs that support those elements. (CSIS Report: 'American Military Culture in the 21st Century')

Then it is likely to assert that the essence of military culture is "how things are thought and done in a military organization" (CSIS Report, xviii). Indeed, in the words of Colin S. Gray: "Culture comprises the persisting socially transmitted ideas, attitudes, habits of mind, and preferred methods of operation that are more or less specific to a particular geographically based security community that has had a unique historical experience."[30] Peter J. Katzenstein takes culture and identity as important determinants of security-related issues. As culture is about identities and loyalties, culture provides each security actor not only a framework through which the "meaning" is constructed, motives, loyalties and interests emerge, and subsequently a "self" is

28 Mark Irving Lichbach and Alan S. Zuckerman, *Comparative Politics: Rationality, Culture and Structure* (New York: Cambridge University Press, 2009) p.5.

29 Donna Winslow, *Military Culture: An Annotated Bibliography* (Ottowa: University of Ottowa, 1999).

30 Colin S. Gray, *Modern Strategy* (Oxford: Oxford University Press, 1999), p.131.

formed, but culture also provides a certain understanding of other actors who are interacting in the same context.[31]

Military culture then determines how soldiers interact with one other, how they fulfill their missions, how they see themselves and others in the civilian world and, perhaps more importantly, what kind of attitudinal framework and behaviours they expect from civilians. Military culture also implies some values such as honour, devotion to duty, service to the nation and subordinating oneself to those in command, and also ceremonial/symbolic behaviour, such as saluting, uniforms and reporting. These are the values, in fact, that one may notice in all militaries of the world, surely within varying degrees, as they are integral parts of military culture for all militaries. Some values may be unique to a particular country. The conceptualisation of technology as an asset that may only be kept at the strategic level in the Russian military, bilingualism in the Canadian military,[32] *Kibbutzim* in the Israeli military[33] and the impact of material superiority, massive firepower and advanced technologies over the US military's fighting style serve as examples of this.[34]

Regarding the integral parts of the military culture, James Burk has developed a model that includes four essential elements: discipline, professional ethos, ceremony and etiquette, and cohesion and *esprit de corps*.[35] Given the difficulty in developing a clear, concise statement of military culture that includes all of the nuances, Burk's model can be used to frame the discussion on military culture.

- **Discipline:** the important features of the disciplinary regime in the military. Includes both the self-discipline of each individual soldier serving in the military, as well as a fair and open military justice system.
- **Professional ethos:** based on the hard lessons of war fighting learned in wars, military operations and exercises. Includes values of duty, which includes the imperative of ensuring that all military actions support and reinforce the basic societal

31 Peter J. Katzenstein, 'Introduction: Alternative Perspectives in National Security', in Peter J. Katzenstein (ed.), *The Culture of National Security: Norms and Identity in World Politics* (New York: Columbia University Press, 1996), p.4.

32 Peter Mansoor, 'The Softer Side of War: Exploring the Influence of Culture on Military Doctrine', *Foreign Affairs* (2011).

33 A kibbutz is an Israeli commune, or intentional community. Due to the reflections of kibbutzim in the Israeli Military, for instance, military uniforms are not as shiny as the ones in Western militaries, the insignia representing ranks and qualifications are not cared for so much in the military system and personal charisma plays a more important role than ranks.

34 Dima Adamsky, 'The Culture of Military Innovation: The Impact of Cultural Factors on the Revolution in Military Affairs in Russia, the US, and Israel', *Stanford Security Studies* (2010).

35 See the discussion of these four factors in James Burk, 'Military Culture', in Lester Kurtz and Jennifer E.Turpin (eds), *Encylopedia of Violence, Peace and Conflict* (San Diego, Academic Press, 1999).

values. Duty includes the concept of accountability to the chain of command, the civilian authority and society. It also entails loyalty to Turkey, superiors and subordinates alike. The pursuit of professional knowledge, self-examination and self-improvement are also essential components of the concept of duty. Integrity refers to doing the right thing in an open and transparent manner, moral and physical courage,[36] loyalty and selflessness.

- **Ceremony and etiquette:** the most visible manifestations of military culture. Every aspect of TAF ceremonies and etiquette, including its style on parade, dress, awards, parades and hierarchical considerations, are important. Cohesion and *esprit de corps* are directly related to ceremony and etiquette. Ceremonies such as the change of command, retirement dinners and badge replacement ceremonies are intended to mark significant moments during an individual's service or in a unit's history. They are also intended to remind serving and retired personnel, and civilians, of the TAF's proud tradition of service and past accomplishments.
- **Cohesion and esprit de corps:** essential for combat effectiveness.

With a strategic-culture centric understanding, the cultural factors internal in the military may be categorised into three main domains:

> **Military as a security organization,** with goals, means and ways of operating
> The classic conceptualisation of the military as a security organisation, as well as the military's role in domestic and international security environments, are all included in this domain. On the other hand, factors external to the organisational boundary of the military may either be the relations between the military and the wider society in which the military is situated, or relations with other governmental and non-governmental organisations, including with international partners and adversaries.[37]
>
> **Military as a social institution,** including its values, roles and organisational structures
> The topic of the military as a social institution overlaps with the topic of the military as a profession. Nevertheless, these two domains can be addressed as two separate areas of research. The military can be studied as any other primary social institution, such as the family and religious, economic, educational and governmental institutions in terms of a system of roles based on beliefs and norms, structures, functions, patterned behaviours and adaptation for change. The military can be studied in terms of how it deals with general social issues, such as the

36 Moral courage is defined as a necessary ethos to do the right things when confronted with difficult choices. Psychical courage is the traditional concept on the battlefield.

37 Charles Moskos, 'From Institution to Occupation: Trends in Military Organization', *Armed Forces& Society*, 4 (1977), pp.41-50.

> changing characteristics of society, the changing place of the military in society, the rise of women in the workforce, diversity and inter-generational attitudes. The military can also be studied as a large organisation in terms of bureaucracy, innovation, adaptation to the changing context, hierarchical boundaries and the impact of technology. However, by applying the method of differences, the goal here should be to concentrate on that which is relatively unique to the military as an institution, instead of what it has in common with other institutions.[38]

In this way, Guy Siebold states the following:

> The statement that the purpose or primary orientation of the military, as an institution of the defense of the society or sovereign is basically true, but it is too abstract. More concrete and useful is the assertion that the primary orientation of the military as an institution and as a set of organizations is to take raw "materials" such as recruits, weapons, systems and doctrine and work with them to produce capable combat units (land, sea and aerospace) ready to engage the enemy on the battlefield.[39]

Military sociology must then ask how that orientation permeates the vision used for planning formal/informal values, structures and processes for the objective of turning these raw materials into capable 'armed servants' in an effective and efficient fashion. This study includes the opinions of the Turkish officer corps on political concepts such as democracy, secularism and civilian control of the military in this domain, meaning the addition of politics into the sphere of what is social. The reason for not addressing politics as a distinct domain, and instead including politics in this domain, is not to intimidate the respondents by asking direct political questions while conducting both the survey and in-depth interviews.

Officership as a profession of arms

The profession of arms can be described in ways typical of any profession; that is, one can study how members of a profession are recruited, selected, socialised, indoctrinated, assigned, trained, promoted, educated and retired. One can also examine how the profession constructs and controls occupational boundaries. The military profession is very hierarchical (as a means of control), heavily socialised (for internal control) and full of explicit rules, regulations, checks and counter-checks for external

38 Guy L. Siebold, 'Core Issues and Theory in Military Sociology', *Journal of Political and Military Sociology*, 29 (2001), pp.140-59.
39 *Ibid.*

control.[40] At the centre of the profession of arms, for instance, is what might be referred to by a cluster of such terms as the military mind, warrior spirit, cohort spirit and military ethos. These terms represent the question for the profession of what it means to be military personnel in a given time and society, or what the profession stands for. Indeed, military ethos of a given time and society is at the sociological centre for study of the profession of arms. Thus, it is important to consider this domain to better elucidate the Turkish military's way of doing things.

Defining the Turkish Armed Forces' Organisational Culture

Defining a specific military culture for the TAF is not an easy task. It is particularly difficult in an organisation as diverse as the TAF with three services, the Gendarmerie Command, the Coast Guard and a force structure based on a mix of professional personnel and conscripts. There is no doubt that each of these 'parts of whole' has developed a distinct culture based on their own unique operational necessities, organisational requirements, historical backgrounds and traditions. In other words, the military culture and organisational climate of a special forces team, an infantry company in the Army, a fighter squadron in the Air Force, a joint operation centre in the General Staff, a military hospital and a military academy will be distinct from one another. At first glance, one may suggest that the result is that there is probably no unitary TAF culture that can be applied across the entire institution. The 'parts' must, however, share an understanding of the core military values and ethos as these are essential to the concept of military professionalism. 'Jointness' is, for instance, a value transcending all services in the TAF's military culture. The cohort spirit, or the common spirit of the same year academy graduates, is another significant value prevailing in all services and putting its stamp on the TAF's military culture. For instance, the Air Force in the TAF tends to be defined as the service 'worshipping at the altar of technology'. The Army, on the other hand, tends to emphasise the soldier over technology and tries to develop a warrior ethos that stresses the team over the individual. Unfortunately, until now, there has not been a single scholarly work addressing the Turkish military's institutional culture regarding CMR, the officer corps' attitudes towards civilians, or their self-categorisation within the political system or in society.

Is the TAF's strategic culture immune to change or not? To show that the TAF's culture is not immune to change, Uğur Güngör, for instance, suggests that international peace operations, which the TAF has been involved in throughout the past two decades, have played a major role in the transformation of the TAF's mentality in line with emerging security conceptualisations. This suggests human, societal

40 Bradley C.S .Watson, 'The Western Ethical Tradition and the Morality of the Warrior', *Armed Forces& Society*, 26:1 (1999), pp.55-72.

and global dimensions of security.[41] As a concluding remark, Güngör asserts that the TAF's high-visibility and large-scale involvement in peace operations such as those in Afghanistan, Bosnia, Kosovo, Lebanon and Somalia has not only enhanced Turkey's soft power image around the globe, but has also increased the experience and know-how of the TAF. Similarly, Abdulkadir Varoğlu placed emphasis on how the Afghanistan experience impacted thinking patterns as well as the modes of operations of Turkish officers. He and his colleagues suggest that, particularly junior Turkish officers, have become adept at working with militaries from other nations, especially if they are deployed in areas that are culturally distant from their own.[42]

In his article entitled 'Turkish Security Culture: Evolutionary or Carved in Stone?', Ali Karaosmanoğlu states that policy misfit has to be minimal in order for change to occur. In a sense, ideational change has to precede institutional change.[43] For him, along with a new understanding of democratisation, Turkish security culture has been moving towards a regime with more political initiative and less direct military influence over politics, which is "a pattern that one may call conditional military subordination to the civilian democratic government" (Karaosmanoğlu, 2013). These works are, in fact, indicators for the argument that the TAF as a security organisation can change and adapt to the changing environment. During the literature review, however, the author did not come across any scholarly works addressing the domains of the military as a profession and the military as a social institution. This gap in the literature does not allow one to reflect more on the TAF, which is now a black box waiting to be explored.

The Cultural Sources of Military Change

Turning to cultural norms within the military, sociological approaches explain change by examining factors within the military itself. For Theo Farrell and Terry Terriff, there are three pathways whereby military change occurs: innovation, adaptation and emulation. Innovation, implying that the military is a security organisation, involves developing new tactics, strategies and structures to adapt to new military technologies. Adaptation involves adjusting existing military means and methods to tune up to newly emerging societal and cultural factors. Adaptation can, and often does, lead to innovation when multiple adjustments over time gradually lead to the evolution of

41 Uğur Güngör, *The Analysis of Turkey's Approach to Peace Operations*, PhD Dissertation, Bilkent University, Department of International Relations (2007).

42 Abdulkadir Varoğlu, Joseph Soeters, Erhan Tanercan and Unsal Sigri, 'Turkish-Dutch Encounters during Peacekeeping', *International Peacekeeping*, 11:2 (2004), pp.354-68.

43 Ali L. Karaosmanoğlu, 'Turkish Security Culture: Evolutionary or Carved in Stone?', in Peter M.E. Volten (ed.), *Perceptions and Misperceptions in the EU and Turkey: Stumbling Blocks on the Road to Accession* (Groningen: CESS, 2009), pp.27–46.

new means and methods. Finally, emulation involves importing new tools and ways of war through imitation of other military organisations.[44]

Farrell and Terriff then propose three basic sources of military change: cultural norms, politics and strategy, and new technology. Cultural norms are inter-subjective beliefs about the social and natural world that define actors, their situations and the possibilities of action.[45] Norms are inter-subjective in that they are beliefs rooted in, and reproduced through, social practice. Norms constitute actors and meaningful action by being situated both in social roles (e.g., military professionals) and social environments (e.g., interstate war versus intrastate conflict). In addition, norms regulate action by defining what is appropriate (given social rules, moral codes, etc.) and what is effective (given the laws of science). In short, norms make meaningful action possible by telling military actors who they are and what they can do in any given situation. In this way, cultural norms define the purpose and possibilities of military change.[46] In the theoretical literature, two approaches have been suggested as the engine for military change. The first is the 'process of planned military change' by 'visionary military elites' who seek to mobilise new ideas and interests behind new beliefs and identities. This process of planned cultural change implies instrumental use of culture by military elites to promote their interests. Edward Rhodes,[47] for instance, suggests that, in the 19th century, the development of a powerful US Navy and US efforts for naval supremacy was an elite-driven process sought for planned change in the country's strategic culture. The second approach emphasises an 'external shock' to the local cultural system that can undermine the legitimacy of the existing normative framework. For instance, some military strategists argue that the development of an anti-militarist strategic culture in post-war Germany and Japan was triggered by complete defeat and humiliation after surrendering in the Second World War.[48] Emily O. Goldman suggests that the strategic necessity rooted from the external shocks of being defeated in a series of wars was the prime motor of change for the Ottoman military in the 18th and 19th centuries.[49]

44 Theo Farrell and Terry Terriff, *The Sources of Military Change: Culture, Politics, Technology*, p.6.

45 *Ibid*, p.7.

46 Peter J. Katzenstein, 'Introduction: Alternative Perspectives in National Security', in Peter J. Katzenstein (ed.), *The Culture of National Security: Norms and Identity in World Politics* (New York: Columbia University Press, 1996), p.4.

47 Edward Rhodes, 'Constructing Power: Cultural Transformation and Strategic Adjustment in the 1890s', in Peter Trubowitz, Emily O. Goldman and Edward Rhodes (eds), *The Politics of Strategic Adjustment: Ideas, Institutions, and Interests* (New York: Columbia University Press, 1999).

48 Peter J. Katzenstein, 'Introduction: Alternative Perspectives in National Security', in Peter J. Katzenstein (ed.), *The Culture of National Security: Norms and Identity in World Politics* (New York: Columbia University Press, 1996), p.215.

49 Emily O. Goldman, 'Western Military Models in Ottoman Turkey and Meiji Japan', in Theo Farrell and Terry Terriff (eds), *The Sources of Military Change: Culture, Politics,*

The second source of change proposed by Farrell and Terriff is strategic; a changing threat to national security. Most scholars recognise that strategic pressures that operate through political processes may lead to military change. Barry Posen, for instance, argues that military change is most likely when strategic considerations, particularly the prospect of a defeat or a change in the adversary's strategy, triggers a political process that is primarily internal to the military organisation.[50]

The last source of military change is technological developments. For some scholars, there is a direct connection between the concept of technological determinism in a Darwinian-like order of succession and military change. Yet sociologists challenge technological determinism as the prime motor for change because they assert that, in the last analysis, social networks determine the success or failure of particular technological designs; the followers of this approach ascribe a much greater role to technology in shaping military change.[51]

Hypotheses Aimed to be Tested in the Research

In light of the above-mentioned theoretical framework, there emerge three hypotheses: one regarding the ideological rigidity of the TAF, one regarding the attitudinal differences among the officer corps and another related to the cross-sectional cultural differences among three force commands.

Hypothesis 1: The TAF is in the process of becoming a more heterogeneous and less ideological military.

In his 2012 piece 'Civil-Military Relations Transformed', Ersel Aydınlı suggests that an ideological split distinguishes officers who favour a rapid and military-directed pace toward modernising and Westernising Turkey from those inclined toward a more gradual approach that trusts civilians more. He says that the former (we might call them the 'absolutists') believe that until Turkish society and politics mature, they must be carefully guided by the strong hand of the state and, above all, by its armed forces. The latter ('gradualist') group argues that coups and other harsh tactics are counterproductive and that working with civilians is a better way of achieving modernisation.[52] Aydınlı then contends that "absolutism among the Turkish military

Technology (London: Lynne Reinner Publishing, 2002), p.74.

50 Barry R. Posen, *The Sources of Military Doctrine: France, Britain and Germany between the World Wars* (Ithaca: Cornell University Press, 1984).

51 Metin Gürcan, 'Drone Warfare and Contemporary Strategy Making: Does the tail wag the dog?', *Dynamics of Asymmetric Conflict*, 6(1-3) (2013).

52 Ersel Aydınlı, 'Civil-Military Relations Transformed', *Journal of Democracy*, 23:1 (2012), pp.100-08.

appears to be in irreversible decline, and the gradualists seem to have won", meaning that the TAF has become less ideological.[53]

The Turkish military, or a *de facto* veto-player of Turkey's political system, has embraced two tasks of guarding the state and protecting its founding principles, particularly the ones emphasising the Kemalist, secular and nationalist character of the state. This grip has played a critical role in influencing the political course of the country – both implicitly and by direct military interventions. Since the first military coup in 1960,[54] the TAF's role in politics has by and large been as the guardian of the state and the whole nation. Eric Nordlinger defines this guardian role as one in which the military aims for governmental control with the objective of maintaining the *status quo* and correcting what they identify as malpractice or a deficiency.[55] According to Nilüfer Narlı, "the military [was] built as a covert guardianship model that permitted it to use various forms of intervention, ranging from a coup to controlling and influencing the civilian political process through formal and informal mechanisms".[56] For Toktaş and Kurt, the military has performed this "self-proclaimed" guardianship mission through securitising Turkey's political problems. On the basis of its conceptualisation and definition of 'national security' and 'threats', the Turkish military constructs the security agenda, setting both internal and external mechanisms to support this agenda. The traditional themes of securitisation in the Turkish case have been political Islam and Kurdish nationalism, which have indirectly pushed the military to become involved in Turkish politics. If the governments did not take sufficient measures to deal with these national security issues, the military threatened to intervene in politics; and, on some occasions, forced civilian governments to resign.[57] Which ideology does then one talk about within the military? The TAF is also seen as the only legitimate guarantor of Kemalist ideology. In order to emphasise the 'guardian' role of the TAF to protect secular, nationalist and modernist characteristics of the nation state, the TAF has always inclined to stress Kemalist ideology in particular, the founding ideology of the Turkish Republic designed for sweeping socio-economic, political and cultural reforms.

Following from this, how did Kemalist ideology shape the military's internal and external affairs? It is first worth recalling that the TAF intervened to 'guard' the Kemalist system four times in the past 58 years – in 1960, 1971, 1980 and 1997.

53 *Ibid.*
54 William Hale, 'The Turkish Republic and its military, 1923–1960', *Turkish Studies*, 12 (2011).
55 Eric A. Nordlinger, *Soldiers in Politics: Military Coups and Governments* (New Jersey: Prentice Hall, 1977), p.22.
56 Nilüfer Narlı, 'Concordance and Discordance in Turkish Civil-Military Relations', *Turkish Studies*, 12:2 (2011), pp.215–25.
57 Şule Toktaş and Ümit Kurt, 'The Turkish Military's Autonomy, AKP Rule and the EU Reform Process in the 2000s: An Assessment of the Turkish Version of Democratic Control of Armed Forces (DECAF)', *Turkish Studies*, 11:3 (2010), pp.387-403.

In 2007, with a controversial press release, or e-momerandum (BBC, 'EU warns Turkish...'), a statement, excerpts from which follow, was published on the TAF's official website regarding the crisis in the Turkish presidential elections:

> The problem that emerged in the presidential election process is focused on arguments over secularism. Turkish Armed Forces are concerned about the recent situation. ... the Turkish Armed Forces are a party in those arguments, and absolute defender of secularism. Also, the Turkish Armed Forces is definitely opposed to those arguments and negative comments. It will display its attitude and action openly and clearly whenever it is necessary ... Those who are opposed to the Great Leader Mustafa Kemal Atatürk's understanding "How happy is the one who says I am a Turk" are enemies of the Republic of Turkey and will remain so. The Turkish Armed Forces maintain their sound determination to carry out their duties stemming from laws to protect the unchangeable characteristics of the Republic of Turkey. Their loyalty to this determination is absolute.

According to Article 35 of the Internal Service Act (1961), which could not be removed until 2013, the primary task of the military was to "safeguard and defend Turkish territory and the Republic of Turkey as designated by the constitution". Because Kemalist ideology in general is enshrined in the constitution, the military's primary task is to 'look after' Kemalist ideology, or the guiding philosophy of the Republic. Moreover, Article 85 of the Internal Service Act states that the "Turkish military shall defend the country against internal as well as external threats if necessary by force".[58] Thus, one may suggest that the military has the self-claimed authority to define threats that present existential danger to the state and its founding ideology.

Is this rigid ideological stance the case for the TAF, or has the TAF been becoming less ideological militarily? This study hypothesises that, for almost a decade, the TAF has been becoming a more heterogeneous and less ideological military.

Hypothesis 2: The attitudes and opinions of junior level officers (lieutenants, first lieutenants, captains, majors) are different from those of senior level officers (lieutenant colonels, colonels, generals).

As no single scholarly piece exists addressing the attitudinal differences within the officer corps, this research cannot provide insights from the literature. This piece of research, however, could provide some factual insights on statistical facts on the origins and characteristics of each and every rank. Among the officer corps, in terms of their origin, there were two types of officer in the TAF a decade ago; that is, military high school/war academy graduates and civilian high school/war academy graduates. Currently, however, there are seven types of officers in terms of their origin in the

58 Metin Heper, 'Civil-Military Relations in Turkey: Toward a Liberal Model?', *Turkish Studies*, 12:2 (2011), pp.241-52.

TAF: military high school/war academy graduates, civilian high school/war academy graduates, civilian university graduates (contracted officers), foreign war academy graduates (the US, South Korea), officers with a non-commissioned officer background and officers with a contracted specialist background. One should also note that the ratio of war academy graduates, the category that constitutes the backbone of the officer corps, has drastically decreased from 90% to 60% from 2006 onwards due to the inclusion of contracted officers in the TAF. It is worth mentioning that, from 2004 onwards, there has been a sharp rise in the ratio of civilian university graduate contracted officers and NCO-background officers within the officer corps. This heterogeneity in the origins would inevitably come up with varying attitudes and opinions when interpreting social realities, yet the TAF have been trying hard to standardise young officers through military education and other means. A decade ago, being appointed as a lieutenant required eight years of education (four years of military high school and four years of military academy), and nearly 80% of all lieutenants were spending eight years in military schools. At the moment, however, Major Y.E., a civilian university graduate, who is working in the Turkish General Staff, notes the following:

> It takes only ten months to commence his service as a lieutenant in the Turkish military. And now, the level of eight-year military school graduates among the total population of the lieutenants in the Turkish military has dropped to 40 percent. Sixty percent comes from different origins.[59]

In light of these statistical facts about the diversifying origin and changing characteristics of the officer corps, this study hypothesises that there are attitudinal differences among ranks within the officer corps.

Hypothesis 3: Each force command (Army, Navy, Air Force) has its 'unique' organis\#ational culture that promotes diversity and heterogeneity within the TAF.

Again, regarding this hypothesis, there is no single scholarly piece in the literature. When turning to mere facts, however, one may easily notice that each force command has different military high schools, war academies for undergraduate education, staff colleges and postgraduate institutions for postgraduate education. Different educational institutions would also mean differentiation in the ways and means of thinking and doing things in each force command. Besides, 'jointness', the key concept which provides opportunities for joint-posts and ways/means of doing things within the TAF, has not been fully achieved in the military, meaning that the great majority of personnel in each force command cannot easily find joint-working environments with the officers from different force commands. The fact that officers are prevented from interacting with other officers from different force commands also constitutes

59 From interview with Major Y.E. conducted on 23 May 2015 in Ankara.

a cultural barrier hindering homogenisation and standardisation of organisational culture within the TAF. In this sense, this study hypothesises that, despite some improvements to achieve jointness, all force commands still have different organisational cultures, thus differentiating ways and means of thinking and doing things.

This research is an exploratory one inductive in nature that seeks to move from specific observations to broader generalisations. These tentative hypotheses presented above address specific research areas that this study seeks to explore and finally end up fostering some general conclusions and theoretical frameworks. The precursor to these hypotheses is the research question of this study: whether the endogenous factors leading to change within the military's organisational culture play a role in the recent civilianisation in the Turkish CMR or not. These hypotheses are formulated to pare down this overall question into something testable for the following empirical chapters.

3

Qualitative Analysis of the TAF before 15 July

This chapter will provide a qualitative analysis of the military's transformation. At the organisational level, this transformation has mainy shown itself in three different domains that can be conceptualised as the following:

- The domain of the TAF as a security organisation.
- The domain of the TAF as a social institution.
- The domain of officership as a profession.

This chapter will be divided into sections to better elucidate the military's transformation in each domain.

The first section touches upon the period of August 2011-August 2012 in which the TAF had, for the first time since the 1990s, a clear understanding that they needed a structural self-check to achieve the objectives of familiarising with and situating themselves within Turkey's changing socio-political context at the domestic level, and to adapt to changes in the global security environment at the international level. This period, which the author also witnessed closely thanks to his post as a project officer at the Turkish General Staff (TGS), started with the TAF's attempt of an assessment of the damage it had done in the last decade. This period thus marked the attempt to both conduct and institutionalise this assessment of the damage process by performing various official workshops within the TGS. Despite the fact that TAF had already been discussing the need for a transformation from the beginning of the 2000s, it is likely to suggest the self-reflecting debate about learning more of the damage caused in the last decade and how to institutionalize a transformation. The main objective of this section is to reveal how the military started conducting a self-check on its own decade-long transformation. Furthermore, this section will show that this reflection is more of a self-check process for the military as it represents the first time that the military has acknowledged that its transformation process is a crucial subject to be scrutinised and managed by its own terms.

The second section will feature an institutional analysis of the Turkish military's transformation as a security organisation throughout the past decade. It will delve into the reasons and *telos* of the military's transformation and reconstruction process, which is called 'Force 2033 Vision'. This section will also explore the implications of how the TAF adapted to Turkey's dramatically changing socio-political context by analysing TGS press releases between 2003 and 2014. Focusing on an interval of 11 years, this analysis will be conducted by using the 'qualitative content analysis' method. This analysis will track changes in the military's communication strategies, particularly the altering in tone, language usage, thematic structures and discourse of TGS press releases. This will allow for great insights into how and why the military changed its strategic discourse to adapt to Turkey's socio-political context. This section will also analyze the TAF's endeavour to increase its visibility on the international stage, a process referred to as the 'internationalisation' of the Turkish military by this thesis, and its relation with institutional transformation.

In an attempt to analyse the military as a social institution, the following section will highlight the TAF's efforts to adapt to Turkey's changing social context by looking at the cases that shed light on the TGS' confrontational interactions with junior-level officers, such as the struggle of NCOs for rights and status within the military, the push for embracing more gender-friendly policies, the increasing awareness of violations of the rights of soldiers as well as the rate of suicides among soldiers, and the loosening of the headscarf ban.

The next section delves into the concept of officership as a profession and insights derived from in-depth interviews conducted with officers at various ranks. Thus, there will be interviews from high-ranking officers such as generals all the way down to the lowest ranks, such as NCOs. Through these interviews, this section will endow noteworthy insights regarding how the officers conceive changes about their profession. A comparison will also be made between junior-level officers (lieutenants, captains and majors) and senior-level officers (lieutenant colonels, colonels and generals) to see better that how these officers conceptualise and describe change in their profession, and analyse how their attitudes and opinions regarding their profession resemble or differ from one other.

The last section, designed as a theoretical discussion, will explore the findings of this institutional analysis within the model of institutional change as proposed by Mahoney and Thelen, as well as the cultural model seeking to explain change within the military as proposed by Farrell and Teriff. The power-distributive perspective explaining gradual institutional change put forward by Mahoney and Thelen provides a framework to explain the above-presented changes of the TAF: as a security actor, as a social institution and officership as a profession.[1] Thus, in this chapter Mahoney and Thelen's model of gradual institutional change will be utilised to explain the transformation the TAF has been experiencing for a decade. After reading this chapter, one would easily notice that, within the TAF, it is evident that what animates change is the

1 James Mahoney and Kathleen Thelen, *Explaining Institutional Change: Ambiguity, Agency and Power*, p.30.

power-distributional implications of institutions. However, the place that one expects incremental change to emerge is precisely in the 'gaps' or 'grey zones' between the rule and its interpretation (division among elites) or the rule and its enforcement (division between elites and subordinate groups). This is an analytic space that other conceptions of institutions (as behaviours in equilibrium, or as scripts) essentially rule out by definition; but, as a practical matter, this is exactly the space in which contests over – and at the same time within – institutions take place. That is, in the domain of the TAF as a security organization, for instance, the High Command (particularly the Chief and deputy Chief of the TGS)[2] meets one as the prime change agent of the top-down transformation. Change in this domain is implemented under the full control of the military elites and mainly shaped by the change in the international security environment. That is why it looks like an elite-driven process that seeks to adapt the TAF to the contemporary global security environment by 'emulating' the ways of thinking and doing things of the other modern security actors in the globe, particularly NATO. In contrast to this, in the domain of the TAF as a social institution, change arises primarily as first commencing from the bottom and developing generally by confrontational interactions between the military elites and junior-level personnel, or emerging with the inclusion of the outside actors in civil society. Change then goes to the top and, by dictating its own reality to the military elites, evolves into a process that the High Command cannot keep under its full control and manage accordingly. In this sense, it is likely to assert that, in this domain, change is to some extent an arbitrary process partly controlled by the High Command and partly driven by random dynamics such as the existence or absence of public awareness and media support to the issue at hand. One should note that, in this domain, the High Command, after first ignoring and then counter-attacking the change-demanding insiders or outside actors, can find no option but to submissively accept the existence of the problem and attempt to adapt its institutional order to fulfill change demands. In the domain of officership as a profession, however, one may talk about an 'agentless change' process as no actor can fully control the attitudes and opinions of the officer corps, which still, for the author, is the case in the post-15 July setting. The differentiation among three domains in terms of change types, change agents, change pathways and change modes therefore creates a power-distributional effect of change in the TAF, which according to this research, yields to gradual institutional change within the TAF.

We start with a general overview of when and how the debate within the military about the need for an institutional transformation started to better elucidate which actors led this process, and which kind of structures and mechanisms were established for the operationalizstion of the institutional transformation.

2 By high command of the TAF is meant personnel at the rank of general/admiral, including the Chief of the General Staff, the Second Chief of the General Staff, Force Commanders and Army commanders. As of August 2015, there were 12 full generals in the TAF.

Transformation of the Turkish Military

The Start of Sophisticated Discussions about the Transformation (August 2011-August 2012)

August 2011 marked the resignation of Chief of the General Staff, General Işık Koşaner, and three force commanders. This moment served as a critical juncture that tempted the TAF to realise the fact, or "grim reality"[3] in the words of a general interviewed, that it needed to conduct a damage assessment (or self-check) and transform itself if necessary. Similar to moving indoors from the cold, this admittance pushed the whole military as an organisation to speed up the necessity of fundamental self-reflection and to examine themselves critically about traditional ways of thinking and doing things. Those taking office after the resignations – the new Chief of the General Staff, General Necdet Özel, and Deputy Chief of Staff General Hulusi Akar – initiated this self-check process within the military.

Immediately following this realisation, the TGS preferred to retreat to its own territory and focus only on issues regarding the military. What would be, then, the main reason for the military's self-check process, which resulted in a strong urge for institutional transformation? The main reason for such a change of strategy was the failure of previous strategies that had been adopted by previous chiefs of the TGS. As a qualitative content analysis of the TGS's press releases indicate, during the period when General Yaşar Büyükanıt was in office (2006-08), the military's attitude towards civilian politics can be called 'direct confrontation' because the military openly challenged the civilian political elites and was in a power struggle with the AKP government. Then, when General İlker Başbuğ took office (2008-10), the military adopted an 'indirect confrontation' attitude in which the TGS tried to place pressure on the political realm and indirectly aimed to shape it by interacting with certain political and civil society actors that the military had already been aligned with. Lastly, in the period during which General Işık Koşaner was in office (2010-11), the military adopted an attitude of 'strained harmony', meaning that military elites bargained with the political actors behind closed doors in the hope of silently getting what it wanted. However, none of these endeavours was able to create enough support for the military at the societal level or produced enough force to change the views of political elites within AKP governments. In an interview conducted with a general in İstanbul, he addressed the failure of these last endeavours of the military – direct confrontation, indirect confrontation and strained harmony attitudes – as the main reasons in failing to be able to bargain with politicians to get what it wanted. In addition, the incompetency of military leaders in solving trials and investigations such as *Sledgehammer* and *Ergenekon* involving its prominent serving or retired officers was apparent. The general highlighted the following:

3 From interview with a general conducted in İstanbul on 17 May 2015.

> These were really hard times for [the] TAF not because of highly tense government-military relations for the last decade, but there has been a lot of pressure on the military both from the media and the judiciary, there have been intensified conflicts with the forces of the PKK between 2005 and 2010 all along with the political instability of the Middle East, which has been in its climax because of the conflicts in Syria and Iraq. In addition to all of these, the military had to cope with the tension between the US and Turkey, which immensely intensified after the Hood Event (*Çuval Olayı*) on the fourth of July, 2003. General Özel rightfully followed a new attitude called **delicate harmony** [emphasized by the author] – mainly seeking for a retreat to the military's own territory – after experiencing the failing of previous attitudes, which had been adopted by Büyükanıt, Başbuğ, and Koşaner. The main principles of this new attitude for the military was being committed to the rule of law, being on lawful ground no matter what, and being indifferent to political developments. I think the reason why he adopted such an attitude lies in the traumatic process that the military went through after the trials and investigations like *Sledgehammer* and *Ergenekon*. After all, the initial discussions regarding the military's obligatory retreat, the strategies to get through this traumatic process, and the institution's continuing transformation took place in the General Staff only towards the end of 2011.[4]

Indeed, in 2011 there was a push for an analysis of the current state of the military as a security organisation, which was called a "damage assessment analysis" by TGS headquarters. In this period, TGS headquarters established new workgroups under each of its directorates.[5] The formation of these groups, which were comprised of officers of lower ranks like captains and majors with academic backgrounds, was a solid indicator of understanding the newly emerging sentiment that was generated by the High Command (the chief and deputy chief of the TGS) for the institutional transformation within TGS headquarters. These working groups allowed for an opening of alternate information channels other than traditional bureaucratic-hierarchical ones. These newly founded workgroups allowed scholarly ways of thinking and doing things and for decision-makers to be fed alternative information channels without institutional constraints. These working groups can be said to have endeavoured to offer unorthodox scholarly analyses to the High Command in the following three fundamental fields:

- The change in the global security environment.
- The change within modern militaries and NATO.
- The socio-political change in Turkish CMR.

4 From interview with the general conducted in İstanbul on 17 May 2015.

5 Main directorates in Turkish General Staff headquarters are as follows: Personnel Directorate (J1), Intelligence Directorate (J2), Operation Directorate (J3), Logistics Directorate (J4), General Planning and Principles Directorate, Warfare Electronic Information System (MEBS) Directorate and General Secretariat.

Analyses and reports were prepared in the assemblies, conducted monthly until August 2012, about the way in which the TAF managed its reputation and the preservation of its image in society, the structural transformation which should be experienced by the TAF as a security actor, counter-terrorism efforts, enforcement of institutional loyalty among TAF personnel and their families, violations of soldiers' rights, soldier suicides and TAF communication strategies. This was then presented to the High Command and the proposals accepted were turned into the executive orders from the TGS chief and issued for full implementation.

Following this year-long process of 'damage assessment', it can be said that two main approaches emerged after discussions to be utilised for crisis management. Yet these two, in fact, contradicted each other.

The first of these was the *status quo*-focussed approach. The main argument of this approach was that anchoring the TAF to the abiding system of foundational values, such as a strictly secular and elitist-modernist world view of Kemalism, without accounting for th changes in the last 10 years in the global and societal dynamics and in the Turkish CMR (especially in the military-government relations), would be the best method for overcoming the crisis period. In this approach, which could be summarised as 'we should anchor ourselves to our traditional values to get out of the crisis period in better shape', the aim was to hold on tightly to the value system adopted by the TAF since the foundation of the Turkish Republic. This value system includes primarily values such as Kemalism, secularism, nationalism, guiding the nation, patriotism and safeguarding the Republic against all internal and external threats. Merely by theset means, the military could escape the 'degradation period' of the last decade relatively unscathed. The defenders of this approach asserted that, particularly in the past few years, public conception and opinion could be manipulated very easily with perception management techniques and changed as desired. In this way, by not adapting to society and public perception, the TAF was ensuring that it would not slide to other ideological and security stances. According to this approach, the TAF's trying to take a position in accordance with public conception, which is prone to manipulation, would be a strategic mistake. Hence, the TAF has to steep its strategy in the value system which constitutes its "essence" or "essential soul"[6] with a *status quo*-focussed approach.

The other approach emerging from the damage assessment process is the 'reformist approach'. This approach argues that the process of change in the global security environment, socio-political changes in Turkey and the change in the Turkish CMR render the transformation of theTAF compulsory. According to the reformist approach, if the TAF cannot go through a structural transformation in light of the 10-year crisis period for adapting to both global and societal change in Turkey, it will fall behind both its age and the society. As a result, it will become an "outdated"[7] army whose

6 From interview with Colonel M. conducted in Ankara on 27 April 2015.
7 From interview with Major T. conducted in Ankara on 12 January 2015.

"legitimacy is being extensively questioned by the society".[8] For this reason, the TAF has to examine changes in the three fields listed below and begin a detailed transformation process both materially (in organisational, tactical and technical terms) and cognitively (in institutional culture and mentality) which handles all of the following:

- The change in the global security environment.
- The societal change in Turkey.
- The change in the CMR.

According to the reformist approach, it is possible for an organisation such as the TAF to self-reflect and self-criticise its existing set of values and norms, which has traditionally been thought to be immune to changes and new interpretations. The main objective in this approach is "transformation without breaking away from the tradition, that is, transformation without changing".[9] The TAF has to revise the value system it gathered from the past, its attitude of conduct, its technical equipment and its standardised operational procedures to become a hi-tech military with strong societal legitimacy. But, according to the reformist approach, "having that transformation incrementally is another obligation".[10]

The most apparent difference between these two approaches is that they have different epistemologies, and thus different modes of interpretation of Turkey's current socio-cultural and political context. The *status quo* logic seems to see the current socio-cultural and political landscape, dominated by the AKP, as a temporary deviant discourse in the history of the Republic of Turkey. Therefore, it would be wiser, for the *status quo* logic, to conform to the traditional value system offered by the Turkish military, and interpret socio-cultural and political realities through the lenses of the TAF's established set of values. For the *status quo* logic, this deviant discourse is peculiar to Turkey, which implies that it is shortsighted when assessing global trends such as the transformation of the nation-state system, the changing relationship between individual and state, the diminishing visibility of militaries in Western societies, constraints on defence budgets, demands for the recognition of cultural and other differences and the rise of identity politics all over the world as a reaction to the homogenising attempts of states. For the *status quo* logic, it would be dangerous to anchor military values in society's current value set, which has been easily shaped by mass media manipulations, and thus should not be trusted. The *status quo* logic is confident that Turkey will return to its original state, or "factory settings",[11] and thus it is important to preserve the established value set of the Turkish military. A retired colonel, for instance, posed the following question:

8 *Ibid.*
9 These remarks were made by General Hulusi Akar in a meeting with the author in April 2013.
10 *Ibid.*
11 *Ibid.*

> To what extent is it proper to trust already-manipulated current societal values, which will be totally different five years later? Then, the "compass" which has been institutionalized in each officer by the military will show the "true path" to where an officer should navigate.

For the *status quo*-focussed approach, officership is a way of life that constantly surrounds him and his family; the officer and his family should bear all material and psychological burdens such as temporary budget deficits, marriage problems, health problems, long and risky deployments or the uprooting of a fast deployment cycle to honour the officership. The reformist approach, in contrast, tends to place more trust in society's current value set than the *status quo* logic, and seems to embrace these values along with the military's established value set. The reformist approach, in this sense, could be defined as an approach that endeavours to accommodate the military's established value set and society's current value set.

In fact, in this period, it was seen that the emphasis that the TAF needs a structural transformation was not only uttered in assemblies in TGS corridors, but was also voiced on other platforms and by the civilian decision-makers. For instance, in his speech on 5 April 2012 at the Staff College, President Abdullah Gül emphasised how "the great transformation observed in strategic balances" changes the traditional conceptions of security and strength in the globe. In his speech, Gül's following statement is noteworthy:

> New threats and opportunities arising at the global level are making new security conceptions and new order searches gain acceleration. As a result of that, we are witnessing all over the world that substantial reforms are being made for the armed forces to obtain the most effective and optimal structure.[12]

According to Gül, the TAF's transformation with a new reformist spirit is compulsory. In this reform, there are three principles that the military must adopt: jointness, prevention of duplications and supply of procurement by the national defence industry at the highest possible level.

Institutionalisation of the reformist approach within the TGS (August 2012-August 2013)

Between August 2012 and August 2013, it is possible to say that, of the two approaches designated after the damage assessment process, the reformist approach came to the

12 See the full text of the speech (in Turkish) at <http://www.tccb.gov.tr/abdullah-gul-konusmalar/371/82551/harp-akademileri-konferansinda-yaptiklari-konusma.html> (accessed 10 April 2015).

forefront of the TGS mainly due to the High Command's reformist sentiment. It is for this reason that the Project Management Department was established in November 2012 as a sub-command directly attached to the TGS deputy chief to contribute scientific analyses to the High Command's decision-making. As its head, the department has a brigadier general with an MA degree in international relations and has a qualified staff with both master's and PhD degrees abroad. The department started to prepare analyses and reports about issues ordered by the High Command. Besides that, the establishment of the Conduct Offices within the directories of the General Staff to help commanders of all directories with decision-making was another indicator of the reformist approach.

This period was when the TGS' structural reorganisation occurred. Substantial reorganisation within the TGS carried out in this period include the appointment of qualified staff to the Press and Public Relations Department, the attachment of new branches and sections (like the Branch of Internet and Social Media) to the Press Department, increasing the cadres of the Armed Forces Operation Command Centre (AFOCC), from which General Staff headquarters follows all the activities of TAF units, and the appointment of a brigadier general as its head. Additionally, in this period, a new approach was adopted about the problems of NCOs serving in the military, which had captured media and public attention. To deal with the well-being and lack of motivation among NCOs, a General Staff NCO office was established as a directly attached branch of the TGS Chief. After the establishment of this office, the TGS Senior NCO post was formed. The offices of the Senior NCO in the headquarters of all force commands were also established.

In addition, between August 2012 and August 2013, the Reputation Management Working Group was established for the first time within the TGS to develop new strategies for managing the reputation of both the internal public opinion of the TAF (TAF personnel, their families and close associates) as well as society as a whole. In the following stages, communication experts, including the author of this thesis, joined the working group. This working group played an important role primarily in increasing the loyalty of TAF personnel to the institution, and secondly in the development of the most effective communication strategies for society.

On the other hand, criticisms were also made within the TGS about efforts to transform during this period. The most important of those criticisms, coming especially from the staffs of the Air Force and Navy, is that one of the most essential principles of TAF transformation as a security actor, 'joint-ness', was not taken into consideration satisfactorily. This criticism emphasises that the Army dominates the management of the transformation process, a dynamic that harms joint-ness for the Air Force and Navy. Especially, no appointments made to the newly established departments and branches in the General Staff directories from naval or Air Force officers have caused serious resistance and discomfort against appropriation of the transformation process. The appointment of generals from the Army as the heads of newly established departments, plus the appointment of staff from the Army to the branch directorates, caused discomfort from the top to the bottom.

In this respect, Captain İ. from the Navy draws attention to the following issues:

> How much joint shall [the] TAF be? The answer to this sincere question is directly related to the vision and the security architecture of Turkey. If the country partly wants to be in a global position and to include commitments promising to protect its citizens everywhere in the world, then the dimension of joint-ness will reach out to a dimension of expeditionary forces starting from the peace, but if a joint-ness covering the framework of an operation field of our surrounding seas and present land borders is to be considered, a joint-ness of less coverage starting from crisis/tension phase can be thought of. However, when the projects [the] TAF is carrying out at the moment and is planning to have at the near future are taken into account, it is impossible to think that the field of interest of [the] TAF is limited merely to our mentioned borders. Thanks to those abilities that will be obtained in expense of billions of Turkish lira, when it is taken into account that we will be able to transport our warplanes to intercontinental distances, our vision must be extended far beyond. If you have that vision, you must be speaking of a force projection. In the face of this situation, your naval forces which has [*sic*] a geopolitical definition of three-fourths of the world, should be larger and you need to approve the transformation of the General Staff headquarters and other crucial bases from land-oriented organizations to naval/air-function-oriented organizations. From now on, the changes in the global security environment dictate to us that the domination of the land forces within [the] TAF is over. In my opinion, the main force of the future is either naval forces or the Air Forces, but certainly not the land forces. In that case, why not does a naval or air general become the General Staff headquarter instead of an Army general?[13]

The Expansion of the Debates about Transformation to Force Commands (August 2013- August 2014)

Between August 2013 and August 2014, debates about the transformation started within the Army, the Navy and the Air Force. To manage the transformation by means of scientific methods and under a single executive branch, branches such as the Project Management Department of TGS headquarters were established in each force command. The aim of establishing each branch, which is directly attached to the force commander, was to provide guidance and consultancy for the force commanders' decisions and executive orders and to ensure standardisations for joint-ness in implementation.

In this period, as one of the first instances of the TAF's structural transformation, the Air Force and Missile Defence Command, which gathers the main fighting units

13 From interview with Captain I.G. conducted on 13 May 2015 in Ankara.

of the Air Force under a single framework of a commandership, was established in Eskişehir on 5 August 2014.[14] As the main affiliation of this commandership, the Vice Commandership and United Air Operation Centres Commandership was established in Diyarbakır to manage air operations from a single centre, and land and naval coordination units were formed in Eskişehir together with the Air Defence Command, which manages air missile defence from a single centre and has the right to engage. Employed with strategic projects in the Air Force, Captain S. makes it clear how Air Force projects have been built up, like the F-35 project, which calls for the need to shift to advanced technology and to net type of war architecture, each of which was used as an instrument of self-confidence:

> The Turkish Air Force is competing and taking concrete steps in the way of being a space power. For example, it is planning to procure 100 F-35A until the year 2021 to replace with the F-34 Phantom II planes in the inventory of the Air Force within the F-35 JSF project which it considers to be the project which will lead the Turkish Air Force up to space. Again, the latest efforts are the clearest indication of a technology-centred transformation, such as a project [to] develop a national warplane, the national air missile project, the Wing Guidance Kit project, which will transform classic ammunition into winged and guided ammunition, as well as advanced mobile and stationary radar projects. Even if we will not see it, the next generation will certainly witness a war in space. Therefore, if Turkey wants to be a great country in the future, it must manage to transform its Air Forces into a space power. This is also our goal.[15]

Again in this period, it is interesting to note that naval forces, which were hit the hardest in the *Sledgehammer* and *Ergenekon* cases, took substantial steps towards transformation to overcome the institutional trauma it had experienced. Employed at the Project Management branch of the naval forces headquarters, Captain İ. comments:

> It is normal that national interests have reached a global projection for a country that aims to be listed among the top 10 economies of the world with its GNP of 2 trillion dollars, which will be one of the 32 countries in the world by entering the league of nuclear power using countries with two nuclear plants, and will obtain the potential of production capacity with its population of 90 million in the year 2023. Right at this point, the Navy, probably the force that best envisages the future, has had a great shift with the pool invasion ship project of $1.2 billion, a military base deployment for Qatar, a capacity increase for Somali, a waving flag

14 For the related press release on the official website of the Turkish Armed Forces (in Turkish), see <http://www.hvkk.tsk.tr/tr/HaberDetay.aspx?IcerikID=6348&ID=93> (accessed 12 April 2015).

15 From interview with Captain S.Y. conducted in Ankara on 12 March 2015.

> at the Asian-Pacific region especially for the last few years, and the acceleration of steps taken to implement this project, which was its last move.[16]

He also emphasizes that the Navy considers these ambitious projects as confidence-building means for its personnel "to grasp the future with a new breath".[17]

Consolidation of Transformation (August 2014-August 2015)

In this period, the most important formal text emphasising the need for a transformation and restructuring was the Defense Reform Report issued with the signature of President Abdullah Gül in August 2014.[18] The transformation activities by the TGS, parallel to the Presidential Defence Reform, were commenced under the tutelage of Abdullah Gül, carried out by a working group composed of veteran soldiers, diplomats and scholars, and shared with the public under the name 'TAF-2033 Restructuring', as it was commonly referred to in the press. These transformations, that were started by the General Staff headquarters long before the Defence Reform studies, were collected under a vision document issued by a civilian political power for the first time, before attempts in other developed countries.[19] It is rather interesting that, for the first time, the Presidency prepared a report emphasising the urgency of the TAF's comprehensive transformation and a restructuring process, rendering this process sustainable. In this document, the reforms realised in the CMR were aligned as follows:

- Civilians were appointed to the Secretariat General of the National Security Council (NSC), the number of civil members of the NSC was increased and the coordination and monitoring authorisation of the NSC was transferred to the Vice Prime Ministry.
- The duties and authorities of the General Secretariat of the NSC were restricted, with the number of military staff in the institution diminished.
- New regulations were prepared for the supervision of military expenditures by the Court of Accounts.
- The field of military jurisdiction was restricted.
- The General Staff Headquarters, the Force Commanders and the Gendarmerie General Commander were added among the people who can be judged by the Constitutional Court with the role of Supreme Court.

16 From interview with Captain I.G. conducted in Ankara on 15 April 2015.
17 *Ibid.*
18 For the full text of the speech (in Turkish) see <http://www.tccb.gov.tr/dosyalar/2014-08-22-SavunmaReformu.pdf> (accessed 13 April 2015).
19 Transformation efforts mentioned in countries like the USA and the United Kingdom were designated under names like 'Horizon 2020' and 'Future Force 2020'.

- The possibility of application to jurisdiction about the dismissal decisions was given, except for the promotion acts of the Supreme Military Council and forced retirements due to lack of position.
- Civilian elites undertook a determining role for the preparation of the National Security Policy Document (NSPD).
- New regulations were prepared for utilisation of the TAF for internal security.[20]

Again in this report, it is interesting that clues in the form of principles were shared about the TAF's transformation and restructuring. According to the report, it was advised to establish working groups about the following subjects and to enter into a sustainable transformation process with the information those groups produced:

- Abilities of the military and structure of the force.
- Method of defence.
- Procurement and logistics of defence system.
- Conscription system.
- Education and training in military schools.
- Source allocation and auditing.[21]

General Staff headquarters established a working group from July 2014, with one person from each force command who had an academic background. As a result of the changes in command structures in August 2015, the 'TAF 2033 Vision' gained pace.

The Collapse of the Reformist Sentiment with the 15 July Uprising: Going back to the old *status quo* or transforming into a new military? That's the Question

As will be discussed in Chapter 5 examining the TAF after 15 July, the putschists killed the reformist sentiment within the military that had flourished after 2010. It is no exaggeration to assert that the putschists, many of whom had become part of transformation efforts in the strategic commands in Ankara, hijacked the TAF's willingness and capacity to transform itself from within. This issue will be addressed in the chapter presenting a snapshot of the TAF after the 15 July Uprising.

20 Cumhurbaşkanlığı Savunma Reformu Raporu (Security Reform Report of Turkish Presidency); for the full report, see <http://www.tcbb.gov.tr/dosyalar/2014-08-22-SavunmaReformu.pdf> (accessed 10 December 2014).

21 *Ibid.*

Public Relations: The field best reflecting change in the TAF

Press and public relations are among the most notable fields indicating that the TAF is attempting to transform itself organisationally. An analysis of the TAF's changing communication discourse, therefore, may constitute an example of TAF efforts for adapting to the changing socio-political context in Turkey.

Nuran Yıldız,[22] a professor at the Faculty of Communication at Ankara University, who was also a consultant in 2009-10 for the Chief of General Staff, General İlker Başbuğ, compares communication strategies of the TAF and other modern militaries in detail in her book *Tanks and Words (Tanklar ve Sözcükler)* and criticizes the TAF's traditional communication architecture. Similarly, Özgür Ekşi, in his report 'General Staff headquarters – Press Relations', critically analyses traditional communication methods and practices among the TAF. In both studies, the criticisms are related to the fact that TAF communication with the media is discrete and one-sided, that reactions against the TAF's accreditation practices can be seen in both the media and in the public, that the language the TAF uses for the public is "peremptory and cliquey", and that both the content and tone used in its occasional political statements is not appropriate.

The TAF started to change its communication architecture since 2010 in the light of those criticisms. The 'Strategic Communication' model, which NATO implemented, has been taken as a base in the TAF's transformation of its communication strategy. For this issue, a 2012 article entitled 'Strategic Communication and Its Applicability in the Security Sector', written by the author of this thesis in 2011, calls for a reorganisation of and a change for the traditional communication architecture of the TAF. From 2009 onwards, the following steps have been carried out in the given order for the institutionalisation of that transformation:

- In 2009, the Press of the General Staff and the Branch of Public Relations under the control of a colonel was upgraded to the level of a department, and a general (Brigadier General Metin Gürak) was appointed to its head. The press and public relations unit, which was working within the Secretariat General as a branch directorate, thus became more important.
- Since 2010, the general who is head of the Department of Press and Public Relations (PRD) started going to the General Staff headquarters for a daily presentation. Press and public relations then started to be conceptualised as an important management function at the TGS.
- In 2010, the number of staff in the PRD was increased, and qualified and experienced personnel in the field were appointed.

22 Nuran Yıldız, *Tanklar ve Sözcükler* (Tanks and Words) (Ankara: Alfa Publishing, 2007).

- Beginning from 2012, the duration in office of the head of the department, which was normally one year, was increased to two or three years.
- Since 2012, analyses which examine the positive and negative visibility of the TAF in the media have been conducted every three months.
- In 2013, civilian positions, which can consult the TGS Chief, were opened.
- In 2013, the content of the website www.tsk.tr, which is the main platform utilised by the TAF to inform the public, was revamped.
- In 2014, due to the increasing importance of social media, the Branch of Internet and Social Media was established. The official Facebook account and YouTube channel of the TAF was also started.[23]

In spite of all those steps, the TAF Chief has stated the deficiency in this field felt by the High Command from time to time. For instance, on 23 October 2013, TAF Chief General Necdet Özel told journalist Murat Çelik:

> We need to go through a deep-scaled change in the field of press and public relations. As the armed forces, we will conduct that work with civilian and professional staff from now on. Besides that, we will also appoint a civilian political consultant again. This person may be from political sciences.[24]

Murat Çelik made the following response to these statements:

> The Commander thinks that there are deficiencies and malfunctions in [the] TAF's communication. In fact, this is a familiar argument we always have seen in his predecessors also. The opinion [is formed] that [the] TAF cannot express itself exactly and, therefore, can't communicate with the public properly.[25]

The most apparent example elucidating the TAF's transformation in the field of press and public relations is the press releases it publishes on its official website. When the press releases the TAF published on its website in the last 10 years are analysed, the change in the strategic discourse the TAF uses with respect to the CMR in terms of content, style and tone is easily recognisable.

23 Metin Gürcan, 'Turkish military wages war on Social Media', *Al-Monitor*, 9 March 2015.
24 See <http://www.gazetevatan.com/murat-celik-853407-yazar-yazisi--bir-yemin-etmissiniz-konusamiyorsunuz-/> (accessed 14 April 2018).
25 31 October 2013. 'Necdet Özel: TSK'ya sivil basın sözcüsü geliyor', T24. See <http://t24.com.tr/haber/tskya-sivil-siyasi-danisman-geliyor,242990> (accessed 10 December 2014).

Content analysis of TAF press releases between 2003 and 2014

The main aim of this section is to demonstrate the TAF's ability to adapt and change according to changing socio-political contexts. To do this, the section seeks to carry out an analysis of the content and tone of the 283 press releases published on the official TAF website, www.tsk.tr, between 2003 and 2014. The TAF's efforts to match its strategic discourse to the changing socio-political context, as well as the overall change in its strategic discourse, are clearly visible through this analysis. From this, we can conclude that unlike what the literature assumes, the TAF is not an institution completely immune to change; it is a social organisation that tries to adapt to changing socio-political contexts.

Why are press releases significant?

The press releases at the TAF's official website represent the official stance of the TAF as an institution, and are therefore prepared through a meticulous process with the utmost care at the TGS. The process begins with the Chief of Staff personally commanding the Head of the PRD to start preparing a draft press release about a given issue. In other words, the chief determines when and on what issues press releases are released. Consequently, the Head of the PRD prepares the first draft in a cohort with a team of communication specialists and others.[26] This draft is then taken to different departments that are deemed relevant, to obtain their views and to coordinate their approval. Finally, the draft is taken to the Deputy Chief for coordinated approval. Should the Deputy Chief approve, the final draft is taken to the Chief of the General Staff. After his approval, the text is released. Should the release contain any pictures and or maps/figures, these too are individually scrutinised by the Chief of the General Staff. It is, therefore, possible to claim that each release reflects both the views of the Chief and the TGS. It is important to remember that these statements are the primary means through which the Turkish military informs civilian politics and society at large, and each sentence and every word of these statements are carefully reflected on before being published. Therefore, one could analyse changes in the TAF's strategic discourse through scrutinising the releases made between 2003 and 2014, under generals Hilmi Özkök, Yaşar Büyükanıt, İlker Başbuğ, Işık Koşaner and Necdet Özel using qualitative content analysis.

An example of qualitative content analysis could be useful to better elucidate the reason why this method was chosen. Under Hilmi Özkök, a press release was published on the TAF website as a reaction to the burning of the Turkish flag by protestors at the Nowruz celebrations on 22 March 2005 in Mersin (*Hürriyet*, 'Thirty-two

26 Under General Necdet Özel's term (2011-15), military judges joined this team.

detained…'). The full text of the release, entitled 'Deplorable insults directed at the Turkish flag during Newroz celebrations', is reproduced below:

> Great Turkish Nation
> A group of individuals who have no sense of values, have taken innocent Newroz, the coming of Spring, to such a level of impertinence so as to attack the symbol of the mighty Turkish Nation, the glorious Turkish Flag, each corner of which has been drenched in the blood of our martyrs.
>
> This is a heinous and treacherous act.
>
> Friend and enemies alike should know that neither this Country's Indivisible Unity nor the glorious Turkish Flag as a symbol of this unity will ever be left unprotected. First, the mighty Turkish Nation and, later, the Turkish Armed Forces that has emerged from among this nation, is prepared, just as their ancestors were, to protect and to secure their Country and Flag to their last drop of blood. It [the TAF] has sworn an oath. Those who misinterpret its solemnity, gravity, and patience, those who act under false pretenses, those who dare to test the Turkish Armed Forces' Love of Nation and Flag, would be better advised to first review the pages of history.

Compare this with nine years later, when the full text of the TAF's response to the taking down of a flag within the premises of a military unit in the Diyarbakir Second Air Force Command (*Hürriyet*, 'Turkish authorities confirmed…') is as follows:

> Following the death of an individual who lost his life on the seventh of June 2014 in Lice, Diyarbakır, certain groups who gathered for the funeral held unlawful demonstrations in the Bağlar province county, on the eighth of June, 2014.
>
> The demonstrating groups have used stones to attack a watchtower located at the Northern District of the Second Air Force Command, located near the cemetery where the funeral in question was being held.
>
> Among demonstrators, some of whom were kids, one individual who had masked his face, jumped over the entrance of the security gate and entered the vehicle control area between two fences, climbing onto the flagpole. Despite the task force sent to the area firing two warning shots into the air and verbally cautioning the individual, they nevertheless took the flag down the pole.
>
> Against such actions that we evaluate to be taken for provocative purposes, using children and women, intending to cause civilian deaths, incite mass demonstrations and overall hamper our capacity for toleration, [the] TAF has sought to respond in a calm and collected manner.
>
> The TAF vehemently condemns the act launched by this individual, who has no sense of value, on the symbol of the mighty Turkish Nation, the mark of our independence, the Turkish Flag, each corner of which has been drenched in the blood of our martyrs. The TAF respectfully assures the public that it will closely follow that the perpetrator behind this attack is found and receives the

appropriate punishment and that no person or group can take down the Glorious Turkish Flag from the pole upon which it waves.

Carrying out a qualitative content analysis of these texts, published by the TAF on two separate occasions, we can note certain striking points.

First, the text from 2005 is dominated by very harsh rhetoric and is addressed directly to the perpetrators. Moreover, the press release is jarring despite events taking place outside military premises. These harsh statements sometimes reach a level of insults, with phrases such as "individuals who have no sense of values", "such a level of impertinence so as to attack the symbol of the mighty Turkish Nation" and "this is a heinous and treacherous act". On the other hand, the text moves on to stress the TAF's strength and decisiveness. The message contains a direct warning that the TAF's honourable stance and patience should not be misinterpreted as a sign of weakness. The text ends with a clear threat, making it possible to claim that the main aim of the text is to teach a lesson to its addressees and underline the strength and deterrence capabilities of the TAF. It is also interesting that the last section contains a veiled reference to history. Interestingly, throughout the message the term 'TAF' is continuously deployed as the subject of sentences, without resorting to a passive voice or indirect speech, thus underlining the TAF as a unitary institution.

The first thing that strikes you about the statement from 2014 is its relatively softer tone, despite referring to an incident committed inside military premises. The second important aspect is that the statement is written in a polite tone and is directed not at the perpetrators but at the public as a whole. It is possible to observe that this statement contains no insulting comments or direct threats, and the basic premise of the statement is to inform the public about the details of how the incident took place. The course of the text first provides the reader a brief summary of the event, following with information on how it came about, and ends by first stressing that "civilian citizens could have been harmed" and later underlining the TAF's efforts to stay "calm and collected" against demonstrations. In the last paragraph, the TAF's belief and expectation that the perpetrators will be apprehended and punished in accordance with the appropriate legal processes is stressed, highlighting that the TAF will be monitoring these developments. Contrary to the first statement, this statement refrains from referring to the TAF in the first person singular and instead opts for the first person plural "we", placing it within passive voice and null subject sentences. This preference has the effect of softening the tone of the statement.

Whereas the first statement could be characterised as directly addressed to the perpetrators, with the TAF making harsh, almost insulting remarks in a threatening and decisive message, the second statement presents itself as an informative text that has been written to the public in general, with a softer tone. In the first statement, the "traitors" are directly threatened and are harshly reminded that the "TAF's solemnity, gravity, and patience" shouldn't be tested, whereas in the second statement the TAF complains about the perpetrators of the event to the public and demands from the authorities that the perpetrators are "captured and receive the appropriate punishment", at the same time reminding, in a soft tone, that the TAF will be closely monitoring the process.

As this preliminary example demonstrates, this study seeks to provide an analysis of the TAF's changing strategy, through a comparison of the content, tone and style of 283 press releases published on its official website between 10 January 2003 and 28 June 2014.

The Period of General Hilmi Özkök (2002-06)

The 5 May 2003 statement is one that refutes media stories. One can define this statement as a harsh criticism of media reports and comments regarding the agenda of the NSC meeting, especially the promotion of generals. The statement leaves the impression of threatening the reader and contains sentences such as "TAF's goodwill in not intervening in debates surrounding everyday politics should not be misinterpreted and abused", highlighting first secularism and second democracy. As it also becomes clear from this statement, the TAF was discomforted by the news stories published around the NSC agenda and general-rank appointments, and found it necessary to express this discomfort with a harsh tone, directly addressing the individuals doing the reporting.

The statement from 22 June 2003 regards military matters. This statement contains an evaluation of global, regional and internal threats, explaining that "the time for a cautious restructuring has come", and declaring that the previously 18-month compulsory military service had been lowered to 15 months. The general style of the statement is structured to give the impression that the duration of the service has been shortened due to the TAF's internal demands. In other words, the statement is notable for giving the impression that the compulsory service has been shortened not due to the efforts of the government, but due to TAF demands. While the statement covertly implies that shortening the service period was the TAF's decision, it also excludes any references to the civilian government.

On 14 September 2003, the Chief of Staff released a statement informing the public that he met members of the YÖK on matters related to military education and higher education. As is obvious from the statement, as of September 2003, a Chief of Staff in Turkey is able to hold meetings with members of the YÖK on the education system, and can publish an online public statement about these meetings.

The statement dated 6 November 2003 criticises the fact that the wife of AKP deputy Mustafa Elitaş, who happens to wear a headscarf, had attended the 29 October Republic Day Reception held at the Kayseri Officer's Club. According to the statement, the headscarf ban on military premises was violated. With this statement, TAF sensitivities about secularism and the ban on headscarves in military areas was expressed to the public.

The statement released on 31 December 2003 can also be categorised as refuting news stories. The statement reads:

> On 30 December 2003, certain media organs have published stories indicating that an MP (member of parliament) has expressed discomfort regarding a photo of Supreme Leader Atatürk as a Field Marshall hanging in parliament, the existence of a Parliamentary Guards Unit ensuring the security of the parliament against outside threats as well as its staff's "food prayers" and "Yes sirs"; adding that the civilianization of the parliament should be initiated by the military and referring the matter to the Chief of Staff.

Although not mentioning him by name, the statement strongly criticises Fehmi Hüsrev Kutlu, the AKP MP in question, both for his anti-secularist rhetoric and his antimilitarist stance. In the following sections, Kutlu's anti-secularist statements are harshly criticised, claiming that anti-secularist acts are fuelled by such statements: "Such irresponsible statements clearly prepare the groundwork for the backward incidents we have witnessed near the İstanbul Fatih Mosque, which has upset us as a nation." The following section of the statement criticises comments regarding the Parliamentary Guards Unit and adds:

> The Chief of Staff, who has served in many modern and democratic countries, has visited many more and has personally observed kings and princes dressed in military uniforms, as well as military officers holding ceremonies in parliaments and ensuring the security of these premises from outside threats. However, the Chief of Staff has never met an individual who interprets this issue within the framework of civilianization of the parliament or who expresses discomforts regarding uniforms and soldiers. The Chief of Staff, the Commander of the Turkish Armed Forces – an organization that is an inseparable part of this nation – representing its every aspect and proudly bearing the title "National Army," expresses deep concerns regarding such rhetoric and events.

The 16 March 2004 statement is about media stories that claimed incidents of profiling during implementation of the Security and Public Order Protocol (EMASYA). This statement refutes these stories and explains that such cases of profiling were conducted beyond the knowledge of the General Staff and that it was an error committed by individual staff. "It is true that in every activity carried out by the staff, certain problems may occur due to human error. The disheartening aspect of this story is that such a problem has been associated with an institution and has been generalized to blame and harm the wrong offices and individuals." Then comes the following interesting statement:

> The Turkish Armed Forces, which is the home of many martyrs and veterans who have sacrificed thousands of lives, arms, legs, eyes for the comfort and serenity of the public, will continue to bury all unjust and bitter criticisms in its memory and heart, trusting the final judgment regarding such criticisms to the good sense of our mighty people, while expressing our gratitude to the positive

> criticisms that give us the opportunity to improve, to celebrate our successes and to increase our diligence.

The statement on 6 May 2014 was published with the purpose of communicating concerns that the changes to the Law of the Higher Education Board would damage the secular education system. This statement demonstrates that, as of 2004, the TAF could directly share its concerns with the public about the secular education system being tarnished. The statement reads:

> Institutions and social aspects whose commitment to the fundamental characters of the Republic are beyond doubt, could not be expected to embrace the changes proposed in this draft law. It is our belief that at a time when Turkey already deals with the utmost delicate issues, clearly the changes in this draft would unnecessarily bring about further serious problems and, therefore, the relevant institutions will treat the matter with the necessary caution and good sense, and, furthermore our Mighty Nation will demonstrate the appropriate sensitivity. The Turkish Armed Forces' thoughts and attitude regarding the Republic's character as a democratic, secular, and social state governed by the rule of law is the same as it has always been and will continue to be so. It is unthinkable for anyone to mistake or to doubt the Turkish Armed Forces' thoughts and attitudes on this matter.

The statement dated 25 May 2004 very harshly responds to corruption allegations regarding the Special Forces construction site in Oğulbey, Ankara. It warns the media that the secrecy of the investigation was being violated. As is obvious from the statement, the TAF is capable of criticising corruption allegations published in the media on the basis that the principle of the secrecy of investigation was being contravened.

Media stories and claims that the scope of the Şemdinli investigation would be expanded to include the generals were harshly criticized in a statement dated 6 March 2006.[27] The statement closes with the sentence, "Legal investigations on the conduct of generals and admirals can only be conducted by the General Staff Military Prosecutor, with the order and approval of the Chief of the Staff", which demonstrates how sensitive the TAF was in 2006 regarding news stories and claims about generals.

In the 20 March 2006 statement, the TAF criticises the prosecutors conducting the Şemdinli investigation. The harsh tone of the statement directed at the prosecutors is immediately striking:

> Against these unjust and mistaken allegations directed at the Turkish Armed Forces, firstly those who are constitutionally obliged to do so should immediately

27 Gareth Jenkins, 'Court postpones Semdinli Hearing once again', *Eurasia Daily Monitor*, 5:109 (2008).

> take a stance against the representatives of the twisted mentality behind these attacks, by revealing them to the public without any heed paid to status, office or standing, by disclosing this attack with all its dimensions, and by taking the appropriate legal action. In this framework, we have already taken the necessary initiative with the relevant authorities, regarding the Public Prosecutor who prepared the indictment. The Turkish Armed Forces is wholly aware of these initiatives planned against it and will continue to pursue the matter till the very end through legal means.

In two statements dated 12 July 2006 and 31 July 2006, the TAF strongly reacted to news stories and claims regarding the resignation of generals prior to the Supreme Military Council in August 2006. The 12 July statement reads: "Media outlets have been publishing stories regarding the resignation of a major-general, which contains stories and commentary that is both misleading in referring to unnamed individuals, and is incriminating of certain institutions and individuals." Read alongside the July 31 statements, it becomes clear that, in 2006, the TAF saw the rank of general as an untouchable position, and therefore felt obliged to publish a statement.

General Analysis of the General Hilmi Özkök Period

In terms of the content analysis of press releases, this study defines General Özkök's period as one of active hostility towards elected civilians. The first years of the statements in the Özkök period, between 2003 and 2004, are mainly focused on foreign policy, as this period saw the 2003 Iraq invasion by the US, disagreements in parliament regarding Turkey's role in the war, the Hood event[28] and tensions with the US. It is significant to note that statements regarding counter-terrorism increased in number, especially after 2004, and stressed that the PKK-KADEK was marginalised and passivised, and that this was the TAF fulfilling its duties. The statements made during the Özkök period present a general attitude of bickering with the media and an effort to respond to any media coverage, news story or claim that is interpreted to be about the TAF. It is equally noteworthy that overtly nationalist and grandiloquent expressions are used to complain to the public at large, of individuals, groups or circles that are evaluated to have written stories siding against the TAF. These statements also often underline the strength and resolve of the TAF, constantly providing a covert message that the 'TAF is aware of everything and is closely watching developments'. Again, especially during 2006, expressions such as "[the] TAF is united in one voice and breath. The attempts to Balkanize [the] TAF are in vain" are repeated once every four statements. It is clear to see that all of the statements released in this

28 For news on the Hood Incident, see <http://news.bbc.co.uk/2/hi/middle_east/3067319.stm> (accessed 4 April 2015).

period respond to any negative claim or criticism directed at the TAF in a harsh and reactionary tone. It is again interesting to note that whereas the statements of this period often contain references to secularism and sometimes to democracy, there are almost no references to the rule of law.

The Period of General Yaşar Büyükanıt (2006-08)

The statement dated 2 September 2006 contains the following: "The claims that an extraordinary protocol was carried out during the parade held on August 30th celebrations at the Atatürk Culture Centre, do not represent the truth." This statement is a good example of the continuing reactionary and harsh attitude taken towards the press that continued under Yaşar Büyükanıt. In other words, the news stories and claims regarding the protocol are still evaluated to merit an official statement.

The statement dated 5 September 2006 contains harsh expressions against the rising public sentiment, perhaps expressed for the first time in 30 years of struggle against the PKK, that 'the TAF is incapable'. The statement is intended to answer the claims that there are insufficient provisions of bulletproof vests, and the harsh comments are noteworthy. "The counter-terror units of [the] TAF are provided with steel vests as per the character and risk assessment of the mission. If necessary, [the] TAF already has the resources and the ability to produce steel vests." This statement is supported with emotional expressions, on the one hand, accusing the originators of the claims and, on the other, making an indirect assertion that can be read as: "We don't need bullet proof vests, and if we did, we would produce them ourselves!"

The statement dated 9 October 2006 responds to allegations that had just surfaced about retired non-commissioned officers who had lost their lives in Ankara receiving different protocols from commissioned officers, and that non-commissioned officers were discriminated against. The statement carries a tone that embraces denial and goes on the counter-offensive, expressing certainty in how the claims were not accurate and that the protocols were in line with relevant legislation:

> A certain newspaper released a story on 8 October 2006 that the funeral proceedings of commissioned and non-commissioned officers in Ankara were being held at different mosques. The allegations in this story are wholly untrue. TAF applies the same principles in all the funeral proceedings of our martyrs, from private to general, without any concern for rank or office. The funeral proceedings of martyrs are held in the mosques determined by the Garrison Command, taking into account the wishes of the martyr's family. The Ankara Garrison has determined the Kocatepe Mosque as appropriate to this end.

The statement released on 1 March 2007 protests against news stories that the views expressed by the Chief of Staff, Yaşar Büyükanıt, during his visit to the US were his "personal views" and stresses that the "views of the Chief of Staff are the views of TAF as an institution".

The statement on 24 April 2007 came just before the more well-known statement that is popularly referred to as the 'e-memorandum' and stresses that the Chief of Staff's comments on the presidential elections were being distorted. It is significant that the statement stresses 'moral values' to the press for the first time. The statement is significant for shedding light on the psychological background of the 27 April e-memorandum. The Turkish General Staff published a memorandum on its official website warning of the danger to secularism.[29] It was the harshest statement by the military since the confrontation with the Welfare Party coalition in 1997 – the 28 February intervention. The e-memorandum stated the following:

> It is observed that some circles who have been carrying out endless efforts to disturb fundamental values of the Republic of Turkey, especially secularism, have escalated their efforts recently.... An important portion of these activities was carried out with the permission and the knowledge of administrative authorities, who were supposed to intervene and prevent such incidents, a fact which intensifies the gravity of the matter.[30]

The last two articles of the 27 April e-memorandum once again read as a confrontational declaration:

> In short, anyone who opposes the view that "How happy is he, who says I'm a Turk," expressed by the founder of our Republic, Great Leader Atatürk, is an enemy of the Turkish Republic and will continue to be so. The Turkish Armed Forces continues to preserve its unshakable determination to fully satisfy its clear and legally-prescribed roles to safeguard these qualities, and is certain in its commitment and belief in this determination.

The 29 May 2007 declaration reads as a harsh negation of certain stories in the press. It is interesting that the statements are on counter-terrorism and that for the first time the name of a newspaper, *Sabah*, is included in a press release.

For the first time the pro-Kurdish Peace and Democracy Party (BDP), without mentioning it and referred to as "a party in Diyarbakır", was criticized and its activities were condemned in a statement published on 9 June 2007.

29 *Ibid*, pp.91-93.

30 In a well-known TV news programme called *32. Gun* broadcast on Channel D on 5 May 2009, the former General Staff of the Turkish Armed Forces, Yaşar Büyükanıt, declared that he wrote the text of the e-memorandum himself.

The statement released on 20 June 2007 criticises news stories regarding a visit by the representatives of the Strategic Research Centre (SAREM) working under the General Staff, to a famous meeting organised by the Hudson Institute in the US.[31]

The statement of 21 October 2007 is the first of five consecutive statements regarding the Dağlıca attack.[32] These statements demonstrate that the TAF suffered from a complete communication failure subsequent to such terror operations with heavy losses, while the general tone of the statements is one of denial and counter-offensive.

The reaction against retired TAF staff and members of the press who criticised the TAF following the Dağlıca attacks is indicated in the harsh comments of the 18 November 2007 statement:

> Certain individuals and media organisations are engaging in hateful and spiteful attacks towards [the] TAF in an unthinkable and unacceptable manner. These individuals are using certain information and experiences obtained in active service, to express wholly distorted or unreal claims and behaviors that are insulting, that tarnish relations of inferiority-superiority within the military, and that destroy the sense of confidence placed in officers and commanders. Ostracizing these individuals from [the] TAF is a natural and precautionary measure to protect this institution.

The statement on 22 December 2007 is the first one to inform the public regarding air operations in northern Iraq. This statement stresses determination and deterrence by sharing images of laser-guided missiles that accurately hit PKK targets in northern Iraq.

The 1 January 2008 statement is the first time the PKK was addressed, with the following harsh comments:

> On the other hand, it bears reminding that the collaborators that support the illegal activities of this organization are responsible, in the highest degree, [for] the citizens, soldiers and security forces whose blood has been spilt.

As the criticisms in the press and public persisted, the TAF abandoned the strategy of denial and counter-offensive, and released the most comprehensive and harsh statement about the Dağlıca attack in 19 January 2008. Below is an excerpt:

> The recent period has seen many news stories and comments being released about [the] Dağlıca attack on 21 October 2007 and the incidents that followed, creating an environment of intense debate. The Dağlıca events have been interpreted in

31 'Belated denial by Turkish military on Hudson scenarios', *Today's Zaman*, 21 June 2007.

32 Ali Ersan Erol, 'From Uludere to Daglıca', Research Turkey Forum, 27 June 2012. See <http://researchturkey.org/from-uludere-to-daglica-impotency-of-the-powerful/> (accessed 20 February 2015).

> different ways according to the past knowledge and experiences, inclinations, and missions of individuals or their affiliated institutions. Certain circles, who have made anti-militarism into a tool of economic gain, are distorting the events for their own purposes. Claims that have been put under doubt, prejudice, and vengefulness are being highlighted while overlooking the fact that a heinous attack in Dağlıca has been overcome through the exemplary sacrifice of the lives and blood of 12 sons of this nation.
>
> The TAF has a well-founded tradition of feedback and self-criticism, and will investigate the Dağlıca events in every detail. After a detailed administrative inquiry, taking the testimonies of all the relevant personnel from every rank, [the] TAF has decided to begin legal proceedings regarding eight soldiers. While an administrative inquiry has been carried out, taking the matter to a trial is desirable in terms of the transparency it provides to members of the media and public. The Turkish Armed Forces' attitude here is the clearest indication of its self-confidence and belief in the rule of law. In fact, the public is acutely aware that the Turkish Armed Forces have never had any doubts carrying unlawful activities to the courts. In this sense, it is unthinkable for the Turkish Armed Forces to discriminate against anyone, and the principle of its evaluation is not based on rank or relations, but rather on personal merits and actions.
>
> Every institution may contain individuals who are at fault. However, in order to talk of institutional fault, we would need to wait for the findings of the administrative and/or legal proceedings.
>
> As these facts remain and the legal proceedings are still under way, [th] TAF leaves it to the public to decide whether the people who find in themselves the authority to incriminate institutions and individuals in their comments are, in fact, committed to the principle of the supremacy of the law.
>
> Moreover, those who try to use this and similar incidents to harm the Turkish Armed Forces and to tarnish its determination in fighting terrorism and protecting the fundamental principles of the Turkish Republic, will find their attempts in vain.

The 22 February 2008 statement informs the public about commencing 'Operation Sun' (*Güneş*) (*Reuters*, 'Turkey launches major...'). A lot of visual material regarding the operation was released in the days following this statement. After releasing the images of the air strikes, the TAF implemented a direct media policy for the first time and produced daily press briefs to inform members of the media.

Another harsh statement was released on 4 March 2008, directed against claims and questions in the media and the public regarding 'Why was Operation *Güneş* brought to an end so quickly? Was it brought to an end with pressure from US?' This statement reads:

> The Chief of Staff and other generals have made their public and media statements in the clearest and most comprehensible manner...

> Despite all this good will and transparency, the comments expressed on 4 March 2008 targeting the Turkish Armed Forces from sources outside the media are interpreted as unjust and uncivil attacks on an institution that is putting up the life of its staff in the struggle against terror.
>
> The Turkish Armed Forces would always avoid entering into debates with institutions and individuals in politics; however, for the first time in its 24 year struggle against terrorism, it is being made the target of such meaningless attacks. These attacks hurt the Turkish Armed Forces' resolve in fighting terror more than the traitors.
>
> The Turkish Armed Forces leave it to the immense prudence of the Turkish Nation to evaluate these attacks directed against it.

In a statement released on 17 May 2008, politician Fikri Sağlar's comments regarding the 'Dolmabahçe meeting' were harshly criticised.[33] The Dolmabahçe meeting was held between Prime Minister Tayyip Erdoğan and Chief of Staff Yaşar Büyükanıt. The content of the meeting has remained a secret (*Hürriyet Daily News*, 'Turkish President: Dolmabahçe…'). The press release stated:

> *Vatan*, a newspaper, has featured an immoral and unfounded new story on its coverage on 17 May 2008 that refers to completely unfounded claims by Fikri Sağlam, originally published in another paper.
>
> As the Prime Ministry has already published a press release on the incident, the General Staff doesn't see it necessary to publish a second one.
>
> However, it is certain that the necessary legal action will be taken against those who have carried out this immoral attack.

The statement published on 18 July 2008 also contains resentful expressions. The statement complains of the increasing level of criticism pointed towards the TAF and contains a call on the public, urging them to take the TAF's side on this matter and actively support the TAF:

> The circles which claim to be defenders of freedom and democracy are looking for the next opportunity to draw the Turkish Armed Forces and its members into disputes, and have become focal points damaging Turkey's stability.
>
> No matter the source, one would naturally expect not only the Turkish Armed Forces but also its real owner, the glorious Turkish nation, to demonstrate their legal and democratic reaction against the unlawful attacks directed towards the Turkish Armed Forces through such news stories.

33 See <http://www.gazetevatan.com/genelkurmay-ve-basbakan-a--fikri-saglar-dan-yanit-179010-gundem/ > (accessed 16 February 2015).

The following excerpt from the 31 July 2008 statement is also interesting:

> In an attempt to make personal gains or damage to the Turkish Armed Forces, we have been receiving letters with false names and signatures that supposedly contain incriminating information about our staff or high command. These attempts to damage the reputation of our members are both unethical and criminal.

When the TAF could no longer pursue those who criticize it through legal means, it opted to stress morality in its statements. This is the first example of an increasing tendency to stress morality.

General Analysis of the Period of General Yaşar Büyükanıt

The period of General Büyükanıt may be defined as a period of direct confrontation. Nearly all of the TAF statements between August 2006 and August 2007 are about foreign policy, as this was a quiet period in terms of counter-terror activities. However, parallel to the increasing number of PKK attacks after May 2007, we see an explosion of statements on the side of the TAF. There are eigh press releases on the Dağlıca event alone. It is also important to note the frequent highlighting of deterrence, technology and determination in statements, supported by the use of maps and images, beginning with statements after the December 2007 air operations. Again, it is worth noting that in the same period, images of the air operations were released to the press which were used as a successful way of countering allegations of "failure and insufficiency of the campaign against terror". Criticism directed towards the early termination of Operation *Güneş*, conducted on the border in February 2008, received an especially harsh reaction. Nevertheless, it is striking to note that the harshest criticism was reserved for news stories and claims regarding the *Dolmabahçe* meetings. None of the statements made during the Büyükanıt period highlight democracy or the rule of law. However, when the TAF recognises that it has legal recourse against claims and criticisms brought towards it, the statements begin to highlight morality and ethics. Moreover, with this period, one begins to see the TAF appeal to public opinion and condemn its critics to the judgment of public conscience. One can also draw attention to the obvious use of nationalist themes in the statements. Again, one can note the very harsh statements directed against the PKK or politicians siding with the PKK.

The Period of General İlker Başbuğ (2008-10)

The first statement of the Başbuğ period expresses that the TAF was closely following the process in the aftermath of 18 September 2008, when military personnel were put in custody.

The statement on 8 September 2008 concerns the Aktütün Raid (*Today's Zaman*, 'Security flaws in Aktütün…').

The statement of 8 October 2008, below, is a harsh response to a news story published in *Akit* entitled 'The general who played golf after Aktütün':

> Certain media organizations have recently published news stories regarding the Chief Commander of the Air Forces, General Aydoğan Babaoğlu.
>
> As the Chief of the Air Staff had been in Antalya, until the evening hours, he was not informed of the casualties suffered during the conflict that broke out in the Bayraktepe period on Saturday, 4 October 2008.
>
> It is upsetting and curious that, despite these facts, this incident was used to tarnish the Turkish Armed Forces without confirming the story first.

Six more statements on Aktütün followed this. The tone of the statement on 12 February 2009 is in colloquial language and is far too personal for an institution. This hints that Başbuğ had personally penned the statement. With this statement, one can observe that the TAF's communication strategy was becoming personalised under Başbuğ. For the first time, the first person plural 'we' was used. It is an attempt to both directly inform the public and take sides on a debate. At the same time, it openly challenges its addressees.

As the excerpts below make clear, the TAF had for the first time begun to ask questions and endeavour to justify its position by appealing to emotional statements:

> If the newspaper in question had access to this information before, why has it waited till 11 February 2009? We hope the members of the media and public acting with common sense will answer this question in a sound manner. Furthermore, we believe that the sources who have leaked or produced the story acted in a haste, bankrupt and helpless manner."
>
> Whereas it is a criminal offence to breach article 157 of the 5271 Code of Criminal Procedure in the name of journalism, why is this offence still being committed? Do the people committing this act have no respect, at least, for ethical values?
>
> We would like to thank print media for their prudence and sensitivity, as the original story that first appeared in a newspaper on 11 February 2009 was by-and-large not reprinted on 12 February 2009, with the exception of a few newspapers…
>
> The Turkish Armed Forces is closely and carefully following the developments, and will stand tall in continuing to fulfill its duties with the whole chain of command united and will refrain from being made to serve the interests of those who would like to provoke it. Our biggest strength is our being the Army of the Turkish nation.

The statement on 15 June 2009 included harsh expressions regarding the document entitled 'Action Plan against Fundamentalism' (*Today's Zaman*, 'Col. Çiçek: Document...').

General Analysis of the 2008-10 General İlker Başbuğ Period

In terms of the content analysis of press releases, Başbuğ's period may be defined as a period of indirect confrontation. It can be summarised as one that started with terror events and ended with arrests and court proceedings. The distinctive aspect of the Başbuğ period is the complete personalisation of the TAF's communication strategy due to the 'Başbuğ effect', as indicated by the excerpts above. The statement portrays an attempt by Başbuğ to integrate the institutional identity of the TAF within his person. Additionally, there exists a visible drop in the number of written statements due to Başbuğ's preference for direct speech and permitting interviews with members of the press. The weekly press briefings conducted during the Başbuğ period also influenced this drop. It is also noteworthy that the statements contain an elitist attitude and do not feature an emphasis on democracy or the rule of law.

This period saw an intensification of the conflict with the PKK and a legal investigation that included members of the military. Some of the most frequently used words were 'PKK', 'terrorist organization', 'Air', 'terror' and 'our planes'.

The Period of General Işık Koşaner (2010-11)

The first statement of the Koşaner period is on 17 December 2010 about the Kurdish language debate. The statement, reproduced in its entirety below, demonstrates that the TAF had been involved on one side in the debate on the Kurdish language.

> The Turkish Republic – the greatest achievement and gift of the Great Leader Atatürk to the Turkish people – is founded on a democratic structure and a legally-sound basis, where popular sovereignty exists and notions such as "unitary state" and "nation-state" are a fundamental aspect of the founding philosophy. Such principles are the basis of the Turkish Republic's achievements today.
>
> The third Article, of the first four entrenched articles of the Constitution contains the declaration that: "The State of Turkey, with its territory and nation, is an indivisible entity. Its language is Turkish."
>
> A common language, culture, and ideal are the most essential elements of nationhood. History presents us with many heartbreaking examples of the results of forgoing a common language.
>
> We are watching with concern, as the founding philosophy of our Republic is brought to a point of being fundamentally changed, through certain recent public debates over "our language."

> The Turkish Armed Forces has always had a role and will continue to play a role in protecting the nation-state, the unitary state and secular state also defined in our Constitution under the title of protecting the independence and unity of the State, the Turkish nation, the Republic, and democracy.

For the first time, in a statement dated 24 January 2011, the principle of the rule of law was emphasised, adding that the case was being followed in silence. Again, it is worth mentioning that the statements below constitute a first in the TAF's attitude towards legal proceedings involving its staff:

> As an institution committed to democracy, rule of law, and constitutional values, the Turkish Armed Forces is following the trial process in patience, silence and calm, despite suggestions to the contrary, and in this framework expresses its belief in the independence and impartiality of the judiciary and its expectation that this process will reveal the truth.

The statement on 7 February 2011 can be interpreted as the TAF signalling that it wants to stay out of politics:

> On 6 February 2011, several media outlets have featured some evaluations by certain leading politicians of two large political parties, concerning the Turkish Armed Forces.
>
> It is saddening to watch these political leaders try to draw the Turkish Armed Forces into ordinary politics, especially as the very same politicians take every opportunity to argue that the Turkish Armed Forces ought to stay out of politics.
>
> In a period when the sources of instability are intensifying around us with no end in sight and the Turkish Armed Forces are doing their utmost to fulfill their security duties in the best manner, it would benefit neither the country nor any political view, to use the Turkish Armed Forces in matters of political debate.
>
> Politicians who would like to win public support for their views would be expected to be more prudent in their statements regarding the Turkish Armed Forces and not pursue politics through the military.

The 6 April 2011 statement complains to the public regarding a court decision not to release the individuals under custody in the Balyoz case.[34] This marks another first for the TAF as it published the full decision of the court on its website alongside its own statement as an appeal to public opinion:

34 Gareth Jenkins, 'The Balyoz Retrial and the Changing Politics of Turkish Justice', *The Turkey Analyst*, 25 June 2014. See <http://www.turkeyanalyst.org/publications/turkey-analyst-articles/item/331-the-balyoz-retrial-and-the-changing-politics-of-turkish-justice.html> (accessed 20 February 2015).

> The legal proceedings regarding a planning seminar held during 5-7 March 2003 in the First Army General Command, as well as the attempts to link this seminar with a plan to allegedly stage a coup, are still underway.
>
> On the fifth of April, 2011, the appeals of 163 military staff still under custody, to be released for a trial without arrest, have been refused for a second time by the appeals court ruling for the continuation of their arrest.
>
> The Turkish Armed Forces have especially avoided statements and actions that may amount to intervening in the legal process, but have made several statements that refrained from effecting the trial, informing the relevant authorities, explaining beyond any doubt, the content of the seminar, how it was conducted, what it included, who it involved through what chain of command. Similar issues are also clearly present in the report prepared by the expert, who was chosen by the public prosecutor.
>
> While these are the facts, it is difficult to understand why 163 retired and serving members of the Turkish Armed Forces are still under arrest.
>
> Therefore, we publish the decision to continue the arrest of these individuals for the purposes of informing the public.

The statement on 26 July 2011 is about the wave of terror that started with the Silvan attack on 14 July 2011, resulting in the deaths of 13 members of the military.

Analysis of the General Işık Koşaner Period

General Koşaner's period, which only lasted a year, can be defined as one of strained harmony, and witnessed the fewest number of statements. Two issues ought to be underlined in these statements: first, the majority of statements concern legal proceedings the staff have been involved in (five of the 13 statements are on this); second, for the first time, we see an emphasis on democracy and the rule of law.

The Period of General Necdet Özel (2011-14)

General Özel's period is one of delicate harmony. The statement on 20 October 2011 regarding the deaths of 24 members of the military (*Today's Zaman*, 'PKK kills 24 security...') during a conflict in Çukurca uses, for the first time, emotional phrases alongside an emphasis on determination and deterrence:

> Members of [the] TAF will continue to serve their country, in a manner that represents our ancestors, under the testimony of our glorious martyrs who have entrusted these lands to our protection...

> We pay our condolences first to the families of our martyrs, then to our Glorious Nation as a whole. May our martyrs' souls rest in peace. We also wish the injured a quick recovery.

The statement dated 2 November 2011 contains the first use of a photograph. The photograph depicts TAF activities following the Van earthquake.

The statement dated 24 October 2011 emphasises the TAF's wish to stay out of everyday debates: "The Turkish Armed Forces have embraced the principle of staying out of everyday debates and, instead, only releasing informative statements to the public, on issues directly relating to them."

The 3 May 2012 statement contains interesting phrases responding to media criticism of the TAF that is evaluated as an attempt to tarnish the TAF:

> Recently, the frequent circulation of news stories, claims, and comments targeting the Turkish Armed Forces, an institution that is wholly focused on its mission, its duties prescribed by legislation and that is fuelled by the drive to fulfill its role of serving its state and Glorious Nation, has come to our attention.
>
> We are sad to observe that these provocative claims and comments that exceed the boundaries of constructive criticism are attempts to harm the morale and motivation of the selfless and heroic members of the Turkish Armed Forces and tarnish their efforts to fulfill their duties in the best manner.
>
> It is regrettable that certain authors, speakers and professional organizations are abusing the freedom of expression and freedom of the press to shamelessly ridicule both our Eternal Commander in Chief, Veteran Mustafa Kemal Atatürk and other military individuals who have made their mark in history, despite their military status, to harm the superiority-inferiority relations, the sense of discipline inside our Army (thought to be one of the most disciplined armies in the world) and to provoke the valuable members of the Turkish Armed Forces through written and spoken statements.
>
> The selfless and heroic members of the Turkish Armed Forces, from the most junior ranks to the most senior general/admiral, will continue to serve our country and the Glorious Nation, without giving in to provocations, in a rock solid unity, and very closely committed to the basic characteristics of our Constitution and our parliamentary democratic system.

The statement on 4 May 2012 is about the improvements made to the employment terms and conditions of NCOs, which is the first comprehensive statement regarding NCOs. With this statement, the TAF can be seen as trying to communicate the message that 'Yes, there are problems regarding NCOs, however, we are trying to address them'.

It is interesting to note the polite tone and emphasis on the rule of law in the 5 September 2012 statement concerning the Balyoz case:

> The tenth High Criminal Court of İstanbul has ruled to convict 324 active duty and retired members of [the] TAF in the trial publicly known as the Balyoz Case.
>
> Taking into account the well-being of the Turkish Republic, the virtue of living under the rule of law and our responsibilities towards our Glorious Nation, we are closely watching the investigations and legal proceedings regarding the members of [the] TAF, with patience, fortitude, cool and calm always avoiding actions that may give cause to misunderstandings.
>
> We deeply share and feel the sadness experienced both by our comrades with whom we have served side by side for years and by their dear family members.
>
> As [the] TAF, we have believed and continue to believe that the trial in question will be resolved equitably, with a definite ruling, as the principles of the rule of law and fair trial necessitate.

Following the first statement on 6 February 2013, a second statement was released responding harshly to stories in nationalist newspapers, which claimed that the "TAF [were] experiencing shortcomings in their chain of command due to the officers that have left as part of the trial process".

The 27 December 2013 statement contains the following excerpt regarding the trial of TAF members:

> Recently, media organizations have featured certain comments and texts concerning the Turkish Armed Forces within the context of a high profile investigation that has grabbed considerable public attention.
>
> The Turkish Armed Forces fulfills the duties and responsibilities ascribed to them in the Constitution and Legislation with the spirit of serving the Turkish Nation in the highest manner outside any political opinion or organization.
>
> In executing its tasks, the Turkish Armed Forces take the principles of constitutional state, the rule of law, and democratic society as its foundation.
>
> In this context, TAF have paid extra care to act within the framework of respecting the law and the independence of the judiciary, and have first and foremost sought to protect the institutional identity and integrity of the Turkish Armed Forces during the investigation and legal proceedings concerning their acting and retired members.
>
> The legal processes concerning the Turkish Armed Forces have been followed according to the duties and responsibilities arising from the relevant legislation and any activity or practice with dubious legal has been reported to the highest decision making bodies and most senior authorities of the state.
>
> The Turkish Armed Forces do not want to be involved in political debates of any sort. However, they will continue to follow closely the developments in matters that concern their institutional identity and the legal standing of their members in accordance with the principles of the rule of law and equity.

The statement on 6 January 2014 contains the excerpt below, and highlights respect for the rule of law in cases concerning the trial of TAF staff:

> As our 27 December 2013 press release indicated, the Turkish Armed Forces have acted in a manner that is in accordance with the necessities of the rule of law, in response to the trial and investigation processes conducted on some of their members. They have refrained from making statements that could be characterized as attempting to influence the trial and have solely shared their views and thoughts with the relevant authorities, [have] presented suggestions, awaited results and as a result [have] not resorted to any legal means thus far.
>
> However, as a result of our institutional and humane responsibilities, we have first released an informative press statement and, on the same day, filed an official criminal complaint about the recent expressions of a figure of political importance in the media.
>
> The aim of this criminal complaint is to investigate the claims being made, to bring clarity, and to alleviate certain grievances in public conscience, reinstating the belief in justice and protecting the rights, dignity and honor of the members of the Turkish Armed Forces.

The statement on 13 February 2014 contained information regarding an NCO seminar.

The statement dated 16 March 2014 emphasised the TAF's attempt to stay out of politics and included the following:

> We are sadly witnessing recent attempts to use various incidents to draw the Turkish Armed Forces into political debates before the local elections.
>
> As we have declared many times, the Turkish Armed Forces is the military of the State of the Republic of Turkey. They receive their support, morale and resources from the Noble Turkish Nation and its glorious history.
>
> The Turkish Armed Forces are of the opinion that they ought to stay out of political debates for the well-being of our State, as well as the peace and security of our Glorious Nation.
>
> The Turkish Armed Forces are determined to uphold their stance of rejecting antidemocratic procedures and practices, respecting human rights, believing in the rule of law and committed to the principle of "a democratic, secular and social state governed by rule of law" indicated in our Constitution.
>
> The dear members of the Turkish Armed Forces are aware of their duties, acting in a sensible, calm manner that avoids all kinds of provocation and political debates, and are continuing to serve our Glorious Nation. They have lost nothing of their power and might.
>
> Moreover, speculative news stories are being featured in certain media outlets about the shooting down of a Syrian aircraft that violated our airspace, despite warnings issued from the authorities in [the] Turkish and Syrian Armed Forces.

The statement issued on 26 March 2014 once again draws attention to the TAF's respect for the rule of law:

> The Turkish Armed Forces are determined in upholding their stance of rejecting antidemocratic procedures and practices, respecting human rights, believing in the rule of law and committed to the principle of "a democratic, secular and social state governed by rule of law" indicated in our Constitution.

Analysis of the General Necdet Özel Period:

The initial stages of the Özel period, between August 2011 and December 2012, are primarily about fighting terrorism. On the other hand, it is interesting to observe the polite tone and emphasis on the rule of law in statements concerning the trial process of TAF staff. It is possible to note a general softening of tone in statements during the Özel period. This period is marked by an informative approach, with statements that sound more polite compared to the elitist tone and self-righteous attitude adopted in earlier statements. Among all the statements analysed in this study, 13 emphasised the rule of law and eight were released in the Özel period.

Analysing the wording of the statements in the Özel period, one can observe that the words 'Türk', 'Chief of Staff', 'air', 'Gendarmerie', "amount' and 'Özel' are among the most frequently occurring. Moreover, we see a relatively greater number and distribution of frequently occurring words in this period.

Overall evaluation of the 283 statements released from 2003-14

In every statement, it is possible to see elements of the character traits of the serving Chief of Staff at the time. For example, fierce criticisms during General Özkök's period of **active hostility** lost their power in General Büyükanıt's period of **direct confrontation**, yet the tone and content of the press releases in General Büyükanıt's period were more aggressive when compared with the following periods. The personalised communication approach in General Başbuğ's **indirect confrontation** period was clearly reflected in the tone and the choice of words of the statements released; the increasing emphasis on the rule of law in the period of General Özel's **delicate harmony** directly corresponds with the character traits of the serving Chief of Staff. In this sense, it is possible to articulate that the TAF's communication strategy is far from being institutionalised and is under the control of the serving Chief of Staff at the time. This presents an obstacle against the development of an institutional stability in the construction of TAF communication strategy. In short, one can observe that the TAF's media and public relations strategy is still under a centrist attitude, just like the 'reserved domain' under the discretion of the Chief of Staff.

On the other hand, as the press releases have been presented consecutively from 2003 to 2014, a general pattern has emerged. One can characterise this pattern in four stages:

- First Stage: Denial of allegations in the media with an elitist attitude and direct threats.
- Second Stage: Counter-offensive and indirect threats.
- Third Stage: Attempt to inform the public with a softer tone compared to early releases, with emphasis on ethics and morality, publicly complaining of those working against the TAF.
- Fourth Stage: Increasing emphasis on democracy and the rule of law, public complaining, a visible softening of tone and communicating sensitivities in a polite manner.

To summarise the general patterns in the statements, there has been:

- A shift in rhetoric from a harsher tone to a softer one.
- An increasing emphasis on democracy and the rule of law.
- A general attitude of being tired of the constant harassment and inquisitiveness of the media and a related desire to stay away from everyday politics.
- A shift from an attitude of demanding to bring authorities to account, to one of informing the public.
- An increasing use of ethic and moral themes.
- A softer tone on statements regarding the Kurdish issue.
- A changing discourse on the fight against terror.
- An increasing tendency to opt for visual material alongside written texts.

In the light of the findings presented above, it is possible to suggest that, between 2004 and 2014, the TAF adapted their strategic narratives and the way they presented these according to the changing socio-political context in Turkey. Namely, the TAF incrementally changed the nature of its strategic discourse from a hard tone to a soft one, and its communication strategy first from direct to indirect confrontation, then to strained harmony and lastly to delicate harmony.

Internationalisation: Driver of the TAF's transformation as a security organisation

Another good example indicating the TAF's efforts to change and, as a security actor, to adapt to new situations in the last decade is its increasing internationalisation efforts. It is evident that, in the last decade, the TAF made deliberate attempts to increase interactions with other modern militaries of the world and sought to assume a more active role on the international scene. Colonel M., being at the end of his three-year mission with NATO, explains this situation:

> The TAF have started to attach more importance to their abroad mission posts from the beginning of [the] 2000s, and, in this frame, they increased the number of personnel cadres for positions abroad. Thanks to that, the visibility of the Turkish Army in NATO missions and exercises such as the ISAF in Afghanistan, as well as Kosovo and Bosnia missions in the Balkans, has increased perceptibly. In addition, I observe that the Turkish military follows the transformation process of NATO and takes important lessons from NATO's experience to be used for its own structural transformation.[35]

Major M., who is currently serving as an adviser to one of NATO's top commanders in Brussels, agrees with the observation of Lieutenant Colonel M. According to Major M., who carries out a crucial consultancy mission at NATO headquarters, one of the fundamental reasons underlying the increase in the number of NATO positions for he TAF and the enforcement of its relations with NATO, is to closely follow NATO's transformation process and to use it for its own transformation process.[36]

> Major M. continues:
> NATO is really vital for us, because it is the only international institution in which we are equal arbiters. We cannot determine the priorities of NATO, but we can block any issue we wish. This is the political part. To me, the military part seems more important. Since NATO is an alliance, it is not a one-to-one fitting system for a country in terms of TTP [tactics, techniques, procedures] but there is much that can be transferred. Most basically, NATO has also an audit and evaluation system, but it does that in accordance with the manuals of force standards. We have lots of instruction documents. In this respect, there are things we are trying to copy from NATO units and military branches and paste to our own procedures within [the] TAF. The job has also a balance section. What is that? In short, everything should not be NATO. We have geopolitical realities, obligations, and opportunities. Other alternatives should always be ready in our hand. The common production of 10 countries called Smart Defense is a good thing, but we must have capacity at the national level. We may not be using that immediately because of prioritizing economic considerations, but we have to have that capacity. At least, we have to have such a long-term plan.
>
> Colonel F. emphasises that the most important thing his commanders wanted him to do was to closely study how NATO actualised the transformation process as a security actor. He continues:
>
> I am one of the people who believes that the experience with NATO will contribute a lot to [the] TAF in the transformation issue. From this point of view,

35 From interview with Colonel M. conducted in İstanbul on 31 May 2015.
36 From interview with Major M. conducted via e-mail on 17-19 April 2015.

Table 2. Summary of the Content Analysis of TGS Press Releases

Name of Chief	Period	Number of Press Releases	Characteristics
Hilmi Özkök	2002-06 **Active Hostility**	**68**	• Direct confrontation with the elected civilians in foreign policy preferences and the counter-terror strategic planning • Bickering with media and efforts to fiercely respond to any media coverage that the TGS considered negative • Emphasis on secular characteristics of the state and nationalist references • Stress on the TAF's strength and deterrence with an elitist intonation • Harsh and reactionary tone to any issue implying that the TAF is not united • No reference to democracy and rule of law
Yaşar Büyükanıt	2006-08 **Direct Confrontation**	**91**	• Direct confrontation with the government on foreign policy choices (particularly 2006-07) • Parallel to the increasing number of PKK attacks like Dağlıca, harsh tone towards critiques • Emphasis on deterrence, determination and use of technology, and first ever use of visual material in press releases • Emphasis on moral principles to counter allegations about TAF preferences and behaviours • No reference to democracy and rule of law
İlker Başbuğ	2008-10 **Indirect Confrontation**	**28**	• Started with terror events and ended with custodies and court proceedings • Personalization of the TAF's communication strategy (use of questions and emotional phrases in the releases) • Attempts to use media outlets and NGOs to influence public opinion • Excessive elitist tone in statements • No reference to democracy and rule of law
Işık Koşaner	2010-11 **Strained Harmony**	**13**	• Attempts to explain legal proceedings against TAF personnel • No counter-attacks or defensive mood in releases • The first emphasis on democracy and the TAF's submission to democratic norms
Necdet Özel	2011-14 **Delicate Harmony**	**83**	• Attempts to explain terror attacks • Polite and softer tone in releases • More provision of information in releases • The first emphasis on rule of law and continuation of emphasis on democracy • No counter-attacks or self-righteous attitude adopted in earlier releases
Total		**283**	

> the methods NATO applies in the institutional transformation and the lessons learned will be very beneficial for the transformation of TAF as well.[37]

It is possible to say that NATO's Rapid Deployable Corps-Turkey (NRDC-T), the TAF's corps allocated to NATO, undertakes the driving role for transport of the institutional transformation experience of NATO to the TAF. A general says:

> One of the most important issues I had concentrated on during my post at this corps was to closely observe the institutional transformation of NATO as a security actor in line with the changing security environment and menaces, and to try to nationalize that experience. Within this scope, we have organized many courses, workshops, seminars and conferences. For example, in my opinion, the "Hybrid Warfare" concept NATO is trying to develop, in fact, fits Turkey's security environment. Therefore, I think that NATO will contribute a lot to us and so it should be followed closely.[38]

Captain Y., who is working in the unit related to the mission abroad at the TGS, states:

> TGS has increased its positions abroad by 30 percent between 2005 and 2015. There is a great increase in the young rank officers going to the 6-month long temporary missions at a lot of international settings, primarily Afghanistan, Bosnia, Kosovo, and Iraq. NCOs abroad were also increased. [The] TAF ensured this increase by both increasing NATO cadres allocated for [the] TAF and also the military attaché and other international observatory mission positions. I think that [the] TAF's increasing their visibility in the international environment is a conscious policy. Because [the] TAF recognized the rapid change of the security environment both in Turkey and also in the world, and attempted to adapt to this change by trying to gain expertise through these missions.[39]

The TAF's graduate-level education abroad

The TAF's process of becoming international is not limited to NATO posts. In the last decade, it has sent nearly 300 officers abroad for post-graduate education, primarily to the US and other Western countries.

The number in the period between 2010 and 2015 is nearly five times that of the previous period from 1990-2000. For example, the TAF started sending successful

37 From interview with Colonel F. via telephone, conducted in January 2015.
38 From interview with the general conducted in İstanbul on 21 May 2015.
39 From interview with Captain Y. conducted in Ankara on 13 December 2014.

lieutenants from the war academies to privileged Western universities for joint PhD educations for the first time in 2010. At the time of writing, almost 60 lieutenants are continuing their joint PhD educations in the US within the frame of this programme. Major H., a PhD candidate in the US, indicates:

> The number of TAF sent to the prestigious universities abroad for post-graduate education has started increasing since 2010. I consider the main reason for that as the need for qualified experts especially in the General Staff and the Force Command headquarters providing scholarly insights for decision making processes and for the effort to increase the quality of the military education.[40]

Captain B, who received his master's education on operational research at the US Naval Postgraduate School in Monterey, California, obtaining his PhD at Bilkent University in Ankara, asserts:

> The TAF is aware of the need for academic personnel both for scholarly decision making support and also for the increase in the quality of education at the military education institutions. Therefore, they attach importance to graduate-level education. But, the TAF is not yet at [the] required level in terms of intellectual capital, particularly at the decision makers' level. In my opinion this situation, in turn, is the greatest obstacle to [the] TAF's transformation. Especially the number of qualified personnel who can be employed is a minute amount. Every qualified personnel is planning to leave [the] TAF.

Major M., who received a master's degree in security studies in the US, agrees with Captain B, underlining the following points:

> Even though [the] TAF increases the number of personnel they send abroad for academic education, I still think that there are structural obstacles in front of their transformation towards an intellectual Army. Probably, the most primary obstacle of those is, in turn, the resistance of TAF generals regarding this issue. For generals, scientific support for the decisions they make is yet a new concept. Hence, the top-level decision makers in [the] TAF are very reluctant to use the intellectual expertise which has started to accumulate in [the] TAF at the post-graduate level. In this situation, the intellectual energy that [the] TAF tries to develop with several altruisms flows out in streams like water, [and] a very small portion of that energy can be used for the benefit of the institution.[41]

40 From interview with Major H. via e-mail conducted on 17 April 2015.
41 From interview conducted on 12 June 2015 in Ankara.

General T. explains why TAF generals, those now in the most important decision-making posts, do not back the scientific decision support:

> This reluctance is somehow related to institutional culture and the codes of the profession for being a general. Most of the generals and especially the ones in the land forces underestimate scientific decision support before issuing an executive order, that is, a decision. In my opinion, this reluctance has two reasons: the first is that the generals consider referring to the scientific decision support as a weakness since they over-relate the administration of an order with their own personalities, and the other is their distant and, to some extent, undermining attitude to scientific support for decision making which stemmed from their occupational backgrounds.

The TAF as a Changing Social Institution before 15 July

The empowerment of gender-friendly policies in the TAF

One of the most obvious examples showing that the TAF has changed over the last 15 years as a social institution is the rise in the number of female personnel and the adoption of more gender-friendly policies by the TAF in recent years.

The TAF made officer cadres available for females by accepting young girls into its war academies in 1992, and staff colleges in early 2000s, and the first female graduates have began to work in all three forces of the military in 1996. According to TGS data, as of November 2014 there were 1,350 female officers in the TAF, some 3.3% of the total number of officers.[42] The TGS objective was to increase this ratio to 5% by 2017; it did not, however, achieve this.[43] The TAF currently employs 96 female colonels, 140 female lieutenant colonels and 360 majors. The military started to recruit female NCOs in 2012. Contractual recruitments of female NCOs largely began in the posts of the Gendarmerie Command;[44] since then, the Army, Navy and Air Force commands have also initiated these recruitments. The TGS wants to further increase the number of female NCOs that today stands at 843 (0.9%). The goal was to increase this ratio to 5% by 2018, meaning the employment of an additional 4,000 female NCOs. To achieve this aim, the military tried to hold more female-friendly recruitment and personnel policies, but again to no avail.

E.O., a female producer working in the media-communication department of the TGS for 15 years, relates the newly emerged vigorous policies about female staff

42 From interview with Captain Y. conducted in January 2015.

43 *Ibid.*

44 For more information, see http://ilan.memurlar.net/ilan/27292 (accessed 13 December 2014).

pursued by the military to rising initial recruitments and the change in their institutional culture.[45] She says:

> I have been working at the General Staff for about 15 years. Especially for this decade, there is a considerable rise in the number of female personnel working at this highest of headquarters. Particularly in the areas in which female presence is actually crucial, the number of female personnel has almost become the same with male personnel.[46]

In 2014, the documentary *Light of Hope*, directed by E.O., was selected for the Jury's Award at the 24th International Defense Film Festival in Rome (*Sabah*, 'Savunma film festivalinden…'). The documentary was about Şenay Haydar, Turkey's first female Gendarmerie commander and senior NCO sergeant, against the backdrop of gender discrimination and violence against women in the small Anatolian town of Mesudiye in Ordu province.[47] She places particular emphasis on the fact that General Necdet Özel, the then-Chief of the TGS, demanded that Şenay Haydar's story about the prevention of violence against women to be shot as a documentary. The idea was widely developed in the TGS.

Haydar worked meticulously with local officials and families. She has been credited with eradicating violence against women among the 40,000 residents of Mesudiye. During the interview, E.O. stressed that the high command has been overwhelmed with Haydar's accomplishments in a small Anatolian town where traditional norms have prevailed:

> NCO Şenay's success, as much as this is due to [her own accomplishments], is also the success of the commanders who have believed in her. Appointing a female NCO as a representative of law and order to a town with 40,000 residents is truly a revolution for the Turkish military.[48]

Over the last five years, there have been wide-ranging changes in the personnel policy of the TAF, with the increased number of female officers and NCOs and, as was the case with Haydar, in assigning female personnel to active field positions instead of just to administrative positions at headquarters.

In an interview, Şenay Haydar says the following:

> I always wanted to be a field commander who makes decisions, instead of working at a desk. I was encouraged by the Gendarmerie General Command.

45 From interview conducted in November 2014 in Ankara.
46 *Ibid.*
47 Metin Gürcan, 'Splitting Gendarmerie from Turkish military: Reform or Bad Timing?', *Al Monitor*, 3 November 2014.
48 Metin Gürcan, 'Turkish NCO fight for their rights', *Al-Monitor*, 12 December 2014.

> When the results [of my employment] turned out to be positive, scores of female officers and NCOs followed in my footsteps.[49]

The deputy commander of the Gendarmerie School in Beytepe, Ankara, notes that, in October 2014 alone, 67 female NCOs were assigned to Gendarmerie Command field posts after completing basic training; another 90 female NCOs and 30 officers were to follow.[50] Captain Hülya Ercan, a teacher of the UH-60 Sikorsky helicopter at Ankara's Gendarmerie Aviation School, is the first female Gendarmerie pilot in Turkey. She states:

> My husband is a captain. I raised my daughters Bensu and Beren without giving up my profession. I actually flew until the third month of my pregnancy with my younger daughter. There are both difficult and good sides of being a woman at [tha] TAF. But I carry out a duty as an operational helicopter pilot, and my commanders absolutely trust me, regardless of my sex. Previously, female officers were not assigned to operational duties like piloting. However, common sense has recently changed, and now you can see female officers at any degree and any place of [the] TAF.[51]

Female colonels usually work at headquarters, while majors are generally unit commanders. Staff Major B. is the commander of the biggest transport fleet of the Air Force Command in Ankara and is also the first female fleet commander. There is an apparent increase of Turkish female staff officers in vital posts in the headquarters of the TAF and NATO. For example, naval staff officer Major Y. was Turkey's current naval attaché in London at the time of writing. Within six or seven years, she may well become Turkey's first female admiral. In an email, she states that she wants to return home after excelling in her current position, and also wants to command a frigate before becoming an admiral.[52]

A colonel from the personnel department of the TGS answered the question of what is behind the Turkish military's decision to increase the number of female officers and NCOs with the following remarks:

> There are two practical reasons and one ideological one. The first practical reason is the relative reduction in the number of personnel called up for compulsory military service; as the Turkish military is moving toward becoming a professional entity, increasing the number of females in the Army makes up for this loss in manpower. The second practical reason is a need for female personnel because

49 From telephone interview conducted on 5 December 2014 in Ankara.
50 From interview conducted on 30 November 2014 in Ankara.
51 From interview conducted on 28 November 2014 in Ankara.
52 Metin Gürcan, 'Turkey's women expand role in the military', *Al-Monitor*, 1 December 2014.

> of a change in security issues the Turkish military is dealing with, notably, the shift from rural to urban areas of the PKK violence in the southeast of Turkey. In addition, there is a need for female personnel in international missions that the Turkish Armed Forces are undertaking in Afghanistan, Kosovo, and Bosnia, among others. To have ranking female officers provides significant advantages in communicating with the local population, especially with women, and carrying out civil-military cooperation projects effectively in the health care and education sectors. Thus, the Turkish Army is determined to establish more effective links with local populations in low-intensity conflict areas and peace support missions. The ideological reason for increasing the number of females in the Turkish military is that the latter has always been the leading cause of modernization and westernization of the Republic. The military sees itself as a pioneer in all transformation processes in society, and more females and an increase in the visibility of their presence in the Turkish military deliver crucial messages – especially to the rural population – on equality for women and a more active participation of women in society.[53]

The Turkish military wants the public to be aware of the rise of female power in military positions. Thus, it brings female staff to the fore in most of the public information activities. For instance, the special news series entitled *Female Power at TAF*, which was produced by Ahu Özyurt, a news editor at CNNTürk, aired in the summer of 2014 and attracted quite an amount of attention.[54] The episodes of this series were serialised as news in the *Hürriyet* newspaper ('*Zor görevlerin kadınları*').

NCOs vs the High Command

The case of NCOs' struggle for their rights and status within the military is another example of how some civil society actors, who gained the power to create public pressure and to set the agenda by taking the support of the civil society and the media, can influence TAF decision-making mechanisms. As of May 2015, 96,228 NCOs served in the Army, Navy, Air Force and Gendarmerie Command, in addition to there being around 100,000 retired NCOs. When taking serving and retired NCOs and their families into account, there are some 800,000 people.[55] In the military, NCOs are intermediary leaders who serve as a bridge between conscripts and officers. Technical and maintenance personnel and logistics experts are all NCOs. NCOs like to describe

53 From interview conducted on 29 November 2014 in Ankara.
54 To watch a chapter of the series see <http://www.cnnturk.com/video/turkiye/tskda-kadin-gucu342> (accessed 16 July 2015).
55 Metin Gürcan, 'Turkish NCOs fight for their rights', *Al-Monitor*, 12 December 2014.

themselves as follows: "Take the NCOs out, and the battalion will starve, planes won't fly, ships won't sail, and tanks will break down."

Tension between the High Command and NCOs first became public in 2012 and centred on two main issues: first, the personal rights of serving NCOs, their status in the TAF and claims that NCOs are discriminated against and treated unfairly; and second, complaints of low pensions among retired NCOs. In 2012, the public and media began to notice that NCOs were engaged in unconventional protest actions unheard of in the Turkish military. The Turkish Retired Non-Commissioned Officers Association (TEMAD) organised protests and became the voice of NCOs. What did NCOs want? As noted above, serving NCOs point to status problems and call for an end to unfair treatment. For example, they are unhappy that their rank is displayed on their arms and not on their shoulders like officers, and that there are variations in campaign ribbons and badges. Furthermore, NCOs are critical of a lack of living quarters, and of tougher and longer working conditions with lower compensation when compared with officers. Retired NCOs have financial complaints. When in service, an NCO is paid US $1,600 monthly, and when retired receives a US $900 monthly pension. NCOs state that they must still work after retirement and that they struggle to make ends meet, even after toiling in state service for 30 years.

NCOs represented by TEMAD engaged in unusual forms of protests, including a two-week fast against discrimination and injustice within the military. One retired NCO, for instance, walked 600km (372 miles) to protest at injustice. NCOs wore black on certain days of the month, demonstrated in front of the parliament and appeared on TV shows and news reports. Nobody expected Turkish soldiers to resort to such actions, but their protests worked and attracted media and public attention.

How did the TAF react to these unexpected protests? The command's response underwent three distinct phases, which can be summarised as the strategy of silence, the strategy of denial and counter-accusation, and the strategy of engagement and rehabilitation.

The first phase: strategy of silence

Founded in 1984, TEMAD[56] initially acted on the views of the TAF and remained a low-profile non-governmental organisation for years. However, TEMAD began to draw the attention of both the media and the public by means of unusual protests against personal rights problems of retired and serving NCOs, against their statute in the TAF, and discrimination and maltreatment against them in the TAF. By May 2014, there were about 72,000 serving NCOs and around 100,000 retired ones as members of TEMAD. When considered together with their families, NCOs are a well-organised community consisting of approximately 800,000 people. The TAF

56 For more information, see the official website of TEMAD <www.temad.org>

at first ignored these protests. Perhaps the most interesting of these actions was an almost two-week death fast by Ahmet Keser, TEMAD Chairperson, and the executive board members, as a stand against discrimination and injustice against NCOs (*OdaTv*, '*Ölüm orucuna başlayacaklar*'). The TAF did not deal with the executives of the TEMAD, which began to draw attention through its actions and statements, and silently watched developments unfold. However, in addition to frequent news reports about NCOs in the written and visual press, continuous articles written by Umut Talu from *Habertürk*, Tunca Bengin from *Milliyet* and Cüneyt Özdemir from the *Radikal*[57] raised awareness on the subject, making the issue a significant one.

It is clearly observed that the TAF preferred not to deal with and to ignore discussions about the personal rights and statute of retired and serving NCOs, and to do nothing about claims and comments about themselves until 2012.

The second phase: denial and counter-accusation

The issue of retired and serving NCOs became a heated one on the public agenda from 2012 onwards. The TAF felt obliged to do something on this issue because of the discussions and claims gradually arousing the attention of the public and media. It primarily issued a written press statement about the issue, which was accepted as a memorandum by TEMAD members:

> It is regretfully watched that the members of the Association of the Retired Non-Commissioned Officers of Turkey has misinformed the public by making idle statements about our non-commissioned officers, which constitute a highly significant force of the Turkish Armed Forces, at certain media organs, and that they have acted outside of the limits of the aim and the acting area of the association so as to provoke our serving staff.
>
> The division of tasks in charge of the statute law is constructed with such statutes as officer, non-commissioned officer, civil servant, specialist gendarme, master sergeant, contractual private soldier, petty officer, and private. All the responsibilities and authorities are accordingly distributed. According to the required criteria, a demand on one of these statutes is a person's own preference. Similar structures are also available at official and private institutions and organizations. In this respect, it is against the nature of military and civil institutions and organizations to describe some rights and authorities given to personnel according to their incomparable statutes, duties and responsibilities as inequality or injustice.

57 For an archive of news and journal articles published about NCOs in the TAF, see <http://www.temad.org/basin.php?k=4> (accessed 24 July 2014).

In this statement, the TAF emphasised that TEMAD had attempted to destroy the TAF's hierarchical order, chain of command and discipline, and had provoked serving NCOs to disobey their commanders. the TAF vehemently condemned such 'treacherous'. They pointed out that being an NCO was one's personal choice, as NCOs knew the statutes from the very beginning of their service. In short, the TAF argued that one accepts the statute of an NCO at the starting point when that person voluntarily commences his/her occupation by knowing what an NCO means in the TAF. Therefore, the problem was not the issue of the statutes of NCOs in the TAF, but the issue of damaging the discipline and chain of command of the TAF by those who voluntarily preferred to be an NCO. This ontological approach by the TAF, that 'there is not a problem of NCO rights and statutes, but the only problem is of breaking the hierarchy and discipline in the TAF by one's using his/her NCO status', continued through 2012 and 2013.

The TAF kept emphasising the same argument in disavowals sent to newspaper columnists having written about NCO rights. For instance, in a disavowal sent to Tunca Bengin, it was underlined that there was not a problem with the personal rights of NCOs in the TAF, only in the intentional commentaries of malicious people who informed the public and the media with unrealistic claims so that they could create the perception that there was a problem in the TAF, and that such news and commentaries aimed at the TAF were not beneficial to the state. In addition, some claims were reflected in the press that the General Staff barred internet access to Umur Talu, who, as a *Habertürk* columnist, frequently wrote about problems experienced by NCOs.

While the TAF's communication strategy can be summarised as denial and counter-accusation, the struggle for NCOs' personal rights, whose lead was taken by TEMAD, aroused a great deal of social media interest. On 17 April 2012, a Facebook group named '*Bu Kadarına da Pes*' (That's Enough) reached 220,000 followers in a short period of time, while the '*Astsubay*' (NCO) hashtag on Twitter contained hundreds of thousands of messages.[58]

In the meantime, retired NCOs from TEMAD held a number of meetings to draw attention to their problems, stating that they had not yet managed to attract enough public support for their cause. Retired NCOs issued strong complaints about their pensions, claiming that they were unfairly lower than those of retired commissioned officers (*Today's Zaman*, 'Retired NCOs seek…'). Retired NCOs also supported their colleagues on active duty. Keser announced his association's support for the protest, and said that it was a grassroots movement and that approximately 200,000 NCOs were organised through social media websites like Facebook and Twitter.

58 See <https://twitter.com/hashtag/assubaylar?src=hash> (accessed 12 June 2015).

The third phase: strategy of engagement and rehabilitation

By the middle of 2013, the TAF ended the second phase and was obliged to step back on this subject, which had gained a rising public awareness with a great deal of press visibility. The TAF first contacted TEMAD, whose executive board members were invited to the General Staff to receive their opinions, and many structural reforms to the TAF were made to enhance the personal rights and statutes of NCOs. The most important of these reforms were the foundation of the Office of the General Staff NCO and the Force NCO offices, which began in 2013.

This system was actually founded in the Air and Naval Forces in 2012 and was carried over into the Land Forces Command. Under the new system, NCOs are assigned as representatives of the Chief of the General Staff to work under the Force Commanders. For example, three non-commissioned officers in the Land Forces, who are directly under the command of the Land Forces Commander, regularly visit troops and have meetings with NCOs of these troops. These NCOs listen to their colleagues' problems and hopes, and report these directly to the Land Forces Commander.

These 'Ombudsman' NCOs, or master sergeants, visit every single troop they are attached to and arrange meetings with all the non-commissioned officers. The aim is to reach all the NCOs in Turkey. In these meetings, not only NCOs' complaints are received, but also their proposals. It is possible for serving NCOs to communicate with these master sergeants, who provide personal contact information to their colleagues to share their grievances. These NCOs of the General Staff have begun to find solutions to the problems they delivered to their force commanders. However, the solutions are still very limited since the majority of NCOs' problems are ones such as personal rights, which can only be sorted out with government decrees. They have already sorted out some issues with the initiative of their commanders.[59]

A master sergeant NCO makes the following points on this matter:

> The struggle of the NCOs serving in [the] TAF for the enhancement of their statutes in the institution and their personal rights is actually important in terms of proving that the institutional culture of [the] TAF can be changed by civil society taking the support of the public and the media. Just as in any modern world military, subordinates' struggle for legal rights is a tough experience due to the hierarchy and discipline at [the] TAF. Legal struggles by especially inferior ranks are not regarded well in a hierarchical institution like a military. However, the Office of the General Staff NCO that I am in charge of at the moment is a good example showing that [the] TAF and their command echelon can stretch and that things which seem unusual and impossible at first view can be institutionalized in line with the requirements. My duty is to deliver general problems and solution suggestions of all the NCOs serving [in the] TAF to the Chief of

59 Zeynep Gürcanlı, 'TSK'da astsubay devrimi (Turkish)', *Hürriyet*, 30 March 2013.

> the General Staff and to relay notifications of the command echelon to NCO fellows without any intermediary. That is my duty, to be like a bridge. I have meeting arrangements with the Chief of the General Staff every week, and I regularly visit all the troops [of the] TAF every month and listen to problems of NCO fellows.[60]

To highlight the TAF's progress regarding NCOs, journalist Balçiçek İlter's interview with General Yaşar Güler, the Deputy Chief of the TGS, on 12 December 2013 presents significant information. To İlter's question about whether or not the NCOs were correct in their demands, General Güler answers: "I can say neither they are right, nor they are not…" İlter says General Güler understands the troubles of the NCOs and acknowledges them to be right. Yet his following words from the interview with İlter are also noteworthy:

> Can a statute of an employee bringing tea in an office be equal to the statute of a general manager? Everything has a hierarchy, a gradation. Well, if someone misconducts his position in that hierarchy, we already spare no effort to do our best about that person like conducting an investigation. All investigations are conducted with an utmost detail and precision. It is not as in the old times, everyone is able to demand justice.

According to İlter, General Güler seemed sincere in his statements, although he emphasises hierarchy and rigid organisational discipline in his words:

> While NCOs are waiting for the enhancement of their personal rights, they have also demanded the names and signs of their ranks. They complain that the names and signs of their ranks are not much different from the ones of privates performing their military service … [and want them to] be carried just like officers' shoulder marks instead of [on] upper arms.

Interestingly, the military organised and hosted the International Senior NCOs' Symposium 2014 in June of that year in İstanbul and İzmir. For TAF NCOs, organising such an activity academically for the first time had an enormous importance. The symposium was considered to contribute a lot to increasing the efficiency of NCOs around the world.[61] Similarly, an NCOs' Seminar was organised in the headquarters of the General Staff in February 2014, attended by senior NCOs serving in the Land, Navy and Air Forces, Gendarmerie and the coast guard. At the seminar, personnel specialized in their fields spoke to those in attendance. The seminar was regarded

60 From interview conducted on 21 May 2014 in Ankara.
61 For the advertisement see <http://www.hvkk.tsk.tr/EN/IcerikDetay.aspx?ID=171> (accessed 28 July 2014).

as profoundly beneficial in terms of spreading the culture of joint-ness, providing occupational development, strengthening communication among the forces and interactive consultation, and it concluded with closing remarks by the Deputy Chief of the General Staff .The final report of the seminar was presented to General Necdet Özel, the Chief of the General Staff.

Civilian activists vs the High Command on allegations about violations of soldiers' rights

Another case indicating that the TAF are able to change their strategic preferences and attitudes in the face of civil society movements supported by the public and the media concerns the matter of soldier suicides and violation of soldier rights since 2012.

Firstly, it is noteworthy to acknowledge one significant item of the public agenda in the period October-December 2011. Uğur Kantar, a soldier serving in northern Cyprus, received imprisonment in a room as a result of a disciplinary punishment, then went into a coma due to maltreatment by soldiers in charge of his imprisonment.[62]. After 80 days, he passed away at the military hospital in Ankara on 12 October 2011. This case brought the claims of maltreatment in the military before the media and the public.

The EU 2013 Turkey Progress Report notes:

> However, instances of ill treatment of conscripts have been continued to be reported and efforts are needed to address this issue. The Human Rights Inquiry Committee of the Parliament opened a monitoring dossier on ill-treatment during military service.[63]

In the quarterly media analysis report for the period of October-December 2011 prepared by the Office of Public Information of the General Staff in 2012, the issue of violation of soldier rights was at the top of the list of issues affecting media visibility of the TAF most negatively. General Necdet Özel, Chief of the General Staff, instructed the subject to be dealt with in detail, and a working group was gathered in coordination with the Personnel Division of the General Staff.

The author, who joined the first coordinated meeting of this working group in 2012 as the representative of the Public Information, observed that the Personnel

62 Soldier Uğur Kantar had been sentenced to seven days in the 'discipline dormitory' known as 'disko' during his compulsory military service in northern Cyprus. Uğur Kantar went into a coma due to torture inflicted on him and was hospitalised to the military hospital GATA in Ankara Province on 25 July 2011.

63 European Union, Turkey 2013 Progress Report, 16 October 2013. For the full report see <http://ec.europa.eu/enlargement/pdf/key_documents/2013/package/tr_rapport_2013_en.pdf> (accessed 12 December 2014).

Directorate (J1) did not attach importance to the issue, and reported this observation in writing to the deputy Chief of the General Staff. The J1 then restarted its personnel management work with the command of the Chief of the General Staff.

In April 2012, the Soldier Rights Platform,[64] a civil society platform based in İstanbul, prepared a report entitled 'Violation of Soldier Rights during Conscription' on the grounds of applications made on the website www.askerhaklari.com between April 2011 and April 2012. According to this report, 432 applications were made on the website in a year; the most common issues were 'suffering an affront' and 'exposure to physical violence'. As also stated in the report, 32 soldiers committed suicide over those 12 months.[65]

Upon the continuation of discussions about the violation of soldier rights and soldier suicides as an agenda item, the working group was extended to include legal experts from the Judicial Advisory of the General Staff and specialist scholars from the Department of War Psychiatry of the GATA. Thus, a further inclusive transformation period had begun. In this regard, military discipline rooms known as 'disko'[66] to the public were removed, and all offences, even those committed during conscription, started to be brought to justice and the courts. The services of Psychological Counselling and Guidance became widespread, a psychological support system named '*Can Dost*'[67] was established and a complaint line was activated through which any military personnel or their family could directly connect to the General Staff in order to convey their problems.

In the meantime, Ayhan Aslan and Fırat Keser, two Turkish soldiers serving as military guards in northern Cyprus at the time of Kantar's death, were sentenced to life imprisonment on 8 July 2012 by the Turkish Kyrenia Military Court in Cyprus. Such a severe penalty is a first, even for the TAF. However, news stories about violation of soldier rights continued to be published throughout 2012.[68]

Between 2012 and 2014, the issues of the violation of soldier rights and soldier suicides preserved their status in the public agenda. On this issue, Major T. states the following:

> In our quarterly analyses between the years 2012 and 2014, the category of the violation of soldier rights and soldier suicides remained among [the] top three in the rank of negative subjects about [the] TAF available in the media. News and columns written in the period of October-November-December of 2012

64 For the official website of the platform see <http://www.askerhaklari.com> (accessed 19 July 2015).
65 See <http://www.askerhaklari.com/genel/bin-100-asker-ihtihar-etti> (accessed 19 July 2015).
66 Disko is the abbreviation of Disciplinary Dorm (*Disiplin KOğuşu*) in Turkish.
67 '*Can Dost*' is a kind of buddy system in which a soldier with a problem is matched with another soldier, who is expected to closely monitor his buddy's behaviours.
68 Lale Kemal, 'Grave violation of soldier rights', *Today's Zaman*, 26 December 2012.

> especially constituted almost 60 percent of the negative visibility of [the] TAF. It is obvious that the public image of [the] TAF was extensively worn [down] in recent times due to this issue. We, as communication professionals, always explained [to] the Personnel Division the importance of this issue since late 2011. They were firstly reluctant to deal with it; however, General Necdet Özel, the Chief of the General Staff, and General Hulusi Akar, the Deputy Chief, extensively thought on this and commenced a variety of new projects for the solutions. I can easily say that the public and media pressures on this topic had a major part in enabling the issue first to be perceived as a problem area in [the] TAF and then enforced [the] TAF to feel requisite to take action for the solution.[69]

High Command vs the headscarf: and the winner is the headscarf

The headscarf had long been a symbol of the power struggle in Turkey between secular elites labelled as the 'centre' and a conservative segment labelled as the 'periphery'. The recent easing of this struggle and the trend toward normalisation is attributed mainly to the Turkish military, which is still the most noticeable representative of the centre and softened its firm stance against headscarves. In a decision dated 20 March 2015 by the High Military Court, the TAF cancelled their rigid practice of prohibiting first-degree relatives (spouse, children and parents) of military personnel from entering military buildings, living quarters, military clubs and social facilities wearing headscarves.

The Higher Military Court's ruling concerns hundreds of thousands of female relatives of military personnel. Infantry NCO Hakan Kayabaşı charged the Ministry of National Defence after refusing his application for a military ID card allowing his wife to enter military housing because she wore a headscarf in her photo on the application form. In its defence, the Ministry surprised everyone by maintaining the ban on headscarves and asking that the case be dismissed. But the court found Kayabaşı's argument justified and the ban to be "against human rights and equality", and ended the practice of denying ID cards to female relatives whose photographs contained headscarves.

Kayabaşı's lawyer, Mehmet Erkan Akkuş, emphasised that the ruling would set a precedent, telling the daily *Hürriyet*: "With this ruling, from now on relatives of TAF personnel with headscarves will not have any problems entering military clubs, social facilities, and military premises. This important decision concerns about 1 million people." With this ruling, the TAF has untangled itself from an issue that seriously lowered its prestige with the public and what were seen as uncompromising and unfair practices that at times violated human rights and the law.

69 From interview conducted in Ankara on 21 January 2015.

One should note that in Turkey, where all male citizens must serve 12 months in the armed forces, the military is an important component of social life. For years, the public severely criticised the ban on conservative Turkish mothers attending their sons' important oath-taking ceremonies in military bases. The mothers, wives or sisters of tens of thousands of soldiers could not see their sons, husbands or brothers being sworn in as a soldier because of the inflexible military rule posted at entrances of military areas: 'No entry with headscarves.'

The AKP has been adept at making political ammunition of the strict rule of the TAF since the party was voted into power in 2002. For example, in 2007, General Aslan Güner, the Deputy Chief of the General Staff, walked out of the protocol line-up while welcoming President Abdullah Gül at the airport to avoid shaking the hand of his wife, Hayrünnisa Gül, who wore a headscarf. The incident made headlines. In 2010, Emine Erdoğan, the wife of Prime Minister Tayyip Erdoğan, went to the GATA Hospital in Ankara to visit a patient and was denied entry because she wore a headscarf, which became another major scandal in the media.

In yet another striking example of the Turkish military's inflexible hard-line attitude to the headscarf, all the officers at the 29 October Republic Day reception in 2010 walked out in protest when guests with headscarves arrived. It was later understood the mass walkout was an order from the High Command that had been interpreted as 'walk out when you see a headscarf'.

The inconsistencies in the military's criteria for headwear at times led to humorous consequences. For example, the attire rule for entry of civilians to military premises that read 'If a woman who comes to a military facility agrees to knot her headscarf under her jaw, she will be allowed entry' became the subject of sarcastic jokes that the TGS categorised traditional headscarves as not threatening to national security but classed conservative headscarves as threatening. This ban applied to Turkish citizens without exception but not to foreign military personnel and their relatives, which was seen as ridiculous.

What caused the Turkish military's ironclad attitude toward headscarves? In an interview, Zeki Sarıgil, an associate professor at Bilkent University, known for his studies on military-society issues, said: "The Turkish military is truly sensitive to uncompromising secularism of absolute separation of what is religious and what belongs to the state."[70] Sarıgil stated that the Turkish military always saw itself as the guardian of uncompromising secularism and couldn't have handled the headscarf issue otherwise. He added: "We can say that we are undergoing an important transformation in civilian-military relations and also in [the] TAF's own organizational culture. One aspect of this change is the softening of [the] TAF's approach to secularism and religious freedoms."

70 Interviews conducted in Ankara with Zeki Sarıgil at Bilkent University on 12 November 2014.

One should not deny the role of the gradual moderation over the headscarf issue in the country as a whole. Sarıgil notes:

> The military as a part of this society feels the need to keep in step with the normalization in society. To preserve its legitimacy, an institution tries to be in harmony with its environment. Until now, academics like myself have focused on the changes in civilian-military relations. Certainly these changes have affected the internal dynamics, opinions, values and tendencies of the military. But there is not much academic study of this headdress change in [the] TAF, which still remains a black box.[71]

Another significant development in the easing of the military rules on appearances ought to be mentioned here. After a decision by the High Command dated 30 March 2015, bearded men can now enter military clubs and social facilities.

In summary, it is right to say that the military is undergoing changes parallel to the changes in society. One should note that, starting with the institutional changes after the softening of headscarf bans in public domains such as parliament (*Aljazeera*, 'Turkish women MPs…'), university campuses (*Daily Sabah*, 'Turkey lifts controversial…'), hospitals, schools (Akyol, 2013) and courts (*The Express Tribune*, 'Headscarf-wearing judge…'), the headscarf issue is no longer at the centre of contentious politics. Such a major change in the civilian domain helps one contextualise better the shifting attitude of the military towards headscarfs.

Officership as a changing profession

In this section, after general assessments of the interviews conducted about changes in the profession of officership, the characteristics of every rank, starting from general down to the lieutenant, will be shared, based on interviews conducted with TAF personnel of that rank.

In his interview, Colonel Z.,[72] who is a 1974 graduate of the Staff College, begins by saying that in his time "officership was seen as chivalry", and continues:

> The officer style had never changed between the years 1970 and 1990. The officers of this period were the very soldiers who were deeply faithful to the Turkish military, disciplined, sacrificed their selves and their families for the military, and performed every order in obedience without questioning. Disobedience to the order of the commander and questioning the order were deemed to be the greatest shame. It cannot be conceived otherwise in the Turkish military,

71 *Ibid.*
72 Interview conducted in Akçay/Balıkesir Military Resort on 2 August 2014.

> everybody respected his superiors and esteemed them. But after [the] 90s, first of all, the education in the Staff College was spoiled. Of course, when the terrorism also began, the officers of the new period got away from the chivalry. The millennium lieutenants of the 2000s are, in turn, much more individualistic. They are questioning every order and they are chasing how they can escape [from orders], or how they can slack. The minds of those young officers do not work like ours.[73]

When he was asked to say the three words he remembered when he heard the word 'officer', Colonel Z. said "motherland, honour and duty". When asked to elaborate on those concepts, he stated that he understood unitary and national state from the concept of motherland, and perceived the fundamental concept of officership and being a soldier when honour was spoken of; by duty, he emphasised that the TAF came even before his personal interests and his family.

Lieutenant A.,[74] with just one year in that rank, emphasizes that he perceives officership as a profession. He is not a graduate of the war academy and is called a 'contractor officer', being a graduate of the Department of Mathematics, Faculty of Arts and Sciences, İstanbul University. He prepared for the public teacher acceptance exams called KPSS (Public Personnel Selection Examination) for almost two years, but did not succeed in the exam and steered for officership instead. He emphasizes with sorrow that he is worried about his becoming an infantry lieutenant and wants to move to one of the branches of artillery or air defence classes since he is a mathematics graduate; however, this is not possible.

Lieutenant A. continues:

> In fact, I am not that much worried about my being an infantry lieutenant. I am aware that a tough professional life awaits me and I will be stationed in three or four year periods. But I think the career opportunities offered by [the] TAF are not offered by any other state institution. I started attending the English course even at this stage. My aim is to take my English to a good level and to go abroad for a course or a mission.

When asked to say three words he remembers when he hears the word 'officer' his answer was "profession, career opportunities and commitment". He states that he preferred officership himself, although he could work at other jobs and, therefore, he perceives it as a profession. Again, he emphasises that the most important factor for his preference to be an officer was the career opportunities the TAF offers, and underlines that he has to serve with commitment in order to reach his goals.

As can be seen in these examples, the perceptions of officership of the retired Colonel Z., who stepped into the life of a soldier with his family's blessing at the age

73 *Ibid.*
74 Interview conducted in Infantry School, Tuzla, İstanbul on 5 November 2014.

of 13, and infantry school graduate Lieutenant A., who could not find a job for two years after graduation and therefore opted for officership, are apparently different.

According to Major N.,[75] who has been a teacher at Kuleli Military High School and Land War Academy for 15 years, perceptions about the profession of officership started to change in the 2000s. Until 20 years ago, although the quality of education was much better in military schools compared to their civilian counterparts, the standard of education in civilian schools developed rapidly during the 2000s, overtaking that in military schools. Major N. stresses that parallel to the increasing diversity of education, development of the private sector, increase in opportunities abroad, increase in the possibilities of scholarship and education support funding, education opportunities have rapidly been improving in civilian life. He states that successful youngsters and their families now aim for civilian education opportunities, and only if no result comes out of those do they go for officership, which they perceive as a "guaranteed public profession". Major N. says:

> I think that the military education system fell behind the civilian [one] between the years 2000 and 2014. Those 15 years slipped away from our hands. I remember, in the year 2000 a delegation from the Robert College in İstanbul visited the Kuleli Military High School to see the school's internal computer network system which they greatly admired. Now we are very behind in education at the high school and undergraduate levels. Having such a situation, the successful children first try the opportunities in the civilian life and go ahead for the officership as the last remedy. Before [the] 2000s, the Army Academy based in Ankara was accepting students up to the 30,000th in the University Entrance Exam, but as of 2014, the academy accepted up to [the] 150,000th student, a fact showing the decreasing quality of the students in the war academies. Before 2000, there were youngsters among the ones taking the university entrance examination who gave up medical faculties, engineering faculties and law faculties of prestigious universities in Turkey [to be] accepted to the War Academies, nowadays the students who are accepted to faculties of arts and sciences or faculties of education of average universities are coming to the War Academies. I know many students [who came] to the War Academies although they were in the top 1,000 rank between the years 1994 and 2000. But now, we are delighted if a student preferring the War Academies is in [the] top 100,000.

A general[76] also agrees with Major N.'s opinions. The general says: "The most important thing distinguishing between us, the old officers, and the youngsters is the time management." He elaborates on this as follows:

75 Interview conducted in Ankara on 14 November 2014.
76 Interview conducted in İstanbul on 30 March 2015.

> We, old officers, are too busy with the daily tasks [to] such an extent that we cannot find the opportunity to educate ourselves and learn new things. Tasks never end. Your own career and family are always the second priority, that is, for 24 hours seven days [a week] you are busy with your job. Therefore, you never have time to update yourself. But young officers of this time are not the same. They are much more skilled than us in terms of time management. They ... can allocate time for themselves and their personal development. They put [in] effort for that. I witness lots of young officers who have hobbies, a pursuit or who are interested in fields other than the officership. Frankly, I like this situation.

According to Captain Y., working at the General Staff headquarters, the increased diversity of officer resources is the most important reason for the change of officer profile. Captain Y. says that while there were only two types of officer in [the] TAF a decade ago (military high school/war academy graduates and civilian high school/war academy graduates), there are now seven types: military high school/war academy graduates, civilian high school/war academy graduates, civilian university graduates (contracted officers), foreign war academy graduates (from the US and South Korea), officers with NCO background and officers with contracted specialist background. The ratio of war academy graduates, the backbone of the officer corps, has drastically decreased from 90% to 60% over five years, and since 2004 there has been a sharp rise in the ratios of contracted officers and NCO-background officers. Captain Y added that 10 years ago, eight years were needed (four years in military high school and another four in military academy) to become a lieutenant, but now for a civilian university graduate it takes only 10 months to commence service as a lieutenant in the Turkish military.[77]

Generalship as a profession

As of May 2014, 343 generals were serving in the TAF. Issues about the profession of generalship elicited from the statements of seven generals (four from the Army, one from the Gendarmerie, one from the Air Force and one from the Navy) interviewed for this thesis are listed below.

In the Turkish military, on average, the position of brigadier general is held by officers between the ages of 48 and 52, major general between 52 and 55, lieutenant general between 55 and 59, four-star general between 59 and 62, and force commander between 65 and 67. It is important to note that there is a difference of 18 years between the average age of brigadier generals and four-star generals, even though both are generals. In this sense, one may talk about generational differences among Turkish generals. Among those who are all graduates of the War Academy, 10% (about 35)

77 From interview with Captain Y., conducted in Ankara on 23 May 2015.

have master's degrees and about 5% have doctorate degrees. Regarding the status of their parents, about 15-20% are sons of primary school graduates (sons of low-degree public servants, workers and farmers); 50-60% are sons of secondary school/high school graduates (low-degree public servants and tradesmen); 10% are sons of bureaucrats, academicians and large-scale tradesmen; and 10% are sons of soldiers (officers and sergeants).

General M. from Ankara emphasises the following about the histories of families of generals:

> I can say that only one-fifth of the families of the generals are from the urban, educated, and intellectual class. Most of the generals are poor fellow Anatolian children coming from villages. In this respect, generalship is a somehow a process of becoming elite.

Another general defines generalship not as a "profession" but as "a lifestyle in which everything is exaggerated":

> Learning is too weak after becoming a general. A general cannot admit his mistake even if he has made a mistake since if he does, his honor of being a commander, which is united with his personality, will be hurt and he cannot bear it. He tries not to have a critical attitude in his relations with his superiors. He does not want to be seen as opposing his commander when seen from outside. A general does not want a "rebellious inferior," which would make him a permanent troublemaker, which he deems a source of problems. The characteristic of searching for mistakes is very dominant among generals, and he has become a general for that reason. Therefore, he is so unsympathetic to both his personnel and to his family. He always thinks that everybody is wrong and he is right. He assumes and approves that it is the most essential part of his job to find and correct mistakes, which he always believes to exist.
>
> Since being very hardworking is praised in his group, he has to be hardworking and seem to be busy all the time. Always being busy with something is the aim of life. Always being available when the commander calls, staying for extra work, going to his unit even on the weekends, the message that "this herd belongs to me." He is in the state of being busy with his unit as much as a shepherd cares about his herd. A general's attachment to [the] TAF is very strong, but the feeling that the unit he is ordering and commanding belongs to himself is stronger. He has no chance to educate himself and learn new things since he is very busy. He is busy with his job 24 hours a day, seven days a week. He has never got time to educate and improve himself.

Nearly 80% of the wives of generals are employed. Nearly 20% of generals speak at least one foreign language (mostly English), but in the generalship foreign languages are forgotten in time (especially in the Army and Gendarmerie, as there is not a huge need for foreign languages in many positions). All of the generals interviewed expressed regret that they could not retain foreign language skills that they had spent so much effort to acquire. However, in parallel with the increase in TAF missions abroad, the generals also stated in the interviews that foreign language has now become a very important criterion for appointments and promotions. Foreign language proficiency has become a compulsory preference due to more international missions and NATO positions. At least 60% of generals have been on a mission abroad for about two or three years (as an attaché or in a permanent mission). All interviewees emphasise that military status and prestige come into prominence in generals' motivation, and it is observed that none of them speak of economic motivation.

General A., interviewed in Ankara, explains this situation as follows:

> For a general, the single most important thing in life is his name and reputation in the institution. Generals know each other very closely without paying regard to force differences. Think of a competition starting from the rank of major, which continues for more than 30 years. The professional careers of the generals are much more important than the other factors such as wife, children, and health. This gives a general both the feeling of being elected and the feeling of commitment. If you ask me who a general is, I would tell you "a committed and highly motivated person." At the same time, this motivation creates an expectation for the next rank. Owing to [this], a general finds the energy in himself to strive for his job and his unit 24 hours a day and seven days a week.

Generals working in the Army and the Gendarmerie have had internal security missions in counter-terrorism, but these missions are less in the Air Forces and do not exist in the Navy. Two generals interviewed in İstanbul indicated that generals are more like doves, but others are more like hawks since they have not seen the region and do not know the public so closely.

The generals, except one of them in the Air Force, perceive NATO positively and think that it increases TAF power and effectiveness in war. A general from İstanbul explains his opinions about NATO as follows:

> NATO is the only place we come face-to-face with modern armies around the world. I consider NATO to be the most important anchor connecting us to the West and the western security system. In fact, I have observed that 90 percent of all generals perceive NATO positively. All of them have a deep understanding of what NATO adds to the Turkish military. Perhaps, 20 percent might oppose NATO for ideological reasons. But this stays only in the verbal realm, and he does not show his opposition in his behaviors.

General A. explains the effects of lawsuit processes such as *Balyoz* and *Ergenekon* on the profession of generalship:

> [The] TAF passed the democracy and sincerity test in the lawsuits involving soldiers. Almost 30 percent of the generals went to the prosecution office and testified in one way or another. Almost 20 percent were arrested, tens of them went to prison. I think this process created much trauma and emotional breakdowns among generals. All the generals tasted the end of impunity and what the law can do with a sour experience. Since then, the emphasis of law is the priority among generals. Especially in the political field, nobody takes the risk of stepping outside of legal bounds. Because now they know very well what will happen to them.
>
> Moreover, in military lawsuits, we could not "play the victim" in any way; therefore, a great opportunity was lost. The best example is Başbuğ. He could not manage the process well. For this reason, we are still an elite mass disconnected from the public. Also, I think that these prosecution and lawsuit processes have caused a paranoia of "not talking to civilians" for some generals. In my opinion, this paranoia has been very harmful for [the] TAF because it has disconnected some generals from the societal change and the civilian one.

Another general continues:

> Although in the 1980s, around 30 percent of generals were rightist and 70 percent were leftist, I think this process of prosecution and lawsuit increased the ratio of rightist generals. Now, the transition to the right is ongoing and, in my opinion, I can say that right and left are balanced.
>
> Although nearly half of the generals in the TAF are still oversensitive about secularism, I can say with sincere comfort that they now think that secularism is not in danger, but it is hard for me to say that they think the same way for the nation-state and the indivisibility of the state. But, while conceding all this, the TAF still needs a mental revolution. The most important factor for this revolution are a "qualified command rank" and effective leadership. On the other side, the acting staff and the technology are sufficient for that job. We were shaken by the fact that we were lagging behind. At this point, getting support from civilians is certainly needed.

Another general, who underlines that cohort spirit (*devre ruhu*) is still very important among the generals, says:

> The cohort spirit is still an important means of peer pressure both in general promotions and also in appointments. At the same time, it is a very crucial self-control mechanism which forces a general to get on well with his friends.

Regarding the level of religiosity among the generals, General S. emphasises:

> A general never externalizes his piety or cannot do that. Therefore, it is almost impossible to measure a general's level of religiosity. In my opinion, 55 percent to 60 percent of generals try to fast, even if they do not fast for the whole period [of Ramadan]. But let us underline that fasting is not a criterion for piety in [the] TAF. Fasting is usually an act of tradition and habit. The percentage of the ones performing prayer, in my opinion, never goes above five percent.

According to General M., there is a great amount of support for the EU among generals, to ensure the success of Turkey's westernisation/modernisation as well as secularism.

General T. stresses the importance of secrecy for generals:

> Every general tries to be secretive, they never share their secrets, all kinds of secrets, even the ones related to their families and health, are state secrets. By that, watching out and never disclosing is targeted. For generals are persons working in an over-competitive environment.

Staff officership as a profession

In his book *Shirt of Steel*,[78] Mehmet Ali Birand defines staff officers as the "cream of the military", praising both the education provided by the Staff College in Levent, İstanbul, and the quality of staff officers. Birand explains how officers are selected for staff education with an exclusive attitude and how hard a procedure the exam there is, as well as the features of the education and the prestigious, brilliant careers of young staff officers who have graduated from War Academies in the Turkish military. Twenty years after his book was written, are Birand's insights still relevant?

First of all, it is possible to define staff officership as a privileged type of officership formed within the TAF to provide a decision-making consultancy for commanders. The Staff College is a military academy that offers post-graduate level (master's and doctorate) education and teaching, and raises staff officers for the TAF. The War Academies founded in 1848 produced their first graduates in 1849.[79] They resumed their education and teaching activities at the campus in Yeni Levent in 1975.[80] In line with the amendments inserted into the Staff Colleges Act in 2003, graduate courses have been initiated at the Service War Colleges, and for the first time in 2007,

78 Mehmet Ali Birand, *Shirts of Steel* (London: IB Tauiris, 1991).

79 Mesut Uyar and Edward Erickson, *A Military History of the Ottomans* (Oxford: Praeger Publishing, 2009), pp.151-53.

80 For the War Academy legislation see <http://www.mevzuat.gov.tr/Metin.Aspx?MevzuatKod=7.5.5847&MevzuatIliski=0&sourceXmlSearch=> (accessed 20 July 2015).

graduates were awarded master's degrees, in addition to a Staff Officer Diploma. In order to meet the requirements of the modern technological world, the War Colleges command inaugurated the much-needed Atatürk War Gaming and Convention Centre on 25 July 2003 to support academic education and training activities, and experiment the joint concepts in a simulated environment as well as exercise and seminar environments.

The Strategic Research Institute (SAREN) of the Staff College has been continuing its education and training activities since 2004 to provide postgraduate (master's and Ph.D) training and certificate programmes and to carry out academic studies. Applications from friendly and allied countries to the War Colleges, which hold a special place among their counterparts, constantly increase every year. More than 1,000 international officers from 41 countries have graduated from the War Colleges since 1995. Today, at the end of a process, which has been shaped by historical developments and experiences, there are five educational institutions within the organisation of the War Colleges command, which is a direct subordinate unit to the Turkish General Staff.[81]

It is necessary to note that every year, only 50-60 officers are selected from the 2,000 Land Force applicants, and only 30-40 from the 600-800 applicants from the Navy and Air Force. They are chosen based on exam results. It is also necessary to emphasise that every year approximately 95% of the colonels becoming brigadier generals are selected from staff officers. Therefore, being a staff officer is a prerequisite for becoming a general.

In the Turkish military, staff officers have a privileged position among officers. Staff officers, constituting roughly 4% of the officer population (around 1,500 of 39,000 officers), have been given priority both in the selection of international cadres and assignment to the rank of general. An officer is entitled to apply for the Staff College exam, which is administered every December, six times during his first lieutenancy and captaincy. The Staff College exam is a very tough one, including military culture, general knowledge (international relations, law and international law, political history and popular agenda, among others) and operational planning sessions. Officers are responsible for memorising about 40 books. Each year, approximately 1,200 officers from all services apply for the exam, and roughly 100 (8% of the total) pass it. After passing the exam, the soon-to-be staff officers pursue a two-year education at master's level in the Staff College in İstanbul. After graduation, the staff officer holds a master's degree on security studies and is deployed to 'staff only' cadres accordingly.

Staff officers are privileged in the TAF, as roughly 90% of its international cadres and 95% of the general cadres are reserved for them. It is also worth mentioning that international posts (*daimi görev kadrosu*) are the most desired position in the TAF as they are a three-year deployment, and an officer could earn up to $7,000 per month

81 For the official website of the War Academy see <http://www.harpak.edu.tr/pageContainer.aspx?PID=1> (accessed 12 July 2015).

when working in this cadre. If an officer could save the half of this monthly payment, which is the case for the majority of officers, it means $120,000 could be amassed after the three-year deployment. There are roughly 300 international cadres of the TAF.

To be a staff officer in the TAF is, thus, the first step to being deployed to an international cadre for three years (maybe another one for a second term) and to be a general. The desire and endeavour of a junior officer to be a staff officer, which means the first and most significant step for the contemplation of a military career in the TAF, is a reliable indicator to assess the extent of idealism of young officers. There has, however, been a drastic decline in applications for the Staff College exam. According to official TAF numbers, in 2012, only one out of four officers applied for the exam, which means the great majority did not even apply.

Staff Major D. says the following about the system of staff officership:

> First of all, let us note that the staff officership exam carried out in December, which takes four days, is a very hard exam. In order to prepare for the exam, you have to remember 40 military source books[82] and about ten general culture books which we call "the white series"[83] down to their points and commas … In this respect, the exam tests fully the memorization skills of the officers, not their judgment and criticism skills. In addition, in the "Military planning at the brigade level" part of the exam, they have to solve military operation problems related with their force. For example, the problems about the land forces are built on attack operation at the level of brigade. In this problem exam also, the analytical judgment skills are needed in a limited amount. The more needed thing is mastery on previously asked questions, that is the archive. I can say that this exam is even harder than the TUS (Expertise in Medicine Exam). At least 1 year of studying with a daily average of 6 hours is necessary. Despite this [amount] of studying, the possibility of not succeeding [after] two years is above 60 percent. In this situation, you already select the hardworking ones who reveal their will to be a staff officer.[84]

It is possible to say that the staff officers are an elitist mass in the TAF, having very high motivation compared to the other officers called 'class officers'. Most of the young TAF officers who are not staff officers gain prestige after becoming staff officers and begin to gain privilege. According to Major D.:

82 Those source books contain basic instructions of all of the force commands and the common instructions that all force personnel must know, which are called 'Common Instructions'.
83 In the category of general culture called the 'white series', there are undergraduate level books in fields such as political history, history of reforms and public administration.
84 From interview conducted in Ankara on 18 December 2014.

> In fact, privileged attitudes ... and primarily the attitudes of generals to the staff officers cause staff officers to feel privileged and despised by others. Otherwise, there is no special education or attitude advice for the staff officer either at the Staff College or at other military units and institutions. Staff officers are always among the top 1,000 people in [the] TAF and therefore embrace [the] TAF. Staff officership is, in my opinion, a status created in [the] TAF upon being the first step in moving towards being a general. I think that the staff officership is built on closely watching the attitudes, conduct, and behavior of prospective generals and their families (wives and children) and not to promote the wrong people. A staff officer cannot behave like an ordinary officer. If someone arises and says "treat me like an ordinary officer, give me that many tasks, I do not want generalship, whatever the rights of the ordinary officer, I only want that," the system lynches him. Because he is harming the staff officership system. Simply, he is the bad example of his breed. His different behavior cannot be accepted. Whilst an ordinary officer showing the same performance is appreciated, the staff officer stating and applying that is punished, perhaps dismissed from the job. But if he does not state that and just behaves like a class officer, he goes on to benefit [from] lots of privileges.[85]

It is interesting that all eight staff officers interviewed in the study stated that professional knowledge and combat in warfare are not effective for the promotion of staff officers. The comment of one staff officer is interesting: "I can argue that civilian experts on military matters may know soldiery better than some generals."

A staff officer at the rank of major says:

> The greatest difference between staff officer and an ordinary officer is his unquestioned obedience and ability to work hard. That is why important posts are allocated to the staff officers. The staff officers, therefore, do the jobs important for the commanders. Issues like audit program, speech notes, gathering together the preparations before the meetings [and] tracking the schedule of the commander are cut out just for staff officers.[86]

Another staff officer attracts attention to the following point:

> The most important task of a staff officer is to learn English after being accepted to the academy. English score is much more important than your overall academic score at the Staff College. Because NATO's posts abroad are appointed through the language score. Therefore, in the Staff College, the smart staff

85 From interview conducted in Ankara on 18 December 2014.

86 From interview conducted in Ankara in May 2015.

> officer candidates study English more than their academic courses and they get the payoff eminently.[87]

One of the wives of the staff officers interviewed also emphasises that staff officership is not a profession, but a lifestyle, including the wife and the children, stating:

> The transformation of staff officership into lifestyle starts during education in the Staff College. This college is an education setting which covers the wives also as much as the officers being educated. Wives learn how to entertain guests, how to eat and drink, what activities to be participated in, and how to select dresses through social activities, such as kermises and meeting days. The aim of this process is preparing the wives to be good general wives. You are held responsible from your market-shopping to service for guests and to the relationship of wives of high rank and low rank officers in the hierarchy; in short, you are held responsible for everything. Everybody knows everybody very well, and nothing remains as a secret in this environment.[88]

Staff Major M., in turn, states the following:

> In my opinion, staff officership should not be abolished. Staff officership education should remain, it should extend and more people should be given this education, the generalship issue should not be perceived as being specific to staff officership; but, on the other hand, the system should invest in the personnel (I am not saying definitely staff officers) from which it will benefit most, without hurting the others. Thinking the opposite of that means not accepting the truth. I do not know how we will establish the difference between equality and justice. Equality means that everybody has equal rights and opportunities, but justice is getting the payoff as much as you invest. The German system is continuing in us and in the Germans. You become a staff officer, it means you are; otherwise, your chance of generalship decreases very much. The French system is also very sharp. They even invest more. Before going to the academy, they have their men conduct internships in a joint base (SHAPE, ISAF, peace mission in Mali, KFOR, etc.). Americans were also going to the academy with [a] 50 percent rate. Now, they increased that to a hundred percent with distance education. My opinion about the staff officership was also rigid before I came here, but I can say that it has softened after I have seen the examples here. The point we need to learn from them is to benefit [from] their skills without having other personnel lose their motivation, or having them lose a little amount, and trying to unlock the payoff of those skills with material and emotional compensations.

87 *Ibid.*
88 From interview conducted in Ankara in June 2015.

> I am saying "trying to" because the social culture is different. Experts criticize sergeants, sergeants criticize officers, fighting class criticizes support class, class officers criticize staff officers, staff officers who have not become general criticize ones who have become generals usually, and ones who have become generals do not appreciate the others.
>
> That exists in our nature, but extra precautions are necessary. A retired general in the US wrote a book saying that 60 percent of the jobs done by the generals are the ones which can be done better by a civilian. We need to concentrate on the motivation of the personnel by taking those into account, by opening other tracks and putting other targets and by making the audit and assessment system a more reliable one. I cannot speak comfortably because I am also in this job (I am leaving staff officership aside), but I spent 6 years in the US, 3 [of] which was with an American general, the state sent me … now, at what point should the needs of the organization and the wishes of the personnel unite?

General T. says the following about the staff officership system:

> To be accepted to the staff officership, to be a graduate of the staff school, to become a general after staff officership is not a job that every brave fellow can do. Both success in the staff officership exam and the staff officership itself requires discipline and patience. Most importantly, it requires dedication. While you are preparing for the staff exam, you will also do your job in the mountains, in the sharp hills, in the posts and in the base. In the evening when you go home, you will steal time from your children, your sleep, your entertainment, your rest, your off-days, your wife, and your friends, and you will read books and study, be it night or day. You will lean on the maps and you will adapt yourself to the scenarios superior than the ones of best scenarists, you will carry out wars on paper, you will win the wars or lose. You will prepare for the staff exam for months; after an exam lasting four days, you will be successful when you get the point enough for reaching the quota. If you cannot achieve this, and you still want to be a staff officer, you will start working over. Assume that you are accepted to the staff officership. You are not done merely succeeding in the exam. The state educates this officer … to be a staff officer as a gentleman with a stone of patience, a cube of secrets, and holding as much information as a library. It has its officer graduated after handling him and raising a perfect man of state. Our war academies are good examples and one of the best in the world. You are not done after graduating from war academies. You have to be ready to conduct missions everywhere in Turkey and throughout the world. When you become a staff officer, you enter into the brain and become one of the nerve endings of the Turkish Army which resembles a living organism.
>
> You work without losing heart, without getting tired, saying no matter if it is day or night and with great commitments also of your wife and of your children, and you serve for your state and your nation and conduct your mission. You

> start the competition for generalship with tens of your classmates and other class members via targeting the best, the most excellent and having the latest information. The weird thing is that there is no general rule saying every staff officer shall be a general. If there are a hundred classmates deserving staff officership, only ten or fifteen of them reach the generalship. The staff officers who cannot be generals go on doing their jobs with their heart and soul until the last moment before their retirement. The staff officers have [a] very high level of commitment. It is not a job everybody can do and stay patient.[89]

Major T., who is a class officer, says the following about the staff officership system:

> Staff officers are the officer group whose basic aim is to become a general. If possible, they want to work in places where their records will not be spoiled, they will not be scratched out, a place where they make their gateway to abroad for permanent missions and a place where they can form a robust network; the most dangerous position for them is to work in troops where there are plenty of soldiers and therefore plenty of problems; the most ideal is to work in the bases or the institutes. Their greatest target is to fill in their pockets even though in little amount, and to have [a] career in the abroad missions without being engaged with the soldiers and therefore the problems and without being scratched out until the end of colonelship. When they become generals and admirals, the situation is a meal fit for a king. Generalship is already a separate world. Of course, the conditions have changed a little bit today, it has become inevitable to think of settling [into] a new civilian life and making alternative plans after the lawsuits experienced. As much as possible, they feel they need to conduct their troop commandership missions, which is often two years, by postponing the problems instead of solving them or taking measures for the side from which damage will come to them. At the very end, there is an abroad mission or base mission awaiting them after that commandership mission, they should be careful not to destroy their admiralship dreams in the long run. When you consider the professional life of 20 or 25 years of a successful staff officer, the duration of commandership is at most seven or eight years while that of the plain officer of the same rank is 15 or 16 years. Of course, all those are generalizations, and reflections present dominant mentality; no matter what happens, there are ones who try to do their jobs in the best way and try to deserve the attribute of commandership.[90]

Captain E., who graduated from the War Academy with a high ranking, carried out his master's in the US and is a successful class officer who worked in the counter-terror

89 From interview conducted in İstanbul on 21 May 2015.
90 From interview conducted in Ankara on 20 June 2015.

zone in east and south-east Turkey, emphasises that he did not take the staff officership exam during any of his six opportunities to do so, did not prepare for the staff officership exam and has no aim of being a staff officer:

> The staff officership system in its present state is losing power and desirability like ice melting in the sun. Now, the dreams or ideals of lots of young officers are not having staff officership or generalship. Now, I see that the officer puts the concepts of academic career, foreign language, hobbies, and family before the staff officership. This is something the system cannot appreciate. If examined, it can be seen that the number taking the staff officership exam decreases every year. Because the successful class officers like me do not want to allocate two years of their life in preparation for that hard exam and two years for enduring the tough education process and spend their following years of their career as staff officers. Staff officership is like a Catholic wedding. Once you get it, you transform and can no longer stand in front of the flowing water. But, I see that the class of "successful non-staff officers" has been rising since the successful class officers do not prefer staff officership.[91]

It is known that the TAF, which has recognised that staff officership is losing its appeal, has been making efforts to increase the desirability of staff officership since 2009 (2009, 'TSK'da Kurmay Subay…'). Within the scope of the revision of the system, it is planned to abolish the War Academy acceptance exam, which is infamous for its toughness, to encourage successful officers, such as Captain E., who do not want to take the exam. In the new system, officers between the ranks of first lieutenant and first captain and those with good records will be invited to the academy. The invited officers will be subjected to education for a year. The successful ones will be staff officers and will partly open the gate to generalship for the following process of their professional life. With this change, the system will both ensure prospective generals are selected from among more officers and will create 'equal opportunity' among the officers. The new regulation, which will reward candidates according to successful records instead of an exam, is still being discussed at General Staff headquarters.

Lieutenant Colonel M. says:

> Staff officership; I think [it is] not delivering enough for the needs of the contemporary Turkish military. Very complex and complicated operations, [and] jointness are very significant today. Although there is a structure in which you have to communicate and cooperate with everybody, we stand separate from those. We need to rise up parallel to today's conditions. The selection and exam system is problematic. Evaluation and assessment requires command plus base experience. With the memorizing mentality, the ones making their asses uneasy

91 From interview conducted in Ankara on 14 December 2014.

> become staff officers. Staff officership is a great problem hindering specialization in decision-making. There is no balance between troop and base missions. It is needed to delegate decision-making processes. Let me note that, in the third corps, the papers for taking the foreign personnel to the airport are signed by the Head of the Staff. The gun charge and discharge stations at the security gates are handled by the Head of Staff of Land Forces Command. Centralization in decision processes is very bad, but this does not fit any more. So, I think there is an urgent need for a significant study about decision-making processes. The presentations of the projects proposed to the decision-makers should be listened to by the owner of that project. The owner of the project should talk to the decision-maker, not the general. The one who knows the issue best will present it to the decision-maker.[92]

The system of staff officership was abolished just after the failed 15 July 2016 military uprising.

Colonelship as a profession

According to data from the TGS's Personnel Directorate (J1), there are a total of about 6,000 colonels in the TAF (nearly 15% of the total number of officers), and around 80% are from the Army. It is necessary to note that the percentage of colonels in the US military is about 3%. In short, the ratio of colonels in the TAF is nearly five times that of the US military.

According to Colonel M., it is possible to separate TAF colonels into three basic groups: staff colonels, successful and still idealist non-staff colonels willing to work, and colonels not doing anything but taking their salaries and waiting for their retirements to kick in. Colonel M. continues:

> The staff colonel group constituting four percent of all the colonels is the group with very high motivation since they are on the way [to] being generals. But this high level of motivation causes great stress on themselves and the people working with them. Because a staff colonel on the path to generalship should not take excessive risks and should not offend the eyes of the commanders. Therefore, staff colonels are excessively careful and status-oriented. Working with them is always difficult. The colonels who are not working and waiting for retirement, I think, constitute 70 percent of the colonels. Since those colonels (especially the land soldiers who conducted missions in counter-terrorism regions for several years) think that they have gotten very tired at their previous missions, they perceive colonelship as a recumbence and retirement process. In my opinion,

92 From interview conducted in İstanbul on 17 April 2015.

> this group of colonels is a great burden for [the] TAF and is one of the biggest obstacles for institutional transformation. The "working and idealist" group of colonels, which I consider myself to be in, in turn, constitutes 25 percent of the complete group of colonels. A portion of those colonels continue to work even though they are emotionally hurt to some degree because they think they could not get the payoff for their sedulity and commitment from [the] TAF. Another portion of colonels try to do their jobs better to deserve the salary they get.

Lieutenant colonelship as a profession

Lieutenant Colonel is an intermediate rank of three years between a major and a colonel in the TAF promotion system. The most crucial task of lieutenant colonels is battalion command. Besides that, lieutenant colonels conduct tasks as project officers at the TGS's and Force commands' directories, and are planning officers at the brigade and corps-level headquarters. Lieutenant Colonel M. states:

> I perceive lieutenant colonelship as a crucial rank where differentiation between the operational and tactical levels starts. This rank, which corresponds generally to the ages of 40-43, should force an officer to decide whether he will resume troop commandership or take [a] place in the base missions. In my opinion, the battalion and fleet commands carried out by lieutenant colonels in [the] TAF are the most crucial operational offices. The lieutenant colonels are responsible for guiding and administering battalions, [and the] smallest self-sustaining regiments as well, in which they contribute to the individual development of their subordinates by communicating [with] each one of them. But I do not consider the promotion policy and the system of promotion to high ranks to be correct. The duration of waiting and promoting everybody to high ranks [is] not good and leads to under-motivation. In my opinion, not everybody should be lieutenant colonel. Besides, I think the waiting duration of three years at the lieutenant colonelship is very short. Lt. colonelship should be a rank in which the decision-makers to take over important missions in [the] TAF are tested.[93]

Lieutenant Colonel M. emphasises that there is quota for entering the Staff College but after graduation everybody is a staff officer, and for him, that kills specialisation. Stressing the need for the TAF's increased involvement in civilian life, he continues:

> As a social institution, we came from the center of it, but we somehow could not get into it. We are not in the social life. The employee lodging systems should be abolished at the places having no security threats. The personnel should be

93 From telephone interview conducted with Lieutenant Colonel M. on 1 June 2015.

> immersed in society. The public does not know he attends Friday prayers. We need to dig to the center of the public and get in there. Let us have a martyr-oriented approach in the ceremonies. Each of us should [make] emotional connections [with people]. We need to foster the social connections via the emotional connections. Physical spreading is compulsory.[94]

Majorship as a profession

Major is a rank with a five-year waiting period covering the ages of 35-40. Battalion commanders, battalion-level planning officers in the brigades and corps, base squadron commanders, fleet and project officers at the headquarters of the TGS's and force commands are majors. Majors are crucial officers providing contact between operational battalions at the tactical level, and brigades and corps at the operational level. Major O., who has been working in the Special Forces Commandership since his second lieutenantship, says the following:

> Since I have spent all my professional life in the special forces, I cannot clearly reflect on what majorship is in the force commands, but we came together with the majors in the land, Navy, and Air Forces for occasions like missions, exercises, trainings, and drills, and I had the chance to observe them closely. For the land forces, the majorship is coded more like a bridge between operating units of team and platoon; and other units such as squadron and brigade. In the Navy and Air Force, nonetheless, majorship is coming to the front with its ship and fleet commandership features. In my opinion, majorship is a hard but pleasing rank having both features of operating and decision-making. That is, it is possible for you to go sporting with the young officers if you like, or if you like it is possible do operation and education planning with the superior officers at the base. Majors have also got an important mission of ensuring a balance between younger officers and NCOs, and older generals and colonels to boost the morale of the Army. Majorship is also a critical career rank in which you look for the answer [to] the question of whether you will resume your career as a decision-making commander or a base officer. But, in my opinion, the fact that this rank covers a long duration of six years diminishes the dynamism and the power of this rank.[95]

94 *Ibid.*
95 From interview conducted in Ankara on 20 April 2015.

Captainship as a profession

Captain is arank with a six-year waiting period, usually covering the ages 30-35.

> Captain T. suggests:
> Captainship is the most loved rank within the military because it is the first for an officer to feel like the company commander, fully and independently in charge of around 80-120 soldiers. Companies are the first independent military units, and generally captains are company commanders. This is also a mediator rank between younger personnel such as conscripts, NCOs, lieutenants, and senior level officers. It is also the most critical rank for an officer to make big decisions for both his career in the military and his personal life. The great majority of officers marry in this rank, and they decide about [their] career path, [with the] most critical decisions about studying the entrance examination of the Staff College, developing language skills for three-year long abroad mission cadres, pursuing [an] academic career or trying to have [a] happy family life. Please also note that this is the very first rank [in which] an officer's political and personal being [is] matured, and his understanding about the socio-economic and political issues [is] settled. When I first joined the Army as a cadet in 1996, for instance, our captain told us that it was forbidden by the law for the members of the armed forces to participate in any kind of political activity. He also added [that] any violation of this rule would result with a discharge from the armed forces. Over the course of my nineteen-year service in the armed forces, I witnessed and realized that members of [the] TAF were an important part of the Turkish politics, usually in a capacity to make important political decisions, [rather than] being discharged [for] participating in it. There is an irony in this issue, which has strongly struck me until this day. The irony is that, while members of [the] TAF have always been strongly inclined to take part in Turkish politics, they (including me) have had almost no courses of [any] sort about political science during their academic endeavors either in the Turkish Military Academy or in the Staff College. While I was attending classes at the United States Naval Postgraduate School to get my master's degree in "Defense Decision Making and Planning," I better recognized my lack of understanding of political theory and politics as a member of [the] TAF along with my desire to research about it in order to get a better grip of political decision-making processes with a special focus on CMR. At the same time, I thought it would be beneficial for [the] TAF, for academia and for my own career to get a PhD in political science because a soldier's research in political science, especially in CMR, would provide a different and new perspective. That is why I applied for a PhD program in a political science department and seek to have an academic career [in] this field.

Lieutenantship as a professions

Lieutenant, the first rank of the profession of officership, is a process of nine years covering the ages of 21-30 (three years as lieutenant, six years as first lieutenant).

Lieutenant.T.S., who was at the Infantry School of the Land Force Command and was in the first year of his profession, says:

> Lieutenantship is the first officership rank in [the] TAF. When you are at the beginning of the profession, you have a lot to learn. I still see second lieutenantship as an education process. In my opinion, this is a good thing. Different perspectives and problem-solving skills thereby enter into [the] TAF. Second lieutenants care more about the material means and career opportunities compared to the high rank officers. For a second lieutenant, improving himself also means contributing to the system. Therefore, many of my friends are searching for master's degree opportunities even now, they are trying to learn foreign languages and trying to improve their hobbies in sports and arts. In this respect, I think officership is seen as a normal profession rather than a lifestyle by a lot of second lieutenants. Of course, being a soldier is a profession requiring commitment and discipline, but all those things are not obstacles for you to have your own life. Investment in yourself also means investment in the system. But, of course, it is not possible for our high ranking commanders to understand that; they still want us to be the same officer of the Cold War years. But those days are left behind, they have now a new generation at hand which questions, does not immediately obey, wishes to understand and to be encouraged and expects to have role models.[96]

Discussion

The power-distributive perspective explaining gradual institutional change put forward by Mahoney and Thelen provides a framework to explain the above-presented changes in the TAF: as a security actor, as a social institution and officership as a profession.[97] The first finding of this institutional analysis is that the TAF does not yet have a comprehensive transformation process consciously designed and controlled by the High Command that covers all three domains. In the domain of the TAF as a security organisation, for instance, the High Command (particularly Chief and deputy Chief

96 Interview conducted in İstanbul on 17 April 2015.

97 James Mahoney and Kathleen Thelen, *Explaining Institutional Change: Ambiguity, Agency and Power* (Cambridge: Cambridge University Press, 2010).

of the TGS)[98] appears to be the prime change agent of the top-down transformation. Change in this domain is implemented under the full control of the military elites and mainly shaped by the change in the international security environment. That is why it looks like an elite-driven process that seeks to adapt the TAF to the contemporary global security environment by 'emulating' the ways of thinking and doing things of other global modern security actors, particularly NATO. In contrast to this, in the domain of the TAF as a social institution, change arises primarily as commencing from the bottom and developing generally by confrontational interactions between the military elites and junior-level personnel or emerging with the inclusion of outside actors in civil society. Change then goes to the top and, by dictating its own reality to the military elites, evolves into a process that the High Command cannot keep under its full control and manage accordingly. In this sense, it can be asserted that, in this domain, change is to some extent an arbitrary process partly controlled by the High Command and partly driven by random dynamics such as the existence or absence of public awareness and media support of the issue at hand. One should note that, in this domain, the High Command, after first ignoring and then counter-attacking the change-demanding insiders or outside actors, can find no option but to submissively accept the existence of the problem and attempt to adapt its institutional order to fulfill changed demands. In the domain of officership as a profession, however, one may talk about an 'agentless change' process as no actor can fully control the attitudes and opinions of the officer corps. The differentiation among the three domains in terms of change types, change agents, change pathways and change modes therefore creates a power-distributional effect of change in the TAF, which according to this research, yields to gradual institutional change within the TAF.

In the domain of changes to the TAF as a security organisation, it can be stated that, especially since 2011, the High Command's 'reformist sentiment', which first emerged at the TGS headquarters and then expanded to the Army, Air Force and Navy headquarters, creates a 'non-compliant sentiment' to the detriment of a traditional *status-quo*-focussed sentiment. It is exactly this increasing non-compliant sentiment expanding within the TGS and force commands' headquarters due to the reformist mood of the High Command that should be taken into account when analysing the very initiation of the TAF's change as a security organisation. That is why one should focus on the compliance behaviour of subordinate ranks to the High Command. Compliance is built into the definition of the institution under consideration. In other words, what institutions do is to stabilise expectations (by providing information about the probable behaviour of others among other methods), and thus enforcement is endogenous in the sense that the expected costs and extent of non-compliance are

98 By High Command of the TAF, it is meant personnel at the rank of general/admiral including the Chief of the General Staff, the 2nd Chief of the General Staff, Force Commanders and Army commanders. As of August 2015, there were 12 full generals in the TAF.

factored into the strategic behaviour of the actors in a particular institutional equilibrium. If, instead, one breaks with a view of institutions as self-reinforcing (through whichever mechanism) and put distributional issues at front and centre, compliance emerges as a variable, which is critically important to the analysis of both stability and change. The need to enforce institutions carries its own dynamic of potential change, and emanates not just from the politically contested nature of institutional rules, but also, importantly, from a degree of openness in the interpretation and implementation of these rules. Even when institutions are formally codified, their guiding expectations often remain ambiguous and are always subject to interpretation, debate and contestation. It is not just that unambiguous rules are enforced to greater and lesser degrees. Rather, struggles over the meaning, application and enforcement of institutional rules are inextricably intertwined with the resource allocations they entail. The above-presented analysis clearly indicates that this is exactly the case for the TAF. The changing socio-political context in Turkey and the changing global security environment, nevertheless, have degraded the power of compliance as the principal institutional driver, and, thus, the prime constant for the TAF to such an extent that compliance has gradually turned out to be a variable for the TAF in the last decade.

Particularly from 2011 onwards after the critical juncture of the resignation of the then-Chief, General Işık Koşaner, along with three force commanders, the new High Command has come to conclude that compliance has become inherently complicated for the TAF by the fact that rules can never be precise enough to cover the complexities of all possible real-world situations. It is worth mentioning that new developments affecting Turkey's socio-political context such as the empowerment of civilian elites, single-party rule for over a decade and emerging public reaction to military intervention in politics have emerged in the last decade. In the same vein, the changes in the global security environment such as increasing complexity and uncertainty in the global system, emergence of hybrid threats, the changing characteristics of global terrorist networks and the military's greater involvement in international peace missions and support missions after man-made or natural disasters, forces the High Command to transform the TAF and adapt to the new context. The changing socio-political context in Turkey and change in the global security environment confound pre-existing rules, and existing institutions may be changed to better accommodate the new reality. These changes can involve rule creation, or may simply entail creative extensions of existing rules to the new reality. Here, it is seen that the High Command has entered into a reformist mood to promote the non-compliant sentiment in the TAF to better grasp the new reality imposed by the changing socio-political context in Turkey and changing global security environment, to the detriment of compliance, once the determining institution within the TAF. The emergence of the 'new reality' and then the High Command's realisation of the need for an acceptance of this new reality with a reformist mood have drastically eroded compliancy, which was adopted as an overarching sentiment in the TAF, and have gradually turned compliance into a variable. 'Non-compliant sentiment' then emerged as the prime driver that has started to define the very essence of institutions within the TAF.

In addition to erosion of compliance from a constant into a variable, other dynamics forcing the High Command to change things is an increasing ambiguity within the TAF. It is possible to assert that especially investigations and trials such as the *Sledgehammer*, *Ergenekon* and *Izmir Spy Case* with which serving officers were involved created an ambiguity about the promotions and appointments of senior-level commanders in the TAF because many detained and arrested senior-level officers had to resign or were relieved by the High Command. This has deeply degraded the traditional institutional mechanisms set for determining the promotion and appointment of senior-level officers.

In short, a non-compliant sentiment emerged because of the High Command's reformist mood first in the TGS, and then expanded to the force commands headquarters, causing the pre-existing determining institution of compliance to turn into a weakened institution. The increased institutional ambiguity caused by legal processes like *Sledgehammer* and *Ergenekon* revealed the necessity of the transformation of the TAF.

How then have these two mega-trends within the TAF as a security organisation influenced the officer corps? It is right to suggest that these two-mega trends have forced each officer to choose one institutional identity in terms of his/her attitude towards institutional change. Unsurprisingly, the portfolio of the identity includes four types of change actor (insurrectionary, symbiont, subversive and opportunist) proposed by Mahoney and Thelen.

Coming to the domains of the TAF as a social institution and officership as a profession, the analysis shows that, in contrast to the domain of the TAF as a security organisation, the High Command is the prime change agent. One may even suggest that there is no solely dominating change agent in these domains. It is the friction between the High Command and the mass-level actors (NCOs or NGOs within the civil society) about change in these domains that appears as the prime trigger of change. What can be said about the nature, characteristics and evolution of this friction between military elites and mass-level actors in these domains? Firstly, it is worth mentioning that, by pumping a great amount of uncertainty into the TAF's institutional setting, this friction has increased the level of ambiguity within the organisation. Increasing ambiguity leads to a non-compliant sentiment and thus mass-level insurrectionary behaviours. The analysis reveals that the military elites have a patterned response to those insurrectionary behaviours. The first stage is the strategy of ignorance, implying the High Command's inaction and silence as it thinks that any response would give credit to those insurrectionary behaviours. The second stage is the strategy of denial and counter-offensive through which the High Command seeks to gain control of the narrative supremacy so as to delegitimise those rival narratives in the eyes of the public. The last stage is the strategy of submission and rehabilitation in which the High Command passively accepts its defeat and seeks venues to engage with the rival actors for rehabilitation and restoration.

One may conclude that, in an organisation like the TAF, change occurs through distributional effects of institutions which trigger distrust to the pre-existing norms and divisions among institutional elite-level power-holders. Or, through elite-mass frictions, change can occur if institutions disadvantage subordinate groups to the point that they organise and come to identify with one another, thereby increasing their power and capacity to break prevailing institutional arrangements. These two mechanisms correspond to the themes of 'divided elites' in the TAF as a security organisation domain, and 'united subordinate groups vs military elites' in the TAF as a social institution level that are emphasised in explanations of change.

Within TAF, it is evident that what animates change is the power-distributional implication of institutions. However, the place that one expects incremental change to emerge is precisely in the 'gaps' or 'grey zones' between the rule and its interpretation (division among elites) or the rule and its enforcement (division between elites and subordinate groups). This is an analytic space that other conceptions of institutions (as behaviours in equilibrium, or as scripts) essentially rule out by definition; but, as a practical matter, this is exactly the space in which contests over – and at the same time within – institutions take place.

The following table summarises the points presented above.

What can one say about the characteristic of change? What are the modes and drivers of change in each domain? Exactly who are the agents behind such changes in each domain? Why do they carry out behaviours that lead to transformation?

As can be seen in the table above presenting a brief summary of this chapter, the change in the Turkish military as a security organisation domain is an elite-driven process in a top-down fashion, and provides no room for arbitrariness. Another important characteristic in this domain is the appearance of 'layering', a change more aiming for incremental transformation of the existing institutional order as the primary mode of change. In this domain, change actors are 'subversive elites' (the High Command and senior-level generals), 'symbionts' and 'opportunists' among the strategic intermediate-level decision-makers (major generals and brigadier generals).

In the domain of the Turkish military as a security actor, there is an effort to reinterpret the existing ways of thinking and doing things without ignoring the existing institutional order. It is evident that starting with the foundation of working groups to conduct damage assessment in August 2011, the High Command's reformist mood created a non-compliance sentiment within the TGS. It is this non-compliance sentiment that led to the emergence of 'subversive' officers in addition to the existing symbionts and opportunists. The working groups formed an evaluation of the last 10 years of the TAF, determined what wrong practices existed in which fields and presented their findings and analysis to the High Command, together with their proposals. In the light of those proposals, the institutionalisation process commenced in fundamental fields such as force structuring and reorganisation, public and press relations, personnel and personnel benefits, military education and international missions. In the following periods, likewise, institutionalisation in the TGS expanded slowly among the lower-level units, starting with the Force Command headquarters.

From those efforts, it is clear that the TAF entered into an attempt at transformation, which seeks to accommodate their traditional ways of thinking and doing things

Table 3. Summary of the TAF's Change as an Institution

	Cases Examined	Characteristics of Change	Mode of Change	Driver of Change	Actor of Change
Turkish Military as a Security Organisation	1.Stages of Change 2011-12: Damage assessment and institutional transformation discussions. 2012-13: Adoption of reformist approach and institutionaliation of transformation in the TGS. 2013-14: Spread of transformation to the Force commands. 2014-15: Consolidation of the transformation. Cases examined: 2. Change in press and public relations. 3.Internationalisation efforts (NATO and post-graduate level education)	An elite-driven process top-down fashion. No arbitrary processes. No pressure from below.	Layering.	Technology+ Internationa-lisation.	Subversive elites and symbionts + opportunist lower senior ranks (brigadiers etc.)
Turkish Military as a Social Institution	Cases examined: • Empowerment of 'Woman Force' in the TAF. • NCO's struggle for their rights and status in the TAF. • Violations of Soldier Rights. • The Headscarf Ban.	Bottom-up and junior-driven processes. The pressure from the bottom as key determiner of the outcomes. Provides room for arbitrariness.	'Drift' and 'conversion' as the modes of change leading to 'passive layering' of the rules/norms by the elites.	Organisational Culture	'Insurrectionaries' at the junior level and 'subversive elites' to appease them. The impact of media scrutiny and public pressure.
Officership as a Profession	Examination of all ranks within the TAF.	Bottom-up and junior-driven processes. The pressure from the bottom as key determiner of the outcomes.	'Conversion' as the mode of change. No written institution. -Fully attitudinal.	Technology + Organisational Culture + Politics	Generals: some symbionts (some parasitical, some mutual). Some subversive, some opportunist. Colonels: great majority symbi-onts, some opportunist. Lieutenant Colonels: subversive. Majors: subversive. Captains + Lieutenants: insurrectionaries.

with changes in the global security environment and socio-political change in Turkey. Therefore, it is possible to suggest that 'layering', the mood defined as 'the introduction of new rules on top of or alongside existing ones', is generally appreciated, because, in this mode, neither change of all the old rules nor ignoring all those is on the agenda. But there exists the establishment of new rules and institutions besides the mass of old rules. A good example of this is the rise of the public and press relations branch to the level of department, and then changing its existing structure and organisation seven times in the four-year period between 2011 and 2015. Another is upgrading the TGS Command Centre to the level of department due to its importance, revising its relations with J-directories and other connected ones and redefining its duties, authorisations and responsibilities without cancelling the old rules. The TAF also integrated the efforts of sending officers abroad and attempted to increase the quality of graduate-level military education with both the military education system and the institutionalisation of support services for the decision-makers in crucial posts.

It is seen that the prime actors of in the domain of the Turkish military as a security organisation are 'subversive elites'. Subversives are actors who seek to displace an institution, but in pursuing this goal, they do not themselves break the rules of the institution. They instead effectively disguise the extent of their preference for institutional change by following institutional expectations and working within the system. From this point of view, it is possible to say that primarily the Chief of the TAF General Necdet Özel in 2011-15 and also General Hulusi Akar (Deputy Chief in 2011-13, Land Force Commander in 2013-15 and TAF Chief from August 2015 to July 2018) played the role of subversive elites and succeeded in forming a strong reformist sentiment within the TAF from August 2011 to August 2015.

With layering, institutional change grows out of the attachment of new institutions alongside existing ones, as mostly happened within the TGS headquarters. While powerful veto players can protect the old institutions, they cannot necessarily prevent the addition of new elements.

The other actors of the transformation in this domain are especially the strategic intermediate level decision-makers at the levels of lieutenant generals, major generals and brigadier generals. They can be defined as 'symbionts' and 'opportunists', the sum of which forms the *status-quo* block. Among this group of 'transformation resisters', the category of 'parasitic symbionts' constitutes the majority because parasitic symbionts wish to retain the formal institutional *status quo*, and strong veto players help to secure this outcome. Besides parasitic symbionts, another group forming the *status-quo* block is opportunists. Opportunists are actors who have ambiguous preferences about institutional continuity. They do not actively seek to preserve institutions. However, because opposing the institutional *status quo* is costly, they do not try to change the rules. Opportunists, instead, exploit whatever possibilities exist within the prevailing system to achieve their ends. The decision to be made by the opportunists, who constitute a large portion of the intermediate level decision-makers, about whether they will present a reformist or pro-*status quo* standing is very important in the transformation of the TAF as a security organisation.

The reorganisation and new force structuring is an important field of change coming to the front in the domain of the TAF as a security organisation. In this domain, the fundamental drives of change appear to be technology and internationalisation. The TAF tries to gain the intellectual capacity to procure, utilise and manage the new capability packages of technology, while trying to increase its international visibility to catch up with the change in modern world armies in the global security environment. From this point of view, it is possible to say that the TAF perceives technology-focussed change and internationalisation as the two driving forces for both material and mental transformation.

In contrast, the process in the domain of the Turkish military as a social institution is not elite-driven and deterministic (or pre-planned), carried out in a top-down fashion. The change in this domain is mostly a mass-driven process in an arbitrary and confrontational fashion. There is a great power gap creating room for arbitrary processes and interactions in this domain, primarily because military elites are not fully aware and capable to manage this domain. Because of this power gap, the actors at the mass level, who can be classified generally as 'insurrectionary' (both serving and retired personnel and their families), can impose their demands of change to the military elites as an organised voice if they can be united, and get the support of the public and press. In the face of such an imposition, the elites give the following responses, as was seen in the case of NCOs' personal rights and violations to soldiers' rights:

- Firstly, imposing that the demands are not legitimate and attempting to degrade the credibility of such demands with counter-attacks.
- Appreciating the existence of the problem, with dialogue attempts.
- Attempting to resolve the problem, building trust with rival actors, institutional and legal arrangements.

In this domain, generally 'drift' appears as the change mood, and sometimes 'conversion'. Since legal regulations are created very late and deficiently in this domain, two methods come forward, either staying non-reactive while the present rules remain the same (drift) or interpreting and practicing the present rules differently (conversion). The best example of drift is the recent softening of the headscarf and beard ban within the TAF, although the official written regulations/institutions have not been amended. It should not be forgotten that the Deputy Chief of the General Staff, General Aslan Güner, left the protocol in 2007 to avoid shaking hands with First Lady Gül, placing the wearing of the headscarf high on the agenda.[99] Although there have been no changes in the formal institutional texts of the TAF such as Military Housing/Lodging Entrance Regulation since 2007, it is seen that there has been a great softening around the headscarf and beard ban.

99 Merve Kavakçı, *Islam Headscarf Politics in Turkey* (New York: Palgrave, 2010), p.5.

The campaign regarding the personal rights and legal status of NCOs was pursued at the conversion mood from the very beginning. Even though they do not like to do very much in the face of pressure, the High Command changed the formal textual institutions for developing rights and privileges of NCOs and for promoting their institutional status with a method that can be defined as 'passive layering'.

The actors of change in the domain of the TAF as a social institution are seen to be the insurrectionaries at the junior level and the subversive elites attempting to soothe them. The demands for change in this domain appear firstly at the mass level generally in an arbitrary way with the attempts of insurrectionaries. The matter attracts the attention of the public and the media to such an extent that the High Command cannot resist this pressure. Demands that captured public attention and were promoted by prolonged news and commentaries in the media forced military elites to change their preferences. Many changes being experienced in the social domain create arbitrary and non-compliant confrontations, with friction between the High Command and mass-level actors, despite the fact that military elites seek to withstand each confrontation. At the end, however, they accept defeat tacitly and try to adapt the institutional structure to the new reality dictated by the mass-level actors supported by the media and the public. In this domain, the fundamental drivers of change are media power and public pressure. Bottom-up demands which can capture media attention.and public support in a prolonged fashion can lead to changes in the strategic culture of the TAF.

In the domain of officership as a profession, the change is completely arbitrary and in a bottom-up fashion. The types and characteristics of change actor of every rank are explained below.

Generals

In the light of the interviews with four serving generals, it is likely to suggest that the great majority of generals are opportunists. About a quarter of them are symbionts and one-fifth are subversives. As the "guardians of the existing system",[100] none of the generals are insurrectionaries. The perceptions and opinions of the generals constituting the High Command about other generals are very important for the promotion and appointment of generals within the TAF. Therefore, generals usually shape their positions in the system according to the perceptions and opinions of the High Command. In this respect, in the period from 2011-15, the reformist mood of the Chief of the General Staff, General Necdet Özel, and Deputy Chief General Hulusi Akar deactivated the traditionally dominant 'pro-*status quo*' sentiment in the TAF and played a role in the domination of the non-compliant sentiment. Investigations and trials such as *Balyoz*, *Ergenekon* and the *İzmir Spying Case* struck the TAF as a

100 From interview with General L. conducted in İstanbul on 12 October 2015.

shockwave, shaking the traditional ways of thinking and doing things, and increased the organisational ambiguity in the organisation. This situation has drastically increased ambiguity in the promotion and appointment processes named 'tradition' (*teamül*), formed over decades by generals who were not sure of their futures and who could be arrested any time because of investigation process. The non-compliant sentiment becoming the dominant one and a high-level organisational ambiguity among the generals caused the formation of a subversive group who are not satisfied with the old order and seeking to create a new institutional order, albeit in a tacit manner.

This characteristic of generals, who are mostly opportunist, makes them each a master player in understanding the dominant sentiment within the TAF and taking a position accordingly. A general suggests that, "For every general, the first dynamic shaping his decisions primarily is his own military career and his next promotion."[101] The most important determiner shaping this dynamic is the perceptions and opinions of the High Command about them. For this reason, it is impossible for the generals to be insurrectionary. Therefore, every general must, above all, be an opportunist carefully analysing the *status quo* challenges in the institution and the ambient political context. Most of the generals have to reflect this opportunism in the decisions they make and their behaviours. A proportion of the generals are parasitic symbionts, believing that they deserve their positions due to their past services and therefore having the opinion that the system 'owes' them. These generals think that the system has to provide them with privileges and prestige due to services they carried out in the past. For the endurance of the present prestige and privileges, they all develop a pro-*status quo* sentiment. For this reason, it is possible to say that the great majority of generals, except the subversives (some 20%), are opportunists and parasite symbionts with a pro-*status quo* and compliant sentiment. However, appointment of the newly formed subversive generals to crucial missions by the High Command, which tries to keep them close by, has become an encouragement, pushing the generals who have an opportunistic latent sentiment towards being subversive. The best example of that issue is the institutionalisation of the decision support departments which were founded in the TGS headquarters and later outstretched to the force commands.

Colonels

For 97% of the officers, colonelship is the last of their professional life. It is seen that the colonels who came to the end of their professional life and started to plan their retirement (this portion is more significant among the land forces) have sacrificed lots of things, both from themselves and from their families, during the weary profession of officership. They therefore want to be comfortable in the rank they 'deserve'

101 From interview with General X, who asked not to be named, conducted in Ankara on 12 September 2015.

in returnfor the price they paid in previous ranks. A great majority of colonels in the TAF are thus of the parasitic symbionts type. The next group among the colonels is the opportunists. Many officers at this rank have a pro-*status quo* focussed sentiment since they are parasitic symbionts. The officers in this rank who do not want to rake risk and responsibility, and also do not want to work too hard, perceive reform as new risks, new responsibilities and an effort to get themselves out of the system as quickly as possible. For this reason, trying to refuse the reform efforts actively or by passive resistance by slowing down jobs is a widespread situation in this rank.

Lieutenant colonels and majors

The great majority of officers of the ranks of major and lieutenant colonel, which cover the ages of 35-45, are subversive, but some of them are opportunist as a small portion seem to be mutual symbionts. The lieutenant colonels and majors are a group that can undertake an important role in the institutional transformation of the TAF in each of the three domains.

Captains and lieutenants

The great majority of captains and the lieutenants, constituting the most crowded group in the TAF, have the image of insurrectionaries. They are definitely in discomfort with the *status quo* and want to change something.

The main drivers of change in this dimension are changes in technology, political context and strategic culture. As a result, changes in the TAF, fed by dynamics independent of one another, are in the domains of:

- A security organization.
- A social institution.
- Officership as a profession, creating a 'power-distributional' effect within the subject of change.

The different change processes shaped by these change modes, actors and drivers are separated from one another, forming a healthy gradual change climate, although the elites are not fully aware of that. It is often seen, especially in the domains of the Turkish military as a social institution and the officership as a changing profession, that institutional change occurs precisely when problems of rule interpretation and enforcement open up space for actors to implement existing rules in new ways.

4

Quantitative Analysis

Historically, the TAF's military service has always been a mixed system with a minority of core professionals and a majority of non-professionals. Today, the TAF is composed of three force commands; the Army, the Air Force and the Navy, as well as the Gendarmerie Command and Coast Guard, yet these last two fulfill their missions under the auspices of the Interior Ministry. As of April 2014,[1] the distribution of the TAF's active military personnel (623,818 personnel including the Gendarmerie Command and Coast Guard yet excluding civilian employees) is shown in the chart below.

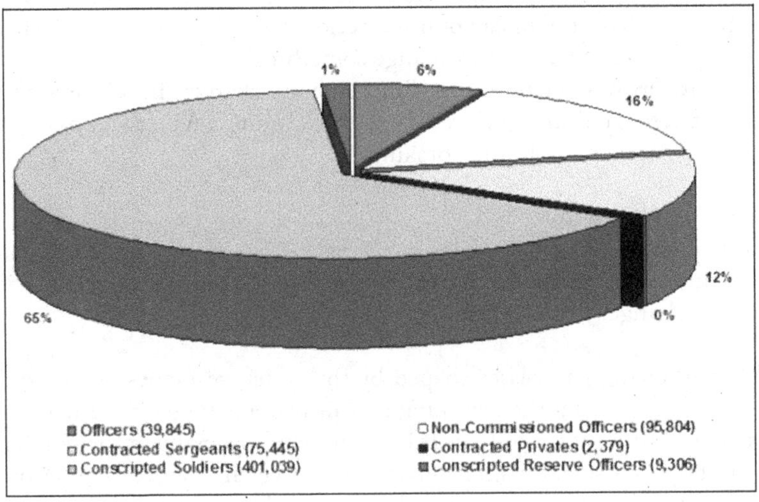

Figure 3 Distribution of the TAF's Active Military Personnel as of April 2014.

1 Please note that there has been no drastic change in the numbers and ratios of the services and ranks within the TAF since April 2014.

In the Turkish military, despite the fact that the officer corps constitutes only about 6% of the total serving personnel, it is the dominating military elite group, similar to other modern militaries of the world. The attitudes, opinions, strategic calculations and behaviours of the officer corps determine outcomes within the TAF. The table below provides the distribution of the TAF's officer corps in terms of ranks and force commands.

Table 4. The service and rank distribution of the officer corps in the TAF as of April 2014[2]

Service	Lt/First Lt	Captain	Major	Lt Colonel	Colonel	General	Total
Army	7,672 (19.2%)	3,561 (8.9%)	3,535 (8.8%)	2,119 (5.3%)	3,936 (9.8%)	196 (0.49%)	21,019 (52.7%)
Navy	1,631 (4.1%)	1,327 (3.3%)	1,126 (2.8%)	528 (1.3%)	725 (1.8%)	48 (0.12%)	5,385 (13.5%)
Air Force	2,723 (6.83%)	1,466 (3.67%)	1,153 (2.89%)	630 (1.58%)	713 (1.78%)	67 (0.16%)	6,752 (16.9%)
Gendar-merie	2,528 (6.3%)	1,393 (3.4%)	965 (2.42%)	494 (1.23%)	497 (1.24%)	31 (0.07%)	5,908 (14.8%)
Coast Guard	348	313	58	29	32	1	781 (1.9%)
Total	14,902 (35.3%)	8,060 (20.2%)	6,837 (17.1%)	3,800 (9.53%)	5,903 (14.81%)	343 (0.86%)	39,845 (100%)

As seen in the table, the distributionof the 39,845 officers serving in the TAF is a clear-cut one. If we set the confidence level as 95% and confidence interval at ±2.5%, our random, representative sample should include around 1,250 officers.[3] One should note that our population (i.e. active duty officers in the TAF) comprises two major strata: rank and service. For a better representation of the population, this study follows stratified random sampling procedure, in which we consider the strata as separate sub-populations and draw a separate random sample from each stratum before combining the results. Stratification is the process of dividing members of the population into homogenous sub-populations before sampling. The principal objective of stratification is to reduce sampling errors, thus making the sample more representative of the population. The strata should be mutually exclusive: every element in the population must be assigned to only one stratum. The strata should also be collectively exhaus-

2 This table was cross-tabulated by data provided by the Personnel Command (J2) of the Turkish General Staff.

3 See Table 2 presented below.

tive, meaning that no population element can be excluded. The primary advantage of stratified random sampling is to provide opportunity to study the stratum variations for each stratum.

Conducting the survey

Table 5. The distribution of the survey sample in terms of service and rank

Service	Lt/First Lt	Captain	Major	Lt Colonel	Colonel	General	Total
Army	427	197	52	7	202	7	892 (63.6%)
	126	42	42	12	22	0	244 (17.4%)
	65	21	28	18	28	0	160 (11.4%)
Gend.	33	17	21	15	18	1	105 (7.4%)
Total	651 (46%)	277 (19.7%)	143 (10.2%)	52 (3%)	270 (19.2%)	8	1,401 (100%)

At the initial phase, three options were taken into consideration as the survey method. The first option was the conduct of the survey by utilising 'formal channels' and within the close control of TAF's chain of command. This option would mean that the survey would be delivered as the annex of an executive order which would be issued by the Turkish General Staff (TGS) directly to the selected respondents via the TAF's formal informing channels. This executive order may have simply forced the selected respondents to complete survey sheets and then send these sheets back to the TGS. However, one should note that it is highly likely to have 'biased survey data' while applying this option due to a general pattern in the TAF's organisational culture, which may be defined as the overreaction of those sub-commanders to any survey directly sent by the TGS to personnel under their command. Simply, in this method, there is a risk that sub-commanders would intervene or influence survey results, which would then yield biased survey data and insights.

The second option would be contacting a civilian survey firm to conduct the survey, which is perhaps the most reliable option among the three. This issue was raised at the initial phase of the research and discussed with the commanders at the highest echelons of the TGS. Unfortunately, the top brass in the General Staff declined this proposal due to the issue of confidentiality on this sensitive research project and their concerns on the reliability of survey results which, in this case, would be collected by civilian employees of the survey firm.

The third option was to conduct the survey with the help of a group of Point of Contacts (POCs), who can create a network of officers to fill out the questionnaires.

The third option is the best among these three as it endows a 'trusted' interaction between the POC, or the surveyor, and the participating officers, a group of 30 officers from different services and ranks. This includes a three-star general and a brigadier general, four colonels from each services, 11 officers from the Army, four officers from the Navy, four officers from the Air Force and five officers from the Gendarmerie Command who were chosen as POCs. Each POC was given a list of 40-45 officers, which only had the required specifications of service type and rank level. One should note that, as they were not given any names, they were asked to pick randomly an officer fitting for the requirements of the list from within their network of acquainted officers. That is, the POCs were not restricted to any rule other than the required specifications, meaning that they were free to choose any officer as a respondent as long as he fitted the requirement in terms of rank and service. As one may give credit, this first-ever survey applied to officers included some questions about their political views and their attitudes towards 'hot' issues such as religion, democracy and the Kurdish question. This means that a certain amount of trust must exist between the POC and respondent to feel comfortable when filling out the survey form.

The surveys were conducted between 15 May and 15 September 2015. At first glance, one may suggest that a four-month period might be a long duration for a survey. However, one should note that the answers of these questions are highly unlikely to be varied within a four-month period.

Content of the survey

The survey to be applied to the participants includes three parts.[4] To gather the base-line information, the first part contains demographic information, including questions on respondents' service and rank, the economic and educational status of their parents, the number of service years spent in missions/trainings abroad, the number of languages known by the respondent and the number of years spent fighting against the PKK. The main purpose of the demographic characteristics of the respondents is to identify associations between these characteristics and attitudes. Would there be, for instance, any statistically significant relationship between the years spent in missions/trainings abroad and the attitudes of the officers regarding democratic and civilian control? Would the number of years spent fighting against the PKK be directly related to the level of satisfaction about the military service? Would the educational and financial status of officers' parents have an impact on their decision to be an officer? Would being a graduate from the War Academy or civilian universities impact the conceptualisation of a 'professional soldier'? Would the ability to speak a foreign language or the level of education make the respondent more open to change and liable to democratic and civilian control?

4 See the Turkish survey in the Appendix.

The first section of the survey's second part includes closed-end questions designed to measure the attitudes of the respondents to issues related to security defence, particularly the mission and role of the TAF, military reform within the Turkish military and their ideas about NATO. The second section contains questions seeking to measure the political stance, religiosity level of the officers and their levels of satisfaction in economic terms.

The third part of the survey includes 36 'yes/no' dichotomous questions. The first eight questions of this section were designed to measure the attitudes of the respondents towards the headscarf issue and confirm or falsify their previous answers about religiosity and the Kurdish question for further reliability. Questions 9-14 were designed to measure the level of trust/satisfaction towards institutions such as the EU, Turkish parliament, media, police and democracy in Turkey. Questions 15-25 were designed to measure ideas about the TAF as a security organization to address issues such as conscription, professionalism, conscientious objection, as well as the service of women and homosexual in the military. The last questions, 26-36, were designed to get a picture of the status of the Turkish General Staff, the independence of the military judicial system, the acceptance of orders violating legal codes, Turkish foreign policymaking, Ataturkism and internet usage.

It is also worth mentioning that the POCs were informed that it was not obligatory for the respondents to answer each and every question, meaning that they may leave blank any questions they did not want to answer. This 'feel-free to leave blank' approach serves the purpose of comforting respondents. One should note, however, that in scholarly terms, these unanswered questions are telling of the 'closed' domains which TAF officers are highly discouraged from commenting on.

At this point, one might be led to ask the following: can this survey presenting a snapshot of the attitudes and opinions of the officer corps as of May-September 2015 be reliable enough to provide scholarly inferences on the changing attitudinal trends of the Turkish officer corps? Military service experience over years would, for instance, change officers, so that colonels, who were the lieutenants of the late-1980s, started the same as the current lieutenants but changed over time due to transformative military mechanisms, such as military education and the military's particular lifestyle. One may then assert that current differences between lieutenants and colonels do not mean change in the distribution of opinions across ranks. There may have been the same distribution of opinion as in the late-1980s if one had applied this design then. This is a grounded reservation that would point to a validity problem in the design, particularly when emphasising generational differences. This validity problem is rooted in the absence of previous research on the attitudes of the Turkish officer corps. This absence of longitudinal data makes it impossible to compare and confirm/confront the findings of this study with other research to generate trend analyses. To overcome this validity problem, this study relies on the triangulation and multi-method approach explained in previous chapters.

Analysis of the survey findings

In the following, a brief analysis will be presented about each question in the questionnaire, followed by a general discussion of this chapter. In the analysis, the Gendarmerie Command, which is affiliated with the Interior Ministry in terms of its duties, authorities and responsibilities, will be included in some relevant questions, but not all.

Distribution of the sample with respect to force commands (services)

Force Command	#	%
Army	892	63.7
Air Force	244	17.4
Navy	160	11.4
Gendarmerie	105	7.5
Total	1,401	100.0

Distribution of the sample with respect to ranks

Rank	#	%
Lieutenant/First Lt	651	46.4
Captain	277	19.8
Major	143	10.2
Lt Colonel	52	3.7
Colonel	270	19.3
General/Admiral	8	0.6
Total	1,401	100.0

Q4. What is the highest level of education you have completed or are currently enrolled in?

	#	%
War academy/University Graduates	990	70.7
Master's (including continuing ones)	335	23.9
PhD (including continuing ones)	72	5.1
No response	4	0.3
Total	1,401	100.0

As seen, the level of education of the officer corps is much higher compared with that of Turkey in general.[5] While 100% of the officer population is a university grad-

5 For more information on this comparison, refer to TUİK's 2014 educational year at <http://www.tuik.gov.tr/basinOdasi/haberler/2015_34_20150609.pdf> (accessed 2 December 2015).

uate, according to data from TUIK in 2014, the ratio of the whole population of Turkey is 11%; while 23.9% of the officers have a master's diploma or are continuing their education, this figure is ony 1% throughout Turkey; and while 5.1% of the officer population has a PhD degree or is studying for one, this figure is just 0.22% in Turkey.

No significant difference between the force commands was found with respect to education levels.

The following table shows education levels broken down with respect to ranks:

Table 6. Education level of respondents with respect to ranks

	Lieutenant /First Lieutenant	Captain	Major	Lt Colonel	Colonel	Total
War Academy/ University	528	172	67	34	182	983
Master's (including continuing ones)	114	91	53	13	64	335
Doctorate (including continuing ones)	6	13	23	5	24	71
Total	648	276	143	52	270	1,389

Majors in the TAF have the highest level of education in the TAF. Thirty-seven percent of majors hold master's degrees, and 16% of all majors are PhD graduates or continuing their doctorate studies. In the light of this result, it is possible to say that the rank of major between the ages of 35-42 is the group that would potentially provide the greatest contribution to the TAF's institutional change in intellectual terms. It is also possible to say that the level of education tends to increase as the rank decreases, down to the rank of captain.

Q5. What type of school did you graduate from?

	#	%
War academy	1,099	78.4
Civilian university	296	21.1
Other (non-commissioned officers or specialised sergeants)	5	0.4
No response	1	0.1
Total	1,401	100.0

Table 7. School distribution with respect to ranks

	Lieutenant / First Lieutenant	Captain	Major	Lt Colonel	Colonel	Total
Civilian University	195	60	7	1	33	296
War Academy	456	216	134	48	237	1,091
Total	651	276	141	49	270	1,387

There is an increase in civil university background among junior ranks, particularly lieutenants and first lieutenants. As of 2014, 30% of lieutenants/first lieutenants serving in the TAF were civil university graduate contracted officers. The insufficient number of lieutenants from war academies to fill the TAF's cadres is being compensated by contracted officers with civilian university background. The recruitment of young civilian university graduates as contracted officers is a source of supply that the TAF has been deliberately concentrating on since 2006. In this respect, the Army has the leading role of positions of platoon/team commander, especially for counter-terrorism, filled with contracted officers. According to the regulation,[6] the contracted officers sign a three-year contract at the beginning of their service, and this contract can be renewed three times, serving nine years in total. After the nine-year period, if the TAF offers and the contracted officer accepts, he gains the right to take the transfer to regular service examination. Those who pass the examination – which has a written test, interview and physical proficiency phases – can continue their service as regular officers up to the rank of colonel.

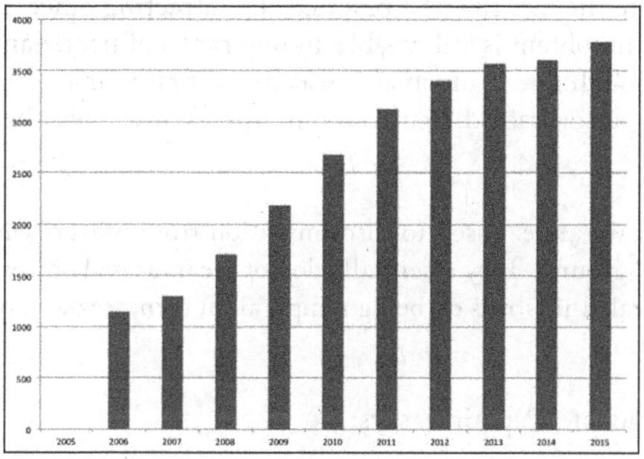

Figure 4 Number of contracted officers in the TAF.[7]

6 For the official regulation of contracted officers (Turkish) see <http://www.mevzuat.gov.tr/Metin.Aspx?MevzuatKod=7.5.11974&MevzuatIliski=0&sourceXmlSearch=> (accessed 14 September 2015)

7 The numbers are taken from the TGS's Personnel Command (J1).

As seen in the table, there were no contracted officers in the TAF as of 2005. By 2015, there were around 3,784 contracted officers in the TAF, a population constituting around 11% of the officer corps.

The following highlights the ratio of contracted officers in each force command:

Table 8. Number and ratio of contracted officers in the TAF

Army	2,108 (11.6%)
Navy	181 (3.4%)
Air Force	572 (9.3%)
Gendarmerie	929 (16.7%)

As one may notice, while the Army has the highest population of contracted officers in the officer corps, the Gendarmerie Command and Air Force have a relatively high population when compared to that in the Navy, a force command which had only been contracting officers for four years.

One should also note that, in terms of the distribution of contracted officers among ranks, the lieutenant/first lieutenant category has the highest number of contracted officers with around 30% of the whole population.

The interview findings suggest that there is a friction between the junior officers (lieutenants/first lieutenants, captains and majors) who have graduated from the War Academy and contracted officers. War Academy graduates do not perceive the contracted officers as 'genuine officers' and they isolate them[8] by calling them 'pouch' (*poşet*), a derogatory term meaning that they are empty beings not fully deserving officership. Despite the fact that the practice of contracting officers has been ongoing for 10 years, this discontent is still visible among ranks of lieutenants/first lieutenants and captains, although not os much as it was in the first years.

Lieutenant S., a contracted lieutenant in the Army, says the following in his interview:

> It is true that we are exposed to discrimination from officers who have a War Academy background. They essentially do not see us as real officers or stress that we are temporal. This stress on being temporal, in turn, weakens our attachment to the institution.[9]

War Academy graduate Captain I. says:

8 From interview with Captain A., who worked as a company commander of the student officer battalion of the Army İnfantry School based in Tuzla, Istanbul, on 16 January 2014.

9 From interview conducted with Lieutenant S. in Istanbul on 21 January 2015.

> The contracted officership has been practiced in the Navy for almost 5 years, but it is still not possible to say it runs smoothly. We have difficulty in seeing the contracted ones as officers. They also do not want to be like us.[10]

Again, an important finding observed in interviews and the questionnaire is that both the quality of education and the level of foreign language in contracted officers are much lower than the officers graduating from the War Academy. The difference in education between War Academy graduates and contracted officers from low-quality universities and not faring well in knowledge of foreign languages, is the most important factor feeding discrimination. For example, while 90% of the officers who graduate from the War Academy know at least one foreign language (mostly English), the proportion of contracted officers knowing at least one foreign language is only about 50%.

Q6. What is your hometown? (Please fill the space below with which ever city you feel is your hometown)

Table 9. Geographic distribution of respondents

Hometown	#	%	Hometown	#	%
Istanbul	104	7.4	Diyarbakır	12	0.9
Eskişehir	61	4.4	Mardin	12	0.9
Ankara	52	3.7	Muğla	12	0.9
Bursa	51	3.6	Muş	12	0.9
Izmir	51	3.6	Sivas	12	0.9
Kocaeli	43	3.1	Aksaray	12	0.9
Rize	36	2.6	Karabük	12	0.9
Edirne	31	2.2	Artvin	11	0.8
Adana	30	2.1	Kastamonu	11	0.8
Konya	29	2.1	Hatay	10	0.7
Kayseri	28	2.0	Kahramanmaraş	10	0.7
Bilecik	27	1.9	Sinop	10	0.7
Kars	26	1.9	Bayburt	10	0.7
Kütahya	25	1.8	Karaman	10	0.7
Kırşehir	24	1.7	Düzce	10	0.7
Ordu	24	1.7	Burdur	9	0.6
Manisa	23	1.6	Gümüşhane	9	0.6
Afyon	22	1.6	Tokat	9	0.6

10 From interview conducted with Captain I. in Ankara on 12 November 2014.

Hometown	#	%	Hometown	#	%
İçel	22	1.6	Şanlıurfa	9	0.6
Denizli	21	1.5	Uşak	9	0.6
Amasya	20	1.4	Isparta	8	0.6
Erzurum	20	1.4	Nevşehir	8	0.6
Samsun	20	1.4	Van	8	0.6
Aydın	19	1.4	Yozgat	8	0.6
Malatya	19	1.4	Bingöl	7	0.5
Adıyaman	18	1.3	Elazığ	7	0.5
Ağrı	17	1.2	Siirt	7	0.5
Trabzon	17	1.2	Şırnak	7	0.5
Antalya	16	1.1	Ardahan	7	0.5
Tekirdağ	16	1.1	Iğdır	7	0.5
Bolu	15	1.1	Kilis	7	0.5
Gaziantep	15	1.1	Osmaniye	7	0.5
Giresun	15	1.1	Kırklareli	6	0.4
Sakarya	14	1.0	Niğde	6	0.4
Yalova	14	1.0	Tunceli	6	0.4
Balıkesir	13	0.9	Kırıkkale	6	0.4
Çorum	13	0.9	Bartın	6	0.4
Erzincan	13	0.9	Hakkari	5	0.4
Bitlis	12	0.9	Zonguldak	5	0.4
Çanakkale	12	0.9	Batman	2	0.1
Diyarbakır	11	0.9			
Total				1,401	100.0

It is seen that the officers disperse proportionally in general, without concentrating on a specific city or region geographically. This is an important point as it shows that no system of segregation exists in the TAF in terms of geographic dispersion and an 'Army-nation' unison, a narrative which the TAF has always been emphasising, is ensured from the geographic point-of-view. When the difference between the force commands is considered, a slight accumulation to those in the Aegean and Marmara regions attracts attention within the Navy and Air Force. The Army, however, has officers distributed evenly from everywhere. Especially for the Air Force, Eskişehir, İstanbul and Bursa; and for the Navy, İstanbul, Kocaeli, İzmir and Bursa, are the leading hometowns of officers. The existence of units/bases in those provinces can be stated as the main reason. There was no significant difference in answers for this question between ranks.

Q7. What is your father's level of education? In other words, what was that highest degree your father obtained?

	#	%
Literate	42	3.0
Primary school	302	21.6
Elementary school	366	26.1
High school	425	30.3
University	242	17.3
Master's	21	1.5
Doctorate	2	0.1
No response	1	0.1
Total	1,401	100.0

According to the results of this question, 29.18% of officers in the Army have fathers whose highest level of education was primary school. This figure is only 5% in the Navy and 12% in the Air Force. The ratio of university and above is, in turn, 15.71% in the Army, 28.12% in the Navy and 28.12% in the Air Force. The highest level of education among officers' fathers was in the Navy, followed by the Air Force and the Army. On average, the father of an Army officer has an elementary school education, the father of an Air Force officer a high school education and the father of a Navy officer a high school or university education. This shows that the parents of officers in the Navy and Air Force are from a higher education and income group compared to the Army. On average, while parents of officers in the Navy and Air Force are mostly from high- and middle-income level, parents of Army officers are mostly in the low- to middle-income level.

The following table shows the level of education among officers' fathers with respect to ranks:

Table 10. The level of education among officers' fathers with respect to ranks

	Lieutenant/First Lieutenant	Captain	Major	Lt Colonel	Colonel	Total
Literate/ Primary school	110	47	28	11	145	341
Elementary school	170	74	39	16	66	365
High school	194	109	53	18	48	422
University/ Postgraduate	177	47	23	6	11	264
Total	651	277	143	51	270	1,392

As can be seen, the level of education among fathers increases as rank decreases. While the ratio of university graduate fathers is 27% for lieutenants/first lieutenants, this figure is only about 4% for colonels.

Q8. Which income bracket does your monthly household income fall under? In other words, how many Turkish Liras does your household receive per month on average, from all sources of income? (All sources of income including money from your spouse's wage as well as any money you may be receiving from rent, etc.)

	#	%
2,500-4,000 TL	537	38.3
4,000-5,000 TL	315	22.5
5,000-6,000 TL	220	15.7
6,000-7,000 TL	177	12.6
7,000-8,000 TL	127	9.1
8,000 TL & above	25	1.8
Total	1,401	100.0

The interview findings indicate that the 'financial situation' is one of the important criteria determining the relation of an officer with the TAF. There is an important difference between officers whose wives are working and those whose wives are not working in terms of the institutional attachment towards the TAF and the importance given to the occupational career. Since the officers whose wives are working are more independent on the TAF in financial terms, it is seen that they perceive officership as an 'occupation' instead of a lifestyle. Major M.G., who resigned from the TAF in 2015, says:

> In order to be able to carry on my academic studies, I chose to resign willingly since I completed 10 years of compulsory service. The most important thing [that]fostered me in taking this decision was that my wife is a teacher working in [the] public sector. If her public service and stable income were not in place, I would not have made this decision so easily.[11]

Major Y., a successful staff major whose wife does not work, says:

> My wife is a university graduate, but she is a housewife. We have two children. She had studied for the Public Staff Selection Examination (KPSS), the exam for recruitment of public servants for three years, but could not get the required score, then she gave up. We are trying to survive with my single salary in the metropolis of Ankara. If I did not live in a flat within military housing but out in a civilian rental house, I would have substantial financial problems. In fact, we

11 From interview conducted with Major M.G.. in Ankara on 22 October 2015.

> are having financial problems now. Sometimes my parents and my wife's parents provide financial aid to us. My single aim is to concentrate more on my military career and to be selected to the three-year long post abroad by increasing my foreign language score. For us, the staff officers, when you get a score that is not very high but about 80, it is possible to go to an abroad post in which you can make a saving of US$2,500 per month. In this situation, you can return from that post as having saved enough money for a house and a good car. Since my wife does not work, going to a permanent post abroad is vitally important for me financially to guarantee my children's future.[12]

Q9. Do you know any languages aside from Turkish? (including those you only have a beginner's or basic knowledge of)

	#	%
I do not know a foreign language	269	19.2
One language	973	69.5
Two languages	152	10.8
Three languages	7	0.5
Total	1,401	100.0

According to the results of this survey question, 68% of Army and Air Force personnel, as well as 88% of the Navy, know at least one foreign language. The decreased foreign language knowledge in the Army and Air Force can be attributed to their higher number of contracted officers than in the Navy.

The following chart shows the knowledge of foreign languages with respect to ranks:

	Lieutenant / First Lieutenant	**Captain**	**Major**	**Lt Colonel**	**Colonel**	**Total**
I do not know	153	49	5	4	58	269
Only one	440	188	114	36	189	967
Only two	57	37	23	11	23	151
Total	650	274	142	51	270	1,387

As rank decreases, the rate of knowing one foreign language or more increases. Knowledge of a foreign language is most prevalent amongst majors, 95% of whom know at least one other language. Of the captains, 82% know at least one foreign language.

12 Interview conducted in Ankara on 21 March 2014.

The ostensible low rate of foreign language acquisition in the lieutenants/first lieutenants can be explained by the number of contracted officers, which is much more than that of the other ranks.

The foreign language score is the most important criteria for an officer to be selected to temporary (up to six months) or permanent (from six months to three years) posts abroad, in which an officer can receive abroad post payments (around US$2,400 for six-month temporary posts and around US$5,000 for two- or three-year permanent posts). Therefore, a great majority of officers, with a pragmatic approach, consider learning foreign languages as the primary condition for financial gain in the TAF. First Lieutenant E. explains the significance of foreign language skills among officers:

> We say in the TAF "eating bread" to imply financial gains. If you want to eat bread, you eat it only through your foreign language skills. Because the greatest dream of an officer or non-commissioned officer is a two- or three-year permanent post abroad from which he can return with $150,000 in his pocket. For that reason, only with your foreign language skill, you can differentiate from your peers in the TAF, and you can have substantial economic gain.[13]

Major G., who can speak five foreign languages, emphasises the following about the importance of foreign language knowledge among officers:

> Now, knowing only English is not enough in the TAF. Many officers are going for a second and even a third language. My interest in learning foreign languages stems from military high school. I receive award payments for all the languages I learned. Four years of my 17-year career was abroad. For an officer, foreign language proficiency means a ticket for going abroad. Therefore, officers who don't know English, in which the competition is tough, behave more pragmatic[ally] and tend towards the increasingly fashionable languages such as Arabic, Farsi, Chinese, Hebrew, and Russian. While [the] average test score for English, which is composed of the average of public servants' foreign language exam score and the listening test score conducted within the TAF, ... is 95, this average falls down to 70 for those other languages.[14]

The tendency among young officers towards learning less competitive languages such as Arabic, Russian, Hebrew and Chinese reveals their pragmatist side. Their tendency towards learning the languages in which the competition is relatively soft, such as German, French, Arabic, Russian, Hebrew and Chinese instead of English, which requires a General Language Exam average score of 90-100, shows the strategic preferences of officers who are focussing on posts and financial expectations.

13 Interview conducted in Ankara on 15 September 2015.
14 Interview conducted in Ankara on 22 August 2015.

Army Major İ., who had been abroad as an assistant military attaché for three years in a central Asian country with a Russian language score of 87, says:

> In fact, I know English but since the scores are very high in English, it was very difficult for me to go abroad with a score of English. I was deployed to a six-months long temporary post in Turkmenistan. I started learning Russian in this post. I knew very well that I could eat bread from Russian. I studied this language for 4 years and, at the end, I was chosen for this three-years long post of assistant military attaché. It took four years of mine to reach this goal. I am not a staff officer. I do not have career expectations in the military but thanks to my Russian, I went to Turkmenistan. With the money I saved in that post, I could buy a good house in the Eryaman province of Ankara and a good car. My wife is also working. Now, I am relaxed in economic terms.[15]

Q.10. Were you acquainted with officers from your family or your friends before you joined the military?

	#	%
Yes	491	35.0
No	910	65.0
Total	1,401	100.0

That 65% of officers were not acquainted with other officers before joining the military reveals that the profession of officership does not have an aristocratic characteristic coming from family and near sphere lineages. This likely suggests that the great majority of officers do not come from elite officer families, and are rather experiencing their 'elitisation process' within the TAF.

The following table shows the preceding question with regard to different ranks:

Table 11. The main reason in becoming an officer

	Lieutenant/ First Lieutenant	Captain	Major	Lt Colonel	Colonel	Total
Yes	189	131	57	22	89	488
No	462	146	86	30	181	905
Total	651	277	143	52	270	1,393

In all ranks, the percentage not having had any officer acquaintances amongst family or friends exceeds 50%. This finding shows that, in the officer corps, there is no favouritism granted to relatives and no patronage on the basis of family relations.

15 Interview conducted in Ankara on 2 May 2015.

Q11. Who was the primary influence in your decision to become an officer?

	#	%
Personal choice	705	50.3
Family's influence	651	46.5
Other people close to me, besides my family	44	3.1
No response	1	0.1
Total	1,401	100.0

As seen, the decision to become an officer in the military is largely the result of the freewill of the person or as a decision made within the family.

The following chart illuminates the distribution among different ranks:

	Lieutenant/ First Lieutenant	Captain	Major	Lt Colonel	Colonel	Total
Personal choice	410	149	66	24	52	701
Family's influence	235	118	66	24	206	649
Total	645	267	132	48	258	1,350

An important finding is that as the rank decreases, the voluntary choice of an individual becomes the most significant factor in the decision to be an officer. While, for instance, the decision to be an officer is the person's own choice for 64% of the lieutenants/first lieutenants, this number is only 20% for colonels.

The findings indicate that the influence of personal choice on the decision to be an officer is increasing. Junior-level officers (lieutenants, captains and majors) tend to choose officership with a more deliberate preference, while senior-level officers (lieutenant colonels and colonels) become officers with a preference shaped by the influence of their family. It is possible to say that the increase of determination of the freewill of the individual and decrease of the family's influence in the decision to become an officer is an important finding, emphasising increased professionalism among the officer corps.

Q12. What was your main reason in becoming an officer?

	#	%
Social status (serving in an institution such as the TAF)	732	52.2
Financial expectations (a secure job)	417	29.8
A training offered by the TAF, opportunity to serve abroad and similar professional career opportunities	223	15.9
The high level of education at the TAF compared to its civilian counterparts	28	2.0
No response	1	0.1
Total	1,401	100.0

As seen from the table, social status (serving in a prestigious institution such as the TAF) mostly accounts for the reason officers decided to join the military, 52% in the Army, 49% in the Air Force and 61% in the Navy, meaning that the Navy is the most idealist force among the three.

Answers from this survey question reveal that financial expectations were the most important reason to join for 33% in the Army, 29% in the Air Force and 17% in the Navy. Following this, it is possible to say that the officers serving in the Army attach the greatest importance to financial expectations.

The reason for the ostensible higher rate of financial expectations in the Army and Air Force is the increased number of contracted officers compared with the Navy. For a specific force, it is observed that as the ratio of contracted officers increase, the option of financial expectations (a secure job) becomes more weighted.

The following tables elucidates the main reasons officers decided to join, broken down by rank:

Table 12. The main reason in becoming an officer with respect to ranks

	Lt/First Lieutenant	Captain	Major	Lt Colonel	Colonel	Total
Financial expectations (secure job)	243 (38%)	74 (27%)	27 (20%)	16 (30%)	56 (21%)	416
Social status (serving in an institution such as the TAF)	269 (42%)	144 (52%)	92 (66%)	29 (56%)	191 (72%)	725
A training offered by the TAF, opportunity to serve abroad and similar professional career opportunities	123 (20%)	57 (21%)	19 (14%)	6 (14%)	18 (7%)	223
Total	635	275	138	51	265	1,364

The table above is important in that it shows variety among ranks. While social status is the determining factor in becoming an officer at the senior level, as the rank decreases, the determining power of social status deceases and the scale slips towards the alternatives of financial expectations and career at the junior level. This finding shows that the officership is transforming from institutional, that is a lifestyle attaching significance to system of values, to a 'profession' in which financial expectations and progress in career gain importance.

Table 13. The split between seniors and juniors with respect to reasons for becoming an officer

	Social status	Financial expectations	Career
Junior-level officers (Lt, First Lt, Captain + Major	48%	33%	19%
Senior-level officers (Lt Colonel, Colonel + General)	70%	22%	8%

Again, when we separate the sample in a dichotomic way as juniors and seniors, the difference in this question becomes even more visible. While social status is the primary reason to be an officer for the great majority of senior officers (70%), for junior officers this ratio decreases by a third and goes down to 48%. There is an increase in the financial expectations and career alternative for junior over senior officers, the difference in the latter alternative being more than double.

Q13. What is the total amount of time you have served in areas actively partaking in counter-terrorism operations as of now (towns in eastern and south-eastern Anatolia, commonly referred to as 'Sark Görevi')?

	#	%
I haven't	552	39.4
1-2 years	229	16.3
2-3 years	249	17.8
3-4 years	127	9.1
4-5 years	105	7.5
5-6 years	77	5.5
6 years or more	62	4.4
Total	1,401	100.0

According to the results of this survey question, 70% of the Army, 42% of the Air Force and none of the Navy officers have been to south-east Turkey at least once to perform counter-terror tasks.

A colonel in the TAF spends five years on average in combatting terrorism. Among majors, this average falls down to three years and to one year among lieutenants/first lieutenants. Combatting terrorism has deeply affected the organisational culture of the Army. During the interviews, it was interesting to note that, among the 47 officers who served in south-eastern Turkey, roughly half of them stated that strict implementation of security-centric incapacitating strategies through military means cannot solve the PKK-initiated violence by itself, and more comprehensive, population-centric approaches should be mobilised by policymakers.

Q14. How successful do you think the TAF has been thus far in combatting terrorism?

	#	%
Not successful	351	25.1
A little successful	565	40.3
Very successful	485	34.6
Total	1,401	100.0

In regards to the military's efforts to combat terrorism, 32% of officers in the Army, 12% in the Air Force, 15% in the Navy and 10% in the Gendarmerie think that the TAF has not been successful in counter-terrorism. This may lead one to ask why this number is so high in the Army. The answer is that the Army carries the heaviest burden of counter-terror operations in south-east Turkey. Amongst officers in the Navy, who never take an active role in combatting terrorism, 43% think that the military has been very successful in combatting terrorism. The figure is 27% in the Army. From this point, it is possible to say that having served and conducted counter-terror operations in south-east Turkey and experienced such incidents negatively influences the assessment of success against terrorism among officers.

The survey results of how successful the military has been at combatting terrorism broken down by rank is shown below.

Table 14. Perceptions on the TAF's success in combatting terrorism with respect to ranks

	Lieutenant/ First Lieutenant	Captain	Major	Lt Colonel	Colonel	Total
Not successful	130 (20%)	104 (38%)	34 (24%)	5	78 (29%)	351
A little successful	240 (37%)	122 (44%)	57 (40%)	19	125 (46%)	563
Very successful	281 (43%)	51 (18%)	52 (26%)	28	67 (25%)	479
Total	651	277	143	52	270	1,393

The officers who most think that the TAF has not been successful in combatting terrorism are the captains, who have the highest rank in that field. One should note that captains are the intermediate decision-makers in counter-terrorism operations. An interesting finding in the questionnaire is that the tendency to find the TAF unsuccessful in combatting terrorism increases as the duration of mission conducted in the counter-terror region increases. The difference between officers with field experiences in south-east Turkey and those who have not served but have listened to stories account for this phenomena, which is counterintuitive.

Q15. As of today, how long have you served outside of Turkey? (including military deployment, education and seminars)

Table 15. The distribution of service for international posts among respondents

	#	%
Never served outside Turkey	754	53.8
0-6 months	342	24.4
6-12 months	165	11.8
1-2 years	76	5.4
2-3 years	42	3.0
3 years and more	18	1.3
No response	4	0.3
Total	1,401	100.0

The figure for officers who have never been posted abroad is 54% in the Army, 52% in the Air Force and 52% in the Navy, meaning that half of officers in all three forces had been abroad for at least six months. The effects of the increase in international posts and the 'becoming international' efforts in institutional transformation were emphasised in the previous chapter. In the interviews conducted, it was stressed continuously by all officers that the TAF had increased its international post in the last decade and that the High Command had been placing special emphasis on internationalisation.

Q16. What is the total number of years you have spent abroad for educational purposes (military or academic)?

	#	%
Never received education abroad	1,059	75.6
0-6 months	238	17.0
6-12 months	54	3.9
1-2 years	33	2.4
2-3 years	8	.6
3 years and more	1	.1
No response	8	.6
Total	1,401	100.0

In terms of being abroad for educational purposes, 21% of the Army, 30% of the Air Force and 36% of Navy officers have been abroad for at least six months for education/training. It is evident that the best force regarding education/training abroad is the Navy, followed by the Air Force and the Army.

Q17. Where have you served abroad? (If you've served in more than one place, please circle all the relevant options)

The country in which the TAF has the greatest amount of personnel abroad due to NATO posts, as well as training and educational purposes, is the US. While the proportion being in the US for educational or posting purposes is 13% in the Army, it is 19% in the Navy and 17% in the Air Force. Afghanistan ranks second in the number of military personnel being deployed for educational purposes, with European countries coming in third at 4%.

Q18. Generally, how satisfied are you with being an officer as a profession?

	#	%
Not at all	318	22.7
A little	754	53.8
Very	328	23.4
No response	1	0.1
Total	1,401	100.0

When asked about how satisfied they were with being an officer as a profession, 26% in the Army responded that they were not satisfied, followed by the Air Force (21%), Navy (15%) and Gendarmarie (11%). In the light of those numbers, it would appear that the Army is the unhappiest force.

The following chart reveals the satisfaction level of being an officer, breaking it down by rank:

Table 16. The distribution of satisfaction with respect to ranks

	Lieutenant/ First Lieutenant	Captain	Major	Lt Colonel	Colonel	Total
Not at all	148 (23%)	72 (26%)	30 (21%)	12	56 (20%)	318
A little	368 (56%)	164 (59%)	85 (59%)	24	113 (42%)	754
Very	135 (21%)	41 (15%)	28 (20%)	16	100 (38%)	320
Total	651	277	143	52	269	1,392

As seen in the table above, dissatisfaction about the profession among officers increases as the rank decreases. There is a clear shift from '"very satisfied' to 'a little satisfied' and 'not satisfied at all', particularly among junior-level officers.

The interviews suggest that for a great majority of junior-level officers, the level of satisfaction is not directly related to financial issues or difficult assignments in remote bases. Instead, it is directly related to the commander with whom they have served.

An officer, on the one hand, who served in a remote base on the border during a rough period could define this as the most satisfying service in his whole career, thanks to the commander he served under. Another officer, on the other hand, who served in a 'preferable' base in the metropolitan city of Istanbul could define this deployment as the grimmest period in his career, blaming it on the commander's attitude towards his subordinates. It is then not hyperbole to assert that there is a direct association between an officer's satisfaction level in a particular deployment and his perception of the commander in charge of the unit in which he serves.

Q19. What has been the most satisfying aspect of your time in the TAF till now? (please choose only one)

	#	%
Social status and job satisfaction	581	41.5
Economic resources	452	32.2
Career opportunities	367	26.2
No response	1	0.1
Total	1,401	100.0

The figure for 'social status and job satisfaction' is 43% in the Army, 43% in the Air Force, 22% in the Navy and 53% in the Gendarmerie. The ratio of the 'career opportunities' making an officer happy is 35% in the Air Force, 46% in the Navy, 31% in the Army and 21% in the Gendarmerie.

Table 17. Satisfaction among senior and junior officers

	Very	A little	Not at all
Senior-level officers (Lt Colonel, Colonel + General)	37%	42%	21%
Junior-level officers (Lt, First Lt, Captain + Major	19%	58%	23%

Table 18. Satisfaction with respect to ranks

	Lieutenant/ First Lieutenant	Captain	Major	Lt Colonel	Colonel	Total
Social status and job satisfaction	199 (30%)	103	70	21	180	573
Financial gains	209 (32%)	70	34	18	36	367
Career opportunities	243 (38%)	103	39	13	54	452
Total	651	276	143	52	270	1,392

As seen in the tables, as the rank decreases, there appears a shift from the option of 'social status and job satisfaction' to that of 'financial gains' and 'career opportunities'. This finding supports consistently the finding of the 12th question regarding motivations as a determining factor in the decision to become an officer. Furthermore, the findings of this table confirm those of the previous one. While morale and social status play a determining role in the satisfaction levels of senior-level officers, the majors do not associate their satisfaction level with morale and social status as much, instead concentrating more on career opportunities and material factors. Lieutenants, on the other hand, are the most economy-oriented category in the survey. One may then suggest that while social status has been on the decline as the determining factor of the level of satisfaction, material opportunities have been on a relative increase.

Q20. What have you always most prioritised during your period of service in the TAF?

	#	%
TAF (my institution)	675	48.2
Myself	371	26.5
My family	354	25.3
No response	1	0.1
Total	1,401	100.0

When this question is considered in terms of forces, 55% of the Navy, 50% of the Army and 40% of the Air Force stated that the TAF is their greatest priority. However, showing the trend of becoming individualistic, 29% of the Army, 27% of the Air Force and 16% of the Navy said 'myself is above all'. For this question also, the effect of the contracted officers in the Army and the Air Force is observed.

Table 19. Prioritisation with respect to ranks

	Lieutenant/ First Lieutenant	Captain	Major	Lt Colonel	Colonel	Total
Myself	263 (40%)	74 (27%)	18 (13%)	7 (13%)	9 (3%)	371
My family	166 (26%)	89 (32%)	45 (31%)	21 (40%)	33 (12%)	354
TAF (my institution)	221 (34%)	114 (41%)	80 (56%)	24 (47%)	228 (85%)	667
Total	650	277	143	52	270	1,392

With respect to ranks, the rising effect of individualism as the rank decreases is seen clearly from the increase in the rate of the option of 'myself' as an officer's priority. For example, the rate of the option of 'myself' among colonels is 3%, among lieutenant colonels and majors it is 13%, it is 27% for captains and 40% for lieutenants/

first lieutenants. As seen in the table, there is an obvious difference in the opinion of officers towards officership. While the great majority of senior-level officers regard officership as a way of life that not only surrounds the officer himself but also has direct impact on his family's life, most junior-level officers reject this conceptualisation of officership, conceiving it merely as a profession which should not shape the whole life of the officer and his family.

Q21. How important is the 'spirit of cohort' (devre ruhu) for an officer?

The 'spirit of cohort' (*devre ruhu*) has never been studied until now in the TAF scholarly literature, despite the fact that it is an important informal institution directly influencing the behaviours and strategic preferences of the officers. The *devre ruhu* can be defined as an officer's gratuitous trust in collaborating with his cohorts, who are closely monitoring and protecting him. Especially, each officer collaborating with them first when he has been newly appointed is an important rule in the TAF. Friends within a cohort generally know each other very well and think they should firstly support each other in every circumstance and situation, and at all cost. This informal institution allows for both swift communication between cohort colleagues and a pressure mechanism that affects the behaviours and strategic preferences of officers. For an officer well known and appreciated, the cohort spirit has a positive effect on promotion, whereas negative cohort spirit can cause obstacles to an officer's career.

However, especially in war academies, the practice of the same cohorts studying in a single battalion or fleet was abolished from 2000. This meant that there would be students from each of the four classes (that is, from four different cohorts) in every student battalion/fleet. This new regulation, called the 'mixed battalion', has greatly weakened the effect of the spirit of cohort. Now, cohort colleagues do not know each other very well as they do not study together as boarding students for four years. The following table shows to what extent officers value the cohort spirit:

	#	%
Not at all	473	33.8
A little	442	31.5
Very much	486	34.7
Total	1,401	100.0

The following table shows the importance each officer places on the cohort spirit, broken down by rank.

Table 20. Importance attached to the 'Cohort Spirit' with respect to ranks

	Lieutenant/First Lieutenant	Captain	Major	Lt Colonel	Colonel	Total
Not at all	373 (57%)	85	13	1	1 (0.4%)	473
A little	201 (31%)	140	58	12	31 (11.5%)	442
Very	77 (12%)	52	72	39	238 (88.1%)	478
Total	651	277	143	52	270	1,393

While 88% of colonels consider the spirit of cohort to be very important, this ratio falls to 19% for captains and 12% for lieutenants/first lieutenants. This research suggests that as ranks decrease, so does the effect of the spirit of cohort on the behaviours and strategic preferences of an officer.

Q22. Do you think that the respect and reputation accorded to officership as a profession is decreasing in Turkey?

	#	%
Yes	1,077	76.9
No	318	22.7
No response	6	0.4
Total	1,401	100.0

With regards to the perception of the military, 83% of the Army responded 'yes' when asked if the respect and reputation accorded to officership as a profession has been decreasing in Turkey, followed by the Air Force (76%), Gendarmerie (76%) and Navy (50%).

Table 21. Perception about the decrease in the TAF's reputation with respect to ranks

	Lieutenant/First Lieutenant	Captain	Major	Lt Colonel	Colonel	Total
Yes	488 (76%)	233 (84%)	105 (73%)	34 (65%)	211 (78%)	1,071
No	157 (24%)	44 (16%)	38 (27%)	18 (35%)	59 (22%)	316
Total	645	277	143	52	270	1,387

It is an interesting finding that a great majority of all ranks answered 'yes' without much differentiation by rank.

Q23. If you currently have or plan to have children, would you want them to be an officer in the TAF?

The question on whether or not an officer would want his children to be an officer in the TAF aimed to measure institutional attachment:

	#	%
Yes	528	37.7
No	873	62.3
Total	1,401	100.0

In response to this survey question, 66% of the Army answered that they would not want their children to be an officer in the TAF, followed by 65% of the Air Force and 53% of the Navy. In the light of those answers, it is interesting to note that the Army had the greatest number of respondents not wanting to have children entering the military.

	Lieutenant/First Lieutenant	Captain	Major	Lt Colonel	Colonel	Total
Yes	196 (30%)	91 (33%)	61 (43%)	22 (42%)	152 (56%)	522
No	455 (70%)	186 (67%)	82 (57%)	30 (58%)	118 (44%)	871
Total	651	277	143	52	270	1,393

Answers to this question again emphasised that as rank decreases, the less likely the officer would like his offspring to become an officer. These answers also go hand-in-hand with the findings from questions about their degree of satisfaction.

These results clearly show the extent to which officership has become an unpopular profession among junior officers. This finding may also be asserted as another indicator of the officer corps' declining commitment to the TAF as a source of high status within society.

Q24. What do you think the TAF's 'primary task' ought to be?

	#	%
Protecting the Republic of Turkey solely from external threats	740	52.8
Protecting the Republic of Turkey from both internal and external threats	661	47.2
Total	1,401	100.0

Table 22. Perception of the TAF's primary task with respect to ranks

	Lieutenant/ First Lieutenant	Captain	Major	Lt Colonel	Colonel	Total
Protecting the Republic of Turkey solely from external threats	450 (69%)	159 (57%)	54 (38%)	15 (29%)	59 (22%)	737 (53%)
Protecting the Republic of Turkey from both internal and external threats	201 (31%)	118 (43%)	89 (62%)	37 (71%)	211 (78%)	656 (47%)
Total	651	277	143	52	270	1,393

This question aims to measure opinions about the TAF's primary task. While no significant difference exists between the forces, there are significant differences between ranks. As ranks decrease, the opinion that the task of the TAF is to protect Turkey from solely external threats tends to increase. For colonels, this figure is 21.8%, whereas it is 89.1% for lieutenants/first lieutenants.

Q25. Do you think the TAF needs serious structural reforms to meet future threats and prepare for possible conflicts?

	#	%
Yes	1,240	88.5
No	138	9.9
No response	23	1.6
Total	1,401	100.0

The Army responded affirmatively about the restructuring of the military with 92% of officers, followed by the Air Force (88%t) and Navy (80%). In total, 88% answered 'yes', which is an important finding showing that officers want a structural reform and are mentally ready for something like that.

Table 23. Perception about the TAF's need for reforms with respect to ranks

	Lieutenant/First Lieutenant	Captain	Major	Lt Colonel	Colonel	Total
Yes	589 (94%)	255 (92%)	130 (90%)	40 (77%)	221 (82%)	1,235 (90%)
No	40 (6%)	22 (8%)	13 (10%)	12 (23%)	48 (18%)	135 (10%)
Total	629	277	143	52	269	1,370

The overwhelming number of affirmative answers in all ranks is indicative that the great majority of officers who participated in the questionnaire agree that the TAF needs serious structural reforms for transformation.

Q26. How optimistic are you about the TAF's power and deterrent capabilities in the global security environment?

	#	%
Not at all	397	28.3
A little	667	47.6
Very	336	24.0
No response	1	0.1
Total	1,401	100.0

Regarding the TAF's current security capabilities on the international stage, 30% of the Army is not optimistic, followed by the Navy (33%), Air Force (25%) and Gendarmerie (15%).

Table 24. The level of optimism about the TAF's deterrent capabilities with respect to ranks

	Lieutenant/ First Lieutenant	Captain	Major	Lt. Colonel	Colonel	Total
Not at all	150 (23%)	90 (32%)	46 (32%)	10 (20%)	100 (37%)	396
A little	323 (50%)	137	66	34	107	667
Very	178 (27%)	50	31	8	62	329
Total	651	277	143	52	269	1,392

The average of 'not at all' optimistic among all ranks is around 30%.

When both the interviews and the questionnaire results are considered, it is possible to say that there is a positive correlation between the duration of posts abroad and the negative opinion regarding international deterrent capabilities of the TAF. That is to say, as officers increase their understanding of the capabilities of other armies around the world while posted abroad, their level of optimism about the TAF's ability as international deterrent declines.

Q27. Which are the most important factors for a 'deterrent and strong Army'? (please choose only one)

	#	%
Qualified personnel	609	43.5
Technology	490	35.0
Qualified commanders	226	16.1
Military morale and cultural values	74	5.3
No response	2	0.1
Total	1,401	100.0

It is interesting to note that the officers who participated in the questionnaire emphasised 'qualified personnel' for a deterrent and powerful Army.

Table 25. Perception about the most important factor for a strong TAF with respect to forces

	Qualified personnel	Technology	Qualified commanders	Military morale and cultural factors
Army	10%	29%	56%	5%
Air Force	18%	60%	15%	7%
Navy	48%	36%	12%	4%
Gendarmerie	13%	25%	53%	9%

As seen from the table, the variety among the forces give clear insights about the cultures of each force command. In the answers given, while the emphasis of qualified personnel predominates in the Navy, the emphasis of technology gains importance with 60% in the Air Force, and in the Army the emphasis of qualified commanders gains importance with 56%.

Q28. How do you think Turkey's membership fo NATO contributed to the TAF's institutional structure (organisational structure, work, institutional culture, etc.)?

	#	%
Positively	992	70.8
Negatively	362	25.8
No response	47	3.4
Total	1,401	100.0

The ratios saying yes are 74% in the Army and Air Force, and 68% in the Navy. The answers show that the positive perception about NATO reaches an overall rate of 70%.

Table 26. Perception of NATO with respect to ranks

	Lieutenant/ First Lieutenant	Captain	Major	Lt Colonel	Colonel	Total
Positively	472 (75.8%)	196 (75.4%)	108 (76%)	39 (75%)	169 (62.8%)	984
Negatively	151 (24.2%)	64 (24.6%)	34 (24%)	13 (25%)	100 (37.2%)	362
Total	623	260	142	52	269	1346

In light of the table above, it is possible to say that the level of positive perception about NATO is the same for all ranks at around 75%, except for colonels with a 62% figure.

Q29. How do you think Turkey's NATO membership contributed to the TAF's effectiveness in battle?

	#	%
Positively	990	70.7
Negatively	366	26.1
No response	45	3.2
Total	1,401	100.0

Finding of this question support the previous question.

Q30 Should Turkey cooperate more with international security organisations other than NATO, such as Shanghai Cooperation Organisation?

	#	%
Yes	1,189	84.9
No	204	14.5
No response	8	0.6
Total	1,401	100.0

Those officers saying 'yes' to further international cooperation are 89% in the Army, 94% in the Air Force, 62% in the Navy and 71% in the Gendarmerie. The overwhelming overall 'yes' total of 84% is as a result of the interest of officers about posts abroad and the fact that internationalisation efforts offer opportunities for both their occupational careers and their finances.

In the interviews conducted, it was also seen that the support of the officers for internationalisation is directly related to their financial expectations and career opportunities.

Q31. Is the recent wave of civilianisation in civil-military relations in Turkey positively affecting the TAF's military power and efficacy?

	#	%
Yes	574	41.0
No	708	50.5
No response	119	8.5
Total	1,401	100.0

The ratio of 'yes' is 47% in the Army, 44% in the Air Force, 28% in the Navy and 45% in the Gendarmerie. The trauma and rage experienced by Navy personnel because of the court cases and prosecution processes experienced by some Navy officers in the last couple of years are seen clearly in the results of this table.

Table 27. Perception about positive effect of civilianisation in the CMR with respect to ranks

	Lieutenant/ First Lieutenant	Captain	Major	Lt Colonel	Colonel	Total
Yes	328 (58%)	116 (44%)	54 (40%)	15 (30%)	60 (22%)	573
No	233 (42%)	145 (56%)	83 (60%)	36 (70%)	206 (78%)	703
Total	561	261	137	51	266	1,276

As can be seen from the table, as the rank decreases, the opinion of officers that civilianisation positively affects the TAF's power and efficacy tends to increase.

This table shows the deep-seated mistrust of the political system among senior officers when it comes to civil-military relations. It is noticeable that while senior officers were inclined to answer this question in a negative way, the captains and especially lieutenants were inclined to answer this question with 'yes'.

Q32. How nationalist would you say you are?

	#	%
Not at all	51	3.6
A little	641	45.8
Very	607	43.3
No response	102	7.3
Total	1,401	100.0

With regards to nationalist sentiment, 42% of the Army, 44% of the Air Force and 46% of the Navy defined themselves as 'very nationalist'.

The fact that an average of 7% from all the forces left this question empty is an important finding, as it shows that stating an opinion about this subject, which is considered to be a political question, can still be a taboo matter in the TAF.

Table 28. Level of nationalism with respect to ranks

	Lieutenant/ First Lieutenant	Captain	Major	Lt Colonel	Colonel	General/ Admiral	Total
Not at all	31 (5%)	4 (1%)	3 (2%)	2 (4%)	11 (4%)	0	51
A little	286 (44%)	139 (50%)	56 (39%)	18 (34%)	140 (52%)	2 (25%)	641
Very	253 (40%)	117 (42%)	81 (56%)	32 (62%)	119 (44%)	5 (62.5%)	607
No response	81 (11%)	1 (7%)	3 (3%)	0	0	1 (12.5%)	102
Total	651	261	143	52	270	8	1,401

These results show there is no significant difference between ranks as regarding the level of nationalism.

Q33. There has existed a long tradition of left-right-centre politics in Turkey. Where in this spectrum would you locate your political views?

	#	%
Centrist	510	36.4
Centre left	287	20.5
Centre right	282	20.1
Right	43	3.1
Left	37	2.6
None	19	1.4
No response	223	15.9
Total	1,401	100.0

As is seen from this table, which measures the political position of officers, 'Centre' is the most preferred answer with 36.4%. The fact that 15.9 percent of participants avoided answering this question is important, since it shows that talking and expressing opinion about politics is still taboo in the TAF.

Table 29. Political stance with respect to force commands

	Left	Centre left	Centre	Centre right	Right	Blank
Army	3%	18%	34%	24%	3%	18%
Air Force	1%	20%	26%	16%	-	37%
Navy	-	35%	43%	4%	-	18%
Gendarmerie	1%	2%	30%	20%	15%	32%

This table shows the Army has the most 'centre right' conservative opinion, whereas the closest force to the left is the Navy. The Air Force is the most unwilling to answer this question, with more than one in three refusing to do so. In addition, it appears that Gendarmerie General Command personnel are graduates of the Army War Academy and are very close to the Army officers.

Table 30. Political stance with respect to ranks

	Lieutenant/ First Lieutenant	Captain	Major	Lt Colonel	Colonel	General/ Admiral	Total
Left	143 (22%)	37 (13%)	12 (8%)	2 (4%)	29 (11%)	0	223
Centre Left	7 (1%)	3 (1%)	1 (0.6%)	1 (2%)	25 (9%)	0	37
Centre	76 (12%)	62 (22%)	38 (27%)	14 (27%)	97 (36%)	0	287
Centre right	232 (36%)	106 (38%)	64 (45%)	24 (46%)	83 (31%)	1	510
Right	165 (25%)	65 (23%)	19 (13%)	7 (13%)	26 (10%)	0	282
None	23 (3%)	3 (1%)	5 (3%)	3 (6%)	6 (2%)	3	43
No response	5 (1%)	1	4 (2%)	1	4 (1%)	4	19
Total	651	277	143	52	270	8	1,401

In this table, the political view shifts from centre to right as the rank decreases.

Table 31. Political stance within the senior and junior officers

	Junior officers	Senior officers	Total
Left	11	26	37
Centre left	176 (26%)	111 (34%)	287
Centre	402 (38%)	108(33%)	510
Centre right	249 (23%)	33 (10%)	282
Right	31	12	43
None	10	9	19
No response	192	31	223
Total	1,071	330	1,401

In this table, the difference between the junior officers and senior ones appears clearly. Especially there are few 'centre right' seniors, while 23% of juniors have chosen this alternative. It is an important point that the overwhelming majority of those giving no response are juniors, showing that young officers are more timid about expressing their political preferences.

As the table shows, while there is homogeneity in the political stance of seniors (mostly nationalist left and social democrat), the political views of majors and lieutenants are more heterogeneous. It is appealing to note that the political views of lieutenants, particularly, are the most varied. It is also significant to note that, during the interviews, while the seniors had a rock-solid stance in terms of their political ideas, the majors, captains and lieutenants were politically confused when defining their stances.

Q34. Which institution first and foremost represents the 'national will' in Turkey?

	#	%
Parliament	1,239	88.4
Government	75	5.4
Presidency	48	3.4
Constitutional Court	16	1.1
No response	23	1.6
Total	1,401	100.0

As seen from the table, an overwhelming majority of 88% has perceived the parliament as the representative of the national will. This shows that the parliament, to which the officers attach special emphasis in an overwhelming majority, has critical importance in the democratic and civilian control of officers. Given the high level of credibility of parliament among officers, it is also possible to suggest that parlimentary commissions should be the mechanisms managing the civilian side of the Turkish CMR.

Q35. Do you think that the principle of 'secularism' is currently under threat in Turkey?

	#	%
Yes	554	39.5
No	688	49.1
No response	159	11.3
Total	1,401	100.0

The fact that half of the officers think secularism is not under threat is an important finding showing that the TAF no longer perceives political Islam as an internal threat. The secularism sensitivity of the TAF has visibly fallen.

Table 32. Perception of whether secularism is under threat with respect to force commands

	Yes	No	Blank
Army	32%	56%	12%
Air Force	40%	46%	14%
Navy	69%	22%	9%

It is seen that there are significant differences between the forces on the matter of sensitivity about secularism. For example, 56% of the Army thinks that secularism is not under threat any more, while for the Navy this figure is only 22%. According to the Navy, secularism is still under threat. This opinion variety is important in that it shows the differentiation in organisational cultures of the forces.

Table 33. Perception of whether secularism is under threat with respect to ranks

	Lieutenant/ First Lieutenant	Captain	Major	Lt Colonel	Colonel	Total
Yes	167 (31%)	106 (43%)	73 (54%)	38 (75%)	166 (64%)	550
No	374 (69%)	139 (57%)	63 (46%)	13 (25%)	95 (36%)	684
Total	541	245	136	51	261	1,234

This question shows that differences exist between ranks, but also that sensitivity regarding secularism decreases along with rank. While 64% of colonels still think that secularism is under threat, only 31% of lieutenants/first lieutenants believe so.

Q36. Do you think that the principle of the 'unitary state' is currently under threat in Turkey?

	#	%
Yes	1,162	82.9
No	201	14.3
No response	38	2.7
Total	1,401	100.0

An overwhelming majority, as much as 82.9%, of officers think that the unity of the state is under threat. It is seen that the officers' threat perception about the unity of the state is much higher than that about secularism.

Table 34. Perception of whether 'unity of state' is under threat with respect to force commands

	Yes	No
Army	87%	13%
Air Force	82%	18%
Navy	86%	14%

While it is seen that there is no significant difference between the forces regarding the sensitivity about 'unity of state', a difference can be spoken of in the distribution among ranks. The rate of 'yes' answers to the question 'Is the unity of the state under threat' is 82% for lieutenants/first lieutenants, 82% for captains, 88% for majors, 75% for lieutenant colonels and 98% for colonels. From those figures, colonels appear to be the rank having the highest sensitivity.

Q.37. Do you fast during the month of Ramadan?

	#	%
I partially do	430	30.7
I don't fast	338	24.1
I try to fast during the whole period of Ramadan	308	22.0
I don't fast (due to health reasons/not in my faith)	139	9.9
No response	186	13.3
Total	1,401	100.0

This question aims to measure the piety/conservativeness level of officers by asking about fasting habits. The ones who partly fast constitute the largest number. The fact that 13.3% of officers refused to answer this question related to piety shows that it is often still taboo in the TAF.

Table 35. Fasting with respect to force commands

	I don't fast	I don't fast (health)	I partially fast	I fast during whole Ramadan	Blank
Army	23%	9%	29%	26%	13%
Air Force	27%	14%	32%	12%	16%
Navy	14%	30%	30%	5%	21%

There is no significant difference between the forces with regards to the fasting question. The answers to this question align with question 33 regarding political preferences, with 26% of Army officers stating that they fast during whole the Ramadan. Again as a characteristic supporting question 33, only 5% of Navy personnel fast during the entire month.

Table 36. Fasting with respect to force ranks

	Lieutenant/ First Lieutenant	Captain	Major	Lt Colonel	Colonel	General/ Admiral	Total
I don't fast	124 (19%)	57 (21%)	41 (29%)	12 (23%)	103 (38%)	1	338
I don't fast (due to health reasons/not in my faith)	41 (6%)	33 (12%)	14 (10%)	4 (8%)	47 (17%)	0	139
I partially do	185 (28%)	95 (34%)	44 (31%)	27 (52%)	79 (29%)	0	430
I try to fast during the whole period of Ramadan.	184 (28%)	58 (21%)	31 (22%)	7 (13%)	23 (9%)	5	308
No response	117 (18%)	34 (12%)	13 (10%)	2	18 (7%)	2	186
Total	651	277	143	52	270	8	1,401

There is significant difference between ranks, and the answers to this question also support the results of question 33. In addition, the tendency of not responding to the question about fasting increases as rank decreases. The number of officers not fasting generally increases as rank increases.

Table 37. Fasting among senior and junior officers

	Junior officers	Senior officers	Total
I don't fast	222 (21%)	116 (35%)	338
I don't fast (due to health reasons/not in my faith)	88 (8%)	51 (15%)	139
I partially do	324 (30%)	106 (32%)	430
I try to fast during the whole period of Ramadan.	273 (25%)	35 (11%)	308
No response	164 (15%)	22 (7%)	186
Total	1,071	330	1,401

As is seen in this table, which aims to analyse ranks in a dichotomic fashion, while 25% of junior-level officers try to fast through the whole period of Ramadan, only 11% of senior-level officers do the same. Some 21% of junior-level officers do not fast, while 35% of senior-level officers do not partake in fasting. These findings also consistently support the findings of question 33, which shows that being conservative increases among officers as their rank decreases.

Q38. Generally, how satisfied are you with your personal economic situation?

	#	%
Not satisfied at all	829	59.2
A little satisfied	527	37.6
Very satisfied	36	2.6
No response	9	0.6
Total	1,401	100.0

The forces not satisfied at all with their personal economic situation are 66% in the Army, 45% in the Air Force and 37% in the Navy. Air Force and Navy personnel receive higher salaries than their counterparts in the Army due to their high level of mission compensations, which is the fundamental reason of the high dissatisfaction about economic status in the Army.

Q39. How has your economic situation changed as an officer over the past few years?

	#	%
Worse	1,153	82.3
Same	236	16.8
Better	10	0.7
No response	2	0.1
Total	1,401	100.0

An overwhelming majority of 82.3% of officers think that their economic situation has become worse in the past few years.

In the remaining part of the questionnaire, the analysis of dichotomic 'yes/no' questions designed for both cross-checking and expanding the questions asked in the previous section are presented.

1. Matters of religion and state ought to be separate

	#	%
Yes	1,398	99.8
No	2	0.1
No response	1	0.1
Total	1,401	100.0

The 'yes' answer received for this question is almost 100%, showing that the overwhelming majority of officers have a high awareness of secularism.

2. Women serving as judges, prosecutors, teachers and police should be allowed to wear their headscarves during public service.

	#	%
Yes	181	12.9
No	1,104	78.8
No response	106	8.3
Total	1,401	100.0

The rate of officers opposing women in public service from covering their heads is more than 78%. Most of the those who answered in the affirmative are contracted lieutenants/first lieutenants in the Army.

3. Female students in primary and secondary education should be allowed to cover their heads in class during lessons.

	#	%
Yes	110	7.9
No	1,177	84.0
No response	114	8.1
Total	1,401	100.0

Officers are overwhelmingly against female students in primary and secondary schools covering their heads, with 84% answering 'no'.

4. I believe in the afterlife.

	#	%
Yes	874	62.4
No	334	23.8
No response	193	13.8
Total	1,401	100.0

This question tries to measure the level of piety directly, with 62% of officers believing in the afterlife. The 13.8% who did not answer the question is meaningful, showing that expressing opinions about piety is still taboo in the TAF.

Table 38. Believing in the afterlife with respect to ranks

	Lieutenant/First Lieutenant	Captain	Major	Lt Colonel	Colonel	Total
Yes	423 (80%)	199 (82%)	90 (70%)	31 (61%)	126 (51%)	869
No	110 (20%)	42 (18%)	37 (30%)	20 (39%)	124 (49%)	333
Total	533	241	127	51	250	1,202

Belief in the afterlife decreases as rank increases. The answers to this question further support the findings related to officers' political preferences in question 33 and fasting in question 37. An overwhelming majority (80%) of lieutenants/first lieutenants believe in the afterlife, but only 51% of colonels.

5. When science and religion contradict each other, I seek guidance from science.

	#	%
Yes	1,294	92.4
No	93	6.6
No response	14	1.0
Total	1,401	100.0

An overwhelming majority of 92.4% of the officers stated that they prefer science in a situation of contradiction between religion and science, which also supports the second question of this section related to religion and the state.

6. I don't approve of income from interest (e.g. receiving returns from money in a bank account).

	#	%
Yes	263	18.8
No	1,036	73.9
No response	102	7.3
Total	1,401	100.0

This question attempted to gauge how religious matters affect financial matters among officers, with 73.9% thinking that it does not go against religion to obtain money from interest.

7. Kurds should be granted the right to be able to use their mother tongue as the language of instruction in education.

	#	%
Yes	100	7.1
No	1,221	87.2
No response	80	5.7
Total	1,401	100.0

Measuring the sensitivity to the Kurdish question, 87.2% of officers opposed the right for Kurds to be able to use Kurdish as the language of instruction in primary school. An overwhelming majority of officers still consider the rights surrounding the use of the Kurdish language from a political point of view but not from the cultural rights point of view.

8. I support Turkey's EU membership process.

	#	%
Yes	925	66.4
No	438	31.4
No response	30	2.2
Total	1,393	100.0

This question was aimed at measuring the willingness about EU membership, and a majority of 66.4% of officers supported the membership process.

In the interviews conducted, it was observed that the majority of officers still attach importance to the EU membership process and westernisation, perceiving them as the preliminary requirement for democracy and modernization in Turkey.

Table 39. Support for EU membership with respect to ranks as follows:

	Lieutenant/First Lieutenant	Captain	Major	Lt Colonel	Colonel	Total
Yes	458 (86%)	190 (70%)	106 (83%)	34 (66%)	126 (49%)	925 (68%)
No	167 (14%)	83 (30%)	37 (17%)	18 (34%)	133 (51%)	438 (32%)
Total	625	273	143	52	259	1,363

9. I trust the parliament.

	#	%
Yes	271	19.3
No	1,104	78.8
No response	26	1.9
Total	1,401	100.0

The purpose of this question was to gauge the military's trust of parliament, with 78.8% of the officers responding 'no'. When this result is compared with the results of question 34, in which 84.4% of officers perceived parliament to be the representative of the 'national will', it is possible to say that there is a perceptional gap among officers between credibility of the parliament and trust of that institution.

10. I trust the police (law enforcement agency).

	#	%
Yes	157	11.2
No	1,239	88.4
No response	5	0.4
Total	1,401	100.0

To the question attempting to gauge the trust of the police as an institution, 88.4% of officers answered 'no'. It is considered that this perception could be explained by mistreatment by the police of TAF personnel, particularly during the last decade in the cases and prosecution processes against serving and retired officers.

11. I trust the media.

	#	%
Yes	99	7.1
No	1,302	92.9
Total	1,401	100.0

When measuribng the military's trust of the media, only 7.1% of those questioned said they did so. This low ratio is considered to be caused by the negative perception and biased attitude of the media.

12. No matter what the circumstances, Turkey should have a democracy.

	#	%
Yes	1,301	92.8
No	96	6.9
No response	4	0.3
Total	1,401	100.0

An overwhelming majority of officers questioned – 92.8% – think Turkey's governing style must be a democracy.

Table 40. Level of internalisation of democracy with respect to ranks

	Lieutenant/ First Lieutenant	Captain	Major	Lt Colonel	Colonel	General/ Admiral	Total
Yes	617 (94.8%)	276 (99.6%)	136 (95%)	51 (98%)	214 (79.3%)	7	1,301
No	30 (4.6%)	1 (0.4%)	7 (5%)	1 (2%)	56 (20.7%)	1	96
No response	4 (0.6%)	0	0	0	0	0	4
Total	651	277	143	52	270	8	1,401

The belief that Turkey must be governed by democracy increases as the officers' rank decreases.

13. I am satisfied with the level of democracy and the functioning of democracy in Turkey.

	#	%
Yes	344	24.5
No	993	70.9
No response	64	4.6
Total	1,401	100.0

Some 70.9% of the officers are not satisfied with the present level and functioning of democracy in Turkey. When this finding is considered together with that from the previous question, the majority of officers (95%) think democracy is the only political system, yet 71% are not satisfied with the current level of democracy in Turkey.

From this result, it is possible to say that there is a strong perception in the minds of officers that there is a democracy deficit in Turkey.

14. Turkey is a military nation.

#	%
1,313	93.7
88	6.3
1,401	100.0

This question tries to measure the prevalence of the opinion of Turkey being a military nation among officers, and an overwhelming 93.7% responded affirmatively.

15. When necessary, the military should seize control and govern the country.

	#	%
Yes	83	5.9
No	1,309	93.4
No response	9	0.6
Total	1,401	100.0

In response to this question, which aims to measure the level of belief in democracy among officers and to cross-check question 12, 93.4% of them said 'no'. This finding shows that answers with question 12 are consistent.

Table 41. Inclination to military rule with respect to ranks

	Lieutenant/First Lieutenant	Captain	Major	Lt Colonel	Colonel	General/ Admiral	Total
Yes	15 (2%)	7 (3%)	10 (7%)	3 (6%)	48	0	83
No	630 (97%)	270 (97%)	133 (93%)	49 (94%)	219 (81%)	8 (100%)	1,309
No response	6 (1%)	0	0	0	3 (1%)	0	9
Total	651	277	143	52	270	8	1,401

When distribution with respect to ranks is considered, it is seen that, discounting the small number of generals/admirals, the tendency to say 'no' to this question increases as the rank decreases. While 81% of the colonels answered 'no', the figure rises to 97% for lieutenants/first lieutenants and captains.

16. Military administrations can be much more effective and successful than civilian ones

	#	%
Yes	152	10.9
No	1,236	88.2
No response	13	0.9
Total	1,401	100.0

The findings of this question, which is included in the questionnaire to cross-check the 12th and 15th questions, are consistent with the previous two questions, with 88.2% of officers rejecting the idea that military administrations can be much more effective and successful than civilian ones.

17. The military's influence in civil politics and government has decreased in Turkey over the past 10 to 15-year period.

	#	%
Yes	1,135	81.0
No	219	15.6
No response	47	3.4
Total	1,401	100.0

In response to this question, which aims to measure the general opinion among officers about civilianization during the last 10 years regarding the military's influence on politics, 81% of officers answered 'yes'.

Table 42. Perception about whether the military's influence decreased in the last decade with respect to ranks

	Lieutenant/ First Lieutenant	Captain	Major	Lt Colonel	Colonel	Total
Yes	534 (87.8%)	237 (86%)	122 (85.3%)	42 (80%)	194 (71.8%)	1,129
No	74 (12.2%)	36 (14%)	21 (14.7%)	10 (20%)	76 (28.2%)	217
Total	608	273	143	52	270	1,346

The tendency to answer 'yes' to whether the military's influence has decreased increases as the rank decreases. While the rate of junior-level officers agreeing with this question is 86.3%, the figure for senior-level officers is 75.9 percent.

18. The total number of soldiers in the TAF should be decreased.

	#	%
Yes	1,145	81.7
No	252	18.0
No response	4	0.3
Total	1,401	100.0

A clear majority of 81.7% of officers responded 'yes' to this question, which aims to measure the opinion about decreasing the number of soldiers in the TAF.

19. Compulsory military service should be abolished.

	#	%
Yes	930	66.4
No	464	33.1
No response	7	0.5
Total	1,401	100.0

In this question, aiming to measure opinions about compulsory military service, 66.4% of officers answered affirmatively, most of which were junior-level officers.

20. Even if compulsory military service continues, the length of service period should be further shortened.

	#	%
Yes	1,186	84.6
No	214	15.3
No response	1	0.1
Total	1,401	100.0

When asked about shortening the length of time for compulsory military service, 84.6 of officers said 'yes'.

21. Imagine that you have sufficient economic wealth and means and your son wants to complete his military service through a payment/fee. Would you approve?

	#	%
Yes	876	62.5
No	517	36.9
No response	8	0.6
Total	1,401	100.0

In response to this question, which aims to measure an important part of the value system of the TAF such as compulsory military service and the level of pragmatism of officers towards this element, 62.5 percent of officers approved that their son could complete military service through payment (*bedelli askerlik*).

Table 43. Perception about military service through payment with respect to ranks

	Lieutenant/First Lieutenant	Captain	Major	Lt Colonel	Colonel	Total
Yes	511 (80%)	171 (62%)	80 (56%)	27 (52%)	85 (32%)	874
No	132 (20%)	106 (38%)	63 (44%)	25 (48%)	185 (68%)	511
Total	643	277	143	52	270	1,385

The tendency to answer 'yes' increases as rank decreases. In accordance with this finding, it is possible to say that there is a shift from an idealist attitude to a pragmatic one regarding a concept that has great value for the TAF, such as compulsory military service.

22. The TAF should be an army constituted of only professional soldiers (that is, volunteer soldiers like paid public servants) like in the USA.

	#	%
Yes	965	68.9
No	434	31.0
No response	2	.1
Total	1,401	100.0

In this question aiming to measure officers' opinions about a professional army, 68.9% of them supported the idea.

Table 44. Perception about 'professional military' with respect to ranks

	Lieutenant/First Lieutenant	Captain	Major	Lt Colonel	Colonel	Total
Yes	547 (84%)	181 (65%)	101 (71%)	34 (65%)	98 (37%)	961
No	103 (16%)	96 (35%)	42 (29%)	18 (35%)	171 (63%)	430
Total	650	277	143	52	269	1,391

It is seen that the tendency to appreciate professional soldiers generally increases as rank decreases. This question also supports findings related to the shift from an idealist officership to a career- and economy-oriented officership.

23. There should be a legal right to refuse military service based on belief, moral views or personal choice (conscientious objection).

	#	%
Yes	162	11.6
No	1,234	88.1
No response	5	0.3
Total	1,401	100.0

An overwhelming percentage of officers (88.1%) think negatively about conscientious objection.

24. The number of female officers and sergeants serving in the TAF should be increased.

	#	%
Yes	920	65.7
No	481	34.3
Total	1,401	100.0

Almost twice as many officers (65.7% against 34.3%) support increasing the number of female personnel in the TAF.

Table 45. Perception about woman empowerment within the military with respect to ranks

	Lieutenant/First Lieutenant	Captain	Major	Lt Colonel	Colonel	Total
Yes	470 (72%)	194 (70%)	92 (64%)	25 (48%)	135 (50%)	916
No	181 (28%)	83 (30%)	51 (36%)	27 (52%)	135 (50%)	477
Total	651	277	143	52	270	1,393

The opinion that the number of female officers and sergeants serving in the TAF should be increased tends to increase as the rank decreases. Looking at this result, it is possible to say that officers have more gender-friendly opinions as the rank decreases.

When it comes to gender approval in the TAF, as seen in the table, there is a direct negative association between the seniority of an officer and his approval of women serving in the military, which means that the approval of women serving in the military has gradually been increasing among junior-level officers. One should also note that, since 1996, women have been actively serving in all services of the Turkish military, even in the combat branches as war pilots in war fleets of the Turkish Air Force and helicopter pilots in aviation units in the Turkish Army. This fact also implies that majors, captains and lieutenants have been more acquainted with working with women officers in their units. Another important element in this issue is that at the time of the survey women had started to serve as non-commissioned officers in the Turkish military for the previous two years, a matter that will eventually increase women's contribution to service-related jobs.

In contrast to officers' gradually and positively changing attitudes on the gender issue, the officers are in rock-solid unanimity when it comes to approval of homosexuals serving in the military. As seen in the table below, it is impossible to assert that the officer corps has been looking for a paradigmatic change on this issue. Nearly all respondents (except for one lieutenant) were extremely conservative on the serving of homosexuals in the TAF.

25. If they want to, homosexuals should be allowed to complete their compulsory service in the TAF.

	#	%
Yes	50	3.6
No	1,349	96.3
No response	2	0.1
Total	1,401	100.0

More than 96% of officers said 'no' to allowing homosexuals to serve in the TAF. Thirty-five of those ones saying 'yes' to the question were lieutenants/first lieutenants, while 15 were captains. Therefore, although in a very minor way, it is possible to say that the tough attitude on this matter softens somewhat as the rank decreases.

26. Atatürkism is the main source of intellectual inspiration for the TAF

	#	%
Yes	1,164	83.1
No	237	16.9
Total	1,401	100.0

An overwhelming majority of 83.1% of officers think that Atatürkism is still the main source of intellectual inspiration for the TAF.

27. An officer in Turkey is always superior to a civilian counterpart of the same education level.

	#	%
Yes	440	31.4
No	961	68.6
Total	1,401	100.0

In this question, aiming to measure the elitist view of officers about society, a great majority (68.8%) think that officers' level of education is not higher than that of civilians.

Table 46. Perception about an 'elitist view' within the military with respect to ranks

	Lieutenant/First Lieutenant	Captain	Major	Lt Colonel	Colonel	Total
Yes	124 (19%)	79 (28%)	49 (34%)	31 (59%)	152 (56%)	435
No	527 (81%)	198 (72%)	94 (66%)	21 (41%)	118 (44%)	958
Total	651	277	143	52	270	1,393

The rate of answering 'no' increases as rank decreases. From this result, it is possible to say that the level of elitist view of society decreases as rank decreases. It is an important finding that 56% of colonels answered 'yes', but only 19% of lieutenants/first lieutenants.

28. The General Staff should operate under the Ministry of National Defence

	#	%
Yes	441	31.5
No	918	65.5
No response	42	3.0
Total	1,401	100.0

In this question, aiming to measure the opinion of officers about operation of the TGS under the Ministry of Defense, although 65.5% of officers said 'no', this ratio falls drastically for junior-level officers: 42% of lieutenants/first lieutenants supported the proposal, but only 18% of colonels.

29. The military judicial system should be abolished to end the distinction between civil and military courts.

	#	%
Yes	544	38.8
No	820	58.5
No response	37	2.6
Total	1,401	100.0

On this subject, which is widely debated by the public and is an important item on the agenda of the Turkish CMR, 58.5% of officers answered 'no' to the question.

30. I would not carry out an order that I think is against the law, legislation or constitution.

	#	%
Yes	1,273	90.9
No	127	9.0
No response	1	0.1
Total	1,401	100.0

In this question, aiming to measure how much the superiority of law is internalised by the officer corps, especially in the last 10 years after court cases in which TAF personnel were judged as suspects, it was desired to learn whether the officers would back the 'executive order' or the 'law' in cases where there exists conflict between the two, in a disciplined and tough organisation like the TAF. The executive order is regulated strictly via formal legal arrangements within the strategic culture of the TAF, and absolute obedience of executive orders without question is one of the important norms in the institutional culture. In the 13th article of the TAF Internal Services Law and Regulation,[16], which is the most fundamental text regulating the attitudes, behaviour and mutual relations of TAF personnel, it is emphasised that 'discipline' is the basis of being a soldier. The definition of discipline is given as "an absolute obedience to the laws, rules and superiors and conformity to the rights of superiors and subordinates".

The notion of absolute obedience to superiors has become an extremely internalised norm within the TAF. In Article 8 of the same law, order is defined as "the oral, written or other type of expression of a demand or prohibition related with the service". Interestingly, in a regulation prepared with the assumption that no order can already contradict with the law, there is no regulation about what to do if an order does contradict an article of law. Although it is stated that it will be related to the service, it is not clearly stated when and under which circumstances an order will not be realised. The norm that order is not questioned but that it is first done, and then if a problem arises the situation is submitted to a superior, is an important standard that has been practiced in the TAF.

16 For the full text of the law (Turkish) see <http://www.mevzuat.gov.tr/MevzuatMetin/1.4.211.pdf> (accessed 12 November 2015).

Table 47. Perception about whether the rule of law is superior when contradicting with orders with respect to ranks

	Lieutenant/ First Lieutenant	Captain	Major	Lt Colonel	Colonel	General/ Admiral	Total
Yes	618 (95%)	264 (95%)	126 (88%)	48 (92%)	210 (77%)	7 (88)	1,273
No	33 (5%)	12 (4%)	17 (12%)	4 (8%)	60 (23%)	1 (12%)	127
No response	0	1 (1%)	0	0	0	0	1
Total	651	277	143	52	270	8	1,401

In this question, aiming to understand the level of opinion about whether an order should be practiced or not when it contradicts the law, the opinion that it should not be carried out when it is believed that it contradicts the constitution and the law generally increases as the rank decreases. In this paradoxical situation, which can be defined as a 'law-order contradiction', 77% of colonels stated that the order should not be realised, rising to 95% for captains and lieutenants/first lieutenants.

These high rates are important since they show that superiority of the law and conformity to the legal arrangements, even if they contradict orders given, has started to appear as a new norm in the TAF.

31. When there is a conflict of opinion between civilian, political decision-makers and the military with regard to security/defense issues. the civilian, political decision-makers should have the final say.

	#	%
Yes	1,092	77.9
No	271	19.3
No response	38	2.7
Total	1,401	100.0

The response to this question, which aimed to measure the opinion about whose decision will be more seriously taken into account when there is a disagreement about security/defence issues, an overwhelming majority (77.9%) of officers think that the final word should be by the civil power. This is also important in showing the change in officers about being subjected to civilian control and attaching importance to the decisions of elected civilians.

32. The Chief of Staff should freely discuss his views with the public at large, including political issues.

	#	%
Yes	739	52.7
No	628	44.8
No response	34	2.4
Total	1,401	100.0

More than half (52.7%) of the 'yes' answers can at first glance be perceived as a contradiction to the principle of democratic and civilian control of the military. But in the interviews conducted, it was observed that every officer is confused about how and by which means technical information about defence/security and the opinions of the TAF should be shared with the public. The declarations of the Chief of Staff appear as the most privileged method in their minds, since there is no idea in the TAF of which other mechanisms information sharing should be carried out by.

33. Besides western countries, Turkey should also initiate and pursue closer foreign policy ties with countries from Asia (Russia, Central Asia, etc.), Africa and the Far East (China, India, etc.)

	#	%
Yes	1,228	87.7
No	164	11.7
No response	9	.6
Total	1,401	100.0

This question, which shows willingness over the issue of internationalism, reveals an important trend in the TAF, with 87.7% of officers leaning towards an extension in foreign politics other than with NATO.

34. I think recent Turkish foreign policy has been successful.

	#	%
Yes	293	20.9
No	1,070	76.4
No response	38	2.7
Total	1,401	100.0

The majority (76.4%) of officers do not agree that foreign policy has been successful for Turkey in recent years.

35. Ataturk's 'thought system' ought to remain the founding block of military education.

	#	%
Yes	1,255	89.6
No	144	10.3
No response	2	0.1
Total	1,401	100.0

A clear majority of 89.6% of officers still attach importance to Atatürkism and want it to remain as the fundamental component of the military education system.

36. I frequently use the internet and social media to follow the news.

	#	%
Yes	1,131	80.7
No	269	19.2
No response	1	0.1
Total	1,401	100.0

In this question aiming to measure the level of access to different news resources, 80.7% of officers said they use the internet to access information and follow the news.

Table 48. Prevalence of internet usage among respondents with respect to ranks

	Lieutenant/First Lieutenant	Captain	Major	Lt Colonel	Colonel	Total
Yes	611 (94%)	231 (83.3%)	105 (73.4%)	39 (75%)	141 (52.2%)	1,127
No	39 (6%)	46 (16.7%)	38 (26.6%)	13 (25%)	129 (47.8%)	265
Total	650	277	143	52	270	1,392

It is observed that there is a significant difference between ranks regarding use of the internet for gathering information and following the news. The use of the internet extends as rank decreases. For example, while the figure is 52.2% among colonels, this number rises to 94% for lieutenants/first lieutenants.

Discussion

In light of the findings from the questionnaire, as of May-August 2015 it is possible to define an average profile of an officer in the TAF as follows:

He is a person who comes from a family of low-medium income, his father has an average education of a high school graduate, he can come from any province of Turkey and he is not likely to have other officers in his family or among his close relatives. He has a salary in the range of 3,500-4,000 Turkish Lira, and while he attaches importance to secularism, the unity of the state is more important. He never trusts the media or the police, but does trust the parliament a little, as to him it is an important platform in CMR. On average, he has spent four years combatting terrorism and (with 50% probability) has spent six months of his career abroad. Furthermore, he considers being an officer an occupation now, even though he had thought it a lifestyle in the past. He now attaches importance to career opportunities in his occupation and financial means, whereas before he was an elite attaching importance to his social status in society. He argues that the TAF should definitely transform and restructure itself, thinking that respect for and trust ino the TAF has diminished in society during the last few years. In this way, he is respectful to democracy and elected civilians, but aware of the 'exceptional' significance of the institution for which he is working and the profession of officership. Following this, he expects respect for himself and his institution from civilians and is aware of the supremacy of law. This means that he cares more about serving within the boundaries of the law than obeying blindly the orders of superiors. As he already knows at least one foreign language (mostly English), he is further trying to learn foreign languages, mostly for career opportunities and as a way to get a better-paying job within the TAF by being posted in another country. His political view has slipped from centrr to centre-right, meaning that he is getting more conservative with time. He sometimes fasts, believes in the afterlife, is nationalist and is not satisfied with his economic status. He has hawkish views about the Kurdish question and his focus has slipped away from institutional attachment to his occupational career and towards financial success. He is further of the mindset that the duration of compulsory military service should be diminished, and does not approve of conscientious objection in the military. He has a definite negative attitude about having homosexuals serving in the military, but a positive attitude toward women serving alongside him. He does not consider Turkey's foreign policy successful and still attaches importance to Ataturkism. Using the internet often, he is curious about technology and relatively open to new possibilities.

In light of the findings of the survey, it is possible to divide the officer corps into two categories: juniors (lieutenants, captains, majors) and seniors (lieutenant colonels, colonels, generals). This split indicates that there is a generational conflict within the TAF. The main factors causing the difference of opinions between junior-level and senior-level officer groups are changes in the social-political context in Turkey and in the global security environment. In the light of the findings, it is possible to list trends causing this split between juniors and seniors.

Shifts influencing the officers' mindset

From idealism to pragmatism

The findings of the survey reveal that, particularly among juniors officers, there seems to be a moral/practical dichotomy, whereas a great majority of seniors tend to opt for idealist discourse. That is, established norms and principles within the Turkish military, such as absolute obedience to the orders of superior commanders, selfless service for the nation, prioritisation of the military rather than the self and practical self-interests such as a personal career and financial expectations seemed to be exclusive in most cases. Junior-level respondents, for instance, in contrast to senior ones who mostly embraced an idealist track, seem to be in a dilemma of pursuing rational practical self-interests to be able improve their lives on a material basis or with career opportunities, as well as adopting the moral principles dictated by the institution. That is why, for instance, that while senior-level officers noticeably dislike post-graduate education and learning foreign languages on the ground that it distracts moral commitment to the military, junior officers are inclined to evaluate their academic career and foreign language skills both to promote their military career and as a potential job opportunity in civilian life. During the interviews, for instance, the seniors tend to define speaking a foreign language as a crucial part of being an elite within society and a qualification for being an elite officer. Among junior-level officers, however, it is clearly noticeable that the respondents have dual motivation to learn a new language: to participate in temporary (six-month) or permanent (two-three year) posts abroad to take part in multinational operations and to apply for international cadres; and to honour his officership with an idealistic stance as well as to contribute to his personal career and financial expectations.

One should note that, as the rank decreases, the rate of the option of social status as the primary reason to be an officer decreases. The increase in the ratios of the options of career expectations and financial gains as the rank decreases shows that idealist expectations and behaviours are being set aside by junior-level officers. As rank decreases, pragmatist preferences and behaviours concentrating on career and financial gain gain prevalence among the officers.

Other indicators that show the transition from idealism to pragmatism is the decreasing significance of staff officership among junior officers and the changing attitudes of staff officers. Staff officers are privileged in the TAF, as roughly 90% of TAF international cadres and 95% of general cadres are reserved for them. To be a staff officer in the TAF is thus the first step to being deployed in an international post for three years (maybe another one year for the second term) and to be a general. Simply, the desire and endeavour of a junior officer to be a staff officer, which means the first and most significant step for the contemplation of a military career in the TAF, is a reliable indicator to assess the extent of idealism of the young officers. It is a fact that applications for the Staff College Entrance Exam, a test administered every December, have shown a drastic decline. According to the TAF's official numbers, in

2012, one out of four officers (25%) applied for the exam, which means that three out of four did not even bother applying. During the interviews, junior-level respondents state that it is a remarkably tough choice to be a staff officer, as any officer desiring to become one should spend two years in preparation for the exam, two years in staff colleg, and then more than 12 years in the 'staff-only cadres'. This career path is defined by a majority of junior-level officers as a process of full sacrifice and absolute militarisation of everything surrounding their life. The great majority of majors and captains who were interviewed emphasised that they did not apply even once for the Staff College Entrance Exam. After assessing the pros and cons of being a staff officer, they concluded that they did not want to bear the burden of staff officership even though it comes with a lucrative opportunity package to promote their military career. More importantly, all staff officers interviewed emphasised that 'material benefits' played a more important role than the career opportunities in their decision of being a staff officer.

Another indicator showing the transition from idealism to pragmatism is the declining importance of generalship among junior officers, whoare now more seeking short-term material benefits instead of long-term objectives such as being a general 20 years down the road. During the interviews, lieutenant colonels and colonels revered generalship as the utmost objective in their career, which was not the case for junior-level officers.

Eighty percent of lieutenants/first lieutenants answered 'yes' to the question: 'Imagine that you have sufficient economic wealth and means and your son wants to complete his military service through a payment/fee. Would you approve?' However, this figure dropped to 32% for colonels. According to this finding, there is a shift from an idealist to pragmatist attitude regarding the importance placed on compulsory military service. Therefore, there is an increase in the tendency to regard shortened military service by payment positively as rank decreases.

From homogeneity to heterogeneity

In terms of their origin, there were two types of officer in the TAF a decade ego; military high school/war academy graduates and civilian high school/war academy graduates. Currently, however, there are seven types of officers in terms of their origin in the TAF: military high school/war academy graduates, civilian high school/war academy graduates, civilian university graduates (contracted officers), foreign war academy graduates (US, South Korea), officers with an NCO background and officers with a contracted specialist background. One should also note that the ratio of war academy graduates, the category which constitutes the backbone of the officer corps, has drastically decreased from 90% to 60% within the last five years. It is worth mentioning that half of the respondents in the lieutenant category were contracted officers from civilian universities, which implies that the trend towards more heterogeneity has accelerated at junior levels. This heterogeneity in the origins inevitably comes up with varying attitudes and opinions when interpreting social realities, yet the TAF has been trying hard to standardise young officers through military education and other means.

Another example showing the process of increasing heterogeneity in the TAF is the differentiation of officers in the land, air and naval forces regarding the TAF's reform process. Some of the factors considered are where a reform process should start, the rates of becoming conservative and expectations from the occupation of officership. According to the results of the questionnaire which was put forward for the first time in the Turkish CMR literature, the organisational cultures of the forces in the TAF are not the same but show differences. For example, according to the findings of the questionnaire, the Army allows institutional reforms such as the need for qualified commanders in decision-making mechanisms, the Navy highlights qualified serving personnel and the Air Force highlights technology. In addition, sensitivity about secularism in the Army is relatively low compared to the Air Force, and is very low compared to the Navy.

Another finding that shows the process of heterogenisation in the TAF is the differentiation between junior-level and senior-level officers regarding their opinions about the compulsory military service system, payment-based military service and the change to professionalism. For example, while 84% of lieutenants/first lieutenants argue for the transformation to a professional Army, this figure is only 37% among colonels.

These findings urge one to suggest that heterogenisation in the TAF is not only in the material domain, but also the cognitive one. The difference of opinion between officers especially shows itself clearly in questions about women participating in the military, compulsory military service, professional military service and payment-based military service.

From centre to centre-right in the political portfolio

A shift from centre to centre-right is observed in the political preferences of the officer corps. It is possible to say that the fact that juniors-level officers are more conservative than seniors and that the Army, constituting 65% of the TAF, has appeared to be the most conservative institution, have influenced this shift.

From secularism to unity of state

Since perceptions of interior threats and the defending of secularism tends to decrease as rank decreases (about 50%) while sensitivity of the unity of state runs high (83%) among all ranks and in all forces, it is possible to say that the main interior security threat in the officer corps is shifting from secularism, as it is defined traditionally, to the unity of state.

From collectivism to individualism

TAF officers shift from a collective to an individualistic point-of-view as rank decreases. According to the findings of the questionnaire, as rank decreases, the primary status of the TAF and the occupation in the officer's life tends to decrease and the tendency of the officer to put himself among the privileges of life increases.

However, it is seen that the influence of guidance of the family and close acquaintances for preference towards the occupation of officership decreases in time, and the person's own preferences increase as rank decreases. In addition, social status as a reason to become an officer in the military is on the decline, while advancing personal careers and financial means serves as a greater motivation .

The most important example showing the transformation from collectivism to individualism is that the determining effect of the 'spirit of cohort' on strategic preferences and behaviours of officers decreases as he rank decreases.

During the interviews, an informal institution was raised that has a significant impact on the opinions, attitudes and even behaviours of the officer corps in the Turkish military – the 'cohort spirit' (*devre ruhu*), which is defined as one of the cores of being an officer by the majority of respondents. This informal institution that attracts considerable scholarly attention yet has never been studied academically, is considered as one of the great enablers of officers to standardise behaviours and as a group to act efficiently, effectively and in a timely manner.

This informal institution that strengthens the 'brothers-in arms' mood of classmates may, therefore, be regarded as the first and foremost antecedent condition of a successful coup attempt among the officer corps. The results clearly show the gradual declining importance of common spirit among same-year graduates. Put differently, this finding confirms the trend from homogeneity to heterogeneity, from a collective mode of thinking and acting to an individualistic one.

From elitist to an egalitarian view of civil society

According to the results of the questionnaire, the elitist view is decreasing among officers as rank decreases, and the egalitarian view – which considers society and the officer corps to be more equal – is, in turn, increasing.

From absolute obedience of orders to respecting the superiority of laws

It is observed that the superiority of laws and obedience to legal regulations, even if they conflict with the orders given, is appearing as a new norm in the TAF after the processes of lawsuits, although 'absolute obedience to orders in every situation and circumstance' is the most important norm in the TAF. The tendency is now for officers to follow legal regulations when contradicting orders are given by the superiors.

It is possible to list those constants which do not create significant differences despite the different forces and ranks as follows:

- High level of positive perception about NATO.
- The opinion that the TAF should immediately go under a process of transformation.
- Technology-centric focus.
- The expectation that religious affairs and state affairs are not to be mixed with each other.
- The expectation that Turkey should be governed by democracy under every circumstance.
- The trust put into science when religion and science contradict each other.
- The opinion that the Turks are a military nation.
- The opinion that the influence of the soldier on civilian politics has decreased in the last 10 years.
- Emphasis on Ataturkism.
- The hawkish standing on any issue regarding the Kurdish question.
- The importance attached to internationalization.
- The worsening economic situation in the last few years.
- A high level of mistrust of the media and the police.
- The opinion that society's respect of the officer as a profession has decreased.
- The negative attitude towards conscientious objection and service of homosexuals in the Army.

In the light of the findings above, there are also constant fields among TAF officers in which no significant differentiation is observed besides the trend which cause significant differences with respect to both the forces and ranks. From this point of view, it is possible to say that changes in the perceptions and opinions of the officer corps are gradual and incremental. In terms of ranks, the split between junior-level and senior-level officers especially evokes interest; regarding the separation between the forces, officers in the Army are behind those in the Navy and Air Force in terms of affairs such as financial and educational status, duration of posts abroad, educational and foreign language status.

Again, while no significant difference exists between the Navy and Air Force regarding the level of conservativeness, belief in the afterlife, fasting and perception of secularism; it is interesting that significant differences between the Army and each of those two forces are observed. In light of the questionnaire's findings, it is possible to say that the Army officers, constituting nearly 60% of the TAF, are more conservative and devout than their counterparts in the Navy and Air Force.

Again, while 39.5% of the officers think that secularism is under threat, an overwhelming majority of 82.9% believes that the unity of the state is under threat. When those two rates are compared, it is possible to say that the primary threat perception for the TAF has transformed from secularism to the unity of the state. A large majority of 82.7% are against giving freedom to use the Kurdish language, giving the impression that a 'Kurdo-phobia' exists in the officer corps.

The fact that 15% of junior-level officers did not respond to questions about political preferences and religious affairs shows that there exists an unwillingness about expressing opinions on these subjects.

In light of the questionnaire's findings, while Army officers emphasise the 'qualified command rank' for the TAF's institutional transformation, it is interesting that Navy officers highlight the 'qualified performing rank' and Air Force officers, in turn, underline 'technology'. It is possible to say that each force has different strategic points of view regarding transformation.

The revelation that 88.4% of officers think that the national will is represented in parliament, but only 19.3% of them trust parliament, is a meaningful finding since it shows the gap between expectation and trust. Also, the findings that only 7.1% of officers trust the media and 11.2% trust the police are important in showing the trust gap in these two institutions in the officer corps.

In the questions, the high level of belief in democracy among the officer corps, especially the fact that 92.9% emphasise that Turkey should be governed by democracy under every situation and circumstance, but only 24.6% are satisfied with the country's level of democracy, is important in terms of showing the expectation of democracy and dissatisfaction with the present situation.

Some 93.4% of officers said 'no' to the statement 'when necessary, the military should seize control and govern the country', while 88.2% disagreed with the statement that 'military administrations can be much more effective and successful than civilian ones'. These findings are promising in showing the high tendency of officers to be subjected to the control of elected civilians. Again, 81% of officers think that the effect of soldiers on civilian politics has decreased during the last 10 years.

While 72% of lieutenants/first lieutenants consider the service of female officers/sergeants positively, this figure is only 50% for colonels. The positive opinion about the service of female officers/sergeants in the TAF is observed to increase as rank decreases. It is interesting that 96.3%are against the service of homosexuals in the TAF.

What are the important findings of the survey that can be assessed with respect to Turkish CMR? First of all, the survey confirms all three hypotheses of the research. Primarily, it is seen that, as rank decreases, there is a shift in the officer corps from the idealist officer attaching importance to value systems to the career-oriented officer focussing mostly on career opportunities and financial gains. The emphasis on secularism and elitist views tend to decrease as rank decreases, but the emphasis on democracy increases. It is also worth mentioning that, as rank decreases, the rigidity of ideological stance weakens among officers and diversification in political preferences increases. The findings reflect a snapshot of the opinions of the Turkish officer corps in the summer of 2015. It is possible to say that the officer corps becomes less ideological as rank decreases and more diversification emerges. Lastly, according to the findings of this survey, there are significant cultural differences between the force commands, especially in terms of political preferences and transformation. According to this picture, in contrast to the assumption that the TAF is a homogeneous and monolithic entity, there are significant differences in points of view and organisational cultures between the force commands, primarily about issues concerning political stances, the extent of conservative ideas and how transformation will take place. The trends in the officer corps can be summarised as from idealism to pragmatism, from homogeneity to heterogeneity, from centre to centre-right in the political spectrum, from secularism to unity of the state as the prime internal threat perception, from collectivism to individualism, from elitist to egalitarian view of civil society and from absolute obedience to orders to respecting the superiority of law. All these differences seem to have caused a change in the TAF's organisational culture.

The findings of the survey also reveal that there exists a split between junior (lieutenant, captain and major) and senior (lieutenant colonel, colonel and general) officers, to such an extent that the attitudes and opinions of the officer corps can be analysed separately under these two categories. In this snapshot, how deep does this cultural split that seems to exist between junior and senior officers affect the organisational culture of the TAF? For example, would it be possible to say that when juniors become seniors, that is after 10-15 years' service, their attitudes and opinions will be just like the seniors of the present time? In fact, in one of the findings of the survey, it has already been seen that officers have a demographic background resembling Turkey in general in terms of criteria of both the geographic distribution and the social and economic status of parents. But it is seen that an 'elitisation' process is ongoing among TAF officers. It is observed that high quality education and importance attached to foreign languages in the military schools are important dynamics shaping the elitisation process in the TAF. One of the reasons underlying the friction between officers having graduated from the war academy and contracted officers from civilian universities of relatively low quality education and not knowing a foreign language is that war academy graduates consider themselves to be more qualified officers. In short, the reason for this friction is seen to be elitisation. In this case, is it possible to anticipate that a present junior officer's attitudes and opinions will resemble those of a present senior officer after years of the elitisation process giving the TAF the ability to transform an officer? In scholarly terms, as this is a first snapshot of its kind in the literature, those seeking to confirm or falsify this assumption do not have data to compare and contrast the findings of this survey with an existing one. If there was existing data, we could at least compare that with this data and could provide scholarly insights about the extent, nature and evolution of the 'elitisation effect' of the TAF. However, this research takes this as a valid point and invites quantitative data-based researchers seeking to snapshot the attitudes and opinions of the officer corps to compare the findings of this survey.

In short, in light of the survey findings, it is seen that the trends of heterogenisation, diversification, softening of political rigidity, strengthening of emphasis on the unity of the state and caring more about supremacy of laws than orders are observed to increase as rank decreases.

So, how do these trends affect Turkish CMR? It is possible at the end of the day to say that these trends affect the organisational culture of the TAF in the light of changing attitudes and opinions of the officer corps. If we also assume that there is a direct association between the TAF's organisational culture and Turkish CMR, it is possible to say that this association is a reciprocal causation between TAF organisational culture and Turkish CMR. The reason for causation to be defined as reciprocal is that the temporal sequence between the TAF's organisational culture and Turkish CMR is not clearly defined and those two variables affect each other reciprocally and continuously.

Another criticism here is how determining the TAF's organisational culture and especially the attitudes and opinions in which junior and senior officerss are observed to diversify in High Command's strategic preferences and decisions seems to shape the Turkish CMR. That is, how determining are the junior officers' attitudes and opinions in the strategic decisions of the High Command? This is an important question. As was also seen in the previous chapter, the High Command recognises that there is currently a trend of change in the TAF as a social institution and officership as a profession but cannot define that and more importantly cannot quantify and measure that trend. But there is a high level of awareness in the High Command that there is a change. The fundamental motivation forcing the High Command to transform is already the change within the socio-political context in Turkey, besides the change in the global security environment. In this respect, the TAF's organisational culture is a fundamental dynamic affecting the strategic preferences and decisions of the High Command.

Snapshot of the TAF before 15 July

In this last section, the findings of the previous empirical chapters are briefly summarised and then merged to provide a comprehensive discussion. Subsequently, the conceptual diagrams presenting configurations explaining change for each domain are provided. In the last section of this chapter, the overall conceptual diagram is presented, including all change domains, agents, modes and pathways, and an endeavour to explain overall transformation within the Turkish military.

Soldiers live and operate separately from the rest of society. To be successful in battle, soldiers must learn to give their loyalty to their comrades-in-arms and put personal considerations aside for the good of the service and the nation they are serving. In doing so, they may nurture *esprit de corps*, a higher sense of responsibility both to uphold the morale of the military as a whole and to cultivate a *sui generis* organisational culture. The soldier's sense of isolation from society should, however, be mitigated with proper means, such as an increased inclusion of civilians in the military, the promotion of civilian housing and family programmes. Nonetheless, the continuous intervention of society into every military-related issue may compromise the military's morale and operational effectiveness.[17] As clearly emphasised in the chapter about theoretical discussions, this dilemma of establishing a mutual balance between two seemingly competing trends has been salient since the emergence of Huntingtonian and Janowitzian formulations. That is, on the one hand, the necessity to provide a space for the military to nurture its organisational culture, its 'way of thinking and doing things' for more professionalisation; and on the other hand, the necessity to prevent the military's isolation from the rest of society so as not to let it become a threat to society and democracy. How is it possible to address this dilemma? As emphasised in the literature review, the first ideal option would be through militarisation of the military by providing an autonomous space to nurture its 'do-it-yourself' values and norms. A second ideal option would be through the civilianisation of the military, which implies the military's embrace of society's values and norms. But what about the working of 'militarisation' emphasising technical transformation and 'civilianisation' emphasszing social change mutually, two processes which at first glance seem to work to the detriment of one another?

The findings of this study show that this is exactly the case for the TAF. That is, as a security organisation the TAF has been experiencing a technical transformation, while as a social institution it is simultaneously in a civilianisation process. Furthermore, in the domain of officership as a profession, the findings suggest that, as of May-September 2015, as rank decreases, there are five trends influencing the professional culture of the officer corps: increasing heterogenisation and diversification of the attitudes and opinions of the officer corps, change from a collectivist mentality to an individualistic one, change from an elitist to an egalitarian view of society, change from absolute obedience to orders to respect for the superiority of the law and, lastly, change from value-centric officership to focussing on financial goals and careers (i.e. a shift from idealism to careerism). For the first time in the literature, the findings of this study indicate that there are differences between the organisational cultures of the Army, the Navy and the Air Force, particularly in the domain of the TAF as a security organisation and on socio-political issues.

Especially in the domain of the TAF as a security organisation, there is a transformation and internationalisation process taking placed driven by the elite run by the High Command (the level led by the Chief of the General Staff and including all four-star generals/admirals in the TAF), as well as by technology. In the current chapter, this research evidently explains why, through which mechanisms and how the High Command has been first trying to institutionalise the reformist sentiment as a foundational dynamic influencing the TGS's organisational culture, and then disseminating this new sentiment to the force commands and lower echelons since 2011. Non-compliant thinking and behaviour, which is the first outcome of reformist sentiment and the primary factor in degrading old ways of thinking and doing things,

17 Nathaniel C. Fick, *One Bullet Way: The Making of A Marine Officer* (New York: Mariner Books, 2006).

starts in the TGS and is then transferred to the force commands. This tacit acceptance (and to a certain extent appreciation) of the non-compliant thinking and behaviour by the High Command in discovering new cognitive templates and models for execution to adapt to the changing international security environment and socio-political context in Turkey has caused the emergence of 'subversive' officers at the senior level (particularly at the colonel, brigadier and two-star general ranks) and 'insurgents' at the junior level. It is possible to suggest that the TAF's security culture has been deeply influenced by this transformation that is still ongoing in this domain.

In the domain of the TAF as a social institution, there exists a transformation influencing the TAF's social culture. This process of change is partly controlled by the High Command and driven by interactions confrontational in nature between the High Command and junior-level personnel, and between the High Command and third-party actors, such as non-governmental organisations like TEMAD and the media. Three cases presented in Chapter 4 that emphasise interactions within the TAF are existing tensions between NCOs and the High Command about the status and rights of NCOs within the system, allegations about soldiers' rights violations and women's status in the TAF. These cases show that if insurgent juniors can get enough media attention and public awareness, then they can impose their will over the High Command, and then can cause changes in the existing institutional order. Furthermore, the submissiveness of the High Command when confronted with outside actors such as politicians, journalists and NGOs is clearly elucidated in Chapter 4 through analyses of the change of tones, content and thematic structures of TGS press releases. In light of the findings of the qualitative content analysis of these press releases, one may easily suggest that the TAF has first submissively softened and then obediently democratised its official discourse to adapt to the changing socio-political context in Turkey in the last decade. As Chapter 5 lucidly highlights, as rank decreases, the trends of heterogenisation, diversification, civilianisation, less ideological and more pragmatic orientations influence the professional culture of the officer corps.

Simply put, while change in the global security environment appears to be the prime driver behind the TAF's transformation in security culture, the fundamental factor influencing the social and professional culture of the TAF is the changing socio-economic and political context in Turkey. The findings of this study elucidate that while the transformation shaping the TAF's security culture seems to be a consciously designed and planned process by the High Command in top-down fashion, the fundamental dynamic influencing the TAF's social culture is the confrontational, and to some extent frictional, interaction between the High Command and juniors, and between the High Command and outsiders. The transformation shaping the professional culture among the officer corps would, in turn, be defined as a more coincidental and arbitrary process of change when compared with other domains. One should also note that, at first glance, the 'militarisation of the military' trend shaping the TAF's security culture and the 'civilianization of the military' trend influencing both the TAF's social culture and officers' professional culture may be seen as conflicting change processes leading the TAF in opposite directions. However, to the contrary, in light of the findings of this research, changes in three different domains are reinforcing, mutually bolstering one another. It is the power distributional effect that emerges as the first outcome of this type of transformation, comprising three different change dynamics in three different domains that semi-independently affect one another. The power distributional effect within the TAF's existing institutional order leads to a 'healthy' environment yielding to a more gradual institutional change within the TAF.

Transformation of the TAF's security culture

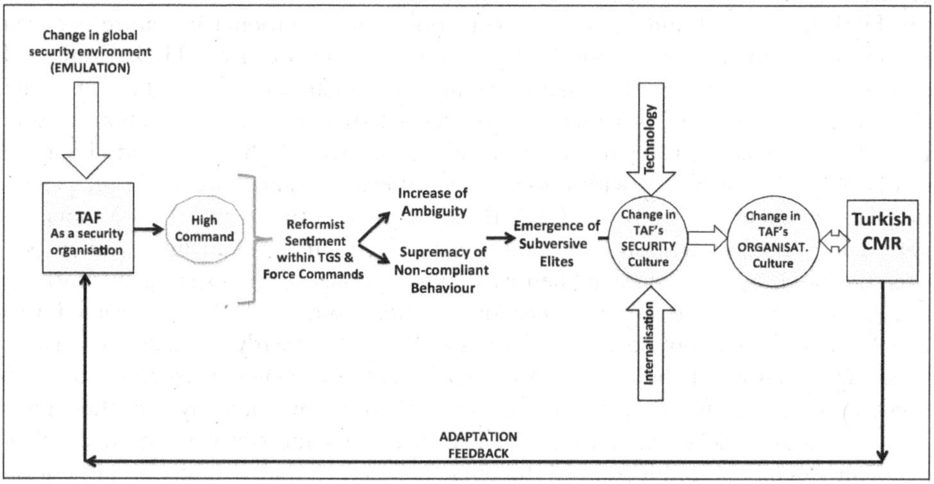

Figure 5 Transformation of the TAF as a security organisation.

As seen in the figure above, the main change actor in the domain of the TAF as a security organisation is the High Command. Following the trends of change in the global security environment, the High Command has been trying to adopt the TAF to the new security environment by aiming to change the TAF's security culture. The reason for this is not to stay behind in the global competition by developing itself continuously and taking into account changes in the other security actors (particularly adversaries). This attempt refers to 'mimetic isomorphism', which implies the tendency of an organisation to imitate another organisation's structure as a response to the challenge of uncertainty due to a belief that the structure of the latter is beneficial. Mimetic isomorphism occurs "when organizational technologies are poorly understood, when goals are ambiguous, or when the environment creates [an] extreme level of uncertainty".[18] When organisations are faced with uncertainty, they may model

18 Paul D. DiMaggio and Walter W. Powell, 'The Iron Cage Revisited: Institutional Isomorphism and Collective Rationality', in Walter W. Powell and Paul J. DiMaggio (eds),

themselves after other organisations, which provide solutions for the problems that are faced by the borrowing organisation. As one may remember from Chapter 3, Theo Farrell and Terry Terriff suggest that there are three pathways whereby military change occurs, which are "emulation", "adaptation" and "innovation".[19] For them, emulation involves importing new tools and ways of war through the imitation of other military organisations. In this sense, emulation is a mimetic isomorphic process. As a security actor, the TAF is trying to learn from other security actors so as to not fall behind, especially not to stay behind its adversaries, in the competition in the global security environment. This study suggests that the TAF has seemed to grasp emulation as the prime pathway of change in the domain of the TAF as a security organisation. That is why the High Command seeks to closely follow transformation processes, particularly in NATO, and is expending a lot of effort in copying and adapting NATO's way of thinking and doing things. It is possible to say that NATO's popularity in the TAF and the high levels of positive perception about it stems from the common opinion that NATO is the primary model for emulation by the TAF. It is NATO that introduces new cognitive templates and new models of execution to the TAF. As a result of the TAF's efforts in copying other security actors, two change drivers arise that directly affects its organisational culture: technology and internationalisation. For further emulation, the TAF is expending a great deal of effort in procuring cutting-edge technology and using that technology. Again, according to the findings of this research, the TAF is trying to familiarise itself with other security actors in the global security environment at the maximum level through internationalisation, which implies getting acquainted with the way in which other modern militaries think and do things. While the driver of internationalisation provides the High Command with the means and know-how to become familiar with the TAF's competition, it also allows individuals to satisfy their career and financial goals. Therefore, internalisation is a win-win driver both at the organisational and individual level.

What about adaptation and innovation, the two other pathways of change proposed by Farrell and Terriff? For them, adaptation involves fine tuning existing military ways and means to newly emerging societal and cultural factors. One may then understand this pathway as the TAF's efforts as a social institution to adapt to Turkey's changing socio-political and economic context. Analyses in this research suggest that the domain of the TAF as a social institution can be described as adaptation, the pathway of change at the domestic level. One should note that adaptation can, and often does, lead to innovation when multiple adjustments over time lead to the evolution of new ways and means. This study contends that the TAF has to improve a lot in terms of innovation, which involves developing ways and means genuinely designed by

The New Institutionalism in Organizational Analysis (Chicago: University of Chicago Press, 1991), p 65.

19 Theo Farrell and Terry Terriff, *The Sources of Military Change: Culture, Politics, Technology* (London: Lynne Reinner Publishing, 2002), p.6.

the TAF both as a security organisation and a social institution. Despite the fact that all modern militaries of the world have been experiencing hard times in finding innovative solutions to meet highly complex challenges,[20] it is possible to suggest that the TAF has not been fully aware of the existence of innovation as a pathway for change. Like any modern military of the world, the TAF thrives on consistent, standard approaches to resolving familiar problems. This explains why the TAF depends on the standardisation of tools, training, methods and organisation. Innovation subverts this standardisation and consistency in the exploration of a new approach (the introduction of variance into the system), as well as (if the innovation is successful enough) in the eventual replacement of the existing cognitive templates throughout the TAF. To make innovation popular in an organisation needs organisational change, which may require cultural change, emphasising the delegation of the decision-making authority, which is something the TAF stills lacks. The reformist sentiment, however, which the High Command, the main change agent in the domain of the TAF as a security organisation, created in the TSG and then let spread to the force commands, caused the questioning of old ways of thinking and doing things at higher echelons. As a result of this sentiment, compliance began to transform from a constant to a variable within the TGS and force commands. Furthermore, due to the reformist sentiment of the High Command appreciating non-compliant behaviour, it is seen that the senior elites with non-compliant thinking and behaviour are being appointed to critical posts close to the High Command in the TGS and force commands. One should note that, in the TAF, those working in critical posts close to the High Command in the TGS and force headquarters are advantageous for promotion as four-star generals know them by name and are acquainted with their specialties and performance. Again, as seen in the interview results, one may suggest that legal processes such as *Ergenekon* and *Sledgehammer* increased the extent of institutional uncertainty experienced in appointments and promotions of senior-level officers, particularly generals/admirals. This increasing uncertainty and non-compliant behaviour which became prevalent among senior-level cadres can be stated as causes of the emergence of four different types of change agents within the officer corps. As explained by Mahoney and Thelen, these four types are 'subversive', 'symbiont', 'opportunist' and 'insurrectionary'. For example, the appreciation of non-compliant thinking and behaviour by the High Command led to the emergence of subversive elites whose overall objective is a gradual institutional change within the TAF without fully abandoning the existing institutional order. Although the ratio of this group corresponds to around 20%[21] of those of their counterparts, the fact that the High Command generally has preferred subversive elites for critical posts at headquarters during the more recent period means these subversive elites having a high chance of promotion. The apprecia-

20 Andrew Hill, 'Military Innovation and Military Culture', *Parameters*, 2015.
21 This percentage was used by a general during an interview which was conducted in Ankara in December 2015.

tion of subversive military leaders for critical posts places the 'subversive officership' in front of senior-level officers as a popular and preferred identity. Those subversive elites and the new reformist and non-compliant habitat they created in the headquarters is the third component affecting the TAF's organisational culture, after technology and internationalisation. The interviews indicate that this habitat started to change the TAF's traditional organisational culture. However, one of the most important points revealed by the interviews and the survey is that the TAF does not have enough qualified support for decision-making among those managing the TAF's security culture transformation. It is possible to define this as the TAF's 'deficiency in intellectual capital'. It is seen that the TAF cannot benefit sufficiently from the human capital composed of majors aged between 36 and 42, who are the best group in terms of academic sufficiency, international experience as well as foreign language proficiency. There is a hierarchy-based perception that knowledge increases the higher the ranking due to the military's strict hierarchy and intra-organisation discipline at higher TAF command echelons, including absolute obedience to orders without questioning them. This perception still exists, despite the fact that it has been gradually decreasing. Due to the dominating opinion that the higher rank knows more and 'if the commanders order like that, there is something he knows' mentality prevalent among officers, the intellectual energy of those subversives, especially that of majors, cannot be fully utilised for the organisational transformation of the TAF. This deficiency in translating the intellectual dynamism of junior-level officers, particularly majors, into the intellectual capital needed for institutional transformation comes across as the greatest obstacle to the TAF becoming an 'intellectual Army'. Even though the High Command is trying to benefit maximally from the majors and captains in the decision-making departments, it is seen that this effort has not yet reached an effective level and institutionalisation in this domain is extremely weak.

The dominant kind of change or transformation in the TAF's security culture has been layering. Due to this approach, which can be summarised as the integration of the newly emerged cognitive and behavioural templates to the existing institutional order without devastating it, the change comes in a gradual and incremental mode. However, due to the fact that the duration of critical posts within the TGS and force commands are generally two years at the level of generals, there is difficulty in ensuring institutionalisation regarding structural transformation. This is mainly caused by the myopic outlook of those military leaders during their fast rotation periods. These short terms in office means that the officers are focussed on daily routines and the short-term tactical picture. They are not able to concentrate on the strategic picture or foresee the future and adapt accordingly.

The groups that have taken a critical stance of the transformation of TAF security culture are the majority of colonels, some brigadier generals and major generals who can be defined generally as symbionts. Aside from those, again the opportunist colonels, brigadier generals, major generals and three-star generals are the actors coming to the stage within the anti-transformation coalition. The fact that the great majority of colonels in the Army are symbionts and there is an abnormal excess number of those colonels at the top immediately appear as an obstacle to change. On the other hand, the *status-quo* oriented mood of opportunist generals puts compliance behaviour in front of us as the fundamental strategic behaviour style, and this behaviour creates a risk-averse sentiment in the TAF. Due to this sentiment, the headquarters in the TAF headed by a general focussing only on daily routines, does not take risks and does not have interest in addressing structural problems, as those problems would mean risk packages.

One of the important findings of this study is that the symbiont and opportunist seniors attach importance to daily routines more than necessary as a risk-aversive style of behaviour. This goes a long way to explaining why the TAF cannot direct its intellectual energy to the structural problems requiring new designs and new ways and means of the management of risks. While symbionts complain about the heavy workload of routine jobs during working hours and emphasise that they are working very hard, opportunists are, in turn, trying to manage the intensiveness of those routine jobs in line with their personal agenda. From this point of view, even though they are complaining a lot, the intensiveness of daily routine jobs is just what the symbionts and opportunists are seeking. Symbionts and opportunists in the TAF state that they cannot allocate their time to structural problems, as they are continuously concentrating on daily routines. However, focussing on daily routines seems to be just the thing that they prefer.

There is an overwhelming percentage of common opinion within the officer corps that the TAF is in need of reform as a security actor. However, each force has different priorities as to what should be reformed in each service. For example, the Air Force thinks priority should be given to technology, the Navy to educating 'qualified practitioner personnel' and the Army to educating 'qualified command ranks'. In terms of the points emphasised, while the Air Force places emphasis on a techno-scientific change, the Navy highlights a practitioner-focussed discourse and the Army underlines a commander-focussed one. From this point-of-view, it seems that the Army is having problems regarding qualified decision-makers.

Again, as is put forward for the first time by this study, difference in organisational cultures of the force commands appears to be one of the foremost problems for the TAF's organisational transformation. For example, there is still no complete agreement within the TAF about 'joint-ness', which is continuously emphasised as one of the most important issues of the TAF's 2033 vision. It is observed that different force commands understand quite different things by the notion of joint-ness. What is meant by joint-ness? At what level and in what size should this joint-ness be? Which abilities should the TAF have while ensuring operative joint-ness? Even if enough resources are obtained for reaching those abilities, how and by what means will this vision be conveyed to political decision-makers? No clear answers have yet been given to those questions within the TAF. As is also seen in the example of joint-ness, not paying attention to the differentiating organisational culture of each force within the TAF's transformation can cause structural friction in the TAF in the near future. In the light of the debate about key concepts such as joint-ness, military transformation, military innovation and adaptation within the TAF, this study contends that each service (Army, Navy, Air Force and Gendarmerie) has its unique cultural framework that promotes diversity and heterogeneity within the TAF.

The transformation of the TAF's social culture

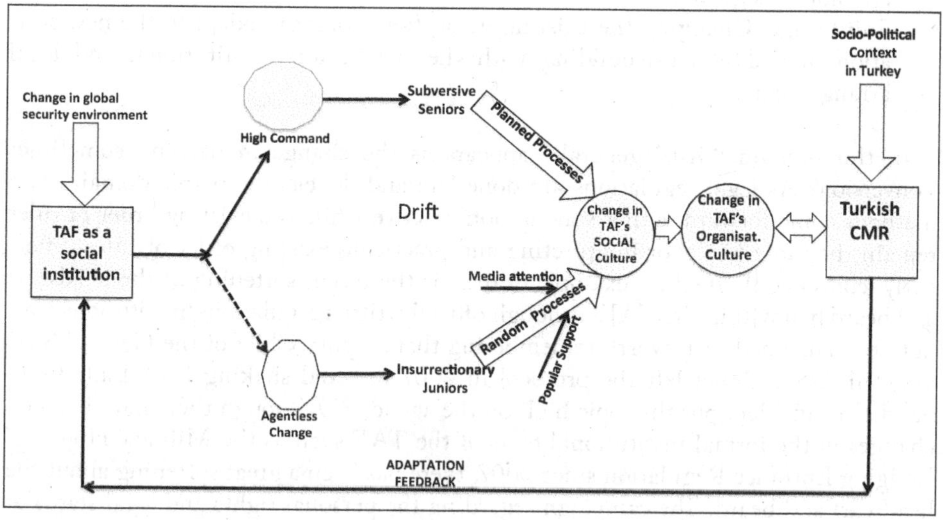

Figure 6 Transformation of the TAF as a social institution.

In contrast to change in the TAF's security culture, the process of change in its social culture appears to be a dual-track construction. This means that change is not solely a pre-planned process driven by military leadership and carried out in a top-down fashion. Change in this domain mostly comes with confrontational interaction between the High Command and insurrectionary junior-level officers and NCOs within the system, as well as outside actors such as politicians, journalists and NGOs in Turkey's socio-political context. It is worth mentioning that change in this domain is partly controlled by the High Command, and to some extent it occurs as non-deterministic sub-processes. Thus, this domain entails and provides room for arbitrariness and randomness. This, in fact, implies that the power-distributional effect is a dynamic shaping TAF social culture. The friction between the High Command and agentless change driven by insurrectionary juniors within the system and outsiders makes the High Command incapable of managing this domain. Due to this friction, the insurrectionary juniors can impose their demands and will for change onto military leaders as an organised voice if they first become united, and then enlist the support of the public and media, emphasising the effect of outside actors. In the face of such an imposition, elites give the following responses as a pattern, as was seen in the cases of NCOs' status problems and rights, violation of soldiers' rights, gender equality and the headscarf issue examined in this research.

- First stage: Counter-attacks imposing that the demands are not legitimate and attempts to degrade the credibility of demand-holders.
- Second stage: Acceptance of the existence of problem and seeking venues to attempt dialogue.
- Third stage: Changing the existing institutional order to adapt to the new situation, including trust-building with the rival actors, institutional and legal arrangements.

In this domain, 'drift' generally appears as the change mode, and sometimes 'conversion'. As legal regulations are done late and deficiently in this domain, two methods come forward, either staying non-reactive while the existing order of rules remain the same (drift) or interpreting and practicing existing order of rules differently (conversion). The best example of drift is the recent softening of the headscarf and beard ban within the TAF, although official written regulations/institutions have not been amended. It is worth remembering that Deputy Chief of the General Staff General Aslan Güner left the protocol in 2007 to avoid shaking First Lady Gül's hand. This incident put the topic high on the agenda.[22] Although there have been no changes in the formal institutional texts of the TAF such as the Military Housing/ Lodging Entrance Regulation since 2007, there has been a great softening about the headscarf and beard. The campaign regarding the personal rights and legal status of NCOs was pursued at the conversion mode at the very beginning. Even though the High Command does not tend to do much in the face of pressure, it changed formal texts for developing the rights and privileges of NCOs and to promote their institutional status with a method that can be defined as passive layering, implying the passivity of the change agent.

The actors of change in the domain of the TAF as a social institution are seen to be the insurrectionaries at the junior level and the subversive military leaders trying to soothe them. The demands for change in this domain appear firstly at the junior level, generally in an arbitrary way with attempts by insurrectionaries. Then it attracts the attention of the public and media, and captures public attention to such an extent that the High Command cannot resist this pressure. Later, those demands, if capturing public attention with the involvement of outside actors like the TEMAD's involvement in the NCOs' struggle for their rights, and if promoted by news and commentaries on the media in a prolonged fashion, may force the military elites to change their strategic preferences. Many changes being experienced in the social domain create arbitrary and non-compliant confrontations or frictions between the High Command and junior-level actors despite the fact that military leaders seek to withstand each

22 Merve Kavakçı, *Islam Headscarf Politics in Turkey* (New York: Palgrave, 2010), p.5.

confrontation. At the end, however, they accept the defeat tacitly and try to adapt the institutional structure to the new reality dictated by juniors and outsider actors. In this domain, the fundamental drivers of change are media power and public pressure. Simply, bottom-up demands that can capture media attention and public support in a prolonged fashion can lead to changes in the TAF's social culture, changes which directly influence the TAF's organisational culture, and thus Turkish CMR.

Transformation of the officer corps' professional culture

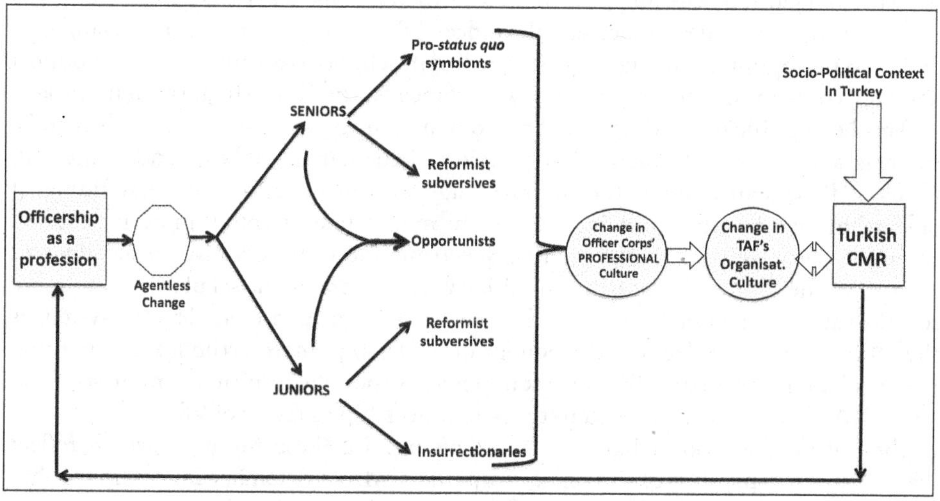

Figure 7 Transformation of officership as a profession.

To start with, one should note that the High Command is not yet fully aware of the existence of this domain; meaning that change in the professional culture of the officer corps is out of the High Command's control. In contrast to change of the TAF's security culture, which is under the full control of the High Command, and change of the TAF's social culture, which is partly controlled by the High Command, the professional culture of the Turkish officer corps is driven by agentless change. The profile of the officer corps has been gradually changing as a result of the change in the source of officers. The continuously increasing percentage of contracted officers is the first driver of change influencing the corps' profile. For example, the Army (11.6%) and Air Force (9.3%) has a higher number of contracted officers compared with the Navy (3.4%), which has a relatively low percentage of contracted officers. Although the policy of contracted officers has been operative since 2006, tension between War Academy graduates and contracted officers is still visible. When contracted officers are compared with War Academy graduates, it is evident that the former have relatively low-quality undergraduate education levels, are deficient in foreign language proficiency, more focussed on financial expectations and tend to have more conservative tendencies.

Again, the findings of this study indicate that the TAF has been becoming a less ideological military. The results of the questionnaire show that the ideological rigidity of an officer weakens as ranking decreases. According to the results of the survey conducted as part of this study, diversification in political views increases as rank decreases, while the perception that secularism is under threat decreases. These findings imply the loosening of traditional ideological principles in the TAF. The only statistically significant difference with respect to ranking and force command is the perception regarding 'the unity of the state', which is something that the officer corps continues to take a tough stance on. The officers' rigid stance on the Kurdish language and their perception of the right to use Kurdish in schools as an 'unacceptable political demand' confirm the officer corps' hawkish stance on the Kurdish question in Turkey.

Another significant finding is a dichotomous split between the seniors (generals, colonels and lieutenant colonels) and juniors (lieutenants, captains and majors) in terms of their stance about the military and political issues and understanding of officership. Senior offiers, for instance, seem more value-oriented, more inclined to sit on the centre-left side of the political spectrum, more conservative on social issues such as women's involvement in the military, care more about secularism, are more sceptical about academic careers and financial opportunities provided by the system as they think that these degrade the honour of officership, more orthodox on anything new, stick to the normative framework imposed by the cohort spirit, are more sceptical about NATO and more inclined to think of officership as a way of life.

The critical question at hand is the following: are these findings, which reflect insights from a snapshot of the officer corps as of May-September 2015 and emphasize change within the universe of the Turkish officer corps as of that summer in terms of generational (ranks) and cross-sectional (force commands) difference, enough to assert that there is a change within the officer corps? To answer this question, what we need is a trend analysis of officer corps' professional culture that requires a comparison of this research's findings with a new snapshot reflecting insights from the universe of the officer corps in the future. This point stresses the need for subsequent research aiming to measure change within the Turkish officer corps with the same survey questions. Then, for instance, we could learn more about what officers at the rank of lieutenant think and what they think at the rank of major. With this comparison of the same group of officers in two different time periods and at two different ranks, then, for the first time in the literature, we could get scholarly insights about the whats, whys and hows of change within the Turkish military. It is also worth mentioning that the findings of this research indicate that there is a elitization process within the TAF. With this comparison, one can get scholarly insights about this process as well. It is also worth mentioning that measuring changes in attitudes and opinions of the same group of officers at two or more different ranks may provide scholarly insights on these two change drivers; that is, how the elitisation process within the TAF and the changing socio-political context in Turkey interact with one another when shaping the attitude and opinion of a Turkish officer.

It is possible to summarize the points explained above with the following chart.

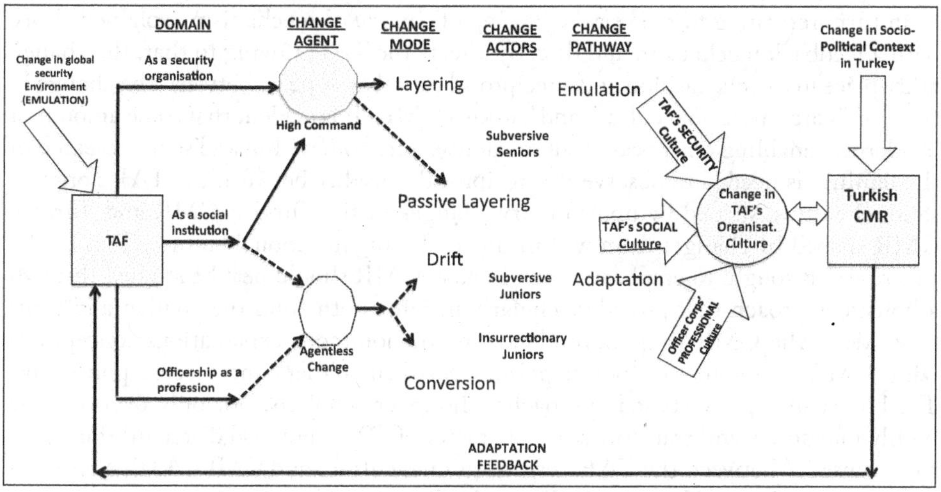

Figure 8 Transformation of the TAF's organisational culture.

The change in the TAF, which was first affected by the change in the global security environment, is occurring in three main domains. The change in the domain of the TAF as a security organisation shaping the TAF's security culture is a deterministic process as it is under the full control of the High Command. The fundamental determinant shaping change in the TAF's social culture is, however, the friction between High Command and agentless change. In the domain of officership as a profession, in turn, change shaping the professional culture of the officer corps is a process running in a completely agentless fashion. In the domain of the TAF as a security organisation, the change mode is generally layering and, sometimes, passive layering. In the domains of the TAF as a social institution and officership as a profession, though, generally drift and conversion appear as the modes of change. Subversive elites exhibiting non-compliant behaviour in each of these three domains, and also subversive and insurrectionary juniors, appear as important change actors. The change processes flowing out from all three domains are ultimately flowing towards the TAF's organisational culture pool through two change pathways: emulation driving the change in the TAF's security culture and adaptation driving its social culture. Lastly, at the end of the day, these incremental changes in the TAF's security and social culture, as well as the professional culture of the officers, directly affect the TAF's organisational culture. The changing organisational culture of the TAF is, in turn, affecting CMR. Turkish CMR is also affected by change in social-political context in Turkey. Simply put, as is seen from the chart above, one should note that there is a bilateral relationship between the TAF's organisational culture and Turkish CMR. This bilateral relationship, in fact, creates a reciprocal causality between the two. The TAF's organizational culture is under the direct influence of its security culture, social culture and the professional culture of the officer corps. The changing Turkish CMR is, in turn, returning to the very beginning of the causal mechanism explained above with a feedback mechanism and directly affects the TAF. Owing to that, the change takes place in a cyclic fashion and a reciprocal causality appears between the change in the TAF's organisational culture and Turkish CMR. It is evident that some amount of insiderness enabling one to carry out social research from within and social research of the familiar is needed to observe this reciprocal causality between the TAF's organisational culture shaped by non-military changes in the Turkish CMR and Turkish CMR shaped by changes from within the TAF's organisational culture. That is why this research sought to emphasise that Turkish CMR should best be studied through a holistic approach that provides scholarly insights both from the civilian and military side of the CMR to go beyond existing dichotomous explanations conceptualizing CMR as a zero-sum power politics between soldiers and elected politicians. The binary and power-based approaches, however scholarly, not only overlook the highly interactive and transformative character of CMR but also disregard the reciprocal causality between the TAF's organisational culture and CMR. As this research obviously elucidates, Turkish CMR is a bi-directional relational concept, meaning that changes in both the civilian and military sides of the relationship may have the capacity to influence the nature, characteristics and evolution of CMR.

5

Turkish Military After the 15 July Uprising

The findings of the previous chapters presenting the Turkish military's snapshot before the 15 July Military Uprising reveal that the transformation of the TAF as a security organisation and as a social institution, and officership as a profession, had been incrementally continuing; and the power distributional effect of the diverging attitudes among officers in terms of their stance towards change, in terms of their worldviews and political affiliations, and in terms of their understanding of officerhip as a profession had already been the case long before 15 July 2016. The bloody uprising, however, that took place on the night of 15 July 2016, was to structurally affect the course of this incremental transformation within the TAF and the very nature of Turkish civil-military relations through military reforms and mass purges.

Indeed, the night of 15 July 2016 will forever be imprinted in the collective memory of Turkish citizens as a night of chaos, horror and fear. As the so-called 'Peace in the Country Council' declared power via state television channel TRT, the fury of helicopters and the abrasive murmur of F-16s over Istanbul and Ankara mixed with a roar of uncertainty across Turkey. Memories of previous coups danced through the minds of those who had lived through the treachery of martial law, torture and worse – the suspension of everyday life. Shocked, frantic and disillusioned, on the night of the attempted coup citizens fled to the streets to gather the essentials – collecting tens of thousands of Turkish liras in cash from ATMs, taking the last scraps of bread from bakeries and crowding the few local markets open after midnight – seemingly readying for an apocalypse of the state. Some, however, grabbed their flags and took to the streets to resist, unwilling to endure what would be a fifth coup for the Republic of Turkey. For the vast majority of the crowd, the live broadcast of President Recep Tayyip Erdoğan's FaceTime call on CNN Türk mobilising civilians to go out on the streets to protest against the uprising had prepared the battleground. This was the ultimate call to arms to protect the decades-long civilianisation of Turkey. The people were called for the first time to elevate their role as the new guardians of democracy after decades of military praetorianism. And it was these new guardians who won, who proved that civilian control of the military would not be reversed.

What happened on the night of 15 July?

For civilians, the first sign of the turmoil came around 10:00 p.m. on 15 July as tanks occupied the two Bosporus bridges and low-flying F-16s were deployed over central Istanbul and Ankara, later bombing a number of buildings around the capital including the Grand National Assembly. For officials, the first sign of the coup came as early as the afternoon. Around 4:00 p.m., the Turkish National Intelligence Organisation (MİT) had intercepted messages from the future putschists, explaining the abnormal activity detected around military bases the day before. Within an hour, the MİT's chief intelligence officer, Hakan Fidan, had warned Chief of General Staff Hulusi Akar of increased military movements that would soon turn into an uprising later that night. It was not long after this, around 9:00 p.m., that Akar himself was taken hostage by the putschists, capturing him in his office and insisting, while holding him at gunpoint, that he read aloud the coup declaration before national television. After Akar refused to participate in the operation, the plotters took matters into their own hands, only to be foiled by the commander of the Istanbul First Army, General Ümit Dündar, who reported to President Erdoğan that a coup was unfolding outside the TAF chain of command. By 11:20 p.m., Prime Minister Binali Yıldırım had echoed the general's words on national television: a military uprising against the government and the top brass of the TAF had officially been launched. Although it seems as if President Erdoğan was the last to know about the coup, having been on holiday in the Mediterranean resort town of Marmaris, by 12:30 a.m. he was able to connect to CNN Türk via mobile video-calling app FaceTime, not only decrying the legitimacy of the coup but also galvanising the population to take to the streets. Within hours, two major bombs had exploded in Turkey – one at Erdoğan's vacated resort within 30 minutes of his flight, a major oversight by the coup plotters, and another on the parliament building – as civilians rose from their armchairs, went out from their homes and flooded the streets in protest. Meanwhile, the battle continued throughout the night. The masses reached the squares, the Istanbul bridges and the government buildings in Ankara. The putschists stood firm against the people, and confrontations of police and civilians against the soldiers flooded the stage with blood. The noise of gunshots ricocheted across the neighbourhoods of central Istanbul and Ankara, as well as military areas. Pixilated television coverage showed a dark cloud of bodies massed across the Bosporus bridge, both firing and strewn across the pavement. The coup was losing ground against the people and the police as civilians, both men and women, lay before the tanks. A defiant population became martyrs of the cause. Around 3:00 a.m., President Erdoğan arrived at Istanbul Atatürk Airport, where he spoke at length against the coup and continued to call for more people to go to the streets, further demoralising the coup plotters. By 6:00 a.m., the surviving contingent of soldiers surrendered at the Bosporus bridge. The uprising had been defeated overnight.

The basic reason for the failed uprising was its premature birth. But how did this happen? First, the uprising was planned for a later date but was moved forward. Then the rescheduled uprising, which was to have started at 3:00 a.m. on 16 July , was moved forward yet again by five hours, to around 10:00 p.m. on 15 July after the attempt was discovered. The first thing to note is that there was no common, basic ideology uniting the uprising participants. There were diverse motivations: various small cliques had personal interests and divergent aims for the TAF. So far the main sentiments that have been discerned are:

- **Gulenist sentiment:** The author suggests that those Gulen-affiliated officers in this group were the bestprepared and mostpowerful and thus played the engine role of the uprising train.
- **Anti Erdogan and antigovernment sentiment**: Looking at the names of detainees, the author wants to emphasise that he personally knows and served together with many of those putschists in the Turkish General Staff headquarters. So it is not hard for him to identify people who resent Erdogan and the AKP government among the putshicsts, despite the fact that they seemingly have no affiliation with the Gulenist network.
- **Selfinterest and pragmatist sentiment:** This tempted those officers who were prioritising their personal military career and attended to the uprising for the promotion of it.
- **Those who were compelled to join the coup by the military culture of absolute obedience to commanders' orders:** This sentiment is particularly visible among the younger cadres like junior officers, military school cadets, conscripts and contracted sergeants.
- **Those forced to join through the use of blackmail and threats by the Gulenist network.**

The primary reason for this premature attempt was because those Gulen-affiliated officers knew the forthcoming Supreme Military Council, which decides on promotions and appointments of generals and admirals, was set to convene in the first week of August 2016. After entering office in early August 2015, one of the most important missions of newly appointed Chief of General Staff General Hulusi Akar was to combat the Gulenists in the TAF, and there had already been several lists circulating with names of such officers. The AKP government favoured a purge of these officers, while the military command was advocating a phased, deliberate process based on solid evidence. Gulen-affiliated officers in the TAF had gotten away relatively unscathed from the 2015 council meeting, but there were sure signs that 2016 would be different.

Developments prior to the Supreme Military Council meeting of 2016 seem to indicate that the divergence of views between the government and the military had been somewhat reconciled. In the last week of June 2016, during the military espionage hearings in Izmir, six serving officers were detained, including an admiral and two generals. Four of the detained officers were consequently arrested. In an earlier military espionage case, also in Izmir, 359 defendants, including serving officers, were all acquitted of charges of keeping secret documents. With the indictments in the previous week's Izmir espionage case, the Turkish judiciary was gearing up to target about 1,000 Gulenists in the TAF, the great majority of whom were senior level officers (major and above), prior to the supreme council meeting. With so many detentions just before the meeting, the government was intending to compel the TAF command to carry out mass purges. When the coup planners learned of that intention, they moved the date to precede the council meeting. This turned out to be a suicidal yet rational move because had they not attempted this uprising, they would have still gone to prison.

It is also evident that putschist leaders had planned to move at 3:00 a.m. to take over by 5:00 a.m., when people would be asleep and the streets would be empty. But this didn't work. Around 4:00 p.m. on 15 July, 11 hours before the coup was to start, the national intelligence service MIT learned from radio and telephone intercepts of TAF personnel known to be Gulenists that some units were gearing up. MIT informed the Chief of General Staff at 5:00 p.m; at a meeting at his headquarters, officials decided to close Turkish air space to all flights as of 6:00 p.m. and bar military units from leaving their barracks. While that order was being written, Land Forces Commander General Salih Zeki Colak was called to the general staff headquarters.

By 7:00 p.m., putschsists realised that their plan was exposed and were able to take General Akar hostage. When Akar refused for two hours to sign an order commanding all units to join the coup action and to go on TV to tell the nation that the Army with its entire chain of command had taken over, they were further delayed. In the end, the plotters couldn't get Akar's signature, so they sent out an order signed by a brigadier general and launched their coup around 9:30 p.m. – that is, almost six hours before the planned time. The first indication of the rash, reckless actions by the Istanbul wing of the uprising was sending small units commanded by junior ranks on to the streets on the pretense of an exercise or fighting terror. These officers, who were trying to coordinate their action through WhatsApp, made a monumental mistake of closing the two bridges over the Bosporus River when everybody was out enjoying Friday night and traffic was heavy. That is when all of Turkey realised an uprising attempt was in the offing.

Meanwhile, the commander of the First Army in Istanbul, General Umit Dundar, and the commander of special forces, Major General Zekai Aksakalli – who could not be persuaded to join the uprising – publicly declared the coup was not a decision of the TAF chain of command, was illegal and had nothing to do with the Army. Their statements were severe blows to the plotters. At 10:00 p.m., the uprising leaders sent some F16s to make lowaltitude flights over Ankara and Istanbul, trying to intimidate people to remain at home. The planes' insane bombing of symbolic places such as the parliament building and presidential compound came when the plotters realised they had lost control. Putschists had no set plans to control the airwaves. Unexpectedly, at 11:00 p.m., Prime Minister Binali Yildirim appeared on TV to inform the public of the uprising attempt, and then at 11:30 p.m., President Recep Tayyip Erdogan called in, urging the public to take to the streets against the coup. He repeated that call at 3:00 a.m. at Istanbul Ataturk Airport, bringing uprising units face to face with an angry public marching into sensitive areas.

Why did the uprising attempt fail on the night of 15 July?

As explained in the previous chapters elucidating the Turkish military's pre-15 July snapshot, endogenous factors had already been shaping the change pathways, change actors' strategic preferences and their way of thinking and change drivers such as hetoregenisation and diversification within the officer corps, a shift from idealist to individualist officer type, officers' more egalitarian view of society and their increasing awareness of democracy and rule of law degrading the military's interventionist mentality, long before the uprising. Those factors seemed to constitute a 'breaking mechanism' preventing the uprising on the night of 15 July from turning into a full-fledged insurgency within the military with the mass participation of officers. Despite the fact that nearly 151 generals (42% of the total 358 generals) were arrested after 15 July, accused of either actively getting involved or pursuing a 'wait-and-see' policy on that night, the agency of those generals could not ignite a pro-uprising sentiment, particularly at the lower echelons of the military among the junior-level officers. Accordingly, the heat of the pro-uprising sentiment at the senior cadres of the military drastically decreased as the ranks dropped. One should also note that among 39,000 officers, the number of those arrested after the uprising was around 1,800, constituting only 5% of the officer corps. It should also be added that only 35 planes, including 24 F-16s, 37 helicopters, 74 tanks, 246 armoured vehicles and three ships were used in the coup attempt, while 3,992 light weapons were used by soldiers during the uprising; relatively low numbers when considering the TAF's total inventory.[1] Furthermore, in many military units, particularly in those in Ankara, Istanbul, Izmir and Malatya, many officers actively fought against and passively resisted the orders of the putschists. Seven officers and NCOs lost their lives and around 40 personnel were severely injured during armed clashes against the puschists within the military units on 15 July. The putschists could not take control of the Gendarmerie Command HQ in Ankara on the night of 15 July, mainly due to ongoing clashes between the putschists and pro-government soldiers. Also, and more importantly, there ws a clash between the Air Forces' Combined Air Operations Centre (BHHM) in the western province of Eskişehir, which had a pro-government stance on the night of 15 July, and Akinci Air Base in Ankara, the putschists-controlled air base that sought to hijack Turkey's airspace control that night.[2] It was this institutional resistance within the military, both at the general staff and service command headquarters and in the operation centres of come critical military commands such as Special Forces Command and Air Force Strategic Air Space Operation Command based in Eskisehir, that played the prime factor leading to the failure of the uprising. Aside from this institutional

1 Ibid.

2 See Sedat Ergin's articles elucidating many interesting insights about the aerial clashes between the putschists and pro-democracy soldiers for the control of Turkey's airspace on 15 July, particuarly 'Aerial wars on the night of the coup attempt', *Hurriyet Daily News*, 23 August 2017.

resistance within the military, the following developments on the night of 15 July contributed to the failure of the uprising:

- The fate of the coup was determined by General Umit Dundar, the commander of the First Army in Istanbul, who called Erdogan, who was on holiday in the Mediterranean resort of Marmaris, to brief him on the events. Thanks to this early warning, Erdogan quickly left Marmaris. The putschists raided his hotel an hour after he had left it. Erdogan's quick departure to Istanbul was one of the key elements in disrupting the coup plans. Dundar appeared calm and informative during the press conference, that was broadcast live on TV, when he declared the uprising illegitimate. He said the attempt was out of the TAF's chain of command and that top commanders were being held hostage by the plotters.
- President Erdogan took the risk of taking about an hourlong flight from Marmaris to Istanbul, which was a relatively secure location for him given his service as Istanbul's mayor from 1994-98 and the First Army's actions to suppress the uprising there.
- Most of the soldiers were conscripts who were told they were being sent out into the streets as part of an exercise or because of terror activity. Small units in the streets made up of young soldiers doing their compulsory military service, who were led by junior commanders, were surprised and disoriented when confronted with the opposition of the police and masses of irate citizens. They quickly lost control.
- The antiuprising reporting of mainstream TV channels offered the government a psychological advantage.
- The efforts of the citizens and police persuaded and compelled the soldiers at strategic points – the bridges over the Bosporus, Istanbul Ataturk airport and Ankara's Kizilay Square, as well as the presidential compound – to end their operations. Coverage by TV channels of this courageous resistance of the people and police reinforced the government's efforts.
- The opposition political parties refused to support the uprising.
- The Land Forces Command, which carries the most weight in the TAF, lacked support of the uprising. One should note that only around 500 officers, constituting just 2.2% of the total of 21,000 Army officers, were arrested for being involved in the uprising.
- The plotters did not have a proper chain of command and could not coordinate their actions; they did not have an operations centre. The junta that appeared to be focussed on Ankara and Istanbul could not exploit the element of surprise it had achieved between 10 p.m. and midnight, which gave the impression that the coup attempt was a hastily hatched kamikaze effort.

Turkish government-military relations after 15 July: reforms and mass purges

The Turkish Land Forces (Army), Navy, and Air Force commands, which had been under full control by the TGS before 15 July, have been brought into the control of the MoD. The MoD now also controls the function of professional military education at the undergraduate and graduate level, force generation/operation planning, military intelligence and logistics. With this change, the TGS, which directly answered to the prime ministry before 15 July, has turned into a coordinator/symbolic agent under the shadow of the presidential palace. Given his determination to create a strong executive presidency, one might suggest that President Erdogan wants to subject the TGS to the presidency; however, a constitutional amendment is still required before this change. This change was not among the 18 amendments voted on in the 16 April 2017 constitutional referendum. Furthermore, through executive decrees following 15 July, important changes have been made in the command-control mechanisms of the TGS and institutional settings of the Turkish military. The Chief of Staff is to be appointed directly by the president, and the president will be able to give orders directly to any commander without going through the Chief of Staff. Ultimately, this change could reduce the position of the Chief of Staff to a coordinator of military affairs and eventually weaken its agency as the commander of the armed forces. In its new and empowered role, the MoD will also be able to choose civilian ministry staff rather than making do with the personnel the TAF has provided. Moreover, the MoD will be the ultimate decision-maker on officer promotions starting from the rank of lieutenant. In addition to the military reforms, four major purges on 27 and 30 July and 2 and 7 September 2016, as well as following purges, dismissed a total of around 7,800 military personnel from the TAF. Since then, speculation has been rife on how these purges, still ongoing as of November 2018 despite the decreasing number being dismissed, have affected the TAF's combat effectiveness and led observers to question whether there will be problems filling critical posts.

Among those personnel purged, 4,690 have been from the Land Force command (87 generals, 2,500 officers, 1,016 NCOs and 1,087 contracted sergeants), 1,075 from the Navy (31 admirals, 646 officers, 368 NCOs and 30 contracted sergeants) and 1,726 from the Air Force (33 generals, 1,103 officers, 536 NCOs and 55 contracted sergeants).[3] In addition, all military cadets from the three military high schools and war academies, in total around 16,000 students, have been dismissed.

In the waves of the purges that started on 27 July 2016, the most affected group has been the commanding elites of generals and admirals. Out of the 348 generals/admirals in the Turkish Army, Navy and Air Force, 151 (42%) were discharged. Among them were two four-star generals, nine lieutenant generals, 30 major generals and vice admirals, and 110 brigadier generals and rear admirals.[4] Among those 151 generals,

3 The numbers were released by the Defence Ministry in early July 2017.
4 Metin Gurcan, 'Will the Turkish Military turn East or West?', *Al-Monitor*, 23 August 2016.

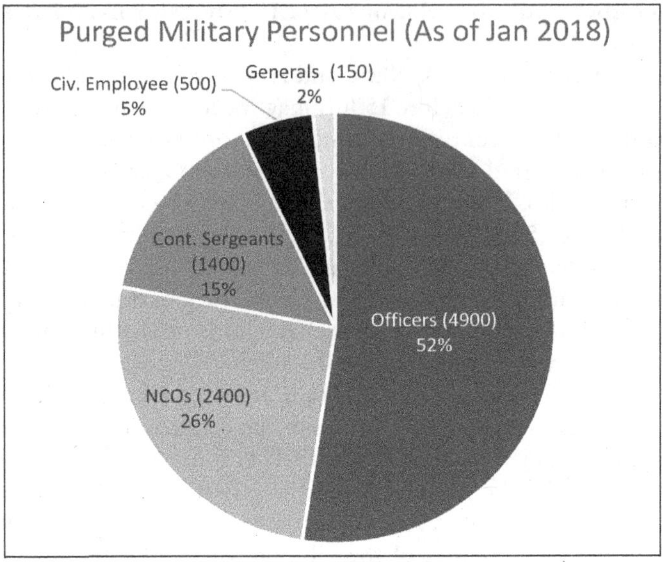

Figure 9 The Distribution of Purged Military Personnel.

nearly 44% of Army generals, 42% of Air Force generals and 58% of Navy admirals were formally discharged.[5] An additional 586 colonels were forced to retire by the Supreme Military Council on 23 August 2016.[6]

The officer group most affected by dismissals is the Air Force combat pilots. As of September 2017, Turkey had 320 combat planes (of which 240 were F-16s), 90 transport planes, seven tanker, and 105 training planes. The following month, after the largest dismissal of about 280 combat pilots, there were only about 300 combat-ready pilots. Before 15 July there were nearly two pilots for each warplane. This ratio was down to 0.8 pilots per plane in September 2017. A similar group affected by the dismissals is the Army's helicopter pilots. About 30 of them, including assault helicopter pilots, have been dismissed. Their absence means a much heavier workload for the remaining pilots, who have major tasks in the fight against the PKK.

Among the dismissals is a disproportionate number of battalion and team commanders in the Special Forces, the Turkish Navy's elite Underwater Assault Unit and the TAF's Combat Search and Rescue personnel. Many Special Forces battalion and team commanders were arrested and dismissed from service on charges of participating in the uprising. Similarly, there are reports of dismissals of a high number of helicopter pilots and other officers and NCOs serving in the Air Force's elite Search

5 Metin Gurcan, 'Why Turkey's coup didn't stand a chance', *Al-Monitor*, 17 July 2016.
6 'Military council retired nearly 600 colonels', *Hurriyet Daily News*, 24 August 2016.

and Rescue teams. The names of these elite military commands tell a lot about the Gulenist cult's strategy of infiltration within the military.

In the Army, most of the dismissals are from the TGS headquarters, service commands in Ankara and from corps and brigades in Istanbul and Ankara, as those were the ones overwhelmingly participating in the 15 July Uprising. The Second Army Command (Malatya) responsible for combatting terror in the south-east, border security with Syria and those who served in Operation Euphrates Shield have been the least affected so far and, with a high probability, will be purged later. This fact tells a lot about the government being pragmatic in their approach during the de-Gulenification of the military. Today, about 20 brigades of the Second Army Command are now operationally active with their new commanders. In the Navy, most of the dismissals were from the command offices in Ankara or personnel serving in rear headquarters. The Navy has been the least-affected service command. Although the TAF appears to be coping with the effects of the dismissals, no one can deny that its most elite forces will need at least two more years to restore their personnel numbers to pre15 July levels.

Did the Gulenist cult have a recruitment pattern in the TAF, as conspiratorial groups are very focussed and deliberate in their recruitment efforts? The Gulenist cult within the TAF may be defined as a religiously motivated 'secret network' with a distinctive utopian religious/political vision that militarised itself through infiltration into critical senior posts of the TAF. The aim of this militarised secret network that played the engine role of the 15 July Military Uprising was to hijack state power by operationalising its cadres within the state's bureaucracy, particularly within the security sector involving the military. As the profile of alleged coup plotter Lieutenant Colonel Levent Turkkan[7] – senior aide-de-camp (ADC) of the Chief of General Staff, General Hulusi Akar – who played a key role in detaining Akar on the night of 15 July 2016, tells us, the Gulenist cult in the TAF sought to gain influence first with the TAF's personnel management system to control promotions/appointments, and then military intelligence,. the military judicial system and military health system so as to promote its hidden agenda of first influencing and then controlling strategic decision-making mechanisms in the TAF with a very deliberate, strictly covert and prolonged strategy implemented by soldiers and their civilian older brothers (*abi*) of the cult operating as a compartmentalised organisation in absolute secrecy.[8] One should also note that this addiction to absolute secrecy, along with the absence of coordinated actions, a common ideology, a joint operations centre and a leader, played a key role in the failure of the 15 July Uprising.[9]

7 Metin Gurcan, "Profile of a dedicated Gulenist in Turkey's military' *Al-Monitor*, 27 July 2016.

8 Metin Gurcan, "Why it is so difficult to decipher the Gulenist network' *Al-Monitor*, 2 August 2016.

9 Metin Gurcan, "Why Turkey's coup didn't stand a chance' *Al-Monitor*, 17 July 2016.

The Gulenist recruitment scene and Levent Turkkan

As for the Gulenists, and their cooptation of the TAF, the group may be regarded as a secret network with a distinct quasi-utopian religious-political vision whose members exploited opportunities to realise its vision through occupying senior military posts, as well as other security roles. Here, intriguing questions arise as to who the Gulenist loyalists actually were, how they were recruited and indoctrinated, and how they could, apparently without hesitation, give up their families and bright futures in the TAF? Moreover, how had they managed to keep their posts without attracting suspicion?

A profile of alleged coup plotter Lieutenant Colonel Levent Turkkan provides some clues. Turkkan first wore the uniform as a military high school cadet in 1989, when he was just 14. He joined the army as a lieutenant in 1997 and would remain an officer for the next 19 years. Between 2011 and 2015, Turkkan served as a junior ADC to Chief of General Staff Necdet Ozel. In August 2015, when General Hulusi Akar took over as head of the TAF, Turkkan was appointed as his senior ADC, indeed the general's closest advisor, with knowledge of all developments and responsibility for arranging the commander's meetings and daily schedule. The ADC likewise reviews and processes all incoming information and documents, and in turn transmits oral and written orders from the commander to others. In rigid armies like the TAF, in which internal hierarchy and discipline are highly valued, whatever the ADC says is treated as his commander's word. In his testimony following the uprising, Turkkan said his first contact with the Gulen movement, in 1989, came when his "older brothers" (*abi*) – fellow Gulenists who had befriended him – prodded him to strive to become an officer. Turkkan said he was supplied in advance with questions on the military high school entrance examination.

He explained further: "In military high school I stayed in touch with older brothers Serdar and Musa. We were meeting once a month to pray and chat. We read Fethullah Gulen's books. My brothers even taught to me how to perform ablution before prayers without being detected, which could have given away my affiliation."

When he moved to the military academy in Ankara, a seven- or eight-month gap in his Gulenist liaisons occurred, which he attributed to his relationship with a girl-friend. Separately, Turkkan said he was not directed to embrace any special political ideology and usually voted for Erdogan's AKP: "When I was in military schools, they didn't assign me any duties. We were told that our only mission was not to be identified."

In describing the absolute secrecy adhered to in the movement, he explained that everyone knew his 'older brother' and carried out certain tasks, but didn't know or ask more. To these 'older brothers', with whom he evidently was not acquainted at all on a personal level, he interestingly displayed complete loyalty. Related here is the point that the Gulenist movement operates according to a horizontal, rather than a vertical, hierarchy. For example, reports suggest that on the night of 15 July many generals were given orders by colonels and even more-junior ranks.

When Turkkan was named ADC, the Gulenist demands spiked, unsurprisingly. Turkkan said he continued to conduct tasks without questioning them, such as recording conversations from and obtaining personal details about commanders. He was even ordered to detain and mistreat his own commander during the coup. Consistent with the larger portrait, Turkkan told the prosecutor that the movement attached importance to compartmentalisation and maintaining its cell structure within the TAF. Gulenistaffiliated officers did not know each other.

Furthermore, Turkkan, like some jihadists, did not hesitate to modify his behaviour to avoid detection. To indicate irreligiosity, he drank alcohol and refrained from fasting during the holy month of Ramadan. In addition, a particular area of Gulenist adeptness, according to investigators, was use of social media, including by imams and others. As well as live couriers, the favourite Gulenist avenues for communication were the messaging applications CoverMe, which erases messages after they are read, and WhatsApp.

A striking example of Gulenist tendencies emerges in the testimony of Muhammed Uslu, a civilian working in the prime minister's office who was also Turkkan's 'older brother'. Amazingly, Uslu received daily recordings from the office of the Chief of General Staff and passed them on to another civilian brother he did not even know. This ethos of blind obedience meant that many TAF officers with master's degrees and doctorates, not to mention high-level security clearances, were passing on their knowledge to anonymous 'older brothers'.

The Gulenist programme, in broader terms, was rooted in gaining influence in the TAF's personnel management system with the aim of controlling promotions and appointments, and thereafter military intelligence, the military judicial system and the military's autonomous healthcare system. It did so to promote its hidden agenda of first influencing and then controlling strategic decision-making mechanisms in the TAF, with a very deliberate, strictly covert and prolonged strategy implemented by soldiers and their civilian 'older brothers'. The organisation thus operated in a compartmentalised way, in absolute secrecy. This addiction to secrecy, one must note, was central to the failure of the overthrow attempt, along with the absence of coordinated actions, a common ideology, a joint operations center and a leader. Once the wheels fell off, the coup operators kept forging forward in an information vacuum, unable to adjust to changing circumstances and adapt their plan accordingly.

The distribution of the TAF's active military personnel (a total of 362,284, excluding the Gendarmerie Command and the Coast Guard, as these two fully attached to the Ministry of Interior after 15 July) is shown in Figure 10.[10] As of February 2017, marking the TAF's last official release of its personnel numbers, 43% of the TAF were

10 Note that there has been no drastic change in the numbers and ratios of the services and ranks within the TAF since February 2017.

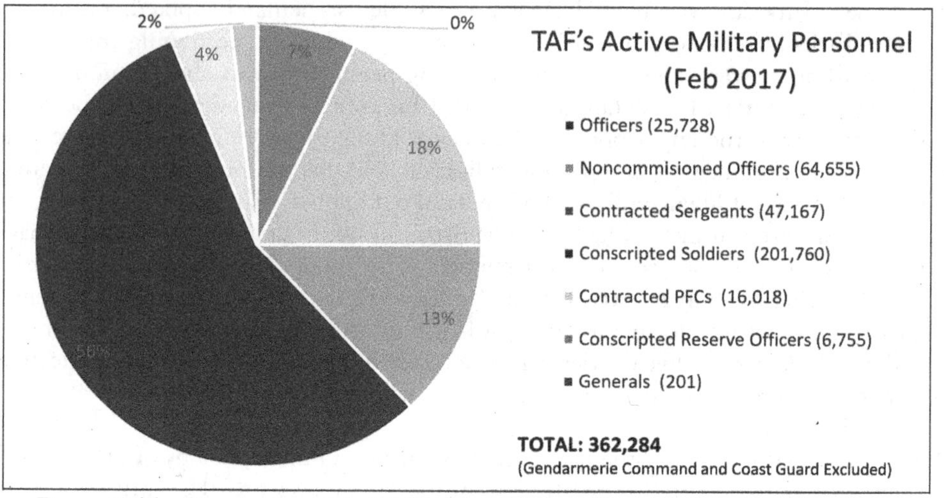

Figure 10 The Distribution of the TAF's Active Military Personnel as of February 2017.

professionals, the remaining 57% conscript soldiers and conscripted reserve officers.[11] When we compare these numbers with the pre-15 July figures from March 2016, we see a 40% reduction in the number of generals, which then numbered 325 across the three branches, and a 20% reduction from a total of 32,451 officers. Particularly, after the dismissal of almost 1,200 staff officers (70%) and the abolition of the staff officer system in August 2016, one would suggest that those staff officers,[12] the most privileged group among the officer corps as they had been given priority in selection of missions abroad, deployment to critical posts at headquarters and assignment to the rank of general, were the second most hard-hit group after the generals. It is not hard to guess that the staff officership system was the prime target for the Gulenist cult to control.

11 See the link http://www.milscint.com/tr/TAFnin-subat-2017-personel-mevcutlari/ (Turkish, accessed 10 October 2017).

12 Before 15 July 2016, staff officers holding an MA degree after their two-year education at the Staff College located in Levent, Istanbul, were the most privileged group among the officer corps in the TAF, as roughly 90% of the international cadres of the TAF and 95% of the general cadres were reserved for them. It is also worth mentioning that an international post (*daimi görev kadrosu*) is the most desired position in the TAF since it is a three-year deployment, and an officer could earn up to $7,000 per month when working in this cadre. If an officer could save half of this monthly payment, which is generally the case for the majority of officers, it means a saving of $120,000 after the three-year deployment. There are roughly 400 international cadres of the TAF.

Civil-Military Relations after 15 July

On the night of 15 July, Turkey bitterly experienced the need to have protection from the military. On this night, Turkey passed a major democracy test that included a coup attempt, the worst terror ever against its citizens, disproportionate use of military power against government institutions and extrajudicial execution attempts on elected civilian elites. Thousands of Turkish citizens who took to the streets that night gave the clearest message: those who came with elections will only leave with elections.

The speed and scale of the reforms have been both swift and strong, sparing few and sacrificing many. Although largely pro-AKP (the ruling Justice and Development Party) protests have been taking place as so-called 'democracy watches' against the coup, society and politicians have largely ignored debating other aspects of democratic civilianisation of the armed forces. Opposition parties have objected to the broad stroke of reforms carried out from under the umbrella of the parliament. There is a gap between civilianisation and democratisation that needs to be bridged.

Turkey has indeed been going through challenging times after 15 July 2016, seeking to diminish those risk factors that would put the country's future at peril. For some, the most effective remedy for Turkey to diminish risk factors is first to formalise and then to institutionalise the executive presidency, the 'practical reality' that has seemed to turn into an 'urgent need' after 15 July.[13] They suggest that the lack of strong government was closely related to the fragmentation of political parties, as a result of parliamentarism and growing friction between various identity groups, which led to periods of instability in Turkey. This chronic instability, in turn, weakened political institutions and made it easier for the military to overthrow democratically elected governments and put democracy on hold.[14] So they concluded that first quickly civilianising and then monopolising Civil-Military Relations (CMR) under the strict civilian control of the elected executive presidency could not only be the solution to prevent the occurrence of another 15 July but could also lead to more effective security forces.[15] One of the prime concerns of the proposed executive presidential system is, however, how close the TAF and other security sector actors such as the National Intelligence Agency (MİT) and Gendarmerie Command and the National Police (EGM) will be positioned relative to the power of the presidency, which has already wielded many executive decrees under the state of emergency and adopted many parliamentary powers. It is worth reminding that, despite the extensive security reforms, around 500 civilians (including 40 foreigners) and 400 members of the

13 Burhanettin Duran, 'The Executive Presidency and Turkey's Future', *Daily Sabah*, 31 January 2017.

14 Burhanettin Duran and Nebi Mis, 'The Transformation of Turkey's Political System and Executive presidency', *Insight Turkey*, Vol. 18/4, 2016, pp.11-27.

15 'Turkey in need of effective executive presidency, Deputy PM Kurtulmuş says', *Daily Sabah*, 7 January 2017.

security forces (soldiers, policemen and village guards) were killed in 25 major terror attacks in Turkey in 2016.[16]

In fact, Turkey's current dilemma of whether to monopolise or democratise Civil-Military Relations to prevent military interventions marks another *problematique* in addition to Feaver's paradox of protection 'by' and 'from' the military. That is, while the monopolisation of CMR enables strict civilian control of the military by the elected civilian president, by implying transfer for power from te military elites to the elected executive presidency, the democratisation of CMR enables diffusion of power among elected president, elected government, parliamentary and civil society actors such as academia, think tanks and media.

It is indeed possible to define the military uprising of 15 July as the act of putschists attempting to hijack state power both to redesign the state apparatus and, in the case of strict Gulenists, to rule people until society adapts to 'Fethullah Gulen's totalitarian political vision militarised by the Gulenist putschits'.[17] These two factors distance the events of 15 July from past coups in the history of the Republic of Turkey, which had sought to topple the elected government and hand over political power to the elected civilians at the end of the day. The events of 15 July then indicates a grim reality: in terms of bureaucratic capacity to challenge the existential threats, 'state rhetoric' and 'state reality' differ in Turkey. The "strong state tradition",[18] which was developed with great trust in its historic background in Turkey, has been painfully revealed to be strong in rhetoric yet vulnerable in responding to existential bureaucratic challenges on the night of 15 July. The public has revealed significant differences between the reality of the state (a state in which the bureaucratic cadres are vulnerable enough to be infiltrated) and its rhetoric (strong state discourse continuously narrated by the state elites), implying attempts to infiltrate the entirety of the state bureaucracy, primarily through the security and intelligence bureaucracy and judiciary, over time by a religiously motivated/pseudo-utopist covert cult supervised/inspired by the US-based cleric Fethullah Gulen. So how can we prevent the occurrence of another 15 July which attempted to 'hijack' the state apparatus? The answer is through monopolising/accumulating power under an executive presidency, enabling strict control of state apparatus or through democratising power so as to create check and balances, institutional oversight and monitoring mechanisms within the state apparatus.

The reforms that have taken place within the TAF following 15 July, with particular emphasis on the meeting of the Supreme Military Council (*Yüksek Askerî Şûra*, YAŞ)

16 Metin Gurcan, 'Does New Year's nightclub attack signal tough year ahead for Turkey?', *Al-Monitor*, 8 January 2017.

17 The author prefers this definition in the light of observations/experiences he had during his service in the Turkish General Staff (2010-15) in which he could interact with many arrested putschist officers allegedly linked to FETO, like Mehmet Disli, Orhan Yikilkan, Muharrem Kose, Osman Kilic, Bunyamin Tuner and Ramazan Gozel, and discuss several issues on the Turkish military's transformation with them.

18 Metin Heper, *Türkiye'de Devlet Geleneği* (Turkish), (İstanbul: Doğubatı, 2008).

on 28 July and the Executive Decrees (KHKs) of 27 and 31 July and 2 and 7 September 2016, were the government's largest recourse for action against the attempted military uprising. The reforms can be classified into three categories, see Table 49.

It is possible to suggest that, given the hastiness and extent of the military reforms, some of which are presented above, this civilianisation process in Turkish CMR seems revolutionary. Simply, the 15 July putschists have broken the ivory tower in which the military once was living in a privileged fashion. Therefore, this paper suggests that these military reforms aiming for revolutionary civilianisation have led to a paradigm shift, from the Huntingtonian one to the Janowitzian one, implying a shift from the professionalisation of an autonomous army which struggles to remain apolitical by its very nature of autonomy, or the Huntingtonian paradigm that influenced the very nature of the Turkish CMR for decades,[19] to a more Janowitzian one – denying the existence of an autonomous military and instead seeking to manage the gap between civilians and military.[20]

The shift from Huntington to Janowitz: the changing Nature of Turkish CMR after 15 July

The literature on CMR revolves around the nature of the relationship between what is civilian (governments, civil society, academia, media, thinks tanks) and what is military. With reference to Feaver, again, CMR "is a very broad subject, encompassing the entire range of relationships between the military and civilian society at every level".[21] There is a problem with explaining the complex relationship between what is civilian and what is military. Historians, political scientists, sociologists, anthropologists and military strategists have all made important contributions to expand the scholarly grasp of the field. Although the work by Samuel Huntington and Morris Janowitz dates back 60 years, it is still relevant for modern debates about CMR. Huntington's *The Soldier and the State*[22] and Janowitz's *The Professional Soldier*[23] *not only methodically combined empirical research on CMR with systematic theorising for the first time, but also led to the emergence of different paths within research on CMR. That is, political science studies of CMR, on the one hand, have mostly followed the Huntingtonian tradition and are mostly concerned with the question of how civilian political leaders can maintain civilian*

19 Ersel Aydınlı, 'Civil-Military Relations Transformed', *Journal of Democracy*, 23(1), 2012, pp.100-08.
20 The work done by both Samuel Huntington and Morris Janowitz dating back 60 years is, indeed, still relevant for contemporary debates regarding Turkish CMR after 15 July.
21 Peter D. Feaver, 'The Civil-Military Problematique: Huntington, Janowitz, and the Question of Civilian Control', *Armed Forces and Society* 23:2 (1996).
22 Samuel P. Huntington, *The Soldier and the State: The Theory and Politics of the Civil Military Relations* (Cambridge: Harvard University Press, 1957).
23 Morris Janowitz, *The Professional Soldier* (New York: Free Press, 1971).

Table 49. Military Reforms since 15 July 2016

Initiated and completed	• Subordinating the Turkish Army, Air Force and Navy to the MoD[1] • Subordinating the Gendarmerie Command and Coast Guard to the Ministry of the Interior[2] • Foundation of National Defence University (NDU) and subordinating this institution to the MoD, closure of military high schools and attachment of war academies and Staff College to the NDU[3] • Revision of officers' promotion and appointment criteria within TAF, making the MoD the final authority on the appointments of all officers[4] • Abolition of the autonomous military health system and independent military judiciary[5] • Civilianisation of the Supreme Military Council with the involvement of deputy prime minister, foreign, justice and interior ministers from the cabinet along with the prime minister, Chief of General Staff, defence minister and the service commanders[6] • Revision of the curriculum of the professional military education system at the undergraduate and graduate levels • Abolition of the privileged staff officer system
Initiated yet not completed	• Sharing of command-control, personnel-recruitment, operations, intelligence, logistics-acquisition, military education and budget management functions/responsibilities between the TGS and MoD in a coordinated and synergistic way mainly due to the TGS's still uncertain status in the security sector architecture • The redesign of the MoD's organisational structure according to the MoD's expanding roles and responsibilities, especially the strengthening of the MoD structure in terms of personnel management (promotion and assignment) and consultancy (decision support), command-control, operation and military intelligence issues, in addition to military education, military procurement, acquisition and budgeting • Empowerment of the institutional agency of the MoD within the security architecture so as to rescue it from the dominance of the TGS • De-Gulenification of the military through purges and dismissals
Desired yet not even initiated	• Ending the ambiguity over the status of the TGS, its roles and missions in Turkey's security architecture • Decreasing the number of TAF personnel • Ensuring joint-ness and full civilian control over the military at all levels • Transition to an all volunteer and fully professional military by increasing contracted sergeant and contracted Private-First-Class (PFC) cadres and abolishing the military draft system • Developing 'civil capacity' in the field of defence/security for the empowerment of the civilian cadres in the MoD, NDU, Undersecretary of National Security and other security sector actors

Notes

1 See Decree No. 669 issued on 25 July 2016 (Turkish) <http://www.resmigazete.gov.tr/eskiler/2016/07/20160731-5.htm> (accessed 11 January 2018).

2 See Decree No. 668 issued on 27 July 2016 (Turkish) <http://www.resmigazete.gov.tr/eskiler/2016/07/20160727M2.htm> (accessed 11 January 2018).

3 See Decree No. 669 issued on 25 July 2016 (Turkish) <http://www.resmigazete.gov.tr/eskiler/2016/07/20160731-5.htm> (accessed 11 January 2018).

4 Metin Gurcan, 'Turkey tells a story with major military personnel moves', *Al-Monitor*, 3 August 2017.

5 Decree No. 669 issued on 25 July 2016.

6 'Top ministers to join Supreme Military Council', *AA News Agency*, 31 July 2016.

control or the subordination of the military under the legitimate elected civilian leadership. Janowitz, on the other hand, concentrates more on the cultural norms, values and societal factors affecting militaries, and the relationship between soldiers and civilians.

During the Cold War, Huntington proposed a solution to reconcile two apparently incompatible social imperatives: the need to construct an institution powerful enough to defend American society against the Soviet threat, and to ensure civilian control at the same time so that this armed institution could not become a threat to the society itself. Simply put, Huntington's solution to this civil-military *problematique* was the maximisation of the separation between what is military and what is civilian. According to Huntington, the way to achieve this is to foster "military professionalism", which is the development of a genuine conservative military mindset focussed on corporateness, social responsibility and expertise in the management of violence.

The field of military sociology following Janowitz's work, on the other hand, has been concerned with the reciprocal influence of the military and society. In *The Professional Soldier*, Janowitz's main message is that, just like other social subsystems, the military is subject to technological, socio-economic and political changes. Therefore, the role and missions, norms and values and, more importantly, self-perceptions of the military's officer corps, as well as the function of the modern military institution itself, should not be considered as constant, or as a 'given fact', but as changeable in line with the prevailing value system and the dominant norms of the greater society. In this tradition, military sociologists focussed on issues such as the bureaucratic organiszation of the military, the sociology of military personnel and their families, as well as the racial and gender integration in the military. Particularly, Janowitz's understanding of military professionalism may be useful in the Turkish case as he sees the institution of the military both as a product of tradition and hierarchy, and more importantly, as an agent shaped by its environment. This understanding provides for a more dynamic grasp of the military as a profession, as a security organisation and as a social institution because it grants agency to the officer corps, and suggests that they are fully aware of their 'influence' on politics and society in addition to being an actual product of them.[24]

For almost the next six decades, both the Huntingtonian and Janowitzian approaches have remained primary points of reference for much of scholarly research in the field of CMR. While military sociology that followed the Janowitzian tradition has become a well-established sub-discipline of mainstream sociology, the Huntingtonian strand has remained as the sub-discipline of the wider discipline of political science.

While Janowitz agrees with Huntington on the separate characteristics of the military and the civilian worlds, he differs from his predecessor on how the military would be denied from posing a threat to democracy and society within which, in fact, it was created. For Janowitz, the military world is conservative and always prone to resist societal changes; therefore, it is highly unlikely that the military will

24 *Ibid.*, p.420.

adapt to changes as fast as society could. Janowitz challenges Huntington's objective control and proposes external intervention, or "subjective control" in Huntington's words, as the most viable instrument that may facilitate the change of the military in a timely and effective manner. Janowitz, who then opposes Huntington's primary assumption that regards the inherent gap between the military and the civilian as it is, seeking to shrink the gap either by civilianisation of the military or the militarisation of society. For Janowitz, the civilianisation of the military, which means equipping the military with the norms and expectations of society, is the wiser strategy to diminish the gap. That is why he encourages the use of conscription and reserve officer training programmes, and collaboration with the military in universities in the realms of education and technological researches so that the broadest level of society's influence on the military may be settled. Simply put, for him, the more societal norms and attitudes are digested by the military, the smaller the attitudinal and behavioural differences between these two worlds are, and consequently the greater the likelihood of establishing and maintaining civilian control over the military. Thus, the key difference between the two is that Huntington separates civilian and military domains, but Janowitz defends the integration or entanglement of those domains. In sum, both Huntington and Janowitz define the civil-military playing field. Huntington implored civilians not to attack the conservative military culture, while Janowitz lamented the consequences of a conservative military drifting too far from civilian society.

New paradigm: less Huntington, more Janowitz

The attempted coup on 15 July has not only shocked and terrorised civilians, but also the military establishment and Turkish CMR as a whole. The extent of this shock has led to this revolutionary reform process, and an equally revolutionary change in Turkish CMR. The comprehensive reforms of the TAF concerning its structure within the government, the judiciary, education, health, businesss and so on have challenged the old paradigm, and demanded a conceptual change: less Huntington, more Janowitz. The 15 July putschists have broken the ivory tower in which the military once was living in a privileged fashion.

Janowitz's depiction of 'the professional soldier' has become a desirable solution in the eyes of Turkish politicians and society. The need to seek a professional military that also engages with the reality of civilians has been one goal of the government's major reforms and restructuring of the military post-15 July. The government has exercised a 'subjective control' of the military in order to orchestrate what it sees as a timely and effective change over an institution in which it has otherwise lost confidence. The reforms carried out in the state of emergency decree laws have severely damaged the privilege of the military, bound it to the politicians in more than a single way and ushered in a new era of civilian control. Moving forward from 15 July, the 'revolutionary civilianisation' process has picked up the Turkish military from Huntington's world and placed it right back down in Janowitz's. Civilians have seen the attempted coup as a clear sign that the military had been living in another world, even in another universe, or maybe just somewhere that didn't have enough wireless coverage to connect to Face-Time. Now the military must live and work within the earshot of the people and the government.

The new paradigm after 15 July does not recognise the autonomous domain of the military; therefore, it seeks to exterminate it rather than manage it. As seen from the above description, the new paradigm cuts off nearly 100 years of Turkish history. The social and cultural norms that the military has been embedded with since 1923 may be eradicated in this new era; as we have seen with the case of the transfer of the military health system to the civilian Ministry of Health. Through the subordination of several posts to civilian offices such as the Ministry of Defence and the Ministry of Interior, the military would be held accountable according to these civilian establishments.

Reforms of the military's judicial process are a definitive narrowing between the military and civilian elements. Efforts to include more military cases in civilian courts had been a main component of the TAF's civilianisation process through Europeanisation in the early 2000s. Abolishing military courts and trials holds the TAF more accountable to civilian standards of justice and law. Talking of abolishing all the military courts in the future would be a complete overhaul of the system.[25]

Reforms in military education have called for a Janowitzian collaboration with the military in universities in the realms of education and technological research. Although the military's privilege of selecting one of the members of the Higher Education Council (YÖK) had been previously removed, the military's autonomous network of high schools and colleges has now been reformed so as to facilitate collaboration on national defence between the military and civilians, synchronizing the civilian and military defence systems in the future.

The Turkish military's institutional identity after 15 July

Modern militaries are complex and *status quo*-oriented organisations that are immune to change as they are strictly founded on both an established institutional setting and a traditionally set framework of values, norms and rituals. Both exogenous and endogenous shocks, however, would change the institutional setting of a military. The uprising on 15 July and mass purges following this, thus, may bring about radical institutional reconfigurations, overlooking shifts based on endogenous developments that often unfold fast or incrementally.

The 15 July Uprising has proven that, just like any other social subsystem, the Turkish military is subject to technological, socio-economic and political changes. Therefore, the role and missions, norms and values and, more importantly, self-perceptions of the

25 Metin Gurcan, 'Nasıl bir sivil-asker ilişkisi? (Turkish)', *T24*, 3 August 2016, (accessed 5 August 2016).

military's officer corps, as well as the function of the modern military institution itself, should not be considered as a 'given fact' or constant but changeable in line with the prevailing value system and dominant norms of the greater society. The endogenous dynamics within the Turkish military, therefore, must be explored in a more dynamic paradigm as reforms and the restructuring process continue to unfold.

In the following section, the change within the Turkish military caused by the shock waves of 15 July in the traditional institutional setting of the military will be discussed. This section seeks to explain the change in the Turkish military from a theoretical framework in which one may see some elements from James Mahoney and Kathleen Thelen's theory of gradual institutional change[26] at the organisational level. This insight then leads to the question: when does endogenous institutional change take place? According to Mahoney and Thelen, institutional change often occurs precisely when problems of rule interpretation and enforcement open up space for different types of pro-*status quo* and reformist actors to displace the existing rules completely, or to implement them in new ways and through new means.[27]

After addressing the questions of institutional change, and elucidating the modes of change that are most likely to drive such a change in diverse institutional settings, one may ask the following question: who exactly are these actors behind such change or blocking it? From a distributional perspective, the first answer would be that there are two types of agents: the losers as the blockers of change and the winners who implement institutional change. When taking into account the fact that the ambiguities inherent in situations and uncertainties existing in institutional enactments force us to move beyond this dichotomous conception, one needs a new framework which can exceed this reductionist conception.

In any institution, one can make generalisations about the affinity between particular types of agents and modes of change. Reformists seek rapid displacement but will settle for gradual displacement. Symbionts seek to preserve the formal institutional *status quo*, but their parasitic variety carries out actions that can cause institutional drift. Pragmatists adopt a wait-and-see approach while pursuing change when it suits their interests.

How can we adapt the approach of Mahoney and Thelen to the case of the TAF? According to them, institutional change can be an unintended byproduct that grows out of a distributional struggle in which no party explicitly had sought the change that eventually occurred. This is exactly the case of the TAF with regard to the purposes of this piece of research. What exactly are the properties of institutions, for instance, that permit change within the TAF? How and why do the change-permitting properties of the TAF allow (or drive) actors to carry out behaviours that foster those changes (and what are these behaviours)? For the TAF, the answer to that question is every

26 James Mahoney and Kathleen Thelen, *Explaining Institutional Change: Ambiguity, Agency and Power*, p.67.

27 *Ibid*, p.13.

single type of process, actor, structure and relation within the domains of the TAF as a security organisation and a social institution, and officership as a profession. Simply put, Mahoney and Thelen's power-distributional perspective of the gradual institutional change model provides a framework to explain the above-presented changes of the TAF: as a security actor, as a social institution, and officership as a profession.

One may conclude that, in an organisation such as the TAF, change first occurs through the distributional effects of institutions and then triggers distrust of the pre-existing norms and divisions among those who hold power at the elite level in the institution. Or, through elite-mass friction, change can occur if institutions put subordinate groups at a disadvantage up to the point that they mobilise and come to identify with one another, thereby increasing their power and capacity to break prevailing institutional arrangements. These two possibilities correspond to the themes of 'divided elites' at the TAF as a security organisation domain, and 'united subordinate groups vs military elites' at the TAF as a social institution domain that are emphasised in the explanations of change above. Unsurprisingly, the portfolio of the identity includes three types of change actors (reformists, symbionts and pragmatists) proposed in the Mahoney and Thelen's approach.

The Turkish military's identity after 15 July

The distribution, as of February 2017, of the TAF s active military personnel (a total of 362,284, excluding the Gendarmerie Command and Coast Guard, given that these two are fully attached to the Interior Ministry after 15 July) is shown in Figure 3.[28] Here, reflecting the TAF's most recent official release of its personnel numbers, 43% were identified as professionals, while 57% were conscript soldiers or conscripted reserve officers.[29] In comparing these figures with those from March 2016, four months before the uprising, one notes a 40% reduction in generals, which then numbered 325 across the three branches, and a 20% reduction from 32,451 officers. Particularly after the dismissal of almost 1,200 staff officers (70%) and the abolition of the staff officer system in August 2016, one would suggest that those staff officers[30] – the most

28 Note that, since February 2017, no drastic change has occurred in the numbers and ratios within the TAF services and ranks.

29 See 'TAF'nin Subat 2017 Personel Mevcutlari', <http://www.milscint.com/tr/TAFnin-subat-2017-personel-mevcutlari/> (accessed 1 February 2017).

30 Before 15 July 2016, staff officers holding a master's degree after their two-year education at the Staff College located in the Levent neighbourhood of Istanbul were the most privileged group among the TAF officer corps. Indeed, they constituted roughly 90% of the international TAF cadres and 95% of the general cadres. Worth mentioning here is that international posts (*daimi görev kadrosu*) are the most desired given that they entail a three-year deployment, during which an officer can earn up to $7,000 per month. By saving half this monthly payment, which most can do, they can amass $120,000 after the full deployment. Roughly 400 officers serve in this international role.

privileged group among the officer corps given that they had received priority in the selection of missions abroad, deployment to critical posts at headquarters and assignment to the rank of general – were the second hardest-hit group after the generals. It is not difficult to surmise that the staff officer system was the prime target for control by the Gulenists.

In determining whether the TAF will truly be transformed by the current process or revert to the *status quo ante*, one can usefully assess the post-15 July stance held by military elites toward change, based on several measures: opinions on military transformation; worldviews and political orientations; service affiliations; ranks; perspectives on officer service as a profession; and views on rank, privilege and status. Such an analysis yields three general categories:[31]

> **Symbionts**: Military elites who have a parasitic and mutualistic relationship with the TAF.
>
> **Pragmatists**: Military elites who only think of their careers and have opportunist relationships with the military. This type of military elites has ambiguous preferences about institutional change. They neither actively seek to preserve the *status quo* nor visibly try to change the rules. Pragmatists instead exploit whatever possibilities exist within the prevailing system to maintain their interests. Pragmatists consistently follow the *status quo* or the trends that are happening inside the institution and fall on the side of what would be the best for their career. Out of all types of military elites, the pragmatists are the most vulnerable to being politicised as they emphasise the short-term, instead of the values of the institutional system or the long-term strategic vision.
>
> **Reformists**: Military elites who are not pleased with the current situation and who want to see the TAF turn into 'something' else.[32] The reformists are enemy to the *status quo* as they are constantly criticising the TAF's culture, organisational structure and the nature of job positions. They also believe that the TAF falls behind (in either technology or tactics/techniques) when compared with global armies. There are two variants of this category:
>
> **Originalist reformists:** According to these more traditionally minded reformists, the current values held by the TAF have diverged from the ideals espoused during the early years of the Turkish Republic (proactive and exclusive secularism, etatism, nationalism, elitism and enlightenment, among others). In order to reach their goals without diverging from the intended path, the current system needs to be completely abolished and then return to the original principles

31 As established and defined by the author.
32 The following groups are two classes of reformist colonels.

(almost like a factory reset). According to this type, the thing that needs to be prioritised and addressed above all else is the mental and ideological system of values within the military.

Progressive reformists: This type, who are not as stuck in the past as the originalist trans- formationalists, thinks that the TAF must move forward with the present situation as it stands now. Generally speaking, the progressives, who do not have as much of a values-oriented approach as the last type, are of the opinion that changes need to be made to society, Turkish CMR and the global security environment.

An example may better illustrate these typologies.

For instance, think about the discussion of whether or not the graduates of imam-hatip schools (high schools with a religious curriculum) should become officers or NCOs in the military. The originalists would not accept this under any circumstance as it would deviate from the 'ideal type'. The symbionts would remain uninterested in this debate, while the pragmatists could either be for or against it depending on the tide of politics and the stance taken by their higher-ups, such as the chief commanders. As for the case of the progressives, they would conduct a cost-benefit analysis. If the analysis revealed that the need for societal change prevailed over the need to stick with the current system, then they would support allowing graduates from imam-hatip religious high schools to become officers and NCOs.

In addition to the typologies among military elites, it is possible to classify the viewpoints and political tendencies of elites as follows:

Table 50. List of prominent ideologies within the Turkish military

	Nationalist	**Globalist**
Rightist	Conservatives (*mukaddesatci*)	Atlanticists
Leftist	Neo-nationalist (*ulusalci)*	Eurasianists

Typically, **Conservatives** do not have knowledge of a foreign language or experience in training in foreign countries, and do not hold offices in foreign countries. They tend not to be concerned with developments in the international system and the global security environment. The conservatives are pro-*status quo*, reactive and are normally pragmatists, but sometimes their symbiont sensibilities can come to the forefront.

Conservatives are nostalgic for the time period before 1923, making the difference between religiosity and nationalism visible (for example, a conservative would allow religious practices such as Friday prayers and fasting inside the barracks and would act in a particular manner such as using prayer beads, talking colloquially and using local expressions). This type of elite officer thinks that areas outside of Turkey's borders are dangerous and views anyone outside of Turkey with suspicion (this can even sometimes include civilians in Turkey).

Atlanticists typically have a pro-NATO and pro-US sentiment, are well-educated, speak fluent English and have undergone at least two years of service abroad. Furthermore, Atlanticists aim at reaching a level of NATO professionalism. Atlanticists think that NATO and its value system, as well as the structure and the conditions of jobs within the US military, are ideal. This school of thought is not that dissimilar to the way in which the originalists think of Republican ideals. Furthermore, the Atlanticists perceive that the TAF is an important part of the Western security environment, with the US in the lead. This type thinks the TAF must rank among the armies around the world in order to increase its presence on the world stage.

Neo-nationalists, in contrast to the conservative, view the period before 1923 as the era of darkness, and do not tend to have high competence in a foreign language or much international experience, similar to the conservatives. For this reason, this type will view anything that happens outside of Turkey with suspicion, and most of the time will lean towards a reactive nationalist attitude over a leftist ideological position. In addition to showing pragmatic tendencies, the neo-nationalists are critical of preserving the TAF's traditional institutional identity and the continuation of the *status quo*, similar to the originalists.

Like the Atlanticists, the **Eurasianists** have a good grasp of foreign languages, a good academic education and at least one post abroad. However, unlike the Atlanticists, the Eurasianists are more independent and anti-American, and thus have a non-aligned stance. They hold the opinion that the TAF should be more independent, and are as anti-NATO as a neo-nationalist is. They believe that the centre of global power should be shifted east. Since the Eurasianist is more well-read, he is not as colour blind as the neo-nationalist.

The vast majority of the senior officers who were forced to separate from the TAF between 2010-14 during the *Balyoz*, *Ergenekon* and the *Izmir Spy* cases were idealists, some were neo-nationalists and some were originalists. There were also more senior officers being promoted who were Eurasianists, and it is known that the Eurasianists had tendencies towards being transformationalists. The TAF had slid to the right during these intellectual purges, which provided FETÖ with an opportunity to take hold of the process, a painful lesson that we have all learned from.

As for the process following 15 July, in contrast we see that those who were on the list to be expunged from the TAF were either conservatives or Atlanticists. It is possible to say from these lists that the FETÖ members nesting in the units showed the characteristics of Atlanticists and were governing the TAF's institutional transformations. These facts emerged during a number of coup plotters' testimonies following 15 July. In addition, a list of those who used the mobile messaging app WhatsApp to plot the coup included a number of military staff who had served in NATO missions. As a consequence of these dismissals, the TAF is now moving 'left' after 15 July. However, the intellectual Left is now much more reactive and nationalist after undergoing such unjust treatment in the previous era, with stronger wills after having been proven right about FETÖ. What is even more important is that the originalist tendency is even stronger than before. The effects of FETÖ on the Atlanticists and the subsequent dismissals were, to a great extent, the reason why so much momentum has been lost.

A critical question remains: will the Europeanists and neo-nationalists attempt to side with the political will to lead the way with their models of transformation (originalists in domestic affairs but independent and Europeanist with foreign affairs), or will the pragmatists and symbionts work to establish stricter control over civilians to return to the *status quo* of pre-15 July? To put it differently, will the political will place a Europeanist view to spearhead the efforts of the TAF's institutional transformation by way of shielding itself from external threats? Or will the pragmatists, symbionts and reformists work amongst themselves to establish something to gather together in order to maintain the *status quo*? In its efforts to rebuild the Army, will the political will and the chain of command want to urgently return to the old TAF or do something new? The answers of these questions are to be relevant indicators when addressing change within the military.

As a caveat, it should be emphasised that it is difficult to separate the above types from each other by certain lines in real life and to explain the military elites with a single approach in terms of their worldviews and differences between how they read the global and their political tendencies. The 'ideal types' above are the basic explanatory approaches and it is necessary to pay attention to the transitions between them in real terms. For example, it is possible that a military elite, who fasts owing to his upbringing by a right-wing nationalist family, might be shifted to the Eurasian approach during his military career, as well as a neo-nationalist elite or nationalist who goes to Friday prayers and uses rosaries, but when it comes to the leanings of the TAF, he might be an an Atlanticist military elite with a pro-NATO and US stance.

One should also note that debates about military transformation in the TAF after 15 July brought to the surface the service commands' conflicting approaches concerning pace, scale and drivers of military transformation. Particularly, the reorganisation of the TAF, military education system, present and future threat perceptions, and military transformation in the light of Turkey's regional and global vision, depend on the provision of 'jointness and interoperability' based on land-sea-air cooperation. In the military reform debates after 15 July, however, each service command seems to understand different things from joint-ness and interoperability. In the light of the findings of his PhD research, the author suggests that the Land Force Command, with a pro-*status quo* stance, tries to preserve the existing privileges in the TAF, whereas the Air Force and Navy Commands, with a reformist stance, strive to end these privileges and want to play the engine role in the TAF's military transformation, a dynamic leading to institutional rivalry among these three.[33] This inter-service rivalry, therefore, caused by the service commands' stance in terms of change after 15 July is among those main factors leading to the fragmentation/factionalisation of the TAF.

33 *Ibid.*

In the wake of 15 July it can be said that, as the "guardians of the existing system, or *status quo*",[34] none of the current crop of generals are insurrectionaries. In the post-15 July setting, not only are the perceptions and opinions of the four-star generals constituting the High Command very important for the promotions and appointments of generals within the TAF, but also the presidential palace's (*kulliye*) evaluation is of critical significance. Therefore, generals usually shape their positions in the system according to the perceptions and opinions of the High Command and, more importantly, President Erdogan's evaluation as he is the ultimate decision-maker at the moment. This careerist stance prevailing among the generals makes each of them a master player in understanding the dominant sentiment within the TAF and taking one's position accordingly – a significant factor explaining the generals' extreme risk-averse attitudes when dealing with the political echelons on domestic politics and military power projection efforts abroad such as controlling the Jarablus-Al Bab-Al Rai triangle in the north of Syria and forward military basing in Qatar, Somalia and Sudan after 15 July. For this reason, except the traditionalists and progressives who represent roughly 25% of the generals – the author's scholarly guess based on his PhD research and interviews with retired and serving generals – it is possible to say that, as of November 2018, the great majority are careerists, having a pro-*status quo* and compliant sentiment leading to full obedience of the prevailing pro-Erdogan discourse. However, one should note that those careerist generals constituting the majority are not devout believers of President Erdogan, meaning that their stance can easily change parallel with the power shifts both in Turkish politics and in CMR.

For around 97% of the officers, colonelship is the last rank to be reached in their professional life. It is seen that the colonels who came to the end of their professional life and started to plan their retirement have sacrificed lots of things, both for themselves and for their families, during the weary profession of officership, and they want to be comfortable in the rank they 'deserve' as the return for the price they paid in past ranks. Therefore, a great majority of the colonels in TAF are free riders.

As emphasised in the previous chapters elucidating the pre-15 July snapshot of the TAF, the great majority of officers at the ranks of major and lieutenant colonel, usually officers aged 35-45, are overwhelmingly progressives with a reformist spirit, but some of them are careerist as a small portion seem to be mutual free riders. This ratio makes the lieutenant colonels and majors the only group that can overtake an important role in the institutional transformation of the TAF when considering the political interference among the higher ranks and intellectual capital deficiency at the lower ranks. Simply, considering the careerist tendencies prevailing among the generals and unexpectedly low quality of the lieutenants recruited from the civilian universities after the 15 July Uprising, the majors and lieutenant colonels with reformist spirit and

34 Interview with a major general in correspondence with the author, Istanbul, 12 October 2016.

intellectual capital are the only group of officers the TAF can rely on for an institutional transformation.

These findings,[35] which could be defined as a snapshot of the Turkish military's officer corps' views, show that, as the ranks decrease, there are some major trends influencing the officer corps. These include diversification of opinions from collectivism to individualism, from an elitist to an egalitarian view of society, and from an idealistic commitment to the military to a focus on financial gain and career opportunities.[36] Yet it is possible to suggest that the great majority of the captains and lieutenants, constituting the largest group in the TAF, have the image of insurrectionaries. They are definitely uncomfortable with the *status quo* and want change.

In short, the military elites within the TAF have been divided in terms of:

- their stance towards military transformation,
- their worldviews and political orientations,
- service affiliations,
- their ranks,
- the way they look at officership as a profession, and
- the way they look at rank, privilege, and status.

The cross-cutting rivalry among these categories creates a power-distributional effect within the TAF. One should note that, unlike the contemporary socio-political context in Turkey in which pro/anti-Erdogan divison has become the dominant cleavage, there exists no pro/anti-Erdogan divide in the Turkish military. The absence of a pro-Erdogan military elite group constitutes the primary obstacle for the 'Erdogan-ification' of the military, or the creation of a military in Erdogan's own image, at least in the coming five to six years. It is therefore very unlikely to expect the institutionalisation of President Erdogan's way of thinking and doing things in the military in the short term, let alone the creation of a TAF in Erdogan's own image. It is also worth noting that the conservative military elites with Islamist leanings, theoretically constituting the most likely group to foster a pro-Erdogan camp in the TAF, lack intellectual capital on how to design and manage a possible Erdoganist military transformation. Ironically, it is the left-leaning traditionalists that have this capacity. Thus, the overall question remains as to whether President Erdogan will ally with the *status quo* bloc at the end of the day or continue his ambitious reforms by siding with the traditionalists, his ideological rival. Either way, it is sure that the TAF needs to continue to pursue transformational demands and build the capacity for it, as well as to continue implementing unfinished and new military reforms.

35 Metin Gurcan, 'A snapshot of the blackbox: a 2015 survey of the Turkish officer corps', *Turkish Studies*, 10 September 2017.

36 *Ibid.*

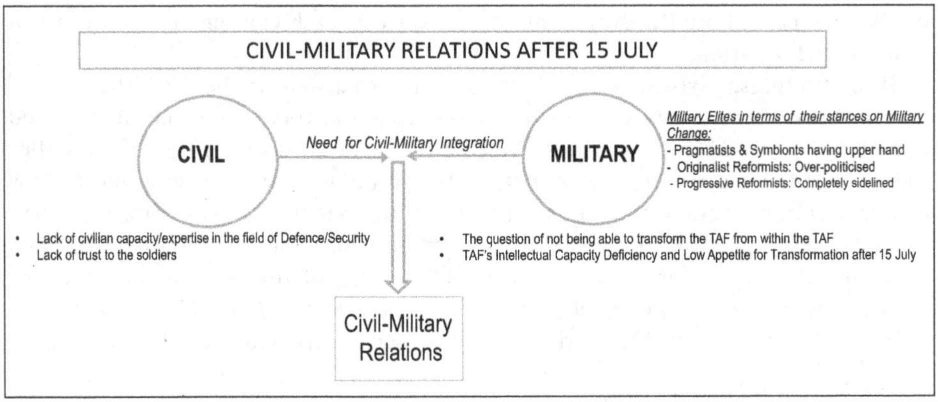

Figure 11 Current Situation in Terms of Civil-Military Relations.

Implementing military reforms within the TAF

According to the civilian bureaucrats working in the security sector,[37] it is very difficult for the TAF to transform itself from inside. The problem of the TAF's inability to do so shows strong military-civilian integration, yet the lack of civilian capacity in the field of defence/security and civilians' ongoing trust problem with soldiers are two main factors blocking this.

It is possible to summarise the current state of the TAF's transformation in Figure 12.

One should note that while the solid lines indicate the command-control structure established after the 15 July Uprising (the Prime Ministry is excluded in the new system), the dotted lines emphasise the existence of the parallel structure caused by the still continuing uncertainty regarding the institutional status, roles and missions of the Turkish General Staff (TGS) and thus led to the institutional friction between the MoD, which traditionally stayed under the shadow of the TGS as an institution merely in charge of procurement, budgeting and drafting yet got the full control of the professional military education system and the operational control of the Land Forces, Navy and Air Force after the 15 July Uprising. It is worth underlining that the optimum share of functions and responsibilities between the MoD and TGS, which has not yet been achieved despite the fact that it has been 19 months since the uprising, constitutes the neurological point of the transformation of the TAF after 15 July, and is thus directly related to the operational effectiveness of it.

37 The interview was conducted in Ankara in May 2017.

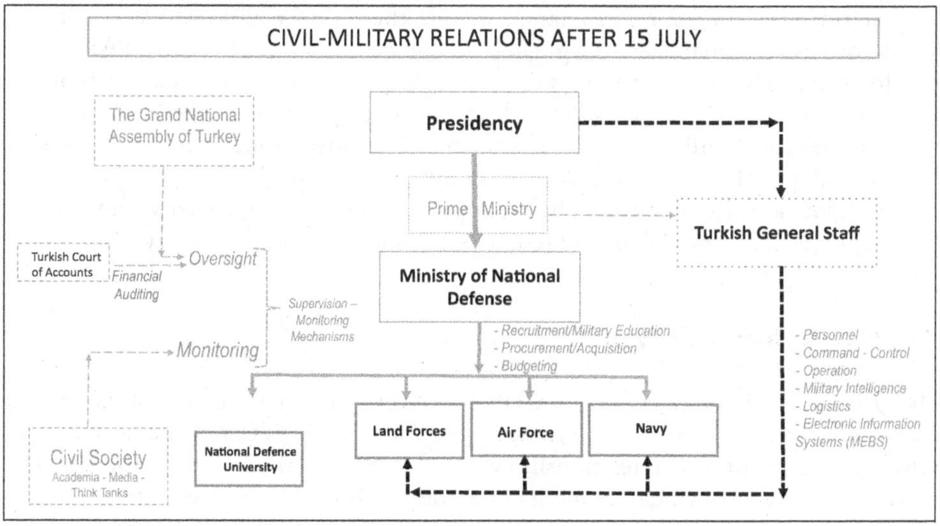

Figure 12 Current Situation in Terms of Civil-Military Relations.

Sources of friction

There are four sources of friction in the post-15 July setting that put extra tension on power relations among military elites, have a negative impact at the strategic/political level and are effective at the operational level. These are:

- The friction between the civilian elites and military elites over the causes, scale and tempo of military reforms after 15 July.
- The rivalry between the MoD and TGS over optimum sharing of functions due to the still ongoing ambiguity on the institutional status of the TGS in Turkey's security architecture.
- The friction between the pro-*status quo* camp (free riders and the majority of careerists) and reformists over pushing for military transformation or preserving the pre-15 July *status quo*. In this track, one should also note the rivalry between the traditionalists and the progressives, and that President Erdogan's indecision, whether to ally with the *status quo* block or the reformists, intensifies this friction.
- The friction among those military elites with differentiating world views regarding the military's new institutional identity, particularly questions about the role of Islam, pro/anti-US sentiment, pro/anti NATO stance, being a part of Western security architecture or going for a 'non-aligned' position in the construction of this new identity.
- Furthermore, because of the still lack of synchronisation between the civilian and military elites, rivalry between the MoD and TGS, and power struggle between

reformist and pro-*status quo* camps among the military elites, the issues in the below-listed domains are the greatest challenges for the post-15 July TAF:

- Joint-ness, civil-military integration and hybridisation of operational functions in multi-domain battle spaces in the TAF for more operational effectiveness.
- A professional military education system at the undergraduate and graduate level so as to quickly tackle the deficiency of intellectual capital.
- Religion/secularism in the military, implying a golden balance between the military's freedom from Islam and religious freedom within the military.

Possible roles for the TGS

How the MoD will build civilian capacity for the effective management of the service commands is yet to be seen. Determining the status of the TGS in the post-15 July setting and its institutional relationship with the presidential office, the MoD and the service commands will help define its new roles/missions as new security architects emerge. In particular, this report examines potential roles for the office of the TGS in the post-15 July Turkish security sector. Three potential roles for the office of the General Staff can be imagined as follows:

- Direct subordination of the TGS to the office of the presidency while preserving its current capacity/organisational structure and retransferring some of its old privileges such as the military education and promotion systems from the MoD to the TGS so as to enable the latter to maintain its full control of the service commands as it had been before the 15 July Uprising. This approach would be the best option for careerist and free rider military elites as it allows them both direct engagement with the office of the presidency and for the TGS to regain its old privileges while retaining the existing ones. One should also note that traditionalists seek to roll back the parliamentary system, while the TGS seeks to regain its old autonomous zones such as the military health system and independent military judiciary and privileges like full control of officers' promotion system.
- Creation of a 'hybrid model' merging the MoD and the TGS for the management of service commands' operational capabilities. This approach would be defined as a half-*status quo*/half reform option that necessitates an incremental institutional change and very delicate management. Hypothetically, this option could be the case if current Chief of Staff General Hulusi Akar would choose to voluntarily retire. It could be possible that the president would appoint Akar as the Minister of Defence while retaining his symbolic post of Chief of Staff when/if a full-fledged executive presidency could be initiated after the presidential election scheduled for 2 November 2019.
- Direct subordination of the TGS to the MoD and transferring its current capacity/organisational structure to the MoD; the TGS's transforming into a mere 'coordinator-agent' with symbolic status in the new security architecture.

> This approach of killing the TGS for more empowerment of the MoD, proposed by many pro-government pundits/experts[38] after 15 July yet not realised, is definitely a big blow to the TAF's institutional continuity. However, such reform seems unrealisable at the moment as the MoD still lacks the civilian capacity and intellectual capital to exterminate the TGS.

As one may easily notice, the ongoing double-headed management at the top of Turkey's security architecture due to the current rivalry between the MoD and the TGS not only leads to an unclear division of labour between the MoD and TGS but also causes duplications in the transformation process, like those we witness in the military education system, procurement and personnel management. This confusion regarding the division of labour between the MoD and TGS has been yielding a number of institutional overlaps and duplications, which have hindered the effectiveness and efficiency of the TAF. These duplications can be remedied through the following means:

- Personnel management, operations, military intelligence, logistics management and Combat Electronic/Information Systems (MEBS) functions should be shared between the MoD and TGS.
- The ongoing institutional uncertainty between the MoD and TGS concerning strategic issues, such as the management/coordination of 'joint-ness' and civil-military integration, should be solved, and it should be decided whether the MoD or TGS should control the management of military reforms.
- It should be decided whether the MoD or TGS will coordinate/control the curriculum of the professional military education system and who will be in charge of the National Defence University.

Changes at the operational level

By examining the Efes 2016 military exercise and Operation Euphrates Shield – occurring before and after 15 July and the personalisation of the TAF, respectively – one can see how the officers' effectiveness is based on the structural and institutional organisation of the TAF and has been affected by the 15 July process. The TAF and the government's lack of clear-cut political directives, coherent civil-military integration, very low levels of joint-ness and power struggle among the military elites has seemed to result in the gradual weakening of the TAF's effectiveness measured at the operational level.

38 Abdulkadir Selvi, "Bakanlar askeri yapilanmayi konustu [Ministers discussed military restructuring]," *Hurriyet,* 15 August 2016.

The Efes 2016 military exercise

From 4f May to 4 June 2016, the most sophisticated combined/joint military drill ever conducted by the TAF took place in the Turkish city of Efes (Ephesus in English), providing insight into the extent of the conventional capabilities of the pre-15 July TAF. First, the exercise provided an opportunity for the military to test the first Turkish-made corvette developed as part of the National Ship Project (MİLGEM), T129 Atak military helicopters and Bayraktar TB-2 armed drones. The purpose of the exercise was to improve joint and combined combat operations including amphibious, air assault and counter-terrorism. As he closely monitored both planning and conducting phases of the drill, the author would assert that the integration of those new weapon systems and platforms was successfully achieved. It is also worth mentioning that, along with Turkey's land, air, naval and gendarmerie forces, some 900 military staff from Turkey's major allies – including the United States, Azerbaijan, Qatar, Saudi Arabia, the United Kingdom, Pakistan, Poland and Germany – participated in Efes 2016, which was watched by 255 delegates from 79 countries.[39] Participating units executed scenarios pertaining to the imaginary country of Arnlad seeking United Nations assistance against invasion by another country. These scenarios required a dynamic mission set to meet the challenges of a multi-domain battle space, including cyber space. One can suggest that the TAF did very well to pass these tests, which included a brigade-level beachhead seizure, counter-terrorism operations and hostage rescue tasks as the special operation mission, humanitarian aid operations for refugees and cyber warfare. The TAF's conduct of the Efes military exercise in May 2018 provided a good perspective from which to compare/contrast the TAF's pre-15 July and post-15 July operational effectiveness at the conventional level.

Operation Euphrates Shield (OES)

Turkey's OES was initiated on 24 August 2016, a month after the 15 July Uprising, and coincided with military reforms directly affecting the nature of CMR as well as mass purges. In the initial phase, Ankara emphasised that the operation was to be limited both in time and scope to maintain border security and confront the Islamic State (IS) as an act of self-defence against terrorism, codified under Article 51 of the United Nations Charter. The operation, however, gradually encroached to the south and ended in the capture of al-Bab, north of government-controlled Aleppo, after 72 days of fierce fighting. OES achieved some successful outcomes on the tactical level, such as familiarisation with how the Islamic State fights and an understanding of the need to blend unconventional and conventional military capabilities, particularly in urban settings. But it was ultimately managed poorly at a political-diplomatic level and suffered from both the TAF's inability to adapt operationally to changing circumstances on the ground and low levels of situational awareness at the operational level.

39 'Turkey showcases domestic military might in Efes-2016 drill', *Daily Sabah*, 30 May 2016.

The operation can be divided into four phases. The initial achievement at the first and second phases of OES arguably led to a gradual shift in the initial objective of clearing and holding only the border line between Jarablus and al-Rai, resulting in an unplanned long-term commitment.

1. 'Capturing Jarablus' (three days): designed and planned as a Special Forces Operation by Major General Zekai Aksakalli, the Special Forces Commander, whose reputation and popularity increased after 15 July as he was considered among those few generals actively resisting the coup plotters.
2. 'Clearing of the border between Jarablus and Al-Rai' (September to early November 2016): OES forces cleared an area of 1,100 square kilometres.
3. 'Encroaching south' (one month, November 2016): OES forces were increasingly exposed to the improvised explosive devices (IED) and anti-tank guided missiles (ATGMs) of the Islamic State.

Before addressing the last point, it is important to point out that this change in the adversary's approach could not be meticulously assessed at the Turkish operation centre in Kilis. The primary factor leading to this assessment failure was the dominance of Special Forces planning personnel in the effort. The gradual evolution of OES from a Special Forces operation to a new type of counter-terrorism operation requiring an optimum blend of conventional armoured units, indirect heavy fire support with tube and rocket artillery and commando battalions, and unconventional capabilities such as guiding proxies for desired tactical outcomes, anti-IED measures, anti-drone warfare and tunnel warfare in urban settings, should have facilitated the introduction of new staff with appropriate expertise at the operation centre, yet this requirement was not fulfilled.

After the killing of three Turkish soldiers in an IED attack in the north of al-Bab on 24 November 2016, just before the beginning of the al-Bab offensive on 30 November, some of the groups within the Free Syrian Army (FSA), Turkey's local partners in the region, deserted due to ongoing rivalries in the FSA and their lack of discipline. After seeing that the al-Bab offensive could not be conducted with FSA groups, the Turkish military deployed a battalion from the 57th Commando Regiment/Sarikamis, a battalion from the Fourth Commando Brigade/Tunceli and two battalions from the First Commando Brigade/Kayseri. Furthermore, all battalions of the 2nd Armour Brigade/Istanbul with Leopard 2A4 tanks and 20th Armour Brigade/Urfa with M60 T tanks were deployed to the theatre of operation. This increase in conventional capabilities also meant the increasing influence of Second Army Commander General Metin Temel in the course of OES. This in turn frustrated General Aksakalli, who saw it as a 'conventionalisation' of the operation which would tarnish his newfound credibility/reputation in Ankara thanks to his active resistance on the night of 15 July. This clique-related friction between generals at the operational level would be the primary factor leading to mismanagement problems during the planning and conduct of the operation.

4. 'Siege and capture of al-Bab' (100 days, between December 2016 and March 2017): IS's establishment of resilient defensive perimeters in urban areas, the use of SVBIEDs (Suicide Vehicle Borne IEDs), tunnel warfare and anti-tank missiles meant the al-Bab offensive should have required a new type of planning. General Aksakalli and his staff at the Kilis Operations Centre, which was overwhelmingly comprised of staff officers with SF background, did not foresee Islamic State's resolve inside al-Bab's city centre, and thus did not accordingly increase numbers of staff officers with backgrounds in conventional war in the planning room. They utterly failed to assess how to increase situational awareness with intelligence-surveillance-target acquisition-reconnaissance (ISTAR) capabilities, provide armour and mechanised support for advancing FSA fighters and close air support to neutralise IS's armoured units and fortified fixed facilities inside al-Bab, as well as indirect fire support involving heavy tube and rocket artillery fire to cover the advancing groups towards IS's heavily fortified defensive perimeters in and around al-Bab.

The very first al-Bab offensive was initiated in early 2017 to capture the Aqil Mountain, the key terrain dominating the north-west of the city centre, without planning and coordination between the units participating in the operation as well as inadequate numbers of armoured/mechanised units and fire support systems – most importantly, without close air support. As one may guess, coordination and confusion at the tactical level among and between Turkish military units and the FSA groups, mainly caused by a lack of operational clarity during the operational planning at headquarters, can be asserted as another factor leading to operational problems. The confusion and inability to respond to the changing nature of OES for the Turkish military suggests Ankara needs to improve coordination between different participants, particularly in urban terrains and against unconventional adversaries like IS.

In comparing the success of the Efes 2016 military exercise to that of the reality of OES, it seems as though Turkey once had the capacity to organise its own missions and operations within the TAF and among international partners; however, since 15 July this capacity has been diminishing.

Losses sustained

According to the TGS's official press release, 69 Turkish soldiers were killed in action (KIA) during Operation Euphrates Shield. Of those total casualties, 40% were caused by VBIED attacks (16 Turkish soldiers were KIA in a single such attack on 22 December), 30% by indirect IS mortar and rocket fire while soldiers were resting in forward operational bases, and 20% by roadside IEDs, particularly inside al-Bab. On 9 February 2017, three Turkish soldiers were accidentally killed by a Russian air strike due to, according to Russian sources, "lack of coordination". One should note that not a single Turkish soldier was killed during armed engagements with

Islamic State fighters. In addition, around 220 Turkish soldiers were wounded, mostly by VBIED and roadside IED attacks. On 17 April 2017, within the Sultan Murad Brigade during OES, FSA groups supported by Turkey suffered 1,000 wounded and around 400 were killed, the majority of whom were from the Ahrar al Sham, Sultan Murad Brigade and Nur al-Din al-Zinki movements. The TGS announced on 31 March 2017 that about 3,000 IS militants and 500 YPG militants were "neutralised" during the operation.

Regarding material losses, on 23 December 2016 a list, allegedly prepared by the Kilis Operation Centre and showing damaged, hit or lost armoured vehicles of the Turkish military, was leaked to social media sites. This leaked list, which was not contradicted by official sources, included 10 Leopard 2A4 tanks, one M-60 A3 tank, three improved armoured personnel carriers (GZPT) and three Cobra armoured vehicles, that were targeted mainly in combat near Aqil Hill, where severe clashes took from late December 2016 to early March 2017. Around 12 ACV-15-type armored personnel carriers delivered by the Turkish military to the FSA were also damaged or captured by IS.

Lessons learned for Ankara:
The confusion and inability to respond to the changing nature of Operation Euphrates Shield by the Turkish military suggests Ankara needs to improve coordination between different participants, particularly in urban terrains and against unconventional adversaries like Islamic State. Urban combat with IS should blend conventional armoured operations and counter-terrrorism operations with elite units. OES demonstrated that Special Forces seem to best serve a secondary role in planning and execution against an unconventional adversary. Accordingly, small-unit battles with combined arms, blending conventional capabilities like armoured warfare, close air support, unmanned aerial vehicles and tunnel warfare, and conventional capabilities such as counter-IED efforts and improved proxy support, will lead to better outcomes in the future.

Mainly due to the mismanagement of the last two phases – advancing to the south and the capture of al-Bab – at the strategic-diplomatic level, Turkey could neither get the full support of the US-led anti-ISIS coalition during the operation nor persuade Russia, the actor with air space dominance to the west of the Euphrates, to allow more effective provision of close air support. The absence of effective coalition support or Russian cooperation during the capture of al-Bab caused operational deficiencies in intelligence-surveillance-target acquisition-reconnaissance (ISTAR) capabilities and medical air transport. The absence of ISTAR capabilities led to increased exposure to highly time-sensitive suicide attacks with VBIEDs, a new threat for the Turkish military, and extremely low levels of situation awareness. Failure in the provision of round-the-clock close air support caused problems with fast and effective responses, particularly to ISIS armour units and safe havens inside al-Bab. Undelivered medical air evacuation in all phases of OES also negatively influenced the moral and motivation of Turkish soldiers who fought on the ground.

Overall, OES can be defined as a tactical success story poorly managed at the operational level and very poorly directed at the political-diplomatic level. OES suffered from both an inability to adapt operationally to changing circumstances on the ground and low levels of situational awareness. OES was in many aspects – in its drivers, conduct, direction, losses sustained, foreign policy implications and consequences – unlike any earlier cross-border operation conducted by Turkey, such as Hammer I and II in 1997-98 and Sun (*Gunes*) in 2008. Despite positive outcomes like the capture of Jarablus and al-Bab, along with improved border control, the evolution of the operation from a special forces to a counter-terrorism operation requiring mixed military capabilities led to a gradual shift in objectives and resulted in an unplanned long-term commitment, a process known as 'mission creep'.

Balancing Civil-Military Relations (CMR), but how?

To ensure the balanced success of CMR, civil and democratic control, effectiveness and efficiency, social legitimacy and the credibility of the military must be guaranteed.

Civil and democratic control

It seems that the rapid civilianisation process implemented across the security sector after 15 July has come to a halt. In the heat of more and more terrorist attacks from the PKK/TAK and ISIL, as well as domestic political debate on the constitutional referendum, the prolonged state of emergency attached to the office of the presidency has debilitated further democratisation of the CMR. The TAF continues to remain bolted to the presidential palace – whether officially or unofficially – and it is unclear when it will be granted any independence or its responsibilities will be tied to other civilian-controlled institutions. As civilianisation does not necessarily mean democratisation, this process can also lead to monopolisation. In the literature on CMR, the link between a sound constitution and institutions with a strong security sector is validated. But what happens when constitutional change leads to the concentration of power in the hands of a single executive office? These pros and cons eventually become a zero-sum game, and we arrive back at the present state of insecurity in which Turkey is living. The opposition (namely the Republican People's Party, CHP) has predicted that constitutional changes will increase polarisation within Turkish society, a claim that the AKP denies.[40] In a full-fledged democracy, constitutional change that deals with shifts in presidential versus parliamentary systems should never be the guarantor of CMR. Successful security sectors exist in both presidential and parliamentary states alike. Support for a political system change should not indicate whether or not one supports the fight against terrorism.[41] This is, arguably, civilianisation/monopolisation

40 'Minister blames opposition for "threatening the public" over Turkey's charter changes', *Hurriyet Daily News*, 31 January 2017.

41 'Voting "yes" in charter referendum could support Turkey's anti-terror fight: Deputy PM Kurtulmus', *Hurriyet Daily News*, 29 January 2017.

(transfer of power from military elites to the civilian elites) but not democratisation (diffusion of power among civilian actors such as an elected president, elected government and parliament, and civil society actors like the media, academia, NGOs and think tanks, so as to enable checks and balances, oversight, monitoring and accountability in civil-security sector relations in a transparent fashion) of CMR.

Effectiveness/efficiency

CMR not only concerns democratisation and civilian control, but also ranks 'effectiveness' – the capacity to implement the policies formulated with the desired results, or 'doing the right things' – and 'efficiency', the achievement of maximum output with minimum inputs (resources) such as personnel, cost and equipment, or 'doing the things right', as central to a healthy CMR model.

The effectiveness and efficiency of not only the TAF but also the security sector as a whole is of the utmost concern in Turkey amid a three-pronged battle against terror. Although within the literature on CMR there are studies on a security sector's capacity to purge massive personnel numbers, such moves are largely based on the age and rank of officers, not strictly on politics.[42] Thus, when we analyse such examples in comparison to the Turkish case, the fact that many officers after 15 July were dismissed or jailed on politically related terror charges must be kept in mind. Moves that purge a large amount of staff within CMR are designed for the sole purpose of sparking innovation and institutional transformation that older cadres had opposed. These moves should not negatively alter the security forces' effectiveness or efficiency on the ground.

Social legitimacy

CMR necessitates a long-term change in the professionalisation of security forces, which is nearly impossible to achieve with a politicised, weakened security apparatus devoid of institutional transformation within its own cadres. Within a democratically oriented CMR process, the social legitimacy of security forces is an essential element in achieving cooperation between security forces, the government and civil society.

As discussed above, the strategic identity of the TAF itself is skewed. On the one hand, the Gulenist political elements have been purged from the TAF; on the other, this has made room for Eurasianist camps within the TAF, and the Army's once pro-NATO, pro-Western cadres have been diminished. With the rising tide of popular anti-Americanism and anti-West sentiment, this has proved an effective strategy for appeasing the nationalist majority of the population; however, creating a temporary scapegoat for the nation's security problems does not contribute to universal social legitimacy of the government's security measures within Turkey.

42 Paul Jackson and Peter Albrecht, *Reconstructing Security after Conflict: Security Sector Reform in Sierra Leone* (Basingstoke: Palgrave Macmillan, 2011).

The credibility of the Turkish military in the global security environment

The implications of the 15 July failed coup attempt are much bigger than the repercussions within Turkish domestic politics. The reality in the post-9/11 era is that armed forces are central actors in many developed democracies and are involved in many different roles: they engage in peacekeeping missions, reinforce the police in fighting crime, support civilian authorities in dealing with natural disasters, conduct search and rescue missions, provide humanitarian assistance, contribute to nation- and state-building efforts in host states and fight against terrorists. Modern militaries are diverse, just like the democracies they serve. Although their micro and macro structure may vary around the world, they are called to maintain their multi-faceted character, no matter their internal crises.[43] Faced with a number of threats and challenges, from battling ISIS and the PKK to securing Turkey's borders and managing the security of nearly three million refugees, the Turkish military and security sector's engagements have ballooned from local to global conflicts. As a member of NATO and other international bodies, it is critical that the Turkish military is in particular continuing to fulfill its international engagements while implementing democratic norms at home. It cannot withdraw and shirk its international duties, for any reason, in the midst of global crises. Turkey's break with the West, particularly its contentious ties with NATO and remarks concerning a potential move toward the Shanghai Five, has overshadowed Turkey's efforts in this regard.

Democratising security or securitising the state?

There are many questions relevant to the state's transformation that have yet to be answered. For example, how can we institute democratic and civilian control over the military? Are Samuel Huntington's concepts of objective and subjective control relevant and applicable for Turkey today, or should we look toward Morris Janowitz's more subjective paradigm?[44] How can we apply institutional control mechanisms, oversight mechanisms and professional norms, which are three components of civilian control? As a step toward the institutionalisation of an oversight mechanism, what could be the role and mission of a defence commission within the Turkish parliament?

Our overwhelming emphasis on CMR in Turkey asserts the essentiality of not only civilian control but also democratic control, effectiveness and efficiency, social legitimacy and the credibility of the Turkish military in the global security environment. Three levels of analysis, therefore, should be carried out in order to analyse the case of Turkey:

43 Paul Shemella, 'The Spectrum of Roles and Missions of the Armed Forces', in Thomas C. Bruneau and Scott D. Tollefson (eds), *Who Guards the Guardians and How: Democratic Civil-Military Relations* (Austin: University of Texas Press, 2006).

44 Metin Gurcan and Megan Gisclon, 'Turkey's Security Sector After July 15: Democratizing Security or Securitizing The State?', *Turkish Policy Quarterly*, Winter 2017.

- Analysis at the **political level**, which, for the author, has been overemphasised through the rhetoric of civilianisation but lacks democratisation.
  The political level includes the struggle to ensure the security sector is dissuaded from using its unique coercive advantage to influence the civilian government, either at its behest or that of civilian groups. At the political level, this paper suggests that the most significant obstacle to CMR in Turkey is excessive politicisation within the sector and the increasing number of partisan elements blocking the achievement of the institutional transformation of the security sector. In accordance with Timothy Edmunds, the separation of party affiliation from security sector execution and personnel actions (i.e., departification) is, therefore, the most significant factor for the conduct of a successful CMR process. Once initial control is established, the political level addresses legislative and documented plans to ensure a long-term framework within which civilians can execute control and oversight of/on the security sector – both civilian leadership of the sector and parliamentary oversight and funding. Unfortunately, when reviewing the current state of Turkey's CMR, one may easily notice the absence of parliamentary institutions' involvement in more effective oversight. It is likely to suggest that parliamentary oversight has lacked the expertise and capability to execute the prescribed oversight roles. As such, most parliamentarians have been content to take direction on defence and security matters, either from the security sector ministries themselves or from their party hierarchies. This limits the level of oversight when those being overseen are providing the guidance. At the political level, another deficiency is the absence of an overarching agent in charge of the prevention of duplications among all actors, coordination of efforts and synchronisation of timing and pace of the reforms. In fact, the Parliamentary Defence Commission would fill this deficiency, yet this has not been the case yet.

- Analysis at the **organizational level**, that implies the establishment of an effective and efficient military.
  The organisational level is concerned primarily with how security sector organisations, particularly the military, adapt to changing organisational circumstances such as the downsizing of the security sector and transition from a conflict-affected organisation to one operating in a post-conflict and ultimately stabile CMR context. Additionally, this level of analysis allows an assessment of the professionalism of the new or transformed security organisations, measured by role, expertise, professional and ethical norms, and responsibility. Particularly, the nurture of professional norms regarding the way of doing things and ethical norms regarding the way of thinking through things within the military is a must for any actor within the sector so as to form a 'bureaucratic' and somewhat politically autonomous institutional culture. At the organisational level, the current move toward assigning officials whose political loyalty prevails over their qualifications has led to the politicisation, and to some extent 'partification' – the opposite of Edmunds' "departification" – of the security sector. This trend

has not only been blurring the thin line between what is 'bureaucratic' and what is political' within the security sector, but also leads to questions about effectiveness and efficiency of the sector as this trend demolishes decentralisation of the decision-making, initiative-taking empowerment of middle-level/local decision-makers, and contingency planning, transparency and accountability within the sector. The trend of excessive centralisation of decision-making within the security sector, which has currently been fighting against three violent non-state actors – FETÖ, the PKK and ISIS – organised and operating as compartmentalised actor-network assemblages, may be dealt another setback, which is, in fact, the consequence of partification of the sector.

- Analysis at the **international level**, implying the Turkish military's credibility in the international arena.
  The international level assesses CMR driven by external actors – other nations or international organisations. On this level, particularly the nature, characteristics and evolution of Turkey's relationship with NATO in general and the Turkish military's relationship with NATO in particular, would matter a lot. If Turkey continues to care for its relationship with NATO, it can copy and paste NATO's transformation efforts to reform its security sector, particularly the military. If Turkey decides to follow a more non-aligned course within NATO, or even strategic preferences independent of NATO's course, then Turkey should be able to foster its national CMR process so as to update its security sector.

One should also note that Turkey currently faces second-generation CMR problems. Limited expertise in government ministries and parliament mean limited ability to exercise control and oversight. Intelligence reform remains elusive as central control resists oversight. Civil society involvement shows limited chance for success and is largely restricted to Ankara. As with the government, civil society faces resistance from within the security sector itself. The media has no oversight capacity or qualified security experts/analysts. There has been limited growth of NGOs and think tanks studying security issues; those that do exist have extremely politicised stances and thus cannot provide unbiased technical insights.

The changes and reforms to the Turkish security sector following 15 July have thus far been a patchwork response to both new and pre-existing problems. There has been little time or concern for reflecting upon the implications and possible future challenges such breakneck changes will precipitate. As Turkey moves on from the immediate aftermath of 15 July, knee-jerk reactions such as mass purges and arrests, institutional change for the sake of change and prioritising civilianisation over democratisation – however justified these actions may be perceived to be by the public or politicians – are not part of a successful recipe for holistic and effective CMR. While there may one day be an expiration date for the state of emergency in Turkey – or perhaps a constitution change instead – the consequences of an executive-dominated transformation will need to be dealt with beyond the present cumulative 90-day periods.

It is imperative to reiterate that a healthy approach to Turkish CMR is one that is well-regulated and transparent. Civil and democratic control, effectiveness and efficiency, social legitimacy and the credibility of the TAF in the international security environment are at risk of falling apart if the present political polarisation continues to affect Turkish CMR. Given the present state of the political environment in Turkey, which has over-politicised the security sector much to its detriment, changes must be seen in these areas in order to achieve democratic civilianisation of security rather than pure civilianisation, which is not necessarily democratic.

Reforms to the security sector should be approached in a pragmatic and holistic manner that reinforces not only the stability of operations on the ground but also the apolitical nature of security itself. The response to Turkey's post-15 July security deficits should not entail the creation of further challenges to stability and democracy. Rather, a proper security sector reform process will not only stop bombs but will also inculcate further democratisation, good governance, economic development, professionalism, conflict prevention and integration with international institutions.

The reforms affecting Turkey's security sector surely mean civilianisation. But civilianisation (transfer of power from military elites to elected civilians) does not automatically mean democratisation (diffusion of power from military elites to the government, opposition parties and civil society to the extent that checks and balances can be created and full accountability and transparency are established) or ensure an effective and efficient security sector on the ground. A healthy balance in the Turkish CMR is one that is well balanced and transparent. Civil and democratic control, effectiveness and efficiency, social legitimacy, legal legitimacy and credibility of Turkey's security sector in the international security environment are at risk of falling apart if the present political polarisation continues. Changes must be seen in these categories to achieve democratic civilianisation of the TAF. In addition to the weakening institutional agency of the General Staff yet increasing personal agency of General Hulusi Akar, these two institutional mechanisms, the above-mentioned actors' stance towards change and differentiation in terms of their world views, correspond to the theme of 'divided elites' within the TAF that would lead to the transformation of the TAF's monolithic institutional identity traditionally represented by the chiefs into a polylithic one, implying the existence of many but separated micro identities within the military.

Particularly, six risk domains in the new Janowitzian paradigm place extra tension on CMR in this new era:

- The absence of constructive scholarly debate about the pros and cons of narrowing CMR to the level of palace(i.e., President Erdogan)-military relations due to the ultra-securitised political context in Turkey. As this narrowing process of CMR to 'palace-military relations' has no clear institutional framework and road map so as to manage the transfer of power, the unintended consequences of this process would negatively affect the effectiveness and efficiency of the military, its social legitimacy – which should encompass whole segments of society in terms of political views – and the military's international credibility.

- Low levels of civilian intellectual capital on security issues and military transformation; more importantly, the civilian elites' reluctance to (and sometimes disrespect toward) military experts' views on military reforms and new CMR.
- The military becoming the primary domain of the debate between conservatives and seculars. This trend pulls the military into the hearth of popular political debates and politicises CMR.
- The friction between civilian elites and military elites over the causes, scale and tempo of military reforms after 15 July shaping the nature of CMR.
- The friction between the pro-*status quo* camp (symbionts and majority of pragmatists) and the reformists over pushing for military transformation or preserving the pre-15 July *status quo* within the military.
- The friction among those military elites with differentiating world views regarding the military's new institutional identity, the role of Islam, pro/anti-US sentiment, pro/anti-NATO stance and being a part of the Western security architecture or going for a 'non-aligned' position in the construction of this new identity. It can be suggested that, in the post-15 July setting, it is evident that what will animate change is the power-distributional implications of power relations among these micro-identities within the military, and the question of how the civilian elites, particularly President Erdogan, engages with them.

Personalisation of Turkish CMR

After Turkey's Supreme Military Council met on 2 August 2017, the personal agency and influence of current Chief of General Staff Hulusi Akar was reinforced to the extent that relations between civilians and the military from now on could better be grasped not from an institutional perspective but by understanding the personal trust and harmony between General Akar and President Erdogan.[45]

The precursory signal of this change came on 19 July 2017, when Defence Minister Fikri Isik was named as a deputy prime minister and Nurettin Canikli, who has an economics background and a strong vision for the Turkish defence industry, was appointed Defence Minister. It was no secret there were sharp differences of opinion between ex-Defence Minister Fikri Isik and General Akar, particularly over the military education system and institutional transformation of the TAF. With Isik's departure, the MoD lost some of its strength against the Chief of General Staff. That is why it's not far-fetched to claim that Akar's standing and influence have been boosted in the TAF, MoD and government, given the support he has received from President

45 Metin Gurcan, 'Turkish military upheaval continues at top levels', *Al-Monitor*, 24 August 2017.

Erdogan. If General Yasar Guler, the incumbent Land Forces Commander reputed for his strong careerist stance, becomes the Chief of the TGS after General Akar in August 2019, Erdogan's policy of controlling the TAF through personal connections and mutual trust will continue until 2021. This extreme personalisation would also mean de-institutionalisation of Turkish CMR and the degradation of the TAF's institutional settings, which, at the end of the day, degrade operational effectiveness.

On 24 December 2016, the government issued Decree No.696,[46] placing the Undersecretariat for Defence Industries (SSM), the Prime Ministry's key institution in charge of the state's defence procurement, as subordinate to the MoD and allocating it nearly $11 billion in the 2018 general budget,[47] under the presidency's (*Külliye*) full control. After this decree, the presidential office's taking full control of the SSM, having power to procure, produce and sign deals for all military and police forces of the country, and the president chairing the Defence Industry Executive Committee – Turkey's top committee deciding on procurement – marks more weakening of the prime ministry's agency in Turkey's defence/security architecture.[48] President Erdogan's move for full control of Turkey's defence industry and decision-making mechanism of the procurement system marks the increasing agency of the presidential office as the new prime actor at the expense of the prime ministry. The question of whether the presidency will mostly engage in the MoD or the TGS to run Turkey's defence/security procurement system will be a decisive factor shaping the end state of the rivalry between the MoD and TGS.

The results of the Supreme Military Council's (SMC) August 2017 meeting on promotions of generals in the TAF would be good indicators of the future course of the Turkish military and CMR.

First, the SMC met on 2 August 2017 under Prime Minister Binali Yildirim in a reconfigured format of four military and eight civilian officials. This means that civilians hold the council majority for the first time. Naturally, this also means that from now on, President Recep Tayyip Erdogan – and not the military – will have the final say in SMC decisions.

The rationale of this logic was that despite the flurry of media criticism of Akar, Erdogan had not expressed support for him and it looked like he would be retired unless he was able to bargain with Erdogan. Akar was one of four branch commanders detained by putschists during the 15 July 2016 uprising. They all could have stayed on in their positions, but three were retired: only Akar retained his post. This indicates he did indeed negotiate a favourable outcome through strategic bargaining. According to the SMC decisions, current Gendarmerie Commander Yasar Guler will lead the Army, General Hasan Kucukakyuz will take over the Air Force and Admiral Adnan

46 See Decree No. 696 issued on 24 December 2017 (Turkish): <http://www.resmigazete.gov.tr/eskiler/2017/12/20171224-22.htm> (accessed 12 January 2018).

47 Metin Gurcan, 'Erdogan takes total control of the Turkish defense industry', *Al-Monitor*, 8 January 2018.

48 *Ibid.*

Ozbal will command the Navy. Therefore, it is likely Akar will retain his post until August 2019. Unless there are major surprises, the current configuration also means Guler, a close associate of Akar, will become Chief of General Staff for the 2019-2023 term. Guler gets along well with members of Erdogan's Justice and Development Party and is known for his hard-line performance against the PKK, which Turkey considers a terrorist group, and the Gulen movement, which Erdogan blames for the coup attempt.

Also attracting attention was a four-hour meeting Erdogan had with Prime Minister Binali Yildirim and a two-and-a-half-hour meeting with Akar a day before the SMC announced its ruling. Most of the SMC decisions were obviously made in those meetings, and that is how the SMC completed its work in four hours, whereas it used to take three days.

Why did Erdogan extend Akar's term of duty? What could Akar have offered him?

We have to acknowledge that since the coup attempt, power plays within the TAF and also between the TAF and civilian actors have continued. Within the TAF, relations over political affiliations, stances over civilian-military relations and attitudes toward military transformation remain unstable. Erdogan is mindful of presidential elections, which are due at the latest in 2019. To retire Akar now could have had disruptive, chaotic effects on these relations. A new debate about Akar's successor and the fallout from the failed coup – complete with more mass trials and continuing purges – could have triggered political polemics affecting Erdogan's re-election aspirations. This is most likely one reason Erdogan chose to keep Akar rather than work with an unknown entity.

Another reason is Akar's successful performance in the struggle against the PKK and the Gulenists, which is the SMC's primary criterion for major promotions and appointments.

During the crisis days after the failed military uprising, Akar positioned himself close to Erdogan and skillfully managed the power struggle in the TAF and pertinent political arguments without much damage. Also, the personal confidence between Akar and Guler, who is expected to replace him in 2019, is a buffer protecting Erdogan against a new crisis with the TAF. In short, until 2023, Erdogan should have smooth sailing without any disruption from the TAF, and he will work on reformatting civilian-military relations and the country's security structure.

Akar has eight years of seniority on Ozbal and six years on Kucukakyuz. Similarly, Guler has six years of seniority over Ozbal and four years over Kucukakyuz. This seniority in the TAF means that until 2019, the dialogues between Akar and the generals will start with 'Sir' and conclude with 'Sir, yes sir'.

The Navy was the epicentre of the earthquake that followed the SMC decision. After the Navy's commander, Fleet Admiral Bulent Bostanoglu, was retired, as per tradition it was expected that the No. 2 ranking officer, Admiral Veysel Kosele, would assume the top spot. Ozbal, who was fifth in the Navy's seniority rankings, bypassed four more-senior admirals, which came as a major shock and is likely to cause grumblings. Ozbal's promotion no doubt dilutes the institutional strength of the Navy compared with the Army and Air Force. It also ensures Akar's control over the Navy will be more pronounced.

This is yet another indicator that the TAF's priority in 2018-19 will continue to be combatting the PKK and the Gulenists. Among the colonels the SMC promoted to brigadier generals are many who were sidelined for a time by false legal cases concocted to make it easier to prosecute Gulenist officers. Also promoted to brigadier rank were some Special Forces members and commando officers, although they were not academically trained staff officers.

An unusual number of colonels, lieutenant generals and major generals had their terms extended, even though they were qualified for retirement. Purges after the failed coup created a significant vacuum between the number of four-star and one-star generals, which could affect the TAF's combat effectiveness.

Conclusion

This book, aiming to open the blackbox of the Turkish military by providing two snapshots before and after the 15 July, emphasizes that not only exogenous factors but also endogenous factors from within the military should be taken into consideration when analyzing the Turkish military's institutional transformation and change in the Turkish CMR. Thanks to its analytical premise (a conceptual model), based on the eclectic theoretical grounding benefiting both from institutional and culturalist approaches, this study has sought an approach from multiple angles (e.g., the TAF as a security organization, as a social institution and officership/profession) as well as from multiple levels (e.g., institutional, individual) and examines their interaction with the use of original and primary data (interviews and surveys). These two snapshots with a perspective from within the TAF are surely not immune to substance-related and methodological weaknesses. One should, however, allow that, despite all these weaknesses, by this contribution the available literature now possesses an empirical piece on the Turkish military, relying on primary data sources that may have a potential to elevate the scholarly debates about the TAF and the Turkish CMR to a more quantitative level. The author wishes to emphasize that it is this elevation for which the necessary literature has been waiting, as has a more lively academic environment for more robust scholarly debate.

The findings of this book falsifies some assumptions in the existing literature about the Turkish military, such as the TAF being a 'fixed' organization immune to change, or that it is a homogenous entity with a rigid institutional order. In light of the findings, this book suggests that one should allow for the possibility that the drivers and characteristics of TAF's organizational culture may change over time, and that different - even sometimes conflicting - point of views, approaches, and ways of doing things may emerge within the Turkish military. In the in-depth interviews, the author observed that the military leaders at this moment feel the power-distributional effect of gradual institutional change within the TAF, albeit they cannot clearly conceptualize and define this, and thus are inlined to concentrate more on TAF's organizational transformation as a security actor. In the quest for this transformation, the military leaders know what to change and why to change, but do not have the methodological expertise to answer the question 'how to change?' This increasingly inward-looking approach has been strengthened with the increased ambiguity in the system yielding to a need for transformation, and is another reason explaining how the Turkish CMR has survived domestic and foreign policy-related crises in the last decade, particularly the 15 July uprising. Thus, one may contend that not only exogenous approaches seek to explain change within the military and in the Turkish CMR over the last decade, but that endogenous factors addressed in the chapters analyzing the Turkish military's snapshot before 15 July, such as increased uncertainty within the system and change in the TAF's security culture, social culture, and the professional culture of the officer corps, would explain the recent civilianization in CMR.

Another interesting finding of the research is that the officer corps, particularly juniors, are not at odds with political Islam, and do not see it as a threat to the secular character of the state. The overwhelming majority of officers, however, perceive that the primary threat is the unity of the state. One may suggest that the ongoing clashes between Turkey and the PKK may be the cause of this increased sensitivity to the unity of the state, instead of the principle of secularism. One may then conclude that, in the coming years, the unity of the state, not the principle of secularism, will be the primary sensitivity that may potentially force the TAF to influence politics either directly or indirectly. It is thus not surprising to expect that debate about the 'Islamization of the Turkish military' is ramped up, and particularly junior cadres of the officer corps, notably amongst the contracted officers recruited after the 15 July uprising and those war academy cadets who were recruited directly from the civilian universities, would be more susceptible to increasing religiosity within the military.

The handling of the Kurdish question by elected civilians seems thus an exceptionally significant dynamic shaping the future of Turkish CMR.

The findings of the survey also reveal that a split exists within the officer corps between juniors (lieutenants, captains, and majors) and seniors (lieutenant colonels, colonels, and generals) to such an extent that the opinions and attitudes of the officer corps can be analyzed separately under these two categories.

What can be said about the future implications of this research? As this research indicates, change within the TAF has been taking place in three domains, and the agents, types, modes, drivers and pathways of change in each domain are not the same as the others. While, for instance, the High Command is the prime change agent influencing the TAF's security culture, its influence is getting weaker in the domains of the TAF as a social institution and officership as a profession. This differentiation among these three domains in terms of the change agent's type, change mode, drivers, and pathways leads to a management challenge for the military elites. The question at hand in this challenge is the following: how, through which mechanisms, and to what extent should military elites preserve this differentiation which yields to gradual institutional change as an 'organic' process and how not to let each domain disruptively affect the others? This challenge implies a synchronization, or to better formulate, an orchestration, problem. First, quantification and then measurement of all three domains for a better orchestration emerges as a must for the TAF. Then the TAF should foster a hybrid setting in which both military and civilian expertise can be fused to one another so as to analyze and interpret the findings derived from each domain. This stage has the challenge of civil-military integration, a complicated process hard to achieve but is needed to project hybrid intellectual capital for a comprehensive and holistic military transformation. The nurture of a hybrid intellectual capital so as to manage each and every domain, and construct structures, processes and relationships to achieve needed orchestration seems to emerge as another challenge to cope with for the TAF, an institution which has an inherent distrust and underestimation of anything coming from the civilian world. The question of how to garner this intellectual capital seems to be a highly relevant question for the High Command, as this research shows, because the TAF has major setbacks in the management of its post-graduate education system. The fact that the intellectual energy of those majors and captains having their post-graduate education cannot be translated into intellectual capital for the management of the transformation appears to be another challenge for the High Command.

For decades, the Turkish military embodied the following characteristics: a staunchly secular modernist perspective blended with nationalist themes, a devout pro-Western mentality prevalent among the officers, a pro-NATO sentiment, dissatisfaction and annoyance with anything civilian, a mutual distrust of politics and the attempt to be outside and above politics, a high sense of moral responsibility, an aristocratic way of officership, soldiering as a way of life, the feeling of isolation from the rest of society, a strong sense of superiority over civilians, as well as a robust 'elitization' process in military schools.

However, after the July uprising these characteristics should no longer be considered as fixed or immune to change. It is evident that the TAF has been very busy in operational terms, with counterterrorism operations both inside Turkey and abroad, border security, peacekeeping tasks in Afghanistan, and force projection efforts abroad like the ones in Qatar, Somalia and Sudan's Suakin Island. In the midst of all this, the institutional settings of the TAF have been strained due to the hasty reforms and ongoing mass purges in the past eighteen months since July 15. The ongoing confusion at the strategic-political level due to the absence of a clear political vision, ambiguity of the TGS's status in the post-July 15 setting, and the state apparatus's transition from a parliamentary system to an executive presidency have aggravated the power struggles and intellectual capital deficiency within the military and increased the low levels of civilian capacity in the security sector. More importantly, all of these institutional challenges coincide with the never-ending crises between Turkey and its Western allies, particularly the United States.

Definitely until August 2018 and most likely until August 2019, we will be discussing civilian- military relations not on their institutional aspects but on the basis of the personal harmony between Erdogan and Akar. This may well be the wisest approach to current and future crises, albeit one that could possibly cause the Defense Ministry to lose some power. However, personalizing decisions could also hamper institutional transformation and military reforms — as well as democratization, transparency and accountability in civilian-military relations

In conclusion, in the post-July 15 setting, what Turkey needs to do is to '*democratize security*,' suggesting the *diffusion* of the state's power among the executive branch, parliament, and civil society by creating effective oversight and monitoring mechanisms so as not to face another hijack attempt such as that of July 15. The course civilian elites have been following, however, seems just the opposite, which is the '*ultra-securitization of state*,' or first *transfer* of power from the military elites to the civilian ones and then *monopolize* it to securitize the state apparatus for the objective of strict civilian control. Thus, the question at hand is this: does it really matter if we define the basket as 'military' or 'civilian' as long as we are inclined to put all our eggs in it? Turkey will surely be a good test case for answering this question and to see whether or not civilianization of the Civil-Military Relations automatically leads to democratization.

As a methodological last note, the author wants to emphasize the need for comparative research, the first objective should be the comparison of its findings with future snapshots of the Turkish officer corps to be taken with a representative sample in order to generate a trend analysis addressing change within the Turkish officer corps.

The second is applying the same methodology and survey to other groups of people within the TAF, such as NCOs and contracted sergeants. By doing so we can gain scholarly insights about different groups of people belonging to two or more different social classes, and then compare the findings to understand whether the same inputs driving change within the TAF influence social classes differently or not. More importantly, if differences exist, then we can concentrate on the 'whys' of the differences.

The third is to apply the same survey of this thesis to a representation of Turkish society to acquire, for the first time in the literature, the civilian-military gaps in Turkey. Policymakers and military elites aiming to develop new models for Turkish CMR should note that we cannot manage a process if we have not first quantified the literature on the Turkish CMR, measured changes both in the civilian and military domain, and lastly, compared different snapshots to generate trend analyses.

The last objective should be to apply the same methodology of this study to examine other militaries of the world. By utilising the methodology this study offers, the change within the Turkish military can be compared with the other modern militaries. With this comparison, one can get scholarly insights about the similarities and differences between different militaries and then generate insights about 'whats', 'whys', and 'hows' into those differences and similarities.

Appendix

İYİ GÜNLER

Bu anket çalışması, Bilkent Üniversitesi Siyaset Bilimi Bölümünde "Toplum-Ordu İlişkileri" konusunda doktora çalışmalarına devam eden Bnb. Metin GURCAN'ın (Cep: ...., E-mail: .... doktora tezi için yapılmaktadır. Hem TSK'da görev yapan subaylara hem de bir benzeri sivillere uygulanacak bu anket çalışmasının temel amacı aynı sorulara TSK personelinin ve sivillerin vermiş oldukları cevaplardan elde edilen verilerin istatiksel analizini yaparak Türkiye'de sivil-asker ilişkilerini daha iyi anlamamıza katkıda bulunmaktır.

Bu ankette, kimliğiniz bizim için önemli değildir. Yani kimlik bilgileriniz, telefon ve birlik adı gibi özel bilgilerinize kesinlikle ihtiyaç duyulmamaktadır. Bu anketin temel amacı; tek tek bireylerin ne düşündüğünü değil TSK'da görev yapan subay kadrosunun genel olarak eğilimlerini ve düşüncelerini anlamaktır. ***Bu amaçla yaklaşık 1500 subaydan oluşan rastlantısal, temsili bir örneklemle çalışmaktayız.*** *Bu araştırmadan elde edilen veriler ve bulgular kamuoyu ile paylaşılmayacak ve tamamen akademik, bilimsel amaçlar için kullanılacaktır. Kısacası soruları büyük bir rahatlıkla cevaplayabilirsiniz.*

Bu bilimsel, akademik çalışma için değerli vaktinizden ***10-15 dakikanızı*** *ayırıp soruları ciddiyetle ve gerçek duygu ve düşünceleriniz doğrultusunda cevaplandırdığınız için şimdiden teşekkürlerimizi sunarız.*

S1. Lütfen ordu içinde bağlı olduğunuz kuvveti **belirtiniz?** (Lütfen sizin için uygun seçeneği daire içine alınız.)
1. K.K.K.lığı
2. Hv.K.K.lığı
3. Dz.Kv.K.lığı
4. J.Gn.K.lığı
5. S.G.K.lığı

S2. Yaşınız:

S3. Şu anki rütbeniz?
1. Tğm./Uğtm.
2. Yüzbaşı
3. Binbaşı
4. Yarbay
5. Albay
6. General/Amiral

S4. Eğitim seviyeniz**, yani mezun olduğunuz veya devam etmekte olduğunuz en yüksek seviyedeki okul nedir?**
1. Harp Okulu/ Üniversite
2. Yüksek Lisans (Devam edenler dahil)
3. Doktora (Devam edenler dahil)

S5. ezun olduğunuz okul (yani kaynağınız**)?**
1. Sivil üniversite
2. Harp Okulu
3. Diğer (astsubay veya uzman erbaş)

S6. Memleketiniz **neresidir?** (Lütfen kendinizi nereli hissediyorsanız o ilin adını aşağıdaki boşluğa yazınız)

....

S7. Babanızın eğitim düzeyi**, yani en son bitirdiği okul nedir?**
1. Okur yazar
2. İlkokul
3. Ortaokul
4. Lise
5. Üniversite
6. Yüksek Lisans
7. Doktora

S8. Aylık hane geliriniz **aşağıdaki gelir gruplarının hangisinde yer almaktadır? Yani herkesin her türlü kazancı dahil evinize ayda ortalama kaç TL giriyor?** (Maaşınız dışında hanenize giren eş maaşı, kira vb. tüm gelirler dahil)
1. (2500-4000 TL)
2. (4000-5000 TL)
3. (5000-6000 TL)
4. (6000-7000 TL)
5. (7000-8000 TL)
6. (8000 TL üstü)

S9. Türkçe dışında bildiğiniz yabancı dil **sayısı (biraz bildiğiniz başlangıç düzeyinde olanlar da dahil)**
1. Bilmiyorum
2. Sadece bir tane
3. Sadece iki tane
4. Üç tane
5. Dört tane
6. Dörtten fazla

S10. Ailenizde veya yakın çevrenizde sizden önce subay ve/veya astsubay olan bir tanıdığınız **var mıydı?**
1. Evet
2. Hayır

S11. Subay olma kararınızda öncelikle kim **etkili oldu?**
1. Kendi tercihim
2. Ailemin yönlendirmesi
3. Ailemin dışında, çevremdeki diğer yakınlarımın yönlendirmesi

S12. Subay olmanızın başlıca nedeni nedir?
1. Maddi beklenti (garantili iş)
2. Sosyal statü (TSK gibi seçkin bir kurumda görev yapma)
3. TSK tarafından sunulan kurs, yurt dışı görev vb. mesleki kariyer fırsatları
4. TSK'daki eğitim kurumlarının sivil emsallerine nazaran daha kaliteli eğitim vermesi

S13. Şu ana kadar terörle mücadele bölgesinde (Doğu ve Güneydoğu Anadolu Bölgesindeki illerde, yani şark görevinde) geçirdiğiniz toplam hizmet süreniz nedir?
1. 0 (Hiç bulunmadım)
2. (-2 yıl arası)
3. (2-3 yıl arası)
4. (3-4 yıl arası)
5. (4-5 yıl arası)
6. (5-6 yıl arası)
7. (6 yıl ve üstü)

S14. Simdiye kadar TSK'yı terörle mücadele konusunda ne kadar başarılı buluyorsunuz?
1. Hiç
2. Biraz
3. Çok

S15. Şu ana kadar toplam yurt dışı görev süreniz nedir (askeri görevler, eğitimler ve kurslar dahil)**?**
1. 0 (Yurt dışı görevinde bulunmadım)
2. (0- 6 ay)
3. (6 ay-1 sene arası)
4. (1-2 sene arası)
5. (2-3 sene arası)
6. (3 sene veya üstü)

S16. Yurt dışında eğitim maksadıyla **(askeri veya akademik) geçirdiğiniz toplam süre?** 1. 0 (Yurt dışında eğitim almadım) 2. (0- 6 ay) 3. (6 ay-1 sene arası) 4. (1-2 sene arası) 5. (2-3 sene arası) 6. (3 sene veya üstü)
S17. Yurt dışında görevli bulunduğunuz yerler? (Birden fazla yerde görev yaptıysanız ilgili tüm seçenekleri işaretleyebilirsiniz) 1. Yurt dışında bulunmadım 2. ABD 3. Avrupa 4. Afganistan 5. Kosova 6. Bosna-Hersek 7. Irak 8. Azerbaycan 9. Somali 10. Ortaasya 9. Ortadoğu 10. Afrika 11. Asya 12. Uzak Asya
S18. Genel olarak subaylık mesleğinden ne kadar memnunsunuz? 1. Hiç 2. Biraz 4. Çok
S19. Şu ana kadar TSK'da sizi 'en çok' **mutlu eden unsur aşağıdakilerden hangisidir? (tek seçenek lütfen)** 1. Sosyal statü ve mesleki tatmin 2. Maddi imkanlar 3. Kariyer fırsatları
S20. TSK'daki hizmetiniz süresince sizin için aşağıdakilerden hangisi her zaman en önde **gelmiştir ?** 1. Kendim 2. Ailem 3. TSK (kurumum)
S21. Sizce "Devre Ruhu **" bir subay için ne kadar önemlidir?** 1. Hiç 2. Biraz 3. Çok
S22. Sizce Türkiye'de askerlik mesleğinin toplumdaki saygınlığı ve itibarı **azalıyor mu?** 1. Evet 2. Hayır
S23. Varsa veya olursa çocuğunuzun **subay olmasını ister misiniz?** 1. Evet 2. Hayır

S24. Sizce TSK'nın "en temel görevi" ne olmalıdır?
1. Türkiye Cumhuriyeti'ni sadece dış tehditlere karşı korumak,
2. Türkiye Cumhuriyetini hem iç hem dış tehditlere karşı korumak.

S25. Sizce TSK'nın gelecekteki tehditleri karşılamak ve olası çatışma ortamlarına hazırlanması için ciddi yapısal reformlara **ihtiyacı var mıdır?**
1. Evet
2. Hayır

S26. TSK'nın küresel güvenlik ortamındaki gücü ve caydırıcılığı konusunda ne kadar iyimsersiniz?
1. Hiç
2. Biraz
3. Çok

S27. "Caydırıcı ve güçlü bir ordu" **için öncelikle hangisi önemlidir (tek seçenek lütfen)?**
1. Nitelikli icracı personel
2. Teknoloji
3. Nitelikli komuta kademesi
4. Askeri moral ve kültürel değerler

S28. Sizce Türkiye'nin NATO'ya üyeliğinin TSK'nın kurumsal yapısına **(teşkilatlanma, çalışma ve kurumsal kültür vb. hususlar) nasıl bir etkisi olmuştur?**
1. Olumlu
2. Olumsuz

S29. Sizce Türkiye'nin NATO'ya üyeliğinin TSK'nın muharebe gücüne **nasıl bir etkisi olmuştur?**
1. Olumlu
2. Olumsuz

S30. Sizce Türkiye, NATO'nun yanında'Şangay İşbirliği Örgütü' gibi diğer uluslararası güvenlik örgütleriyle askeri alanda işbirliğini güçlendirmeli mi?
1. Evet
2. Hayır

S31. Türkiye'de son dönemde sivil-asker ilişkilerinde yaşanan sivilleşme süreci TSK'nın askeri gücünü **ve** etkinliğini **olumlu yönde etkiliyor mu**
1. Evet
2. Hayır

S32. Siz kendinizi ne kadar milliyetç*i* **biri olarak görürsünüz?**
1. Hiç
2. Biraz
3. Çok

S33. Siyasi açıdan Türkiye'de yıllardır bir sağ – sol – merkez diye bir gelenek var. Siz kendinizi siyasi görüş olarak nerede tanımlarsınız?
1. Sol
2. Ortanın solu
3. Merkez
4. Ortanın sağı
5. Sağ
6. Hiçbiri

S34. Türkiye'de "milli iradeyi " öncelikle hangi kurum temsil eder?
1. Cumhurbaşkanlığı
2. Parlemanto
3. Hükümet
4. Anayasa Mahkemesi

S35. Sizce günümüzde Türkiye'de "laiklik" ilkesi tehdit altında mı?
1. Evet
2. Hayır

S36. Sizce günümüzde Türkiye'de "üniter devlet" ilkesi tehdit altında mı?
1. Evet
2. Hayır

S37. Ramazan ayında oruç tutar mısınız?
1. Oruç tutmam
2. Tutamam (sağlık gerekçesiyle, inancı dışında olduğu için)
3. Kısmen, bir miktar tutarım
4. Bir aylık orucun tümünü tutmaya çalışırım

S38. Genel olarak kişisel ekonomik durumunuzdan ne kadar memnunsunuz?
1. Hiç memnun değilim
2. Biraz memnunum
3. Çok memnunum

S39. Son yıllarda bir subay olarak ekonomik durumunuz nasıl bir değişim gösterdi?
1. Daha kötü
2. Aynı
3. Daha iyi

S40. Bu bölümde aşağıda bir dizi ifade okuyacaksınız. Bu ifadeler hakkındaki görüşlerinizi katılıyorsanız "EVET" katılmıyorsanız "HAYIR" şeklinde belirtiniz lütfen?*Lütfen size uygun seçeneği X ile işaretleyiniz.*	EVET	HAYIR
1. Din ve devlet işleri birbirinden ayrı olmalı.	( )	( )
2. Hâkim, savcı, öğretmen, polis gibi görevlerde çalışan kadınlar kamu görevleri sırasında başlarını örtebilir.	( )	( )
3. 'İlk ve orta öğretime' giden kız öğrenciler ' sınıfta, ders sırasında' **başlarını** örtebilirler.	( )	( )
4. Ahirete, **yani yaşamdan sonra öbür dünyanın varlığına inanırım.**	( )	( )
5. Din ve bilim **çeliştiğinde rehberim bilimdir.**	( )	( )
6. Faizi, yani bankaya para yatırıp karşılığında belli bir para almayı tasvip etmem.	( )	( )
7. Kürtlerin kendi dillerinde eğitim (yani ana dilde eğitim**) hakkı kabul edilmelidir.**	( )	( )
8. Türkiye'nin Avrupa Birliği (AB) üyelik sürecini **destekliyorum.**	( )	( )
9. Parlamentoya **güveniyorum.**	( )	( )

10. Polise (emniyet) teşkilatına **güveniyorum.**	( )	( )
11. Medyaya **güveniyorum.**	( )	( )
12. Her hal ve şartta Türkiye demokrasiyle **yönetilmeli**	( )	( )
13. Türkiye'de demokrasinin geldiği düzeyden ve demokrasinin işleyişinden memnunum.	( )	( )
14. Türkler asker millettir.	( )	( )
15. Gerektiğinde asker yönetime el koyabilmeli ve ülkeyi yönetebilmeli.	( )	( )
16. Askeri yönetimler sivil yönetimlere göre çok daha etkin ve başarılı **olabilir.**	( )	( )
17. Türkiye'de son 10-15 yıllık dönemde askerin sivil siyaset ve iktidar üzerindeki etkisi azaldı.	( )	( )
18. TSK'daki toplam asker sayısı azaltılmalı.	( )	( )
19. Zorunlu askerlik **kaldırılmalı.**	( )	( )
20. Zorunlu askerlik uygulaması devam edecekse bile süresi daha da kısalmalı.	( )	( )
21. Düşünün ki yeterli maddi gücünüz, olanaklarınız var ve oğlunuz bedelli/paralı askerlik yapmak istiyor. Siz bunu onaylar mısınız?	( )	( )
22. TSK, ABD'deki gibi sadece profesyonel askerlerden (yani maaşlı memur gibi gönüllü askerlerden) **oluşan bir ordu olmalı.**	( )	( )
23. İnançları, ahlak anlayışı veya kişisel tercihleri nedeniyle askerlik hizmetini vicdanen reddedip, askere gitmemek (yani vicdani ret) **bir yasal hak olmalı.**	( )	( )
24. Kadın subay ve astsubayların **TSK'daki sayısı arttırılmalı.**	( )	( )
25. İsterlerse eşcinseller **de TSK'da zorunlu askerlik görevini yapabilmeli.**	( )	( )
26. Atatürkçülük **,TSK'nın temel fikir kaynağıdır.**	( )	( )
27. Türkiye'de bir subay her zaman aynı eğitim seviyesindeki sivil emsallerinden üstündür.	( )	( )
28. Gnkur.Bşk.lığı, Milli Savunma Bakanlığı'na (MSB) bağlanmalı.	( )	( )
29. Sivil ve askeri yargı ayrılığının sona ermesi için Askeri Yargı sistemi **kaldırılabilir.**	( )	( )
30. Hukuka, kanunlara uymadığını ve anayasaya aykırı olduğunu düşündüğüm bir emri **yerine getirmem.**	( )	( )
31. Savunma ve güvenlik konularında sivil, siyasi karar alıcı ile asker arasında bir görüş ayrılığı olursa son söz sivil, siyasi karar alıcıya ait olmalı.	( )	( )

32. Genelkurmay Başkanı siyasi konular da dahil gerekli gördüğü her konuda görüşünü kamuoyu ile serbestçe paylaşabilmeli.	( )	( )
33. Türkiye, Batı ülkeleri dışında Asya (Rusya, Ortaasya ülkeleri vb.), Afrika ve Uzak Asya'da (Çin, Hindistan vb.) da dış politika alanında açılımlar yapmalı.	( )	( )
34. Son dönemde Türk dış politikasını başarılı buluyorum.	( )	( )
35. Atatürkçü Düşünce Sistemi askeri eğitim sisteminin temel unsuru olarak kalmalı.	( )	( )
36. İnternet ve sosyal medyayı haber takibinde sıkça kullanırım.	( )	( )

Bibliography

Primary Sources

Interviews

The interviews with 80 serving officers from all ranks and force commands.

Survey

The survey sheets of 1,240 serving officers from all ranks and force commands.

Secondary Sources

Adamsky, Dima, *The Culture of Military Innovation: The Impact of Cultural Factors on the Revolution in Military Affairs in Russia, the US, and Israel* (Stanford Security Studies, 2010).

Akay, Hale, 'Türk Silahlı Kuvvetleri: Kurumsal ve Askeri Boyut', in Ali Bayramoğlu and Ahmet İnsel (eds), *Almanak Türkiye 2006-2008 Güvenlik Sektörü ve Demokratik Gözetim* (İstanbul: TESEV Yayınları, 2009).

Akay, Hale, 'Turkiye'de Güvenlik Sektörü: Sorular, Sorunlar, Çözümler (Turkish)', TESEV Report, 22 (2009).

Aknur, Müge, 'The Impact of Civil-Military Relations on Democratic Consolidation in Turkey', in Müge Aknur (ed.), *Democratic Consolidation in Turkey* (Boca Raton: Universal-Publishers, 2012), p.234.

Akyol, Mustafa, 'Turkey considers new peace process with PKK', *Al-Monitor*, 3 January 2015.

Aydınlı, Ersel, 'A Paradigmatic Shift for the Turkish Generals and an End to the Coup Era in Turkey', *Middle East Journal* 63 (4) (2009), pp.581-96.

——, 'Ergenekon, New Pacts, and the Decline of the Turkish Inner State', *Turkish Studies* 12:2 (2011).

——, 'Civil-Military Relations Transformed', *Journal of Democracy* 23 (1) (2012), pp.100-08.

Aydınlı, Ersel, Özcan, Nihat Ali and Akyaz, Doğan, 'The Turkish Military's March Towards Europe', *Foreign Affairs* 85 (1) (2006), pp.77–90.

Balcı, Bayram, 'Turkey: Local Elections Gave Huge Victory to Erdogan', *Foreign Policy Journal*, 3 April 2014).
Beeson, Mark, 'Civil-Military Relations in Indonesia and the Philippines: Will the Thai Coup Prove Contagious?', *Armed Forces & Society* 34 (2008), pp.474-90.
Bilgin, Pınar, 'The Securityness of Secularism? The Case of Turkey', *Security Dialogue* 39 (6) (2008), pp.593-614.
Birand, Mehmet Ali, *Shirts of Steel* (London: IB Tauiris, 1991).
Burk, James, 'Theories of democratic civil-military relations', *Armed Forces Society* 29 (1) (2002), pp.7–29.
Canan-Sokullu, Ebru, *Debating Security in Turkey: Challenges and Changes in the Twenty-First Century* (London: Lexington Books, 2013), p.293.
Capoccia, Giovanni and Kelemen, R. Daniel, 'The Study of Critical Junctures: Theory, Narrative, and Counterfactuals in Historical Institutionalism', *World Politics* 59 (2007), pp.341–69.
Carreiras, Helena and Castro, Celso, *Qualitative Methods in Military Studies* (London: Routledge Press, 2014), pp.18-24.
Center for Strategic and International Studies Report, *American Military Culture in the 21st Century* (Washington DC: The CSIS Press, 2000), p.xviii.
Centre for European Security Studies, *Turkish Civil-Military Relations and the EU: Preparation for Continuing Convergence* (November 2005).
Cindoğlu, Dilek, 'Headscarf Ban and Discrimination: Professional Headscarved Women in the Labor Market', TESEV Report (2011).
Cizre, Ümit, 'The Justice and Development Party and the Military: Recreating the Past after Reforming it?', in Ümit Cizre (ed.), *Secular and Islamic Politics in Turkey: The making of the Justice and Development Party* (London: Routledge, 2008), pp.132-71.
——, 'Disentangling the Threads of Civil-Military Relations in Turkey: Promises and Perils', *Mediterranean Quarterly* 22 (2) (2011).
——, 'Demythologyzing the National Security Concept: the Case of Turkey', *Middle East Journal* 57 (2) (2003), pp.216-17.
Cook, Steven, *Ruling but not Governing: The Military and Political Development in Egypt, Algeria, and Turkey* (Baltimore: Johns Hopkins University Press, 2007).
Cooker, Christopher, *The Warrior Ethos: Military Culture and the War on Terror* (New York: Routledge Press, 2007), p.12.
Creswell, John W. and Clark, Vicki Plano, *Designing and Conducting Mixed Methods Research* (SAGE Publication, 2010), pp.58-64.
Demirel, Tanel, 'Civil-Military Relations in Turkey: Two Patterns of Civilian Behavior Towards the Military', *Turkish Studies* 4 (3) (2003), pp.1-25.
——, 'The Turkish Military's Decision to Intervene: 12 September 1980', *Armed Forces and Society* 29 (2) (2003), pp.253-80.
——, 'Lessons of Military Regimes and Democracy: The Turkish Case in a Comparative Perspective', *Armed Forces and Society* 31 (2) (2005), pp.245-71.
Denzin, Norman, *The Research Act in Sociology* (Chicago: Aldine, 1970).

Desch, Michael, *Civilian Control of the Military: The Changing Security Environment* (Baltimore: Johns Hopkins University Press, 1999).

DiMaggio, Paul D and Powell, Walter W., 'The Iron Cage Revisited: Institutional Isomorphism and Collective Rationality', in Walter W. Powell and Paul J. DiMaggio, (eds), *The New Institutionalism in Organizational Analysis* (Chicago: University of Chicago Press, 1991), p.65.

Duran, Burhanettin, 'The Executive Presidency and Turkey's Future', *Daily Sabah*, 31 January 2017.

Duran, Burhanettin and Nebi, Mis, 'The Transformation of Turkey's Political System and Executive presidency', *Insight Turkey* 18, no.4, (2016), pp.11-27.

During, Simon, *The Cultural Studies: Reader* (London and New York: Routledge, 1993).

Farrell, Theo and Terriff, Terry, *The Sources of Military Change: Culture, Politics, Technology* (London: Lynne Reinner Publishing, 2002).

Feaver, Peter D., 'The Civil-Military Problematique: Huntington, Janowitz, and the Question of Civilian Control', *Armed Forces and Society* 23 (2) (1996).

—— and Seeler, Erika, 'Before and After Huntington: The Methodological Maturing of Civil-Military Studies', in S.C. Nielsen and D.M. Snider (eds), *American Civil-Military Relations: The Soldier and the State in a New Era* (Baltimore: Johns Hopkins University Press, 2009).

——, 'Civil-Military Relations',*Annual Review of Political Science* (1999), p.211.

——, *Armed Servants: Agency, Oversight and Civil-Military Relations* (Cambridge: Harvard University Press, 2003).

Fick, Nathaniel C., *One Bullet Way: The Making of a Marine Officer* (New York: Mariner Books, 2006).

Finer, Samuel E., *The Man on Horseback: The Role of Military in Politics* (New York: Praeger, 1962), p.62.

Gidengil, Elisabeth and Karakoç, Ekrem 'Which matters more in the electoral success of Islamist (successor) parties – religion or performance? The Turkish case', *Party Politics* (2014).

Goldman, Emily O., 'Western Military Models in Ottoman Turkey and Meiji Japan', in Theo Farrell and Terry Terriff (eds), *The Sources of Military Change: Culture, Politics, Technology*(London: Lynne Reinner Publishing, 2002), p.74.

Göle, Nilüfer, 'Secularism and Islamism in Turkey: The Making of Elites and Counter-Elites', *Middle East Journal* 51 (1) (1997), pp.56-88.

——, 'Gezi – Anatomy of a Public Square Movement', *Insight Turkey* 15 (8) (2013).

Gray, Colin S., *Modern Strategy* (Oxford: Oxford University Press, 1999), p.131.

Güney, Aylin, and Karatekelioğlu, Petek 'Turkey's EU Candidacy and Civil-Military Relations: Challenges and Prospects', *Armed Forces and Society* 31 (3) (2005), pp.439-62.

——, 'The Military, Politics and Post-Cold War Dilemmas in Turkey', in Kees Koonings and Dirk Kruijt (eds), *Political Armies: The Military and Nation Building in the Age of Democracy* (London and New York: Zed Books, 2002), pp.162-75.

Güngör, Uğur, *The Analysis of Turkey's Approach to Peace Operations*, PhD Dissertation (Bilkent University, Department of International Relations, 2007).
Gürcan, Metin, 'Strategic Communication and its Applicability in the Security Sector', *The Journal of Security Strategies* (Turkish War Academy) 15 (2012), pp.99-139.
——, 'Drone Warfare and Contemporary Strategy Making: Does the tail wag the dog?', *Dynamics of Asymmetric Conflict* 6 (1-3) (2013).
________, 'Turkish military unhappy with parliament's lack of Guidance', *Al Monitor*, 6 October 2014.
——, 'Splitting Gendarmerie from Turkish military: Reform or Bad Timing?', *Al Monitor*, 3 November 2014.
——, 'Military presence increases in the Eastern Mediterranean', *Al Monitor*, 5 November 2014.
——, 'Turkish government, military at odds over Gulenists', *Al Monitor*, 24 November 2014.
——, '$8,700 will let young Turks "buy out" their military Service', *Al Monitor*, 10 December 2014.
——, 'Turkish NCOs fight for their rights', *Al-Monitor*, 12 December 2014.
——, 'Turkey's women expand role in the military', *Al-Monitor*, 1 December 2014).
——, 'Turkish military wages war on Social Media', *Al-Monitor*, 9 March 2015.
——, 'Turkish hawks want to settle past injustices', *Al-Monitor*, 20 March 2015.
Gürcanlı, Zeynep, 'TSK'da astsubay devrimi', *Hürriyet*, .30 March 2013.
Gürsoy, Yaprak, 'The Impact of EU-Driven Reforms on the Political Autonomy of the Turkish Military', *South European Society and Politics* 16 (2) (2011), pp.293-308.
——, 'The Final Curtain for the Turkish Armed Forces? Civil-Military Relations in View of the 2011 General Elections', *Turkish Studies* 13 (2) (2012), pp.191-211
——, 'The changing role of the military in Turkish politics: democratization through coup plots?', *Democratization* 19 (4) (2012), pp.735-60.
——, 'Turkish Public Attitudes Toward the Military and Ergenekon Case: Consequences for the Consolidation of Democracy', European Institute, Working Paper No.5 (2014).
Hale, William, *Turkish Politics and the Military* (London: Routledge, 1994).
—— and Özbudun, Ergun *Islamism, Democracy and Liberalism in Turkey: The Case of the AKP* (New York: Routledge, 2010), p.91.
——, 'The Turkish Republic and its military, 1923–1960'. *Turkish Studies* 12 (2011).
Harris, George S., 'The Role of the Military in Turkish Politics Part I', *The Middle East Journal* 19 (1) (1965), p.59.
——, 'The Role of the Military in Turkey in the 1980s: Guardians or Decision Makers?', in Metin Heper and Ahmet Evin (eds), *Democracy and the Military in Turkey in the 1980s* (Berlin: Walter de Gruyter, 1988), pp.177–200.
Heper, Metin and Güney, Aylin 'The Military and the Consolidation of Democracy: The Recent Turkish Experience', *Armed Forces& Society* 26 (2000), pp.635-57.

——, 'The Justice and Development Party Government and the Military in Turkey', *Turkish Studies* 6 (2005), pp.215-31.
——, 'Civil-Military Relations in Turkey: Toward a Liberal Model?', *Turkish Studies* 12 (2) (2011), pp.241-52.
Hill, Andrew, 'Military Innovation and Military Culture', *Parameters* (2015).
Huntington, Samuel P., *The Soldier and the State: The Theory and Politics of the Civil Military Relations* (Cambridge: Harvard University Press, 1957).
Huntington, Samuel, *Third Wave of Democracy: Democratization in the Late Twentieth Century* (Norman: University of Oklahoma Press, 1991).
Idiz, Semih, 'Turkey's military is angered by Ankara's Peshmerga move', *Al-Monitor*, 31 October 2014.
——, 'No chance Turkey will be kicked out of NATO', *Al-Monitor*, 11 November 2014.
Jakob, Alexander, 'On the Triangulation of Quantitative and Qualitative Data in Typological Social Research: Reflections on a Typology of Conceptualizing "Uncertainty" in the Context of Employment Biographies', *Forum: Qualitative Social Research* 2 (1) (2001).
Janowitz, Morris, *The Professional Soldier* (New York: Free Press, 1971).
Jenkins, Gareth, *Context and Circumstances: Turkish Military and Politics* (Oxford: Oxford University Press, 2001), p.15.
——, 'Context and Circumstance: The Turkish Military and Politics', *The Adelphi Papers* 41 (337) (2001), pp.21-35.
——, 'Continuity and Change. Prospects for civil-military relations in Turkey', *International Affairs* 83 (2) (2007), pp.339–55.
——, 'Court postpones Semdinli Hearing once again', *Eurasia Daily Monitor* 5 (109) (2008).
——, 'Poll suggests military still the most trusted institution in Turkey', *Eurasia Daily Monitor* 5 (25) (2008).
——, 'The Balyoz Retrial and the Changing Politics of Turkish Justice', *The Turkey Analyst*, 25 June 2014. See http://www.turkeyanalyst.org/publications/turkey-analyst-articles/item/331-the-balyoz-retrial-and-the-changing-politics-of-turkish-justice.html (accessed 20 February 2015).
Kalaycıoğlu, Ersin, 'Kulturkampf in Turkey: The Constitutional Referendum of 12 September 2010', *South European Society and Politics* 17 (1) (2011), pp.1-22.
Karakaş, Eser, 'State Protocol and Politics', *Today's Zaman*, 8 November 2012.
Karaosmanoğlu, Ali L., 'Armed Forces And Democracy', Bilgesam Publications, 2011.
——, 'Transformation of Turkey's Civil-Military Relations Culture and International Environment', *Turkish Studies* 12:2 (2011).
——, 'Turkish Security Culture: Evolutionary or Carved in Stone?', in P.M.E. Volten (ed.), *Perceptions and Misperceptions in the EU and Turkey: Stumbling Blocks on the Road to Accession* (Groningen: Centre for European Security Studies, 2009).

Katzenstein, Peter J., 'Introduction: Alternative Perspectives in National Security', in Peter J. Katzenstein (ed.), *The Culture of National Security: Norms and Identity in World Politics* (New York: Columbia University Press, 1996), p.4.

Katznelson, Ira, 'Periodization and Preferences: Reflections on Purposive Action in Comparative Historical Social Science', in James Mahoney and Dietrich Rueschemeyer, (eds), *Comparative Historical Analysis in the Social Sciences* (Cambridge: Cambridge University Press, 2003), pp.270-301.

Kavakçı, Merve, *Islam Headscarf Politics in Turkey* (New York: Palgrave, 2010), p.5.

Kemal, Lale, 'Grave violation of soldier rights', *Today's Zaman*, 26 December 2012.

Keyman, Fuat, 'Post-vesayet, Sivillesme, Demokratiklesme (Turkish)', *Radikal*, 15 January 2015.

——, 'The AK Party: Dominant Party, New Turkey and Polarization', *Insight Turkey* 16 (2) (2014), pp.19-31.

—— and Öniş, Ziya, *Turkish Politics in a Changing World: Global Dynamics and Domestic Transformation* (Istanbul: Bilgi University Press, 2007), pp.9-34.

Krippendorff, Klaus, *Content Analysis: An Introduction to its Methodology* (Newbury Park: Sage Publications, 2004).

Kuru, Ahmet T., 'The Rise and Fall of Military Tutelage in Turkey: Fears of Islamism, Kurdism, and Communism', *Insight Turkey* 14 (2) (2012), pp.37-57.

Lagendijk, Joost, 'The Times are Really Changing in Turkey: Security Matters', *Newsletter from the Centre of European Security Studies*, 12 (2010).

Letsch, Constanze, 'Turkey military chiefs resign over Sledgehammer "coup plot" arrests', *The Guardian*, 30 July 2011.

Lichbach, Mark Irving and Zuckerman, Alan S., *Comparative Politics: Rationality, Culture and Structure* (New York: Cambridge University Press, 2009), p.4

Linz, J.J. and Stepan, Alred C., *Problems of Democratic Transition and Consolidation: Southern Europe, South America, and Post-Communist Europe* (Baltimore: Johns Hopkins University Press, 1996).

Lion-Perlin, David, 'Turkish Civil-Military Relations: A Latin American Comparison', *Turkish Studies*12, 2 (2011).

Mahoney, James and Thelen, Kathleen, *Explaining Institutional Change: Ambiguity, Agency and Power* (Cambridge: Cambridge University Press, 2010).

Mansoor, Peter, 'The Softer Side of War: Exploring the Influence of Culture on Military Doctrine', *Foreign Affairs* (2011).

Mardin, Şerif, 'Center-Periphery Relations: A Key to Turkish Politics', *Daedalus* 102 (1) (1972).

McCargo, Duncan and Ayse, Zarakol, 'Turkey and Thailand: Unlikely Twins', *Journal of Democracy*, Vol. 23/3 (2012).

Michaud-Emin, Linda, 'The Restructuring of the Military High Command in the 7th Harmonization Package and its Ramifications for the Civil-Military Relations in Turkey', *Turkish Studies* 8 (1) (2007), p.36.

Moskos, Charles, 'From Institution to Occupation: Trends in Military Organization', *Armed Forces & Society* 4 (1977), pp.41-50.

——, *Soldiers and Sociology* (US military Research Institute for the Behavioral and Social Sciences, 1988).
——, Williams, John Allen and Segal, David R. (eds), *The Postmodern Military: Armed Forces after the Cold War* (Oxford University Press, 2000). Also Moskos, Charles, 'Military Systems in Twenty-First Century and New Trends', presented at Turkish Military Academy, 2 June 2003.
Narlı, Nilüfer, 'Aligning Civil-Military Relations In Turkey: Transparency Building in Defense Sector And the EU Reforms', Transforming National Armed Forces in South East Europe – from the Social to the Military Challenge, 9th Workshop of the PfP Consortium Study Group'Regional Stability in South East Europe', Lt Col Mag. Ernst M. Felberbauer, Mag. Predrag Jureković, Prof. Plamen Pantev (eds).
——, 'Changes in the Turkish Security Culture and in the Civil-Military Relations', *Western Balkans Security Observer* 14 (2009), pp.56–83.
——, 'Concordance and Discordance in Turkish Civil-Military Relations', *Turkish Studies* 12 (2) (2011), pp.215–25.
Nordlinger, Eric A., *Soldiers in Politics: Military Coups and Governments* (New Jersey: Prentice Hall, 1977), p.22.
Oruçoğlu, Berivan, 'Why Turkey's Mother of All Corruption Scandals Refuses to Go Away', *Foreign Policy*, 6 January 2015.
Pelt, Mogens, *Military Intervention and a Crisis Democracy in Turkey: The Menderes Era and its Demise* (London, New York: I.B. Tauris, 2014).
Pope, Hugh, and Pope,. Nicole, *Turkey Unveiled: A History of Modern Turkey* (Woodstock: The Overlook Press, 2000), p.322.
Posen, Barry R., *The Sources of Military Doctrine: France, Britain and Germany between the World Wars* (Ithaca: Cornell University Press, 1984).
Przeworski, Adam, *Democracy and the Market: Political and Economic Reforms in Eastern Europe and Latin America* (New York: Cambridge University Press, 1991).
Rhodes, Edward, 'Constructing Power: Cultural Transformation and Strategic Adjustment in the 1890s.', in Peter Trubowitz, Emily O. Goldman and Edward Rhodes (eds), *The Politics of Strategic Adjustment: Ideas, Institutions, and Interests* (New York: Columbia University Press, 1999).
Rosen, Stephen Peter, *Winning the Next War: Innovation and the Moden Military* (Ithaca: Cornell University Press, 1994).
Sarıgil, Zeki, 'Europeanization as Institutional Change: The Case of the Turkish Military', *Mediterranean Politics* 12 (1) (2007), pp.39-57.
——, 'Civil-Military Relations Beyond Dichotomy', *Turkish Studies* 12 (2) (2011), pp.265–78.
——, 'The Turkish military: Principal or Agent?', *Armed Forces & Society* 40 (1) (2014), pp.168-90.
Şatana, Nil, 'Transformation of the Turkish military and the path to Democracy', *Armed Forces & Society* 34 (3) (2008), pp.357-88.

——, 'Civil-Military Relations in Europe, the Middle East and Turkey', *Turkish Studies*, 12:2 (2011), pp.279-92.

Siebold, Guy L., 'Core Issues and Theory in Military Sociology', *Journal of Political and Military Sociology* 29 (2001), pp.140-59.

Şimsek, Ayhan, 'Turkey's top general offers new vision of military, democracy and secularism', *Southeast European Times* (2014).

Tank, Pınar, 'Turkey as a "Special Case" for the EU: Will the Generals Retreat from Politics?', *Security Dialogue* 32 (2) (2001), pp.217-30.

Taştekin, Fehim, 'War on Gulenists undermines Turkish Diplomacy', *al-Monitor*, 26 January 2015.

Toktas, Şule, 'The Impact of EU Reform Process on Civil-Military Relations in Turkey', http://www.setav.org/document/Policy_Brief_No_26_Sule_Toktas_Umit_Kurt.pdf (accessed 10 December 2009).

—— and Kurt, Ümit Kurt, 'The Turkish Military's Autonomy, AKP Rule and the EU Reform Process in the 2000s: An Assessment of the Turkish Version of Democratic Control of Armed Forces (DECAF)', *Turkish Studies* 11 (3) (2010), pp.387-403.

Uyar, Mesut and Erickson, Edward, *A Military History of the Ottomans* (Oxford: Praeger Publishing, 2009), pp.151-53.

Varoğlu, Abdulkadir, 'Volunteering for Risk: The Culture of the Turkish Armed Forces', *Armed Forces& Society* 31(4) (2005).

Varoğlu, Abdulkadir, Soeters, Joseph, Tanercan, Erhan and Sığrı, Ünsal, 'Turkish-Dutch Encounters during Peacekeeping', *International Peacekeeping* 11 (2) (2004), pp.354-68.

von Clausewitz, Carl, *On War* (Princeton: Princeton University Press, 1984), p.9.

Watson, B.C.S., 'The Western Ethical Tradition and the Morality of the Warrior', *Armed Forces & Society* 26 (1) (1999), pp.55-72.

Winslow, Donna, *Military Culture: An Annotated Bibliography* (Ottowa: University of Ottowa, 1999).

Wright, George, 'Greek Cypriot leaders reject Annan plan', *The Guardian*, 22 April 2004.

Yalçınkaya, Haldun, 'The Nongovernmental Organizations – Military Security Collaboration Mechanism: Afghanistan NGO Safety Office', *Armed Forces & Society* 39 (3) (2012), pp.489-510.

Yıldız, Nurcan, *Tanklar ve Sözcükler* (Tanks and Words) (Ankara: Alfa Publishing, 2007).

Index